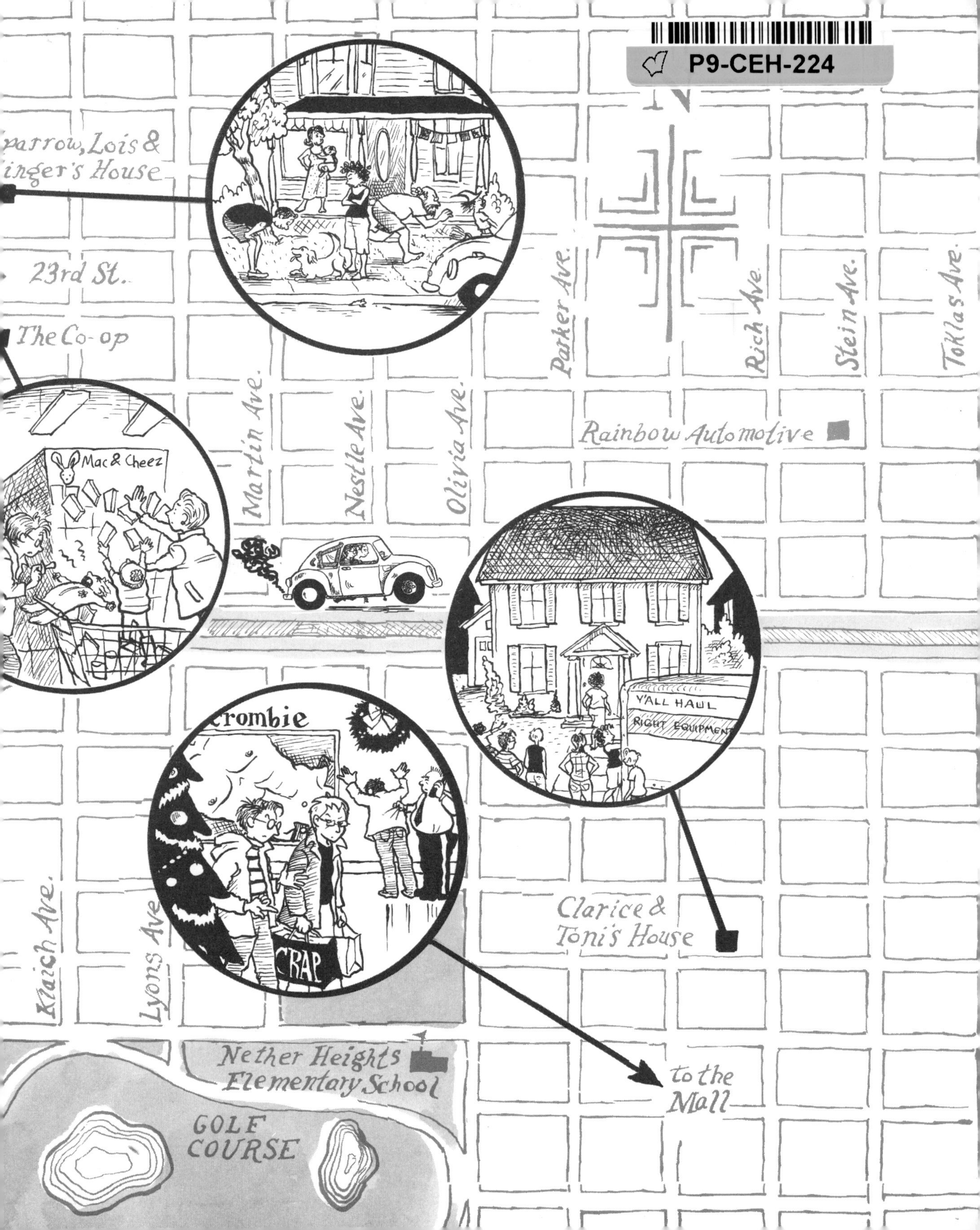

parrow, Lois &
inger's House
23rd St.
The Co-op
Mac & Cheez
Martin Ave.
Nestle Ave.
Olivia Ave.
Parker Ave.
Rich Ave.
Stein Ave.
Toklas Ave.
Rainbow Automotive
rombie
Y'ALL HAUL
RIGHT EQUIPMENT
CRAP
Clarice &
Toni's House
Klaich Ave.
Lyons Ave
Nether Heights
Elementary School
to the
Mall
GOLF
COURSE

THE **ESSENTIAL** DYKES TO WATCH OUT FOR

ALSO BY ALISON BECHDEL

FUN HOME

INVASION OF THE DYKES TO WATCH OUT FOR

DYKES AND SUNDRY OTHER CARBON-BASED LIFE FORMS TO WATCH OUT FOR

POST-DYKES TO WATCH OUT FOR

SPLIT-LEVEL DYKES TO WATCH OUT FOR

THE INDELIBLE ALISON BECHDEL

COMPLETE DYKES TO WATCH OUT FOR: VOLUME ONE

HOT THROBBING DYKES TO WATCH OUT FOR

UNNATURAL DYKES TO WATCH OUT FOR

SPAWN OF DYKES TO WATCH OUT FOR

DYKES TO WATCH OUT FOR: THE SEQUEL

NEW, IMPROVED! DYKES TO WATCH OUT FOR

MORE DYKES TO WATCH OUT FOR

DYKES TO WATCH OUT FOR

THE ESSENTIAL DYKES TO WATCH OUT FOR

ALISON BECHDEL

HOUGHTON MIFFLIN HARCOURT
BOSTON NEW YORK 2008

WWW.HMHBOOKS.COM

LIBRARY OF CONGRESS CATALOGING-IN-PUBLICATION DATA

BECHDEL, ALISON, DATE
[DYKES TO WATCH OUT FOR. SELECTIONS]
THE ESSENTIAL DYKES TO WATCH OUT FOR /
ALISON BECHDEL.
P. CM.
INCLUDES INDEX.
ISBN-13: 978-0-618-96880-0
ISBN-10: 0-618-96880-6
1. COMIC BOOKS, STRIPS, ETC. I. TITLE.
PN6728.D94B475 2008
741.5'6973-DC22 2008036784

PRINTED IN THE UNITED STATES OF AMERICA

MP 10 9 8 7 6 5 4 3 2 1

CONTENTS

Cartoonist's Introduction

TICK
TICK
TICK
Today is
APRIL
28
MONDAY
ATOMIC-CLOCK.COM
1:43 PM
4.28.2008
GOOD GOD.
BRIDE of DYKES TO WATCH OUT FOR
DYKES TO WATCH OUT FOR STRIKE BACK
DTWOF: The Curse of the BLACK PEARL
NASCAR DTWOF
DAWN of the DTWOF
PERIMENOPAUSAL DTWOF

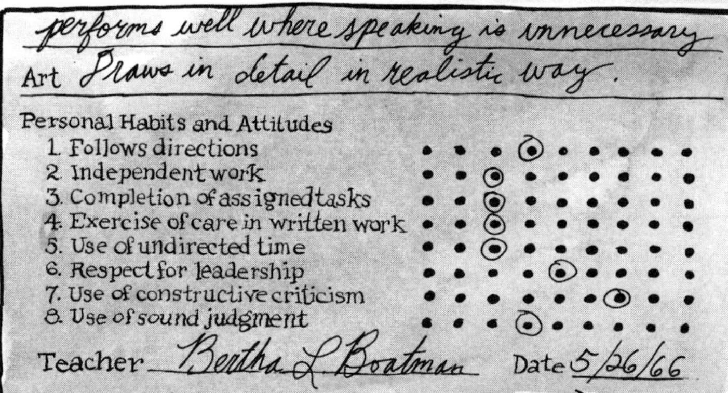
performs well where speaking is unnecessary

Art Draws in detail in realistic way.

Personal Habits and Attitudes

1. Follows directions
2. Independent work
3. Completion of assigned tasks
4. Exercise of care in written work
5. Use of undirected time
6. Respect for leadership
7. Use of constructive criticism
8. Use of sound judgment

Teacher Bertha L Boatman Date 5/26/66

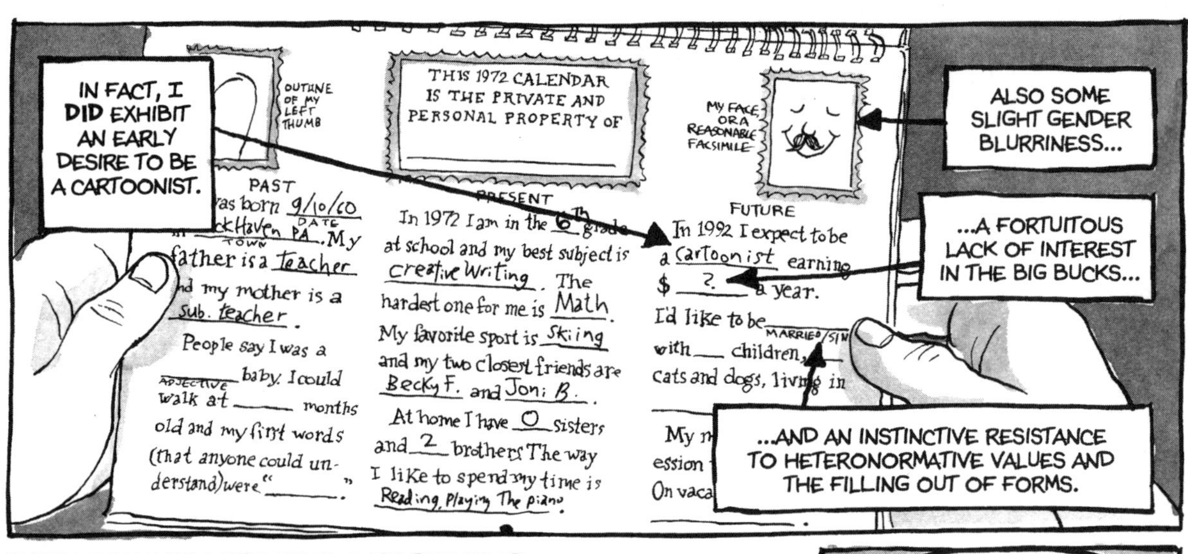

BUT SOON ENOUGH, STRONGER HEADS PREVAILED.

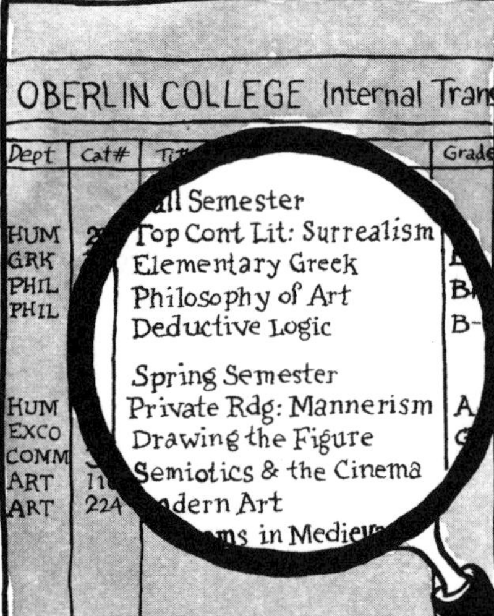

UNOFFICIALLY, OF COURSE, I WAS MAJORING IN SOMETHING OF EVEN MORE DUBIOUS MARKETABILITY.

A FIELD OF STUDY THAT ENGAGED BOTH INTELLECT AND INSTINCT IN A FUSION SO HEADY...

...SO VISCERAL...

...INDEED, SO ALL-CONSUMING...

...THAT IT WAS NO SURPRISE I FAILED TO GET INTO ANY OF THE GRADUATE ART PROGRAMS I'D APPLIED TO.

ool of the Art Institute of Chicago

RISD

Yale University
School of Art

Dear Applicant:
Have you considered dental school?

YES, MY FRIENDS. I ATTENDED THE MFA PROGRAM OF THE **STREETS**.

ARMED WITH NOTHING BUT A HAZY MANDATE TO SPEAK THE UNSPEAKABLE, I LANDED IN *NEW YORK CITY*.

EVERYONE SEEMED TO HAVE THINGS PRETTY MUCH UNDER CONTROL.

I WAS ADRIFT THAT SUMMER. AIMLESS, LOST, AT SIXES AND SEVENS. IN SHORT, BEWILDERED.

I SAW THAT, IN FACT, THERE WAS PLENTY OF REVOLUTIONARY FERMENT STILL AFOOT.

THIS UNRULY PAGEANT, THE SHEER VISUAL PLENITUDE OF IT ALL, INDUCED A STRANGE YEARNING IN ME.

THE WRITERS I WAS DEVOURING SEEMED ABLE TO ACHIEVE THIS, TO APPREHEND THE RICH, TRANSFORMATIONAL QUALITY OF LESBIAN EXPERIENCE AND GET IT DOWN ON THE PAGE.

IN MY SPARE TIME, I GAVE WRITING A WHIRL.

SINISTER WISDOM

Box 660 Amherst, Massachusetts 01004

July 23 1982

Dear Alison Bechdel,

We're sorry to be returning this, but we feel that it's the kind of writing that may be important for the writer, but is not sufficiently dense or rich for us to consider publishing it. In a way, it reads as if you and the various girls or women to whom you've been attracted are the only people in the world. And even these people are not followed through -- were you able to

I WAS A WRITER AND AN ARTIST!
KAPOK KAROUSEL
RRRRRRRR

SKREEEK!
WANDA WILLING THE CAT TO MOVE
WORDS CREPT INTO MY DRAWINGS OF LESBIANS.

ONE DAY, FOR SOME REASON, I ADDED NOT JUST A CAPTION BUT A TITLE AND A NUMBER.

DYKES TO WATCH OUT FOR, PLATE NO. 27
KER-CLUNK!

I HAD NOT ACTUALLY DRAWN TWENTY-SIX OTHER DYKES TO WATCH OUT FOR, BUT THE FAUX TEXTBOOK TONE INSPIRED ME. A CATALOG OF LESBIANS! I WOULD NAME THE UNNAMED. DEPICT THE UNDEPICTED!

AND BY FOLLOWING A METICULOUS INDUCTIVE METHODOLOGY, I WOULD DERIVE A *UNIVERSAL LESBIAN ESSENCE* FROM THESE PARTICULAR EXAMPLES.
flip

MY FIRST CARTOON WAS PUBLISHED IN THE 1983 LESBIAN PRIDE ISSUE OF THE LOCAL FEMINIST NEWSPAPER.
Twyla is appalled to learn that Irene is a morning person.
KA-CHUNK

READERS SEEMED TO LIKE IT, AND THIS EGGED ME ON.

BUT TO BE HONEST, IT WAS SO COMFORTING TO SEE MY QUEER LIFE REFLECTED BACK AT ME, I WOULD HAVE KEPT DRAWING THESE DYKES TO WATCH OUT FOR JUST FOR MYSELF.

It seems to me that you are searching for acceptance and have seized on what seems at this time the easiest solution.

BUT ONE DAY IN 1999, I RAN ACROSS THAT OLD REJECTION LETTER FROM ADRIENNE RICH.

I hope this is helpful. Don't be put off, or discouraged. Writing is a very long, demanding training, more hard work than luck. Strength to you.

In sisterhood,

SHE SAID SHE WAS FAMILIAR WITH MY COMIC STRIP. AND FURTHERMORE...

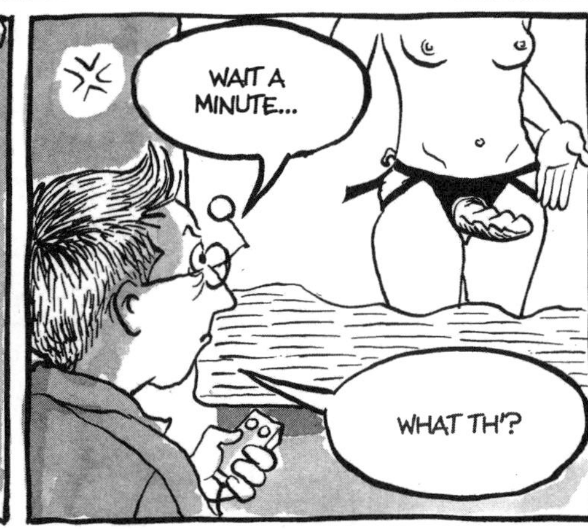

ONCE YOU SPEAK THE UNSPEAKABLE...
...IT BECOMES SPOKEN!
CONVENTIONAL.

BORING!

HAVE I CHURNED OUT EPISODES OF THIS COMIC STRIP EVERY TWO WEEKS FOR DECADES MERELY TO PROVE THAT WE'RE THE SAME AS EVERYONE ELSE?!

HERE. YOU DECIDE. ESSENTIALLY THE SAME?
the ESSENTIAL Dykes to Watch Out For
OR ESSENTIALLY DIFFERENT?
25 COUNT 'EM 25 COPIES
ESSENTIAL DYKES TO WATCH OUT FOR
HOEDOWN MUFFIN, PUBLISHER

MAKE YOURSELVES COMFORTABLE. CLEARLY, I NEED TO RETHINK THIS THING.

BACK TO THE DRAWING BOARD.
ARCHIV
RUSTLE RUSTLE
MOST DISCONCERT-ING.

&$@#

THE **ESSENTIAL** DYKES TO WATCH OUT FOR

IS MO A HOPELESSLY ROMANTIC **IDEALIST**, TRAPPED IN THE **HARD-NOSED, FAST-PACED WHIRLWIND** OF **MODERN LESBIAN LIFE**? *OR IS SHE JUST A* ***DRAG***? STAY TOONED!

MO'S LIFE HAS TAKEN A **TURN** FOR THE **WORSE**. STILL WITHOUT A LOVER, SHE HAS ALSO LOST HER **JOB** AND BECOME THE VICTIM OF A REGRETTABLE **HAIRCUT!**

A RESOURCEFUL WOMAN, SHE DOES NOT GIVE IN TO DESPAIR, BUT KEEPS HERSELF BUSY.

BUT WHEN **NO MAIL** ARRIVES, EXCEPT FOR A **REJECTION** LETTER FROM A PROMINENT LESBIAN-FEMINIST **LITERARY** JOURNAL... EVEN OUR **HEROINE'S** RESILIENT NATURE IS TESTED!

SHRED!

SHE TURNS TO HER FAITHFUL FRIEND **LOIS** FOR SUPPORT.

MO, RELAX! YOU'RE GETTING ALL WORKED UP.

OF COURSE I'M GETTING WORKED UP! I'M **ANXIOUS** AND **TENSE** BECAUSE I HAVEN'T HAD **SEX** IN TEN MONTHS!

THAT'S EASY FOR **YOU** TO SAY. WHAT AM I GONNA DO TILL **THEN**? LO, WHAT'S THAT WEIRD **NOISE**?

OH, THAT'S JUST **GREAT!** YOU KNOW, I **DON'T** UNDERSTAND HOW PEOPLE CAN LIE AROUND **MAKING LOVE** WHEN THERE'S SO MUCH **MISERY** AND **DESOLATION** IN THE WORLD!

THAT'S **REAL PROFOUND**, LOIS. THANKS A **LOT**. I HAVE TO GO WATCH **OPRAH WINFREY** NOW. AT LEAST **SHE** HAS SOME UNDERSTANDING OF THE WORD **COMPASSION!**

WILL HER FRIENDSHIP WITH **LO** SURVIVE MO'S **HARD TIMES?** **IS** LIFE A CYCLE OF **UPS** AND **DOWNS**,...OR DOES MO JUST HAVE BAD **KARMA?** AND THE **CRUCIAL** QUESTION: IS SHE A **DRAG**, OR **WHAT?!**

HIGH ANXIETY
©1987 BY ALISON BECHDEL
ONE NIGHT AFTER KARATE CLASS...
DON'T YOU SEE THE IRONY OF YOUR SITUATION, MO? YOU MIGHT BE MISERABLE NOT HAVING A JOB...

BUT WHAT'S THAT COMPARED WITH THE MISERY OF HAVING ONE? WHY DON'T YOU COME OVER FOR DINNER TONIGHT? I TOLD TONI YOU WOULD.
SURE, CLARICE.
SNAP!

HI ANTONIA.
WELL, IF IT AIN'T THE KARATE KIDS!

STILL JOB HUNTING, MO?
GROAN
RIGHT.
SHE'S KINDA ANXIOUS & DEPRESSED. LET'S TRY AND CHEER HER UP!

OVER THE LENTIL STEW...
GEE, MO... SINCE YOU'RE COLLECTING UNEMPLOYMENT, WHY DON'T YOU JUST TAKE TIME OUT TO DO SOMETHING YOU REALLY LIKE?! ENJOY YOUR FREEDOM!

YOU'RE RIGHT! GODDESS KNOWS HOW MUCH LONGER IT'LL LAST! DOESN'T THE INCREASING CONSERVATISM IN THIS COUNTRY WORRY YOU?

IT MAKES ME FEEL KIND OF SCHIZOPHRENIC... HERE WE ARE, GOING ABOUT OUR LITTLE COUNTER-CULTURE LIVES, RIGHT?

BUT OUT THERE IN THE REAL WORLD THEY'RE BOMBING ABORTION CLINICS... HOLDING NAZI AND KKK RALLIES... TRYING TO QUARANTINE PEOPLE WHO MIGHT HAVE AIDS!

THEY'RE MAKING SECRET WEAPONS DEALS TO ILLEGALLY FUND SO-CALLED "FREEDOM FIGHTERS" AND CALLING IT "THE LORD'S WORK"!!

WE'RE LIVING IN A PROTESTANT POLICE STATE AND ALL I'M WORRIED ABOUT IS GETTING A JOB SO I CAN HELP PERPETUATE THE PARANOID PATRIARCHAL DEATH CULTURE!

YOU TWO ARE ABSOLUTELY RIGHT! THANKS FOR THE LENTILS! I HAVE TO GO HOME NOW AND RETHINK MY PRIORITIES!

SLAM!
GREAT! NOW I'M ANXIOUS & DEPRESSED!
IF I WEREN'T SO PRINCIPLED, I'D SAY IT'S HIGH TIME SHE GOT HERSELF A GIRLFRIEND!

MO & CLARICE IN...
the HOAX
©1987 BY ALISON BECHDEL

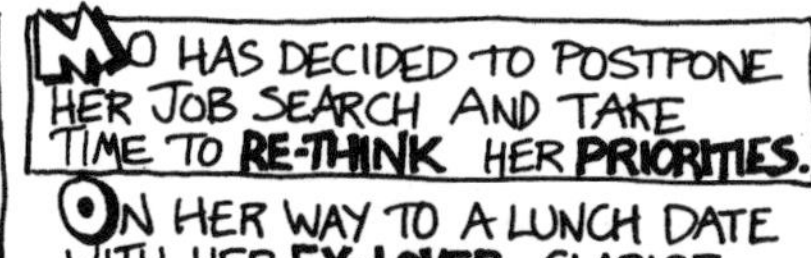
MO HAS DECIDED TO POSTPONE HER JOB SEARCH AND TAKE TIME TO RE-THINK HER PRIORITIES.

ON HER WAY TO A LUNCH DATE WITH HER EX-LOVER, CLARICE...
JADED... I'VE BECOME SO JADED. WHERE DID ALL MY REVOLUTIONARY FERVOR GO?
SCUFF
SCUFF
4

I REMEMBER WHEN CLARICE AND I CAME OUT TOGETHER IN COLLEGE... WE WERE SO EXCITED, SO RADICAL, SO COMMITTED TO DISMANTLING THE PATRIARCHY! CLARICE STILL IS... BUT SOMEWHERE ALONG THE LINE, I STOPPED FIGHTING...
BARBER SHOP
OPEN

HEY, MO! SO HOW'S THE PRIORITY CHECK GOING?
PAINFULLY. HOW'S LAW SCHOOL?
SAME OLD SHIT. STUDYING MY ASS OFF.

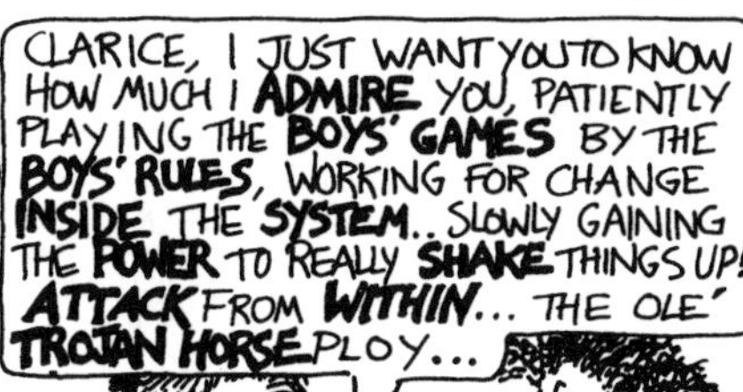
CLARICE, I JUST WANT YOU TO KNOW HOW MUCH I ADMIRE YOU, PATIENTLY PLAYING THE BOYS' GAMES BY THE BOYS' RULES, WORKING FOR CHANGE INSIDE THE SYSTEM.. SLOWLY GAINING THE POWER TO REALLY SHAKE THINGS UP! ATTACK FROM WITHIN... THE OLE' TROJAN HORSE PLOY...

Y'KNOW, MO, I'M REALLY GETTING INTO MY CORPORATE TAX CLASS LATELY!
LISTEN... IF I WENT INTO CORPORATE LAW, I COULD MAKE $70,000 MY FIRST YEAR OUT OF SCHOOL...
WHAT?
Cafe Topaz

UH... JUST TO PAY BACK YOUR LOANS, RIGHT? THEN, AFTER A YEAR YOU'LL GO WORK FOR LEGAL AID, RIGHT?

WELL, I DUNNO... TONI AND I ARE THINKING OF BUYING A HOUSE AND HAVING KIDS... YOU NEED MONEY FOR THAT.

CLARICE! OLD COMRADE! WHAT ARE YOU SAYING?!
GODDESS KNOWS, US WOMEN OF COLOR HAVE A HARD ENOUGH TIME IN THIS COUNTRY... WHY SHOULDN'T I ENJOY THE FRUITS OF MY LABORS? GET A MICROWAVE, A VOLVO STATION WAGON...

CLARICE! I DIDN'T THINK IT COULD HAPPEN! YOU, OF ALL PEOPLE! MY LAST HOPE!
...PRIVATE SCHOOLS FOR THE KIDS,.. QUIET EVENINGS WITH TONI, PORING OVER OUR STOCK PORTFOLIO...

CLARICE! SNAP OUT OF IT! JESUS, WHERE ARE THOSE DEPROGRAMMERS WHEN YOU NEED ONE?!
MO, RELAX! I'M JUST PULLING YOUR LEG!

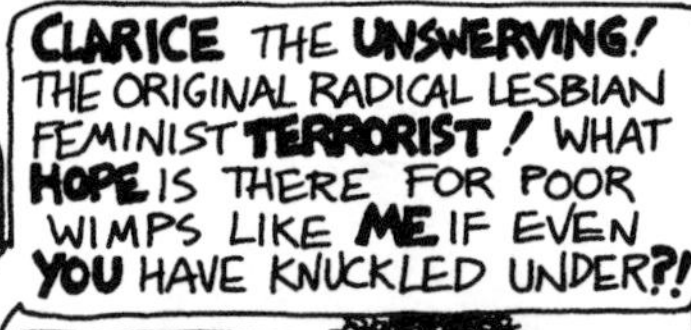
CLARICE THE UNSWERVING! THE ORIGINAL RADICAL LESBIAN FEMINIST TERRORIST! WHAT HOPE IS THERE FOR POOR WIMPS LIKE ME IF EVEN YOU HAVE KNUCKLED UNDER?!

MO, I SAID I WAS KIDDING! LIGHTEN UP!

I MAY AS WELL SEE IF THE C.I.A. IS HIRING!
UH... WHY DON'T I COME BACK LATER?
GOOD IDEA.

IT'S MO AGAIN! AND SHE'S HAVING...
NO SEX
©1987 BY ALISON BECHDEL

LIFE PLODS ON FOR OUR AMOROUS HEROINE.
...HER EYES DARK WITH DESIRE, MONIQUE LICKED THE MELTED PAPAYA ICE CREAM FROM URSULA'S FINGERS. "I WANT YOU," WHISPERED URSULA HOARSELY, USING HER FREE HAND TO FUMBLE WITH THE ZIPPERS OF MONIQUE'S BLACK LEATHER FLIGHTSUIT...
SIGH.
VANILLA LEATHER LOVE
5

THE NEXT MORNING FINDS MO AT HER FAVORITE LESBO HANGOUT, CAFE TOPAZ...
...ALMOST A YEAR SINCE MY LAST SEXUAL ENCOUNTER, AND STILL NO SIGN OF MS. RIGHT...

MY PENT-UP EROTIC ENERGY IS DRIVING ME CRAZY... I'M ATTRACTED TO EVERY DYKE I SEE... THEY'RE ALL SO... SO SEXY...

THE WAY THEY LAUGH...

THE WAY THEY WALK...

THE WAY THEIR JEANS FIT...

HERE COMES A HAPPY COUPLE... LOOKS LIKE THEY JUST ROLLED OUT OF BED... THEY WERE PROBABLY MAKING LOVE ALL NIGHT LONG.

I STILL DON'T SEE WHY WE HAVE TO GO TO A THERAPIST --A COMPLETE STRANGER-- TO DISCUSS OUR PRIVATE PROBLEMS!
BECAUSE WE'RE NOT GETTING ANYWHERE ON OUR OWN! WHEN WAS THE LAST TIME WE MADE LOVE?!
Menu

WILL YOU STOP PRESSURING ME ABOUT SEX?
PRESSURING YOU? IS IT TOO MUCH TO ASK THAT WE MAKE LOVE EVERY ONCE IN A WHILE? YOU USED TO ENJOY IT!

I DO ENJOY IT! JUST NOT ALL THE TIME!
ALL THE TIME?! AT THIS POINT I'M GRATEFUL FOR ALTERNATE BANK HOLIDAYS!!
RADAR EAR

WILL YOU PLEASE KEEP YOUR VOICE DOWN?

HERE'S YER PANCAKES! ANYTHING ELSE?
CAN I PLEASE LICK THE MAPLE SYRUP FROM YOUR FINGERS?
UH... NO, THANKS.

IT'S CLARICE & TONI! AND THEY'RE...
GETTING RESPECTABLE
©1987 BY ALISON BECHDEL

ON THE PHONE WITH MO ONE MORNING...
...BLAH, BLAH...WHINE... NO GIRLFRIEND... NO SEX.. WHINE... BLAH, BLAH...
I KNOW, MO. BUT IT'S SPRING! THINGS WILL START HAPPENING AGAIN!
BYE, DARLING!
GRAPE GRAVEL

I GUESS SO... SO HOW ARE YOU AND TONI?
JUST GREAT! YOU KNOW, I DON'T THINK I'VE EVER BEEN SO HAPPY! IN FACT,..

THAT'S NICE. WELL, I HAVE TO GO READ THE PERSONALS NOW. THANKS FOR LISTENING, CLARICE!

ON CAMPUS THAT DAY...
IT'S GREAT TO SEE YOU, CLARICE! IT'S BEEN MONTHS! SO, ARE YOU & TONI STILL TOGETHER?
UH... LAST I HEARD, WE WERE.

LATER IN THE AFTERNOON...
...MY OTHER GIRLFRIEND ANGELA IS KIND OF UPTIGHT ABOUT ME SEEING NAOMI. ANGELA'S A REAL LINEAR THINKER. SHE CAN'T SEEM TO TRANSCEND THE MONOGAMOUS MINDSET.
GEE, LO. THAT'S ROUGH.

FINALLY, BACK AT THE RANCH...
JUNE! I'M HO-OME!
IN HERE, WARD!
TONI, AM I STILL YOUR ONE AND ONLY?
I THINK SO. WHY?

I WAS AFRAID MAYBE SINCE THIS MORNING YOU DECIDED THAT MONOGAMY WAS TOO LINEAR, AND SO YOU TRANSCENDED IT.
WELL... IT IS KIND OF UNCOOL... BUT I THINK YOU'RE STUCK WITH ME.

WHY IS IT SO UNCOOL? WE DON'T GET ANY CREDIT, TONI! WHEN I RUN INTO SOMEONE I HAVEN'T SEEN IN A WHILE, IT'S ALWAYS "SO, ARE YOU TWO STILL TOGETHER?" LIKE THEY EXPECT US TO BREAK UP!

AND NO ONE WANTS TO HEAR ABOUT HOW HAPPY I AM WITH YOU. THEY'RE ONLY INTERESTED IN ROMANTIC STRIFE!

SO, NOW WE NEED A SUPPORT GROUP FOR HAPPY COUPLES?
YOU KNOW WHAT I MEAN! I DON'T EXPECT ANYTHING FROM THE STRAIGHT WORLD, BUT YOU'D THINK AT LEAST OTHER DYKES WOULD VALIDATE OUR RELATIONSHIP!

WELL... STRAIGHT COUPLES GET RESPECT WHEN THEY MARRY. MAYBE WE NEED TO MAKE SOME KIND OF SYMBOLIC AFFIRMATION OF OUR COMMITMENT TO ONE ANOTHER!
YOU MEAN...

YES! LET'S OPEN A JOINT CHECKING ACCOUNT!
OH, DARLING! BUT THIS IS SO SUDDEN!

ANGST IN RIGHT FIELD
8
©1987 BY ALISON BECHDEL

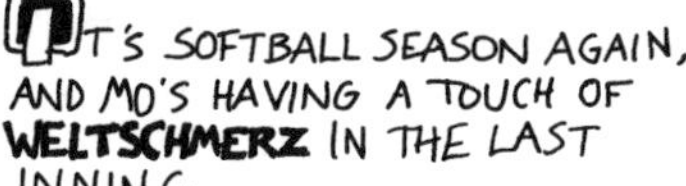
IT'S SOFTBALL SEASON AGAIN, AND MO'S HAVING A TOUCH OF WELTSCHMERZ IN THE LAST INNING...

IT'S SO PEACEFUL OUT HERE...

BATWIMMIN
YOU'D NEVER SUSPECT THAT SOMEWHERE POLITICAL PRISONERS ARE BEING TORTURED, PEOPLE ARE STARVING, CHEMICALS ARE SPILLING, MISSILES ARE PILING UP... NOPE! HERE IN THE HEART OF THE BEAST, EVERYTHING'S JUST HUNKY DORY!

SOUTH AFRICA, CENTRAL AMERICA, AND THE MIDDLE EAST ARE ALL FAR AWAY. WE CAN WATCH THEM SAFELY ON THE NEWS EVERY NIGHT...

AND WHEN SOMETHING GETS TOO CLOSE TO HOME, THE NETWORKS FIND WAYS TO KEEP IT PALATABLE AND UNINFORMATIVE...

LIKE CALLING OLIVER NORTH AND HIS HENCHMEN 'KEY PLAYERS' IN THE IRAN-CONTRA DEAL, INSTEAD OF SOMETHING LESS POSITIVE LIKE 'CRIMINALLY INSANE HYPERMILITARY @*#*! WARMONGERS!'
SMEK!

'KEY PLAYERS'! HMPH! MAKES 'EM SOUND LIKE GODDAMN FOOTBALL HEROES! LIES! CORRUPTION! HYPOCRISY!

AND PEOPLE SWALLOW IT! WELL, WHAT DO I EXPECT FROM A NATION THAT EQUATES TRUTH AND BEAUTY WITH HALLMARK CARDS? A NATION OF MINDLESS CONSUMERS GOBBLING UP NATURAL RESOURCES AND LEAVING ALL THIS SHIT BEHIND!

I MEAN, THE GLOBAL CLIMATE IS CHANGING BECAUSE WE'VE FUCKED UP THE ENVIRONMENT SO BAD!
KIK

I WONDER WHICH WILL COME FIRST, THE NEXT ICE AGE OR NUCLEAR HOLOCAUST?
IS SHE FINALLY LOSING IT?

HOW CAN WE STAND HERE PLAYING SOFTBALL? I MEAN, WHAT'S THE POINT?!?
BATWIMMIN

PLOP!

THAT'S THE GAME! WE WON!
WHAT A CATCH, MO!
FOR A POINTLESS GAME, IT HAS ITS MOMENTS.
BATWIMMIN

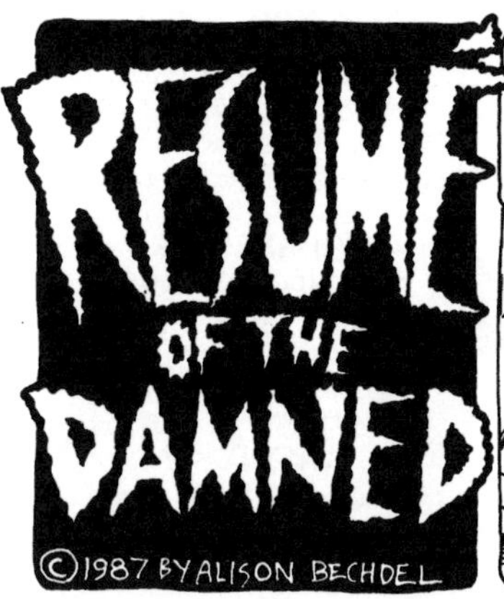
RESUME OF THE DAMNED
©1987 BY ALISON BECHDEL

THANKS FOR COMING OVER, LOIS! MY UNEMPLOYMENT RUNS OUT IN A COUPLE WEEKS AND I GOTTA GET MY RESUMÉ TOGETHER.
NO PROBLEM, MO OLD PAL! I'M GOOD AT THIS KIND OF THING!
END APARTHEID
DIVEST NOW
9

OKAY. LET'S START WITH YOUR LAST JOB.
PROOFREADER AND PRODUCTION ASSISTANT FOR THE NOW-DEFUNCT GAYLY FORWARD NEWS.
...AND BEFORE THAT?
OFFICE ASSISTANT AT THE ABORTION RIGHTS ACTION COUNCIL.

UH... OKAY. AND BEFORE THAT?
DELIVERY-PERSON FOR THE COMMON WOMON (THAT'S WITH AN 'O') BREAD COLLECTIVE.

HM... THIS ISN'T SOUNDING TOO PROMISING.. HOW ABOUT VOLUNTEER WORK?
WELL, I HAVE GOOD EDITING SKILLS FROM MY TWO YEARS ON THE STAFF OF THE LESBIAN RAG...

I GOT EXPERIENCE DOING COUNSELING WHEN I VOLUNTEERED AT THE BATTERED WOMEN'S SHELTER...

AND I HAVE FACILITATING AND ORGANIZING SKILLS FROM PLANNING DEMONSTRATIONS WITH THE CLARA LEMLICH MEMORIAL AFFINITY GROUP AND GRAFFITI GUERRILLAS!

MO, MO, MO... HAVEN'T YOU DONE ANYTHING LESS, UH... LESS PROGRESSIVE?
WHADDAYA MEAN?

I MEAN, WHO'S GONNA HIRE YOU WITH A RESUMÉ LIKE THIS? C'MON MO, THINK! YOU MUST HAVE DONE SOME WORK WHICH HAD LITTLE OR NO SOCIALLY REDEEMING VALUE!

WELL JEEZ, LOIS! I'M NOT TRYING TO GET A JOB WITH THE STATE DEPARTMENT!

OKAY, FINE! BE DOWNWARDLY MOBILE! GET ANOTHER LOW-PAYING JOB IN SOME IDEALISTIC, GOODY-TWO-SHOES ALTERNATIVE ORGANIZATION! SEE IF I CARE!

BY THE WAY, WE NEED ANOTHER CASHIER AT THE WOMEN'S BOOKSTORE. $5 AN HOUR, NO BENEFITS. WHY DON'T YOU COME BY DURING MY SHIFT TOMORROW AND APPLY?
WHAT A PAL!

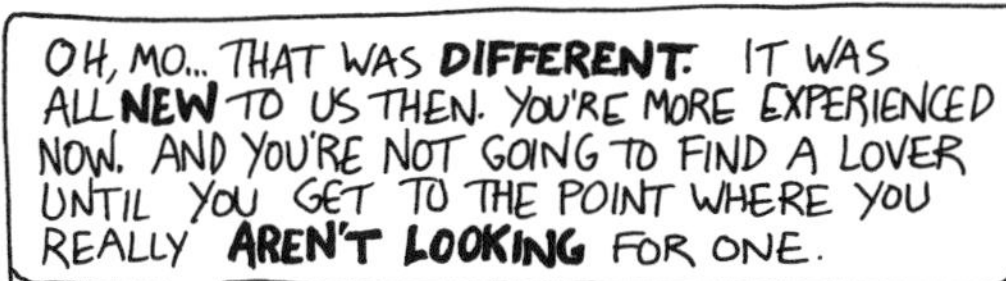

IS MO GOING TOO FAR? IS SHE STARTING TO REPEL HER FRIENDS AS WELL AS POTENTIAL LOVERS? WILL SHE GET HER ACT TOGETHER? BEAR WITH HER A LITTLE LONGER, AND MAYBE YOU'LL FIND OUT!

PRIDE & PREJUDICE
©1987 BY ALISON BECHDEL

WHAT A GREAT DAY FOR A MARCH! LOOK...THERE'S MO!

HEY, MO! HAPPY GAY PRIDE! I WANT YOU TO MEET MY FRIEND HARRIET FROM THE CENTRAL AMERICAN TASK FORCE!
HEY, CLARICE, TONI! HI, HARRIET.
!!

NICE TO MEET YOU, MO! WE WERE JUST AGREEING THAT GAY PRIDE DAY IS OUR FAVORITE HOLIDAY OF THE YEAR.

YEAH? MINE TOO! BUT DON'T YOU THINK THE WHOLE THING IS GETTING KIND OF CONSERVATIVE?

DON'T YOU SEE THE INFLUENCE OF REAGAN AND AIDS? THIS COUNTRY IS IN POLITICAL RETROGRADE AND GAY PRIDE IS GOING ALONG WITH IT!
FIGHT AIDS NOT GAYS
UH-OH... HERE SHE GOES...

LOOK AT THIS MARCH! WE'VE STOPPED SAYING "WE'RE QUEER AND HAPPY THAT WAY, SO YOU'D BETTER GET USED TO IT."
GAY & LESBIAN CATHOLIC MARTYRS
...SOON TO BE SAINTS!

NOW IT'S MORE LIKE, "SEE, WE'RE JUST AS PATRIOTIC, GOD-FEARING, AND RED-BLOODED AS THE REST OF YOU WHOLESOME AMERICANS."
I'M A YANKEE DOODLE DAN-DY... A YAN-KEE DOODLE, DO OR DIE!
MEN'S CHORU

RELIGION! PATRIOTISM! FINANCIAL SECURITY! DOESN'T ANYONE REALIZE?! WE'RE CONSPIRING IN OUR OWN OPPRESSION! WHERE HAS OUR OLD SPIRIT AND OUTRAGEOUSNESS GONE?!
LE$BIAN INVESTMENT BANKERS

MO, THERE'S PLENTY OF SPIRIT AND OUTRAGEOUSNESS HERE! WILL YOU LIGHTEN UP AND TAKE A LOOK AROUND? YOU GET SO WORKED UP, YOU ONLY SEE THE THINGS THAT SUPPORT YOUR DEPRESSING THEORIES!
FUCK GENDER

JEEZ! MAYBE YOU'RE RIGHT! MAYBE I OTTA JUST WANDER OFF INTO THE CROWD AND STOP RUINING THE MARCH FOR YOU GUYS!
IS SHE ALWAYS LIKE THIS?
YOU GET USED TO IT.

©1987 BY ALISON BECHDEL

AT LONG LAST, OUR HEROINE HAS REJOINED THE RANKS OF THE **GAINFULLY EMPLOYED**.

IT'S SATURDAY AFTERNOON AND SHE'S JUST FINISHING HER FIRST WEEK OF **CASHIERING** AT **MADWIMMIN BOOKS**.

MO IS IN A PARTICULARLY GOOD MOOD BECAUSE TONIGHT IS THE FIRST BIG SOCIAL EVENT IN WEEKS... THE BENEFIT DANCE FOR THE **LESBIAN HEALTH COLLECTIVE**!

AFTER A QUICK SUPPER...

MO BEGINS HER **GROOMING RITUAL** WITH GREAT **ANTICIPATION**.

FINALLY, SHE'S DRESSED...

...AND ON HER WAY.

BUT **HORRORS**! IN HER **EAGERNESS**, MO HAS ARRIVED **RIGHT ON TIME**!!

STAY TUNED TO DISCOVER THE OUTCOME OF THIS MOST **AWKWARD PREDICAMENT**!!

EVENTUALLY, THINGS BEGIN TO PICK UP. MO POUNCES ON THE FIRST FAMILIAR FACE SHE SEES.

SUDDENLY NERVOUS, MO FINDS HERSELF STRANGELY UNABLE TO MAKE LIGHT, FRIENDLY CHIT-CHAT!

YEAH... INCREDIBLE, HUH?
COVERT OPERATIONS! FALSE DOCUMENTS! "PLAUSIBLE DENIABILITY"! I'VE NEVER HEARD SO MANY REVERSALS IN MY LIFE! DECEPTION IS A VIRTUE! LAWBREAKERS ARE PATRIOTS! C.I.A.-BACKED MERCENARIES ARE FREEDOM-FIGHTERS!
WHAT CHOO WANT... BABY I GOT! WHAT CHOO NEED... YOU KNOW I GOT IT!

WHOA! LISTEN, MO. YOU'RE REALLY CUTE WHEN YOU START RAVING WITH INDIGNATION, BUT IF YOU KEEP TAKING THE 6 O'CLOCK NEWS PERSONALLY, YOU'RE GONNA GIVE YOURSELF AN ULCER!

CUTE?! SHE THINKS I'M CUTE!
IF YOU DON'T LIKE WHAT'S GOING ON, GO OUT AND ORGANIZE! DEMONSTRATE! REFUSE TO PAY YOUR TAXES! DON'T SIT AROUND WHINING!
OMIGOD! IS SHE FLIRTING?!

THEY DANCE A FEW SONGS, THEN GO THEIR SEPARATE WAYS... BUT BEFORE THE NIGHT IS OUT, THEY MEET AGAIN.

ON THE BUS HOME, OUR HEROINE IS STRANGELY ELATED...

LET'S JOIN CLARICE & TONI AS THEY SPEND SOME...
"QUALITY TIME"
TOGETHER!
14
©1987 BY ALISON BECHDEL

IT'S WEDNESDAY MORNING...
UGH! NOT AGAIN! DIDN'T WE JUST WAKE UP YESTERDAY?
BEEPBEEPBEEP!
BEEPBEEPBEEP!
ZNK.

CAN YOU DRIVE ME TO SCHOOL? I HAVE SOME LAST-MINUTE WORK TO DO BEFORE MY TORTS EXAM.
OKAY, BUT HURRY UP. I'VE GOT TO DROP THE TRUCK OFF WITH THE MECHANIC ON MY WAY TO WORK. THE MUFFLER'S SHOT.
TAMPAX
SKRITCH SKRITCH

CAN I BORROW SOME UNDERWEAR?
THIS IS MY LAST PAIR! I THOUGHT YOU WERE GOING TO DO THE LAUNDRY YESTERDAY!

DAMMIT! NO MILK! I HATE EATING DRY CEREAL!
HAVE YOU PAID THE PHONE BILL? WE GOT A FINAL NOTICE YESTERDAY.
DISCONNECTION

THE TOAST!
¡AY!

OH, NO!
WHAT?
WE FORGOT OUR ANNIVERSARY AGAIN! MONDAY WAS OUR FIFTH!
CRUNCH CRUNCH
SCRAPE SCRAPE
TORTS
DATES

WELL, LET'S CELEBRATE TONIGHT, THEN.
I CAN'T. THE WOMEN OF COLOR ANTI-VIOLENCE PROJECT IS MEETING AT 8.

OH, WELL. I SHOULD GO TO KARATE CLASS ANYWAY, AND MO WANTS TO HAVE DINNER WITH ME. HOW ABOUT TOMORROW NIGHT?

I HAVE THERAPY TOMORROW NIGHT.
THERAPY? I THOUGHT YOU WERE FINISHED WITH THERAPY!

FINISHING. I'M IN THE PROCESS OF FINISHING. DON'T YOU LISTEN TO ME ANYMORE?
HOW COULD I LISTEN TO YOU? WE HAVEN'T HAD TIME FOR A CONVERSATION IN WEEKS!

HELL! IT'S LATER THAN I THOUGHT! THE ALARM CLOCK MUST BE SLOW AGAIN! I DON'T HAVE TIME TO DROP YOU OFF.
HAPPY ANNIVERSARY! BYE!
SAME TO YOU. BRING HOME SOME MILK.

IS MO OVER-REACTING? IS LOIS UNDER-REACTING? THE DEBATE HEATS UP IN OUR NEXT EPISODE!

STAY TOONED!

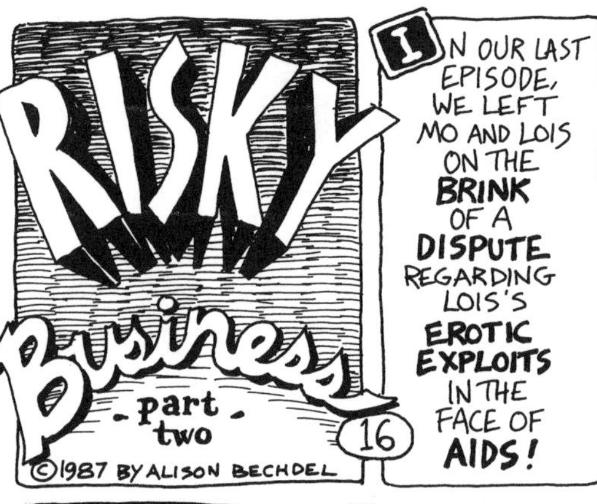
RISKY
Business
-part two-
16
©1987 BY ALISON BECHDEL
IN OUR LAST EPISODE, WE LEFT MO AND LOIS ON THE BRINK OF A DISPUTE REGARDING LOIS'S EROTIC EXPLOITS IN THE FACE OF AIDS!

STOP HAVING SEX?! WHAT'S WITH YOU, MO? HAVE YOU BECOME A FUNDAMENTALIST SINCE I LAST SAW YOU?!
LOIS, THE REASON LESBIANS ARE LOW-RISK IS BECAUSE, IN GENERAL, WE DON'T HAVE A LOT OF CASUAL SEX. BUT YOU SEEM BENT ON SINGLE-HANDEDLY REVERSING THAT TRAIT!

THAT'S BULLSHIT! SINCE WHEN HAVE YOU BECOME AN EXPERT ON THE RATE OF CASUAL SEX IN THE LESBIAN COMMUNITY, SISTER CELIBATE?

LOIS'S HOUSEMATE GINGER STEPS INTO THE FRAY...
OOH! LOW BLOW, LOIS! BUT YOU ARE WRONG, MO. SLEEPING AROUND ISN'T WHAT CAUSES AIDS... IT'S A VIRUS.

PART OF THE REASON DYKES ARE LOW-RISK IS BECAUSE IT'S JUST HARDER TO TRANSMIT DISEASES SEXUALLY BETWEEN TWO WOMEN THAN WHEN THERE'S SPERM BEING ABSORBED.

THANK YOU, GINGER.
HARDER, I SAID. NOT IMPOSSIBLE. REMEMBER THE TIME YOU CAUGHT THE YEAST INFECTION FROM THAT WOMAN VISITING FOR THE WITCHCRAFT CONFERENCE, AND THEN YOU GAVE IT TO ANGELA?

YEAH! SO THERE, MS. DON JUANITA!
HUH! I FORGOT ABOUT THAT... JEEZ, MAYBE I SHOULD'VE TALKED ABOUT THIS STUFF WITH AMARYLLIS... ER,... AMETHYST... BEFORE WE SLEPT TOGETHER...

I GUESS WE ALL GOTTA START TALKING ABOUT IT.
YEAH, GREAT. I HAVE A HARD ENOUGH TIME ASKING FOR A DATE LET ALONE GRILLING SOMEONE ON HER SEXUAL HISTORY.
WELL, LOOK ON THE BRIGHT SIDE, MO. IT GIVES YOU SOMETHING NEW TO WORRY ABOUT!

THE BALL IS IN OUR HEROINE'S COURT! IT'S BEEN SEVERAL WEEKS SINCE THE DANCE WHERE HARRIET GAVE MO HER PHONE NUMBER... BUT MO IS STILL DELIBERATING OVER WHETHER TO FOLLOW THROUGH...

EN ROUTE TO THE **MARCH ON WASHINGTON,** OUR STALWART BAND OF TRAVELERS PAUSES BRIEFLY IN THE **HEARTLAND** OF **AMERICA**...

I **HATE** USING THE BATHROOMS IN THESE PLACES...THIS **5-YEAR OLD** JUST ASKED HER MOTHER IF I WAS A **BOY** OR A **GIRL**!

BACK ON THE TRAIL...

OUR HEROINE IS THANKFUL FOR THE **CROWDED CONDITIONS**!

Bringing it Home
©1987 BY ALISON BECHDEL
BACK FROM THE **MARCH** ON **WASHINGTON**, MO IS APOLOGIZING TO HER BOSS AT **MADWIMMIN** FOR MISSING WORK.
WELL, WE MANAGED TO SCRAPE BY WITHOUT YOU, MO. AFTER ALL, IT WAS FOR A GOOD CAUSE.
GOD, IT WAS **INCREDIBLE**, JEZ! HALF-A-MILLION OF US! WE TURNED THAT **CREEPY, IMPERIALIST CAPITAL** INTO A WHOLE DIFFERENT **WORLD**!

FOR **ONE WEEKEND** WE HAD A GLIMPSE OF REAL **FREEDOM**. IT WAS LIKE BEING 100% QUEER AND **PROUD** OF IT, BUT AT THE SAME TIME NOT BEING **QUEER** AT **ALL** ANYMORE... Y'KNOW?

YEAH, I **DO** KNOW. I WASN'T EVEN THERE BUT I CAN SURE FEEL THAT **ENERGY**!
MO! YOU'RE **BACK**!
HEY, LOIS! YEAH, I GOT HOME LAST NIGHT. SOME **LESBERADO WITCHES** WE WERE IN **JAIL** WITH GAVE US A RIDE IN THEIR **WINNEBAGO**!

JEZANNA, YOU WOULDN'T HAVE **RECOGNIZED** OUR **UPTIGHT LITTLE MO**! WE'RE ALL READY TO **LEAVE** AFTER THE MARCH, BUT **SHE** DECIDES TO STAY ON FOR THE **CIVIL DISOBEDIENCE**! NO RIDE HOME, NO **BAIL MONEY**, NO AFFINITY GROUP!

WELL, **HARRIET** AND I REALIZED DURING THE MARCH THAT WE REALLY HAD NO **CHOICE**... IT WAS JUST A NECESSARY THING TO DO.
HARRIET, EH? NO DOUBT THE SAME HARRIET WHOSE **PHONE NUMBER** YOU'VE BEEN **FONDLING** FOR WEEKS... SO, YOU GOT **ARRESTED**?

"YEAH... WE GOT THROUGH THE POLICE BARRICADE ON THE STEPS OF THE **SUPREME COURT** AND HAD A SYMBOLIC **KISS-IN** WITH ALL THESE **WILD WOMEN**!..."
EQUAL JUSTICE UNDER LAW

"I WAS **KISSING HARRIET** WHEN THE ARRESTING **OFFICERS** PULLED US **APART**!"
CROSS

IT WAS SO... SUCH A **REVOLUTIONARY GESTURE**!
YEAH, I'LL **BET**!

IT'S JUST WONDERFUL TO HAVE SUCH AN **EMPOWERED** EMPLOYEE, MO. NOW YOU CAN START MAKING SOME REVOLUTIONARY GESTURES WITH **THIS**.

BUTT REACTION
20
©1987 BY ALISON BECHDEL
BRUNCHING AT CAFÉ TOPAZ, MO HAS SHOWN ABSOLUTELY NO INTEREST IN CLARICE AND TONI'S DISCUSSION ABOUT U.S. AID TO THE CONTRAS...
ARE YOU FEELING ALL RIGHT, MO?
HUH? OH, YEAH. I'M FINE...
UH... SO, TELL ME EVERYTHING YOU KNOW ABOUT HARRIET. IS SHE INVOLVED WITH SOMEONE?
MO, FER GODDESS' SAKE! YOU SPENT A NIGHT IN JAIL AND DROVE HALFWAY ACROSS THE COUNTRY WITH HER... SURELY YOU GOT BEYOND SMALL TALK!
WELL... IT DOESN'T SEEM LIKE SHE HAS ANY PRIMARY-TYPE PERSON... SHE MENTIONED AN EX-LOVER, BUT SHE NEVER ACTUALLY SAID SHE WAS AVAILABLE!
I MEAN, WHAT IF I ASK HER ON A DATE DATE BUT SHE THINKS IT'S JUST A FRIENDLY DATE... WHAT IF I MAKE A FOOL OF MYSELF?!
MO, TRUST YOUR INSTINCTS! YOU'LL BE ABLE TO TELL IF SHE'S INTERESTED OR NOT!
BUT IT'S BEEN SO LONG! HOW DO I KNOW IF MY INSTINCTS ARE STILL WORKING?
OKAY, MO. AS A RULE, I DON'T LIKE PASSING ALONG THIS KIND OF INFORMATION, BUT I SEE YOU NEED SOME ENCOURAGEMENT. THE OTHER DAY HARRIET REMARKED TO ME THAT YOU HAVE, AH... I BELIEVE HER PHRASE WAS, 'A CUTE BUTT'.
WHAT?! SHE SAID WHAT? WHEN? WHY?!!
WHAT DO YOU THINK SHE MEANT?
I KNEW I WOULD REGRET THAT.
INSTINCTS, MO. TRUST YOUR INSTINCTS.
LATER THAT DAY...
CUTE? CUTE LIKE KITTENS AND BABIES? CUTE LIKE NICE?... OR CUTE LIKE,... HOT?!! I WONDER IF SHE LIKES ME?!

By The Book
21
©1987 BY ALISON BECHDEL
HARRIET, STILL IN PROFESSIONAL DRAG FROM HER JOB, DROPS BY **MADWIMMIN BOOKS** AFTER WORK ONE SNOWY EVENING.
I HOPE SHE'S **WORKING** TODAY! WHAT A **DRAG** IF I CAME OVER HERE FOR **NOTHING**...
OPEN

HEY, MO! HOW ARE YA? NICE TO **SEE** YOU!
HARRIET! HI! WHAT'S HAPPENING?

UM... I'M LOOKING FOR A COPY OF "THE **WHEAT-FREE GUIDE** TO **CREATIVE VISUALIZATION** IN **CO-DEPENDENT PAST-LIFE RELATIONSHIPS**."
HUH. JEEZ, I NEVER **HEARD** OF THAT ONE... WONDER IF IT'S IN **SPIRITUALITY** OR **COOKING**... WHO'S IT **BY**?

I DUNNO. I MADE IT UP. I REALLY JUST CAME BY TO SEE YOU.
PHEW! YOU HAD ME **GOING** THERE FOR A MINUTE! USUALLY I'VE AT LEAST **HEARD** OF A **TITLE**, EVEN IF WE DON'T **STOCK** IT.... **WHA-AT?!**

MOMENTARILY STUNNED, OUR HEROINE QUICKLY REGAINS HER COMPOSURE.
I **SAID**, I JUST CAME BY TO SEE **YOU**.
REALLY? UH... I MEAN, UM, WE'LL BE CLOSING IN A FEW MINUTES... ARE YOU **HUNGRY?** WE COULD, UM... HAVE **DINNER?**

GREAT! I'D **LOVE** TO... I'LL BROWSE AROUND TILL YOU'RE READY.

JEZANNA! THAT'S **HER!** THAT'S **HARRIET!** SHE CAME BY TO **SEE** ME! WE'RE GOING OUT TO **DINNER!**

HUH. SHE'S DRESSED LIKE THAT FOR DINNER WITH **YOU?**
AW, THOSE ARE JUST HER **WORK** CLOTHES. SHE INVESTIGATES **HUMAN RIGHTS COMPLAINTS** FOR THE **STATE**... ISN'T SHE **GORGEOUS?**

I'LL CLOSE OUT, MO. GO ENJOY YOUR BIG DATE.
THANKS, JEZ! SEE YOU TOMORROW!

SO, WHAT DO YOU FEEL LIKE? ETHIOPIAN? MEXICAN? MACROBIOTIC?
HOW ABOUT THE **TOPAZ?**
BUT OF COURSE! SHALL WE?

DINING AT CAFÉ TOPAZ, MO & HARRIET **APPEAR** TO HAVE FINALLY GOTTEN IT TOGETHER. BUT IS IT A **DATE**, OR IS IT JUST A **FRIENDLY DINNER?** ONLY **MORE** TIME WILL TELL...

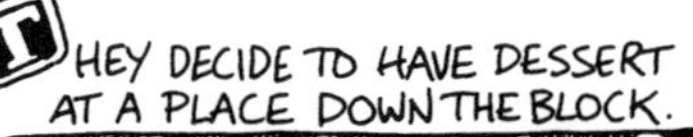

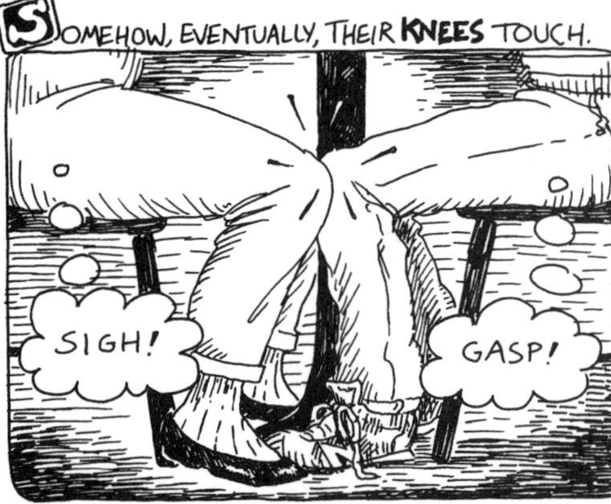

AFTER DECLARING THEIR MUTUAL **ATTRACTION**, OUR HEROINES RETURN TOGETHER TO **MO'S APARTMENT** UNDER THE PRETENSE OF **WARMING** HARRIET'S **FEET**.

HARRIET HAS JUST REFUSED MORE **TEA**.

HAVING DECIDED, UPON FURTHER DISCUSSION, THAT SAFER-SEX PRECAUTIONS WERE NOT **NECESSARY**, MO AND HARRIET PROCEEDED TO INDULGE IN A **WIDE RANGE** OF AMOROUS EXPLORATIONS. SHORTLY AFTERWARDS, WE FIND MO PONDERING HER NEW **NON-CELIBATE** STATUS.

JEEZ, THAT WAS **NICE**... I GUESS I DIDN'T **FORGET HOW** AFTER ALL...

HOW CAN SHE **SLEEP?** I CAN **NEVER** SLEEP IN A STRANGE BED... **OR** WITH A STRANGE **PERSON** FOR THAT MATTER... PARTICULARLY WHEN THEY'RE LYING ON MY **ARM**...

WITH ZEN-LIKE PATIENCE, OUR HEROINE PERSEVERES INTO THE NIGHT AS HER **ARM**, IF NOTHING ELSE, **DOZES OFF**.

...SO **NOW** WHAT? IS THIS JUST A CASUAL **THING** FOR HER? MAYBE SHE DOES THIS ALL THE **TIME**... MAYBE SHE'S **INCAPABLE** OF **COMMITMENT**, OR WORSE YET, **NON-MONOGAMOUS** ON **PRINCIPLE**!

...OR MAYBE SHE THINKS THIS MEANS WE'RE **MARRIED**! WHAT IF SHE STARTS CRITICIZING MY **TABLE MANNERS** AND ASKING ME WHAT I'M **THINKING ABOUT**! I DON'T THINK I'M **READY** FOR THIS...

HER THOUGHTS RUN ON IN THIS MANNER TILL NEARLY **DAWN**...

I WONDER IF SHE WANTS TO HAVE **CHILDREN**... SHE **SEEMED** TO LIKE THE **CATS**... I THINK MY **MOTHER** WOULD LIKE HER..

HUH? WAS I ASLEEP?
ASLEEP?! I WAS BEGINNING TO THINK YOU WERE IN A COMA!

OH, WOW... WHAT TIME IS IT?
A QUARTER PAST TEN. RELAX! IT'S SATURDAY!
SHIT! I WORK SATURDAYS... I HAFTA BE AT THE BOOKSTORE IN FIFTEEN MINUTES!

SO CALL IN SICK!
I CAN'T! JEZANNA DEPENDS ON ME!

SO GET UP AND GET DRESSED ALREADY.
I CAN'T! YOU FEEL SO NICE!

JUST HOW STRONG **IS** OUR HEROINE'S MORAL FIBER **ANYWAY?** STAY TUNED!

COMMUNIQUÉ
26
ALTHOUGH SHE IS EXPECTED TO OPEN THE DOORS OF MADWIMMIN BOOKS TO THE PUBLIC IN TEN MINUTES, MO IS UNABLE TO WRENCH HERSELF FROM HARRIET'S EMBRACES!
©1988 BY ALISON BECHDEL

CAN'T YOU CALL LOIS AND HAVE HER OPEN UP FOR YOU?
NO, NOT LOIS! SHE SAW US LAST NIGHT AND SHE'D KNOW WHY I WAS LATE.

SO?
SO KNOWING LOIS, IT'LL BE ALL OVER TOWN BY NOON. I'LL CALL ARIADNE. SHE OWES ME A FAVOR.

HI, GINGER. IT'S ARIADNE. I HAFTA CANCEL OUR BRUNCH DATE. I'M WORKING FOR MO THIS MORNING. NO, I DUNNO... SHE JUST SAID 'SOMETHING CAME UP.'
LESBIAN BED DEATH
JOAN HOOLIHAN

MORNING GINGER!
HI, NAOMI! SAY, GUESS WHO DIDN'T SHOW UP FOR WORK THIS MORNING AFTER WE SAW HER AT THE TOPAZ WITH HARRIET LAST NIGHT... METHINKS THE CHASTE MAIDEN MO FINALLY GOT LAID!

...ORGANIC BLACK BEANS $1.55...
HEY, TONI.. DIDJA HEAR ABOUT MO & HARRIET?
SOY JUICE

HONEY! I PICKED UP SOME HOT NEWS AT THE CO-OP!
SO SUE ME
NIGHT COURT
IMPOSING LEGAL TOME
FROWST

HEY, LOIS! GUESS WHO FINALLY DID IT!
DAMN.

MEANWHILE, MO TEARS HERSELF AWAY...
MMM... -SMAK- WE HAFTA STOP...
YEAH, I KNOW -SLURP- I'LL BE LATE AGAIN.

AND ARRIVES AT THE BOOKSTORE BY NOON, JUST AS LOIS DROPS IN!
♪HEL-LO, MO!♫ YOU LOOK FLUSHED. 'JA WORK OUT THIS MORNING OR SOMETHING? Y'KNOW, I COULD REALLY GET INTO AN EXERCISE PROGRAM LIKE YOURS!

GREAT, LOIS. GREAT. I'M REALLY IMPRESSED. I THINK THIS COMMUNITY JUST SET THE LAND SPEED RECORD FOR GOSSIP MONGERING!
DETAILS! I WANT DETAILS!

I THINK WE SHOULD CONTINUE THIS DISCUSSION WHEN WE'RE BOTH MORE RATIONAL. I'M GOING TO WORK.

SURE! RUN AWAY FROM A LITTLE HONEST CONFLICT! GO PROCESS IT WITH YOUR GROUP! AND DON'T EXPECT ME TO SAVE YOU ANY TURNIP LOAF!

COLD FEET
30
©1988 BY ALISON BECHDEL
CLARICE?
MMNH.

CLARICE, I'M PREGNANT.
WHAAT?!

RELAX. I WAS JUST **TESTING.** LISTEN, THOUGH. I'VE BEEN THINKING A **LOT** ABOUT THIS LATELY. I WANT TO HAVE A **BABY**.
WELL, YEAH, ME TOO. SOME DAY WE WILL.

WE'VE BEEN SAYING THAT FOR **YEARS** NOW. I'M **THIRTY**, CLARICE. EVERY DAY MORE OF MY **OVARIAN FOLLICLES** ARE DYING OFF! IF WE'RE GONNA DO IT, IT HAS TO BE **SOON**.

JEEZ, TONI! I'M STILL IN **SCHOOL!** WE DON'T HAVE ANY MONEY... OR ANY **SPERM,** FOR THAT MATTER... WE CAN'T RUSH **INTO** ANYTHING!

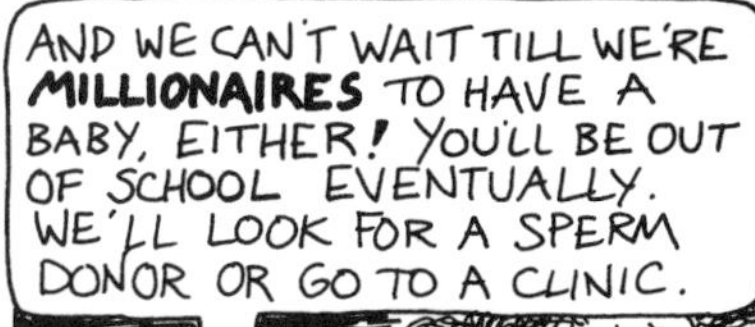
AND WE CAN'T WAIT TILL WE'RE **MILLIONAIRES** TO HAVE A BABY, EITHER! YOU'LL BE OUT OF SCHOOL EVENTUALLY. WE'LL LOOK FOR A SPERM DONOR OR GO TO A CLINIC.

BUT WHERE WOULD WE **PUT** A BABY? WHAT IF WE WANTED TO **TRAVEL?** WHAT IF WE JUST WANTED TO GO TO A **MOVIE?** OUR LIVES WOULD NEVER BE THE **SAME!**

THAT'S PART OF THE **IDEA.** I LOVE YOU VERY **MUCH,** CLARICE! I THINK WE HAVE A LOT TO **OFFER** A KID!

I DUNNO, HONEY... I GUESS DEEP **DOWN,** PART OF ME THINKS LESBIANS WERE CREATED FOR **OTHER PURPOSES** THAN RAISING **CHILDREN!**

LIKE **WHAT?** BEING **DRILL SERGEANTS** OR **DOG BREEDERS?!** THAT'S DOWNRIGHT **HOMOPHOBIC**, CLARICE!
UH... I **MEANT**... DON'T YOU THINK WE SHOULD WAIT TILL I'VE DONE SOME **THERAPY?** HOW CAN I BECOME SOMEONE'S **MOTHER** UNTIL I RESOLVE MY **OWN** CHILDHOOD?!

IF I DIDN'T **KNOW** YOU BETTER, CLARICE, I'D SAY YOU WERE **SCARED**.
TRY **MAD** WITH **TERROR**.

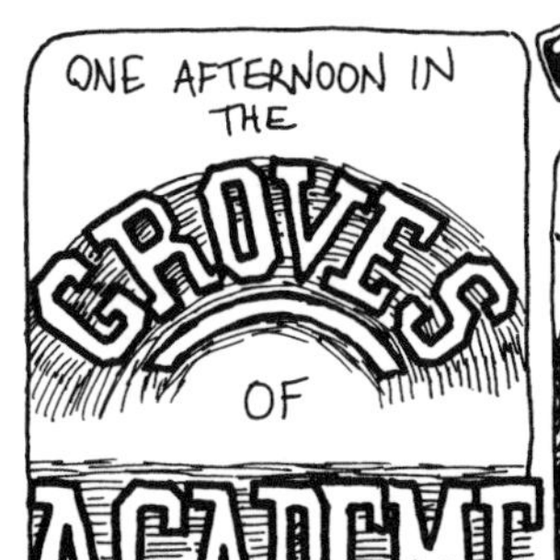

WE NEED TWO PEOPLE TO TAKE THIS WHEELCHAIR AND MAKE SURE THESE WORKSHOP LOCATIONS ARE REALLY ACCESSIBLE.

TROUBLE in Paradise
32
©1988 BY ALISON BECHDEL
AFTER A GRUELING DAY AT WORK AND SCHOOL, OUR DYNAMIC DUO REGROUPS FOR DINNER AT THE TOPAZ.

LOOK, CHICA! THERE'S A GROUP OF LESBIANS MEETING TO TALK ABOUT HAVING BABIES. LET'S GO! MAYBE IT WILL HELP YOU TO FEEL LESS SCARED.
UH...GROUP?
CLASSIFIEDS

EVERY TUESDAY NIGHT AT THE COMMUNITY CENTER.
OH, TOO BAD. TUESDAYS ARE THE COMMITTEE NIGHTS FOR THE GAY AND LESBIAN STUDIES CONFERENCE.

OH, OF COURSE. HOW SILLY OF ME TO THINK PLANNING A BABY COULD TAKE PRIORITY OVER PLANNING A FOUR-DAY CONFERENCE.
Cafe Topaz

TONI, BE REASONABLE! I'VE ALREADY COMMITTED MYSELF TO THIS! AND I DO WANT US TO HAVE A BABY, BUT I CAN'T STAND THIS CONSTANT PRESSURE!
OPEN

HEY, CLARICE!
GINGER! HI! HOW ARE YA? THIS IS MY LOVER, TONI.

HI, TONI. SAY, CLARICE, WE JUST HAVE TO GET TOGETHER FOR SOME GOSSIP ABOUT THE CONFERENCE ONE OF THESE DAYS!
I'D LOVE TO. WE COULD GO OUT FOR COFFEE AFTER THE MEETING TUESDAY.

YOU GOT YOURSELF A DATE! SEE YOU THEN... NICE MEETING YOU, TONI.

GINGER, HUH? SHE WAS FLIRTING WITH YOU, WASN'T SHE?
FLIRTING? TONI, WHAT IS THE MATTER WITH YOU? I THINK THIS BABY STUFF HAS GONE TO YOUR BRAIN!

HAS TONI TAKEN LEAVE OF HER SENSES... OR IS SOMETHING INDEED AFOOT? DON'T MISS THE NEXT GRIPPING EPISODE!
MENU

FATAL ATTRACTION

33

TONI IS MAKING A SUDDEN TRIP TO **SAN JUAN** FOR HER GRANDMOTHER'S **FUNERAL**.

THE **WORST** THING IS, MY ABUELITA WAS THE ONLY **SANE** MEMBER OF MY ENTIRE **FAMILY**.

I KNOW, HONEY. CALL ME IF THEY START TO DRIVE YOU CRAZY. I WISH I COULD COME **WITH** YOU.

GATE 78

THAT EVENING, CLARICE ATTENDS A MEETING OF THE **ACCESSIBILITY COMMITTEE**.

WE STILL NEED ANOTHER SIGN-LANGUAGE INTERPRETER FOR THE PANEL DISCUSSION, **"LESBIANS AND GAYMEN WORKING TOGETHER; TACTICAL TEAM OR TOTAL TRAVESTY?"**

NO, WE DON'T. MARIA SAID **SHE** COULD DO IT.

BUT WE ALREADY **HAVE** A WOMAN SIGNING. WE NEED A **MAN** FOR **PARITY**, ESPECIALLY ON **THIS** PANEL!

MATTERS DRAG ON...

BUT WE ONLY **HAVE** ONE MALE INTERPRETER, AND HE'S DOING THE MEN-**ONLY** WORKSHOP, **"SENSUAL, SALACIOUS & SAFE"** IN THE SAME TIME-SLOT!

AFTER AN APPARENT **ETERNITY**, THE MEETING ADJOURNS.

FRIENDLY ADVICE
34
©1988 BY ALISON BECHDEL
I'M GLAD YOU COULD COME OVER, MO. I REALLY NEED TO TALK TO YOU... UH... WHAT WOULD YOU THINK IF I HAD AN AFFAIR WITH GINGER?
WHAT?
I'M SO ATTRACTED TO HER! I CAN'T DESCRIBE IT... IT'S LIKE... GRAVITY... FATE... DESTINY!
WHAT?!
SHE FEELS THE SAME TOWARD ME. WE TALKED ABOUT IT LAST NIGHT.
CLARICE, WHAT ABOUT TONI?
WHAT ABOUT HER? THIS HAS NOTHING TO DO WITH MY COMMITMENT TO TONI! IN FACT, I THINK IT WOULD BE UNHEALTHY FOR OUR RELATIONSHIP IF I DIDN'T ACT ON THESE FEELINGS FOR GINGER! BESIDES, TONI'S STILL IN PUERTO RICO.
WHOA, CLARICE... CLARICE? ARE YOU IN THERE, OR HAVE YOU BEEN POSSESSED BY AN ALIEN?
MEANWHILE...
YEAH, I KNOW SHE'S INVOLVED WITH TONI. BUT I DON'T WANT TO MARRY HER, I JUST WANT TO SLEEP WITH HER!
WELL, I'VE NEVER BEEN ONE TO DISCOURAGE PEOPLE FROM FOLLOWING THEIR SEXUAL INCLINATIONS, BUT...
EXACTLY! IT WOULD BE WRONG TO REPRESS THESE FEELINGS FOR CLARICE!
LISTEN TO ME, GINGER! I SPEAK FROM EXPERIENCE. IT'S NOT A GOOD IDEA TO GET INVOLVED WITH MARRIED WOMEN!
BUT LOIS, THEY'RE NOT MONOGAMOUS! THAT'S ONE OF THE THINGS I ADMIRE ABOUT CLARICE. SHE DOESN'T JUST THEORIZE, SHE LIVES HER CONVICTIONS!
WE'RE HAVING DINNER TONIGHT. WHAT LOOK SHOULD I GO FOR? SCHOLARLY OR SEDUCTIVE?
HOW ABOUT SELF-DESTRUCTIVE?
THAT EVENING...
¡TONI! ¿QUIÉN LLAMAS POR TELÉFONO? ¿TU NOVIO?
RING!
RING!
RING!

CLOSE ENCOUNTER
A TIP O' THE NIB TO PAT WINICK
35
© 1988 BY ALISON BECHDEL

HEEDLESS OF THEIR FRIENDS' ADVICE, CLARICE AND GINGER FIND THEMSELVES AT THE POINT OF NO RETURN.
WANNA COME IN? LOIS AND SPARROW WON'T BE HOME TILL LATE.
SURE.

IGNORE THE MESS. IT'S MY THESIS.
WHAT'S IT ABOUT?

IT'S ABOUT HISTORICAL TRENDS IN DOMINANT-CULTURE CRITICISM OF AFRO-AMERICAN LITERATURE...

...WITH A FOCUS ON THE CRITICAL RESPONSE TO THE INFLUENCE...UH..

...OF THE ORAL TRADITION IN, UM... CONTEMPORARY FICTION BY BLACK WOMEN... MMM..
SMAK

TWO HOURS AND FIFTEEN MINUTES LATER...
OOPS! 'SCUSE ME!

I HOPE YOU KNOW WHAT YOU'RE GETTING INTO, GINGER, THAT'S ALL I HAVE TO SAY.

SLAM!

GINGER... I HAVE TO LEAVE IN CASE TONI CALLS IN THE MORNING... UM... I HAD A GREAT TIME.
ME TOO. YOU BUSY TOMORROW?

UH... YEAH. TONI'S FLIGHT GETS IN AT 6.
ARE YOU GOING TO TELL HER?
TELL HER WHAT?
HAS CLARICE BEEN POSSESSED BY AN ALIEN? WHAT'S GOING ON HERE, ANYWAY?! DON'T TOUCH THAT DIAL!

In the HEAT of the NIGHT
© 1988 BY ALISON BECHDEL
36
IT'S BEDTIME AT HARRIET'S APARTMENT...
I JUST CAN'T BELIEVE IT! WHY IS CLARICE DOING THIS?
I DON'T KNOW! SHE AND TONI SEEMED SO HAPPY!

THEY'RE MY ROLE MODELS, HARRIET! DON'T THEY REALIZE THEY HAVE A RESPONSIBILITY TO ME TO STAY TOGETHER?!

MO, STOP. IT'S TOO HOT TO RAVE.
THAT'S IT! IT'S THE GREENHOUSE EFFECT! THIS OPPRESSIVE HEAT IS CAUSING HORMONAL IMBALANCES AND CLARICE IS ONE OF THE FIRST VICTIMS!

I MEAN, DOESN'T IT BOTHER YOU, HARRIET? TO SEE AN ESTABLISHED, LONG-TERM LESBIAN RELATIONSHIP -- ONE THAT YOU LOOK TO FOR EXAMPLE AND INSPIRATION -- TO SEE IT JUST BITE THE DUST?!

MO, I THINK YOU'RE OVERREACTING. WHO SAID THEY WERE BREAKING UP?

WELL, JEEZ... I MEAN, CLARICE SLEPT WITH GINGER WHILE TONI WAS AT HER GRANDMOTHER'S FUNERAL! HOW SLEAZOID CAN YOU GET?
WOULD YOU LEAVE ME IF I SLEPT WITH SOMEONE ELSE?

WHO?! WHO IS IT?!

WHOA! IS THIS THE SAME WOMAN WHO WAS RECENTLY HOLDING FORTH ON HOW COUPLEHOOD SHOULD BE ABOLISHED IF WE HOPE TO REACH OUR TRUE HUMAN POTENTIAL?!
DON'T QUOTE ME OUT OF CONTEXT, HARRIET! WHO ARE YOU SLEEPING WITH?!
The Nation

BESIDES YOU? LEMME SEE... UH... NO ONE, AT THE MOMENT...
HAR·RI·ET!

THE IN-TERRO-GATION
37
©1988 BY ALISON BECHDEL

CLARICE HAS JUST PICKED TONI UP AT THE AIRPORT.
SO, DID YOU HAVE FUN WHILE I WAS GONE? ANY WILD AFFAIRS?
WHAAAT?!
SWERVE!
SCREEE

RELAX! JEEZ, I WAS JUST KIDDING SWEETHEART!
SORRY! I... UH... SO HOW WAS IT SEEING YOUR FAMILY?

PRETTY BAD. WITH MY GRANDMOTHER GONE, THERE WAS NO ONE TO STOP THEM ALL PESTERING ME ABOUT WHEN I'M GETTING MARRIED. THE FUNERAL WAS A CIRCUS.
AIRPORT

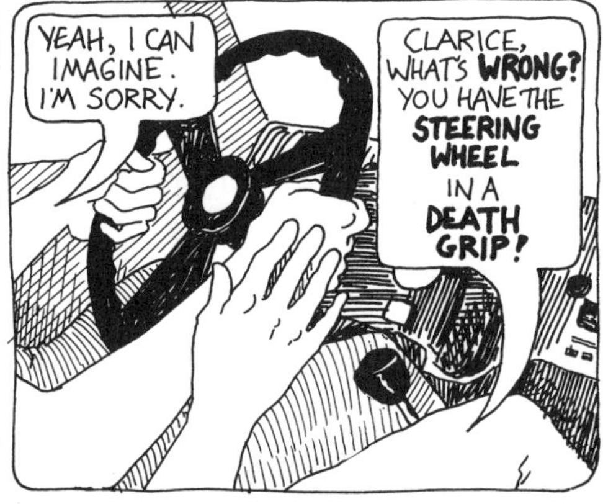
YEAH, I CAN IMAGINE. I'M SORRY.
CLARICE, WHAT'S WRONG? YOU HAVE THE STEERING WHEEL IN A DEATH GRIP!

TONI... I WENT OUT WITH GINGER LAST NIGHT.
I REMEMBER, YOU MADE A DATE FOR COFFEE. SO?

SO, I MEAN... WE DIDN'T JUST HAVE COFFEE. WE... WE HAD DINNER.

WHAT? WHAT ARE YOU SAYING? YOU MEAN, YOU'RE ATTRACTED TO HER?
WELL... YEAH.

DID YOU TELL HER YOU WERE? IS IT MUTUAL?
UM... YES. YES.

I KNEW IT! I KNEW SHE WAS FLIRTING WITH YOU!
TONI...

SO WHAT HAPPENED? DID YOU KISS HER GOODNIGHT?!
UM... YES.

JESUS, CLARICE. I CAN'T BELIEVE YOU'RE SITTING THERE TELLING ME THIS!
DON'T CRY, TONI!

On a long walk with Clarice, Mo relies on her inborn **tact** and adroit **interpersonal skills** to broach a **delicate subject**...

That evening...

AND WE'VE GOT TO SPEND THE NEXT **TWO MONTHS** BEING ASSAULTED WITH **HYPOCRITICAL HYPE** AS TWO MORALLY BANKRUPT **WHITE BOYS** GEAR UP FOR ANOTHER **ELECTORAL FARCE**!

JUST DESSERT
44
©1988 BY ALISON BECHDEL

ON THE RARE OCCASION OF THEIR ALL HAVING NOTHING **BETTER** TO DO, OUR HOUSEMATES GINGER, LOIS & SPARROW **SPEND** AN **EVENING** TOGETHER.

WHAT A ROTTEN MOVIE. WANNA GET SOME DESSERT?
SURE.
OK, BUT I JUST WANT SOME TEA.
Let Them Eat Cake

I'LL HAVE A CHOCOLATE **ORGASM** AND A CUP OF COFFEE
UH... I'LL HAVE THE TRIPLE TASMANIAN DEVILSFOOD **DELIGHT** AND AN ESPRESSO.
MINT TEA AND A **BRAN** MUFFIN, PLEASE.

I THOUGHT YOU WERE **OFF CAFFEINE**, GINGER!
AND I THOUGHT **YOU** WERE ALLERGIC TO **CHOCOLATE**.
I DON'T KNOW **WHY** YOU GUYS **EAT** THIS STUFF IF YOU **KNOW** IT'S **BAD** FOR YOU! DON'T COMPLAIN TO **ME** ABOUT YOUR **HEADACHES** AND **INSOMNIA**.

A SHORT WHILE LATER...
SO GINGER, I HAVEN'T RUN INTO **CLARICE** IN OUR BATHROOM LATELY... WHAT'S UP?
WE'RE NOT SEEING EACH OTHER... TURNS OUT SHE SLIGHTLY **EXAGGERATED** HOW NONMONOGAMOUS HER SCENE WITH **TONI** IS.

AW, GINGER, THAT'S TOO BAD... I'M SORRY. IN FACT, I'M **SO** SORRY THAT I WILL NOBLY REFRAIN FROM SAYING 'I **TOLD** YOU SO.'
YEAH, YEAH. **I** KNOW. BUT I DON'T HAVE ANY **REGRETS**. LIKE I TOLD YOU, I JUST WANTED TO **SLEEP** WITH HER, NOT GET **MARRIED**.

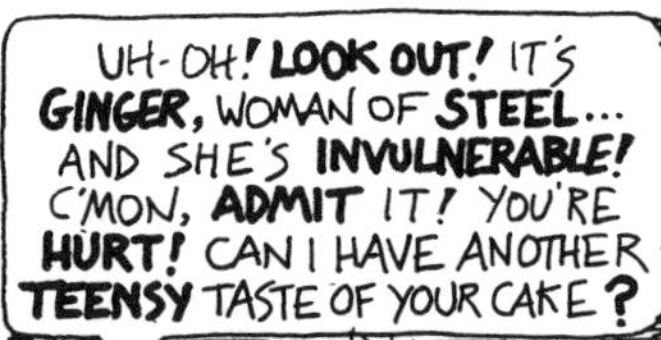
UH-OH! **LOOK OUT!** IT'S **GINGER**, WOMAN OF **STEEL**... AND SHE'S **INVULNERABLE!** C'MON, **ADMIT** IT! YOU'RE **HURT!** CAN I HAVE ANOTHER **TEENSY** TASTE OF YOUR CAKE?

ACTUALLY, I'M KIND OF **RELIEVED** IT DIDN'T WORK OUT. I'M **SICK** & **TIRED** OF ROMANTIC MELODRAMA. THERE ARE **OTHER** THINGS TO LIFE, AFTER ALL.

YOUR PROBLEM, GINGER, IS THAT YOU'VE NEVER WORKED THROUGH YOUR BREAK-UP WITH **PHYLLIS**. YOU SHOULD JOIN A **THERAPY** GROUP. ARE YOU GONNA **FINISH** THAT, LO?
TAKE IT. I'M STARTING TO **HALLUCINATE**.
URP

SPARROW, YOU WOULD RECOMMEND A THERAPY GROUP IF I HAD **HEMORRHOIDS!** NOPE, I'M GOING TO TRY SOME GOOD OLD-FASHIONED **CELIBACY** AND FINISH MY **THESIS!**

YOU **TELL** HER, GINGER! C'MON, WE BETTER HURRY HOME BEFORE WE **CRASH!**
YEAH, I FEEL KINDA **SPEEDY**... D'YOU THINK THEY PUT **SUGAR** IN THE BRAN MUFFINS HERE?

Tête à Tête
©1988 BY ALISON BECHDEL
45
MO IS HARD AT WORK DURING A SATURDAY **SALE** AT **MADWIMMIN BOOKS**.
♪ WE HAVE A GROO-VY KIND OF ♪ LOVE ♫

HEY, GINGER! HOW YA **DOING**! HAVEN'T SEEN **YOU** AROUND IN A WHILE!
HI, MO. OH, I'VE BEEN KEEPING A **LOW PROFILE**, THROWING MYSELF INTO MY WORK, THAT KIND OF THING.
MACHO TROLLOPS EROTIC FICTION
PIGS & GEESE

I... UM, GINGER, I DON'T WANT TO, LIKE, INVADE YOUR **PRIVACY**, BUT I JUST WANNA SAY I **KNOW** ABOUT YOU & **CLARICE**, AND I HOPE IT DOESN'T GET IN THE WAY OF **OUR** BEING FRIENDS.

THANKS, MO. THESE THINGS CAN BE SO MESSY, WITH PEOPLE **TAKING SIDES** AND NOT **SPEAKING** TO EACH OTHER. TOO BAD CLARICE & I DIDN'T THINK OF THAT BEFORE WE HOPPED IN THE SACK.

WHAT'S **WRONG**?
GRINGO BY RENA FAE GREEN

OH, NOTHING! I WAS JUST GONNA SAY YOU SHOULD CHECK OUT THE **75% OFF** BOOKS IN THE **BACK**... **WAY** IN THE BACK OF THE STORE...
MACHO STRUMPETS NEUROTIC FICTION

CLARICE! TONI! OUT SHOPPING TOGETHER? THAT'S SO **NICE!** SO **DOMESTIC** AND **SETTLED!** C'MERE AND SEE MY **WINDOW DISPLAY!**
WHAT'S WITH YOU?
IN A MINUTE, MO. I WANT TO SEE IF THERE'S ANYTHING GOOD IN THE 75% OFF BIN FIRST.

OH, THERE'S **NOTHING** BACK **THERE!** JUST DUSTY OLE' **SCI-FI** BOOKS AND BORING **BIOGRAPHIES** THAT NOBODY WANTED IN THE FIRST PLACE... **JUNK**, THAT'S ALL!

MO, **RELAX!** I CAN DECIDE FOR **MYSELF** IF IT'S JUNK!

MO, **WHAT** IS GOING ON?

OH, **SHIT**.
75% OFF BOOKS →
LESBIAN COUPLES
LESBIAN EX-LOVERS

HELLO, GINGER.
UM, HI, TONI.

HI, CLARICE. THANKS FOR THE **TIP**, MO... YOU GOT **ALL KINDS** OF SURPRISES BACK THERE! I'M GONNA **DISAPPEAR** NOW, SO YOU CAN ALL **RELAX** AGAIN. BYE-BYE.

CIVIC DUTY
46
© 1988 BY ALISON BECHDEL
HEY MO! C'MON! IT'S LATE! TIME TO GET UP!

GET UP? WHAT FOR? I'M NOT GETTING UP UNTIL THE ELECTORAL COLLEGE IS ABOLISHED AND GEORGE BUSH IS IMPEACHED!
BUT SWEETIE, YOU'LL GET BEDSORES.

I'M NOT GETTING UP TIL ISRAEL AND PALESTINE FIND A TWO-STATE SOLUTION, AND APARTHEID IS COMPLETELY OVERTHROWN.
YOU'RE JUST GONNA LIE THERE? MAYBE A HUNGER STRIKE WOULD ATTRACT MORE MEDIA ATTENTION!

I'M SERIOUS, HARRIET! I JUST CAN'T DO IT ANYMORE. I CAN'T GET UP ONE MORE DAY AND GO OUT INTO A WORLD WHERE ATROCITIES ARE BEING COMMITTED EVERY MINUTE WITH THE TAXES I'M WORKING TO PAY!
WHY SHOULD I BE A PRODUCTIVE MEMBER OF A SOCIETY THAT THRIVES BY OPPRESSING EVERYONE ELSE IN THE WORLD?
Y'KNOW, YOU'RE ABSOLUTELY RIGHT! I THINK YOU'VE HIT ON A VERY SYMBOLIC FORM OF PROTEST HERE!

YES! AS A CITIZEN OF A PRIVILEGED COUNTRY, RENOUNCE THE POWER YOU HAVE TO ACTIVELY DISSENT AND EDUCATE! JUST STAY IN BED! THAT'LL SHOW THOSE REPUBLICANS A THING OR TWO.

WHAT A MEANINGFUL WAY TO EXPRESS YOUR SOLIDARITY WITH THE PEOPLE WHO ARE SLEEPING FIVE TO A MATTRESS IN REFUGEE CAMPS AND SHANTYTOWNS AND PRISONS! CAN I GET YOU ANOTHER BLANKET BEFORE I LEAVE?

ALL RIGHT, ALL RIGHT! I'M UP ALREADY!

WHATEVER HAPPENED TO BRIBING YOUR LOVER OUT OF BED WITH HOT BLUEBERRY MUFFINS?
SMAK!

LOIS IN ACTION
©1989 BY ALISON BECHDEL
ONE AFTERNOON AT THE BOOKSTORE...
THANKS FOR STOPPING BY, EMMA, AND SAY HELLO TO JEROME FOR ME.
OKAY, JEZANNA. IT WAS NICE SEEING YOU, AND THANKS FOR YOUR HELP!
BYE.
BYE!
JEZANNA! HOW COME YOU DIDN'T INTRODUCE ME?! COULDN'T YOU SEE ME LEERING?!
GIRL, DON'T EVEN THINK ABOUT IT!
WHY NOT? YOU'RE NOT SEEING HER, ARE YOU? WHO IS SHE? AN EX?
FORGET IT! SHE'S GOT A HUSBAND AND TWO KIDS!
OH YEAH? WELL SHE WAS SURE DOING SOME HEAVY BROWSING IN THE LESBIAN SECTION! WHAT'D SHE BUY?
NONE OF YOUR BUSINESS! GIMME THAT!
AH HAH! "THE COMING OUT STORIES" "SURPASSING THE LOVE OF MEN," "LESBIAN SEX"... LOOKS LIKE YOUR FRIEND IS DOING SOME, UH... RESEARCH, RIGHT?
SALES LOG
LOIS, I'M SERIOUS. STAY AWAY. I'VE KNOWN EMMA FOR YEARS NOW, EVER SINCE I WAS A STUDENT OF HER HUSBAND'S. YOU'VE HEARD ME TALK ABOUT JEROME, MY BLACK STUDIES PROFESSOR?
OH, SO SHE'S MARRIED TO SAINT JEROME. HUH?
MADWIMMIN MEMBERSHIPS $25
YEAH, WELL... NOW SHE THINKS MAYBE SHE'S A DYKE AFTER ALL... SHE'S IN A VERY VULNERABLE STATE, AND THE LAST THING SHE NEEDS IS YOU COMING ON TO HER LIKE A TON OF BRICKS.
OKAY, OKAY! I CAN TAKE A HINT!
GOOD.
CA-CHING
NCR

POETIC LICENSE
50
© 1989 BY ALISON BECHDEL

LOIS ACCOMPANIES GINGER TO A READING BY A RENOWNED LESBIAN POET AT THE UNIVERSITY.

WHY AM I DOING THIS?! I HATE POETRY! I MUST BE REALLY BORED!
YOU'RE SUCH A PHILISTINE, LOIS! A LITTLE CULTURE WILL DO YOU GOOD!

YEAH, SURE. SITTING AROUND WITH A BUNCHA PSEUDO-INTELLECTUALS PRETENDING TO UNDERSTAND WHAT SOME WACKO POET IS EMOTING ABOUT HAS ALWAYS BEEN MY IDEA OF A GOOD TIME!

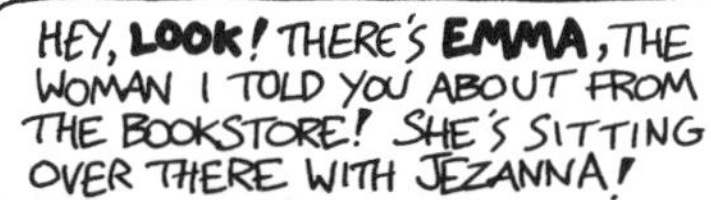
HEY, LOOK! THERE'S EMMA, THE WOMAN I TOLD YOU ABOUT FROM THE BOOKSTORE! SHE'S SITTING OVER THERE WITH JEZANNA!

SHHH! IT'S STARTING!

I LICK THE DELICATE PEARL...
SHE'S MARRIED TO A MAN, BUT JEZANNA SAYS SHE'S JUST COMING OUT! ISN'T SHE HOT?!
DO YOU MIND?! SOME OF US CAME TO LISTEN!

...OF YOUR NAVEL / THE EXPANSE OF YOUR BELLY / A BEACH AT DAWN...
TIGHTASS ACADEMICS!

MAYBE I CAN MAKE SOME EYE CONTACT.
...YOUR DESIRE A TIDAL POOL...

WHOA! SHE'S... SHE'S STARING RIGHT AT ME! CAREFUL, LOIS, DON'T LOSE YOUR COOL!
...RIPE, LIQUID CORAL...

OMIGOD! WAS THAT A WINK?! DID SHE REALLY JUST WINK AT ME?
...AS THE WAVES CREST, SUBSIDE...

... LAP / AT THE EDGE. THE LINGERING SCENT / OF SEAWEED.

CLAP CLAP CLAP!
WELL, YOU CAN'T CALL THAT POEM DRY AND INTELLECTUAL! SHE HAS A WAY OF REALLY BRINGING HER SUBJECT ALIVE, DON'T YOU THINK?
I DIDN'T HEAR A WORD SHE SAID... BUT MY OPINION OF POETRY READINGS HAS DEFINITELY IMPROVED.
CLAP
CLEP!

a very warm Reception
51
©1989 BY ALISON BECHDEL

EXCITED BY A STEAMY BOUT OF OCULAR FLIRTATION DURING A POETRY READING, LOIS SEEKS OUT HER INAMORATA AT THE RECEPTION AFTERWARDS.

THERE SHE IS! WITH JEZANNA OVER BY THE WINE & CHEESE! C'MON!
LOIS, YOU SAID JEZANNA TOLD YOU TO LEAVE THIS WOMAN ALONE! I DON'T THINK SHE'S GONNA TAKE KINDLY TO YOU FORCING YOURSELF ON THEM!
SIGN IT 'TO LORNA WITH LOVE'

LEAVE THIS TO ME, GINGER.

JEZANNA! HI! FANCY MEETING YOU HERE! YOU KNOW MY HOUSEMATE GINGER, DON'T YOU?

OH. HI, GINGER. HI LOIS. I NEVER THOUGHT I'D SEE YOU AT A POETRY READING.
WELL JEZ, I THINK IT'S ALWAYS IMPORTANT TO TRY NEW EXPERIENCES.. IT KEEPS LIFE EXCITING, DON'T YOU AGREE?

I DON'T BELIEVE WE'VE MET! I'M LOIS!
CHARMED. I'M EMMA. DON'T YOU WORK WITH JEZANNA? I'VE SEEN YOU AT THE BOOKSTORE.

OH! WHY, YES! I DO WORK WITH JEZANNA. I'M THE MERCHANDISING CONSULTANT FOR MADWIMMIN!

MERCHANDISING CONSULTANT?! LOIS, YOU'RE A CLERK! LISTEN, EMMA, I REALLY HAVE TO GET HOME AND WALK MY DOG. LET'S GO!
OKAY. LET ME JUST FINISH THIS. I'LL BE RIGHT THERE.

SO YOU'RE A CLERK! THAT MUST BE FASCINATING!
OH! WELL,.. IT HAS ITS MOMENTS. UM... WHAT DO YOU DO?

I'M A CHEMICAL DEPENDENCY COUNSELOR.
OH! UM... I'M NOT AN ALCOHOLIC... I JUST HAVE A GLASS OF WINE NOW AND THEN AT, YOU KNOW, RECEPTIONS AND THINGS!

DON'T WORRY. I WON'T ARREST YOU. THAT'S A LOVELY EARRING YOU'RE WEARING.

EMMA! I HATE TO DRAG YOU AWAY LIKE THIS, BUT IF WE DON'T LEAVE RIGHT NOW, I'LL HAVE TO FACE FIFI'S REVENGE. NICE SEEING YOU, GINGER! G'NIGHT!

I'LL SEE YOU AT WORK TOMORROW. WE HAVE SOME SERIOUS CONSULTING TO DO.

The Wager
52
©1989 BY ALISON BECHDEL
JEZANNA, THE MORE YOU TELL LOIS TO STAY AWAY FROM YOUR FRIEND EMMA, THE MORE INTERESTED SHE GETS! YOU KNOW HOW LOIS IS!
YEAH, I DO KNOW HOW LOIS IS! THE AVERAGE LENGTH OF HER RELATIONSHIPS IS THREE NIGHTS! I JUST DON'T WANT EMMA TO GET HURT.
OFFICE
POSTCARDS .75
I DUNNO, JEZ. EMMA SOUNDS LIKE SOMEONE WHO CAN TAKE CARE OF HERSELF.
OFFICE
BOOKS
MAYBE. THE OTHER THING IS, I JUST DON'T WANNA GET STUCK IN THE MIDDLE, Y'KNOW? I'M TOO OLD FOR THIS EMOTIONAL TUG-OF-WAR STUFF.
OH. YEAH, I FORGOT, YOU'RE FRIENDS WITH EMMA'S HUSBAND, TOO.
AFTER ALL, I KNEW JEROME FIRST. WHEN I GOT TO COLLEGE I'D NEVER MET A BLACK ACTIVIST BEFORE. HE POLITICIZED ME! AND IT WAS THROUGH HIS CLASSES THAT I EVENTUALLY CAME OUT. I JUST FEEL A CERTAIN LOYALTY TO HIM.
IT'S NOT THAT I DON'T SUPPORT EMMA EXPLORING HER LESBIANISM, BUT I'M DAMNED IF I'M GONNA PLAY MATCHMAKER FOR HER!
UH-OH. DON'T LOOK NOW, YENTA, BUT THINGS JUST MIGHT BE OUT OF YOUR HANDS.
HI, JEZ!
JEZ, I'M GONNA TAKE MY BREAK NOW. EMMA & I ARE RUNNING NEXT DOOR FOR COFFEE. I'LL BE BACK IN 15 MINUTES.
SMART WOMEN FOOLISH CHOICES
WHAT CAN YOU DO? THEY SEEM PRETTY DETERMINED.
HELL-BENT IS MORE LIKE IT. GUESS I JUST GOTTA LET NATURE TAKE ITS COURSE.
LOOK ON THE BRIGHT SIDE! ACCORDING TO YOUR STATISTICS, IT SHOULDN'T LAST MORE THAN THREE NIGHTS!
NCR
$5 SAYS LESS THAN A MONTH.
WELL... I'M NOT A GAMBLING KINDA GAL AS A RULE... BUT $2.50 AND YOU'RE ON.

Swept Away
53
© 1989 BY ALISON BECHDEL
LOIS TAKES A QUICK BREAK FROM THE BOOKSTORE...
Deli
GOOD COFFEE, HUH?

LOIS, I THINK YOU'RE A VERY ATTRACTIVE WOMAN AND I'D LIKE TO SLEEP WITH YOU.
GAK!

AHEM! YOU DON'T-COFF- FOOL AROUND, DO YOU?

NO, BUT I'D LIKE TO.
UM, JEEZ, EMMA... I'D LIKE TO SLEEP WITH YOU TOO... I'M JUST NOT USED TO WOMEN BEING SO DIRECT, Y'KNOW? I MEAN, THERE ARE CERTAIN FORMALITIES WE USUALLY GO THROUGH!

I DIDN'T MEAN TO SHOCK YOU. IT'S JUST THAT I'VE SPENT SO MUCH OF MY LIFE DOING THINGS FOR OTHER PEOPLE... NOW THAT I KNOW WHAT I REALLY WANT, I DON'T WANT TO WASTE ANY TIME.

EVERY MOMENT IS PRECIOUS.
UH... JEZANNA MENTIONED SOMETHING ABOUT YOU HAVING A HUSBAND AND TWO KIDS...

YES, JEROME AND I HAVE JUST SEPARATED. MY KIDS ARE 12 AND 18. JAMES IS STAYING WITH HIS FATHER AND AMELIA IS AWAY AT SCHOOL. SHE'S A LESBIAN TOO.
MADWIMMIN BOOKS
Deli
OPEN

UH-HUH, RIGHT. I DUNNO, EMMA... I SUDDENLY FEEL LIKE I'M IN A PLAY. ARE YOU FOR REAL?
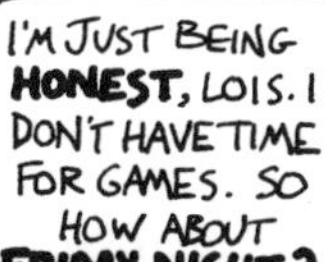
I'M JUST BEING HONEST, LOIS. I DON'T HAVE TIME FOR GAMES. SO HOW ABOUT FRIDAY NIGHT?

UH... FINE, OKAY.
7 O'CLOCK. DINNER AT MY NEW APARTMENT? HERE'S THE ADDRESS. I HOPE PIZZA'S OKAY. I'M NOT SET UP TO COOK YET.

7 O'CLOCK. SURE... UM... SEE YOU THEN?
I'LL BE COUNTING THE HOURS. BYE-BYE.

AFTER the FACT
54
©1989 BY ALISON BECHDEL
THAT WAS REALLY NICE, LOIS.
SO, HAVE I CONVERTED YOU?
WELL... IF I HADN'T DECIDED TO CONVERT BEFORE I EVEN MET YOU, YOU JUST MIGHT HAVE.
YEAH? WOW. CAN I HAVE A CIGARETTE?
NO. SMOKING IS A TERRIBLE HABIT.
LISTEN, YOU MAY BE OLDER THAN ME, BUT YOU'RE NOT MY MOTHER.
YOU'RE ABSOLUTELY RIGHT. I DON'T KNOW WHAT I WAS THINKING. HERE.
NO THANKS.
SUIT YOURSELF.
UM... IT WAS REALLY NICE FOR ME TOO.
YOU PROBABLY DO THIS ALL THE TIME.
WELL, YEAH ... BUT NOT AS MUCH AS EVERYONE THINKS. AND THIS TIME WAS DIFFERENT, KINDA.
OH? WELL, LISTEN... I HAVE A BIG DAY TOMORROW AND I NEED TO GET SOME SLEEP. ALONE.
OH. SURE. OF COURSE. WELL... I'LL BE GOING THEN.
COME HERE.
I'LL CALL YOU, OKAY?

WE'LL INVITE ALL OUR FRIENDS... SHOULD WE WEAR GOWNS OR TUXEDOS? WE COULD EVEN GO ON A **HONEYMOON**..

at the Salon
63
© 1989 BY ALISON BECHDEL

SO HOW'S YOUR LOVE LIFE, CASANOVA?

ROTTEN. I SEEM TO BE LOSING MY TOUCH.
NO LURID TALES OF SEDUCTION FOR ME THIS TIME?

NOT UNLESS YOU WANT TO HEAR ABOUT MY BREATHLESS NIGHTS SPENT PASSIONATELY WAITING FOR THE PHONE TO RING.
LO, THIS DOESN'T SOUND LIKE YOU! IS IT THE WOMAN YOU WERE DROOLING OVER LAST TIME? OLDER, MARRIED?

YEAH. WE HAD ONE DATE. PIZZA AND SEX ON HER FOLD-OUT COUCH.
HOW WAS IT?
SNIP

WELL, I COULDA DONE WITHOUT THE ANCHOVIES, BUT SHE ORDERED BEFORE I GOT THERE.

ANCHOVIES ON YOUR FIRST DATE? KINKY!
DON'T YOU THINK IF SHE DOESN'T WANNA SEE ME SHE COULD AT LEAST HAVE THE DECENCY TO SAY SO TO MY FACE? D'YOU THINK I SHOULD CALL HER?

...SO, LIKE, HE KEEPS CALLING ME. I DUNNO WHAT TO DO. WHAT WOULD YOU DO?
TELL THE PATHETIC JERK TO GET LOST. BELIEVE ME, HON, YOU CAN'T MINCE WORDS WHEN YOU'RE TRYING TO DUMP SOMEONE.

ON SECOND THOUGHT, CALLING HER MIGHT NOT BE THE WISEST OPTION. BUT WHAT CAN I DO? I CAN'T STAND THIS SUSPENSE!
BZZZZ

WHY DON'T YOU SEND HER A TELEPATHIC MESSAGE THAT YOU WANT TO SEE HER?
YEAH, SURE.
MIKO, YOUR NEXT APPOINTMENT IS HERE!

HI, EMMA! HAVE A SEAT, I'LL BE WITH YOU IN A MINUTE! LOIS, DON'T JUMP LIKE THAT WHEN I'M TRIMMING YOUR EARS!
BZZZZZZ

AFTER A SURPRISE ENCOUNTER AT THE HAIR SALON, LOIS HAS ARRANGED TO MEET EMMA FOLLOWING HER APPOINTMENT.

The SPAT
65
©1989 By Alison Bechdel
LET ME GET THIS STRAIGHT. EMMA SAYS SHE'S INVOLVED IN A PRIMARY RELATIONSHIP WITH SOMEONE NAMED DOROTHY.
RIGHT.
BUT SHE'D LIKE TO SEE YOU ON THE SIDE.
WELL... I PREFER TO SAY 'MORE CASUALLY.'
LOIS, IF I LIKE SOMEONE SO MUCH I WANNA BE INVOLVED WITH HER, THEN I WANNA BE INVOLVED WITH HER, FER GODDESS' SAKE! NONE OF THIS 'SECONDARY RELATIONSHIP' BULLSHIT!
I SAID CASUAL, NOT SECONDARY.
OCTOBER
PSYCHO-BABBLE
WHEN GOOD THINGS HAPPEN TO BAD PEOPLE
CODE-PENDENT FER SURE
HOW CAN YOU EXCHANGE INTIMATE BODILY FLUIDS WITH SOMEONE AND CALL IT CASUAL?!
LISTEN! JUST BECAUSE YOU AND HARRIET INSTANTLY MERGED IDENTITIES DOESN'T MEAN THAT'S THE ONLY WAY TO DO THINGS!
WHADDAYA MEAN? HARRIET AND I HAVE PERFECTLY HEALTHY BOUNDARIES!
YEAH, SURE! YOU CAN'T EVEN GO TO A MOVIE WITH ME UNLESS YOU CHECK WITH HARRIET FIRST!
UM... EXCUSE ME...
NCR
MADWIMMIN MEMBERSHIPS $25
BUT...
BUT NOTHING! YOUR TIME'S NOT YOUR OWN! AND I'VE NOTICED THE PRONOUN 'WE' CREEPING INTO YOUR VOCABULARY AN AWFUL LOT LATELY!
AHEM!
SO WHAT! MAYBE I LIKE CHECKING WITH HARRIET! MAYBE I LIKE SAYING WE!
MAYBE YOU'D LIKE A LOBOTOMY TOO!
OKAY LOIS! LET EMMA JERK YOU AROUND! I'M TIRED OF TRYING TO HELP YOU!
UM... MAYBE YOU COULD HELP ME THEN.
HELP LIKE YOURS I CAN GET ON CABLE TV! ALL YOU DO IS PREACH!
LISTEN, I'D LIKE TO BUY THIS BOOK IF IT'S NOT TOO MUCH TROUBLE...
AWRIGHT! KEEP YER SHIRT ON!
JEEZ! DID SOMEONE GET UP ON THE WRONG SIDE OF THE BED TODAY?
THE DANCE OF ANGER

Exclusive En-gagement
68
©1989 BY ALISON BECHDEL

HOW ABOUT EARLY SPRING? OR JUNE! JUNE WOULD BE ROMANTIC!
Whirlpool

OR WE COULD WAIT FOR OUR EIGHTH ANNIVERSARY AND DO IT THEN.
WILL YOU STOP? WE HAVEN'T DECIDED YET WHETHER WE'RE DOING IT AT ALL.
ZING!

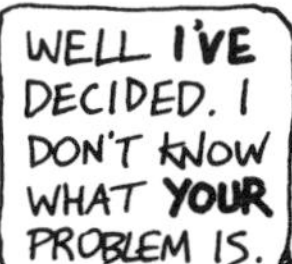
WELL I'VE DECIDED. I DON'T KNOW WHAT YOUR PROBLEM IS.

CLARICE, EXCUSE ME IF I SEEM HESITANT. ONE MINUTE YOU'RE HAVING AN AFFAIR AND LYING TO ME... THE NEXT, YOU WANT US TO DRESS UP IN WHITE SATIN AND SWEAR EVERLASTING MONOGAMY IN FRONT OF EVERYONE WE KNOW.
CHANGE

WILL YOU LET GO OF THE THING WITH GINGER? IT WAS NOTHING! DOESN'T THE FACT I'VE BEEN IN THERAPY WITH YOU FOR SIX MONTHS COUNT FOR ANYTHING?
ALL RIGHT. I'M SORRY. BUT WHY THE SUDDEN URGE TO GET MARRIED? A CEREMONY WON'T MAKE US MORE COMMITTED THAN WE ALREADY ARE.

IT'S A RITUAL, TONI! IT MEANS PUBLIC RECOGNITION OF OUR RELATIONSHIP!
IT JUST HAS SO MANY NEGATIVE CONNOTATIONS. MARRIAGE IS ABOUT PROPERTY TRANSFER AND CREATING STATE-APPROVED NUCLEAR FAMILIES.

WHY MIMIC IT? WE WON'T EVEN GET A STATE-APPROVED TAX BREAK!

TONI, FOR US IT'LL BE ABOUT LOVE.
NO. FOR YOU IT'S ABOUT FEAR. YOU THINK A COMMITMENT CEREMONY IS SOME KIND OF TICKET TO ETERNAL SECURITY.
DAMP
BURNT
25¢ FOR 10 SEC.
CLIK

LOOK, I JUST WANNA MARRY YOU!

SCUM SUDZ

THERE. YOU GOT YOUR PUBLIC RECOGNITION. SATISFIED?

IT'S NOT JUST ABOUT SECURITY, TONI... THINK OF THE PRESENTS!
PRESENTS?! WELL WHY DIDN'T YOU SAY SO?

a
SERIOUS PARTY
©1989
BY ALISON BECHDEL
69

IT'S JEZANNA'S ANNUAL COMING OUT PARTY, AND THE GANG'S ALL HERE!
WELL, MO... YOU CAME OUT TO YOUR PARENTS LAST YEAR. WHAT'S YOUR **NEXT STEP** GONNA BE?
AW, JEZ, I'M SICK & TIRED OF COMING OUT! LIFE'S HARD ENOUGH WITHOUT HAVING TO TELL THE **PLUMBER** YOU'RE A LESBIAN. WHY KNOCK OURSELVES OUT?

BECAUSE EVERY TIME YOU **DON'T** COME OUT, YOU LET SOMEONE GO ON THINKING THEY DON'T KNOW ANY GAY PEOPLE! IT MAKES US **INVISIBLE!**

BUT IT'S NOBODY'S BUSINESS WHO I SLEEP WITH! IT'S A **PERSONAL MATTER!**
PRETTY TO THINK SO! BUT IN THIS CULTURE YOU'RE **PRESUMED** TO BE SLEEPING WITH THE **OPPOSITE SEX** UNTIL PROVEN OTHERWISE!
k.d. lang
TRACY

DON'T WASTE YOUR BREATH, JEZ. SHE'S GOING THROUGH SOME WEIRD **REACTIONARY PHASE**. FRANKLY, I'M WORRIED. SHE JUST LET HER **GREENPEACE** MEMBERSHIP LAPSE, AND SUBSCRIBED TO **MS.** INSTEAD.

THINK OF IT, TONI! WHAT BETTER WAY TO COME OUT TO OUR FAMILIES THAN BY ANNOUNCING OUR **COMMITMENT CEREMONY!**
YEAH, THAT'S WHAT WE THOUGHT. BUT MY FATHER REFUSED TO COME WITNESS A "CRIME AGAINST NATURE."
AT LEAST **MY** FOLKS SENT US A **GIFT** — TWO SETS OF TWIN-SIZE SHEETS.

EMMA!
LOIS! I WAS HOPING YOU'D BE HERE! I'M STILL WAITING FOR YOUR ANSWER!

WELL, UM... I'VE DECIDED THAT **YES**, I **WOULD** LIKE TO GO OUT WITH YOU CASUALLY. NO STRINGS ATTACHED.

OH, GOOD! I'D LIKE YOU TO MEET MY PRIMARY PARTNER DOROTHY! HON, THIS IS LOIS!
OH, REALLY? SHE'S A BIT **YOUNGER** THAN I EXPECTED.

HOW NICE TO SEE YOU ALL GETTING ACQUAINTED! LOIS, COULD YOU HELP ME IN THE KITCHEN FOR A MINUTE?

I OWE YOU ONE.
IT WAS JUST GOOD HOSTESS TECHNIQUE. BELIEVE ME, IF THIS WASN'T MY PARTY, I'D HAVE GRABBED A FRONT ROW SEAT.

an Unusual Plight

CLARICE AND TONI ARE JUST RETURNING FROM THEIR SUPPORT GROUP FOR LESBIANS IN **MULTICULTURAL RELATIONSHIPS.**

SHEESH! IF THAT'S SUPPORT, I DON'T THINK I EVER WANNA SEE **ANTAGONISM!**
OH, COME ON! EVERYONE WAS **VERY** SUPPORTIVE... EXCEPT **TANYA**, OF COURSE.
FEBRUARY
RALLY

DO YOU THINK SHE'S RIGHT? ARE WE JUST MAKING A PATHETIC BID FOR APPROVAL FROM A RACIST, IMPERIALIST, MISOGYNISTIC, HETEROSEXIST SYSTEM THAT WANTS TO **DESTROY** EVERYTHING WE STAND FOR?!

CLARICE, TANYA SAID THE EXACT SAME THING ABOUT YOU GOING TO LAW SCHOOL AND ME BEING A **C.P.A.!** IT NEVER BOTHERED YOU BEFORE!
BOYCOTT

WELL YEAH, BUT...
OKAY. **WHAT** IS GOING ON?

YOU'VE BEEN PESTERING ME FOR **MONTHS** ABOUT HAVING A COMMITMENT CEREMONY... I FINALLY AGREE, AND **NOW** YOU'RE HAVING SECOND THOUGHTS!

I JUST WANNA MAKE SURE YOU **REALLY** WANNA GO THROUGH WITH IT.

CLARICE! YOU **DIDN'T!**

YES, I DO! AND AFTER ALL THIS, **YOU'D** BETTER WANT TO GO THROUGH WITH IT TOO!

OKAY, OKAY... AS LONG AS YOU'RE CERTAIN IT'S THE RIGHT THING...

SHRIEEEEK!
I'LL BE YOUR LAWYER IF YOU'LL BE MY ACCOUNTANT.

3's a crowd
80
©1990 BY ALISON BECHDEL
... AND THAT'S WHAT MY PROBLEM IS! MY FAMILY WAS DYSFUNCTIONAL!
OW! HARRIET, THAT TICKLES!
... SO ANYA THINKS MAYBE MY ANXIETY STEMS FROM REPRESSED ANGER AT MY MOTHER ...
HALF AN HOUR LATER...
WANT A BACKRUB?
NO THANKS, SWEETIE. I'M IN THE MIDDLE OF AN EXCITING PART.
THE DRAMA OF THE GIDDY CHILD
MMM... HOW EXCITING IS IT?
HARRIET! JEEZ! YOUR HANDS ARE FREEZING!
THE DRAMA OF THE GRUMPY CHILD
MO, IT'S BEEN A MONTH!
YOUR HANDS HAVE BEEN COLD FOR A MONTH? DID YOU TELL YOUR CHIROPRACTOR?
THE TRAUMA of The GUILTY CHILD
A MONTH SINCE THERE'S BEEN ANY SEXUAL ACTIVITY IN THIS RELATIONSHIP!
WHADDAYA MEAN? WHAT ABOUT THAT NIGHT WE HAD ARTICHOKES FOR DINNER?
THAT WAS FOUR WEEKS AGO!
OH.
WELL JEEZ, HARRIET! WHADDAYA WANT? I MEAN, A LOT'S BEEN GOING ON FOR ME LATELY, WHAT WITH THERAPY AND ALL... I JUST DON'T FEEL LIKE HAVING SEX!
MROWL!
I KNOW THAT, MO, AND I'VE BEEN TRYING NOT TO PRESSURE YOU, BUT A MONTH IS A LONG TIME!
WELL CAN'T YOU, LIKE, TAKE CARE OF IT YOURSELF TILL I'M IN THE MOOD AGAIN?
THAT'S NOT THE POINT! I WANNA BE CLOSE TO YOU!
BUT WE ARE CLOSE! WE'RE RIGHT NEXT TO EACH OTHER!
THEN WHY DO I HAVE THE DISTINCT SENSATION THAT YOUR THERAPIST IS LYING HERE BETWEEN US?
THE TRAUMA of The NOT-SO GIFTED CHILD

ALL IN THE FAMILY
81
©1990 BY ALISON BECHDEL
WHERE ARE YOU OFF TO, LOVERGIRL?
IT'S EMMA'S BIRTHDAY. SHE'S HAVING A FEW FRIENDS OVER FOR CAKE. D'YOU THINK IRISES ARE TOO OVERSTATED?
SPLUT

THAT DEPENDS IF HER MAIN SQUEEZE IS THERE OR NOT.
WELL... SHE DIDN'T SAY DOROTHY WAS COMING..
ARF.

... BUT IF SHE DID, I'M SURE WE'D ALL CONDUCT OURSELVES IN A CIVILIZED MANNER.
YEAH, RIGHT. WELCOME TO THE NINETIES.

LOIS! COME IN! THE OTHERS JUST ARRIVED!

JAMES, DARLING, PUT LOIS'S COAT IN THE CLOSET.

COOL! DO YOU HAVE A BIKE?
UH...YEAH, A TEN-SPEED. THIS IS JUST A FASHION STATEMENT.

LOIS, I THINK YOU'VE MET MY PARTNER, DOROTHY, AND THIS IS MY EX-HUSBAND JEROME AND MY SON JAMES...
DAD! LOOK! I'M A HELL'S ANGEL!

... MY DAUGHTER, AMELIA...
SO YOU'RE MOM'S OTHER GIRLFRIEND!

... AND HER LOVER SHEILA.
YO.
I CALL HER SHE-RA! LOOK, SHE-RA! I'M A HELL'S ANGEL!
Give Blood. Play Rugby.

LOIS! IRISES! HOW SWEET. AMELIA, PUT THESE IN WATER.

WE'RE OUTTA VASES, MOM. I'LL JUST STICK THEM IN WITH THE OTHERS.
HAPPY DAY! Jerome

WELL! SHALL WE EAT CAKE?
SHE-RA! LEMME DOWN!

Mo STARS IN
A Breach of Etiquette
©1990 BY ALISON BECHDEL

WHERE ARE THEY? MY STIR-FRY IS RUINED!
YOU SHOULDA WAITED TILL THEY GOT HERE TO START COOKING. I RECALL MENTIONING SOMETHING TO THAT EFFECT ABOUT 40 MINUTES AGO.

YEAH, WELL IT WOULDN'T HAVE BEEN A PROBLEM IF THEY SHOWED UP WHEN THEY WERE SUPPOSED TO.
DING DONG!

HI! MMM... SMELLS GOOD! WHAT'S FOR DINNER?
SZECHUAN VEGETABLE PULP!

HI CLARICE! HI TONI!
LISTEN, I'M SORRY WE'RE LATE. WE, UH... LOST TRACK OF TIME. TONI SORTA SEDUCED ME WHEN I GOT HOME FROM SCHOOL.
HEY, I JUST WANTED A QUICKIE! YOU'RE THE ONE WHO SUGGESTED WE TAKE A FOAMING LAVENDER LOVE BATH!

OH, GREAT! THEY WERE MAKING LOVE WHILE MY STIR-FRY DECOMPOSED!
MO, FOR GODDESS' SAKE! WILL YOU TRY AND BE CIVIL? LET GO OF THE @#*%@ STIR-FRY!

I MEAN, YOU'D EXPECT THIS SORT OF IRRESPONSIBILITY FROM SOME LOVESICK NEW COUPLE! BUT YOU GUYS ARE IN A RESPECTABLE, LONG-TERM RELATIONSHIP! YOU'RE NOT SUPPOSED TO HAVE SEX!
YEAH, I KNOW. BUT OUR HORMONES HAVE KINDA GONE CRAZY LATELY.
IT'S BEEN LIKE FALLING IN LOVE ALL OVER AGAIN EVER SINCE WE STARTED PLANNING OUR COMMITMENT CEREMONY.

PUH-LEEZE! NOT AT THE DINNER TABLE!
MO, WHAT IS THE PROBLEM? JUST BECAUSE WE'RE NOT HAVING SEX DOESN'T MEAN NO ONE ELSE CAN!

HARRIET! I CAN'T BELIEVE YOU'RE DISCUSSING THIS IN FRONT OF COMPANY!

HMM... HAVE YOU TRIED SEX TOYS? OR ACTING OUT YOUR FANTASIES?
DO YOU WANT OUR THERAPIST'S NUMBER?

COULD WE JUST EAT, PLEASE?
IT'S OKAY. THESE LIMP, GREY THINGS ARE STRING BEANS, NOT NIGHTCRAWLERS.

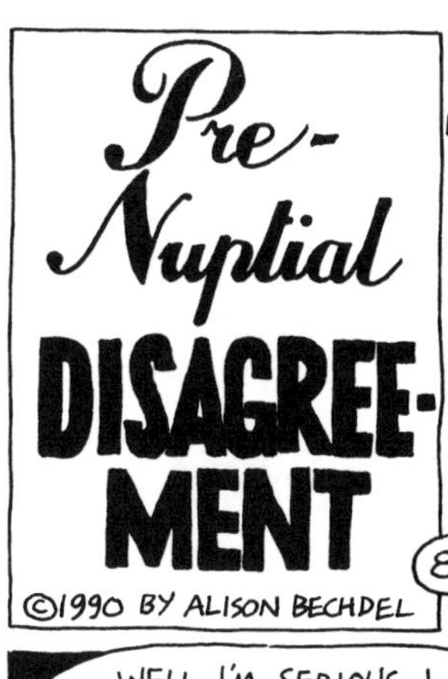
Pre-Nuptial DISAGREEMENT
85
©1990 BY ALISON BECHDEL

WHAT I DON'T GET IS, PROMISING SOMEONE YOU'LL NEVER SLEEP WITH ANYBODY ELSE, FOREVER. TALK ABOUT TERMINAL TEDIUM! I'D GO STIR CRAZY!

I DUNNO, LOIS. I ENVY CLARICE AND TONI. MAKING A COMMITMENT TO MONOGAMY SOUNDS KINDA EXCITING.
WHOA! LOOK OUT, LOIS! JEZANNA'S BEEN POSSESSED BY JUNE CLEAVER!
MADWIMMIN BOOKS
WIN DEX
THE BLACK WOMEN'S HEALTH BOOK

WELL I'M SERIOUS. I THINK PROMISING TO BE EXCLUSIVE OPENS UP A WHOLE NEW WORLD OF POSSIBILITY AND ADVENTURE AND INTIMACY.
OH NOOO! THE 'I' WORD!
NCR

WELL I THINK THEY'RE CLINGING TO AN OBSOLETE HETEROPATRIARCHAL CONSTRUCT... MARRIAGE IS ABOUT OWNERSHIP AND DOWRIES AND STUFF! I MEAN, GROSS!
CAN YOU IMAGINE? THE SAME LOVER...FOR ETERNITY!
VISA
MADWIMMIN MEMBERSHIP $25

THEY'RE EVEN EXCHANGING RINGS, CAN YOU BELIEVE IT?

YOU KNOW, MO, UNDERNEATH THAT HARD-LINE ATTITUDE I THINK YOU'RE BEING JUST PLAIN HETEROSEXIST!
WHAT, ME HETEROSEXIST?
BOOK O' THE MONTH
THE BLACK WOMEN'S HEALTH BOOK
EVELYN C. WHITE, ED.
from
WALRUS PRESS

YOU'RE RESPONDING JUST LIKE YOU'VE BEEN PROGRAMMED TO! TWO WOMEN LOVE EACH OTHER AND WANT TO AFFIRM THAT LOVE PUBLICLY, SO YOU TRASH THEM FOR IT!
BUT... BUT...

A REALLY POLITICALLY CORRECT PERSON WOULD SUPPORT THEIR COMMITMENT WHOLEHEARTEDLY!
?

SO WHAT ARE YA GIVING THEM, JEZ?
A COMBINATION WATER-SAVING SHOWER HEAD AND CAPPUCCINO MAKER. HOW 'BOUT YOU?
WIN DEX

I'M GIVING THEM A COPY OF MY PERSONALLY RESEARCHED CATALOG OF FEASIBLE LESBIAN SEXUAL POSITIONS. GODDESS KNOWS THEY'LL NEED IT. WHAT ABOUT YOU, MO?

I DUNNO. I CAN'T DECIDE BETWEEN THE COMPLETE DONNA REED SHOW VIDEOCASSETTES AND THE T-SHIRTS THAT SAY "HERS" AND "HERS TOO."

Getting Committed
86
©1990 BY ALISON BECHDEL
THE BIG DAY HAS ARRIVED.
Clarice Desmona Clifford and Antonia Norma Ortiz request the honor of your participation in a Circle of Commitment Ritual and Barbecue Saturday
SO, HOWZIT FEEL TO BE GOING TO YOUR OLD FLAME'S WEDDING?
HON, ONE MISGUIDED ROLL IN THE HAY WITH CLARICE HARDLY MAKES US OLD FLAMES. I THINK SHE AND TONI WILL BE VERY HAPPY AND I WISH THEM WELL.
THAT'S THE SPIRIT, GINGER. PUT A BRAVE FACE ON IT. WHO KNOWS? MAYBE YOU'LL CATCH THE BRIDAL BOUQUET!
WHY DON'T YOU GO CATCH A YEAST INFECTION.
TA DA! HOW DO I LOOK?
GREAT, SPARROW. GIDGET GOES TO A RITUAL.
WHERE DID YOU GET THAT?
ADAM LENT IT TO ME. IT'S HIS RADICAL FAERIE PARTY FROCK. ZIP ME UP?
MEANWHILE, THE SITUATION BETWEEN MO AND HARRIET IS RAPIDLY DETERIORATING.
AW, HARRIET.. I FEEL STUPID IN THIS! I'M JUST GONNA WEAR MY STRIPED TANK TOP.
LOOK, YOU CAN'T SHOW UP IN SOMETHING YOU WEAR EVERY DAY! CLARICE & TONI ARE PLEDGING THEIR LIFELONG COMMITMENT TO ONE ANOTHER! IT'S A MOMENTOUS OCCASION!
I STILL DON'T GET IT! THEY'VE MADE IT EIGHT YEARS TOGETHER! WHY DO THEY FEEL THE NEED TO OBSERVE THIS ABSURD, PSEUDO-HET FORMALITY?!
NO ONE'S FORCING YOU TO COME, MO. WHY DON'T YOU JUST STAY HOME IN YOUR STRIPED SHIRT AND THOSE EVERLASTING JEANS?
YOU USED TO THINK I LOOKED CUTE IN JEANS.
...AND OUR BETROTHED COUPLE IS BREATHLESS WITH ANTICIPATION AS THEY PREPARE FOR THEIR CEREMONY...
THERE'S STILL TIME!
WE CAN JUST CALL EVERY-ONE AND SAY WE'RE TERRIBLY SORRY BUT SOMETHING CAME UP AND WE HAVE TO LEAVE TOWN!
...BUT WHAT ABOUT THE FIVE GALLONS OF BABA GANOUSH, AND ALL THOSE TOFU PUPS?
SHIT. I FORGOT. WELL, I GUESS WE'LL JUST HAVE TO GO THROUGH WITH IT, THEN.

A TIP O' THE NIB TO LINNEA STENSON

87

HAVING **QUASHED** THEIR LAST-MINUTE **RELUCTANCE**, OUR STARRY-EYED BRIDES NOW FIND THEMSELVES IN THE **BACK YARD** SURROUNDED BY A LOVING CIRCLE OF THEIR NEAREST AND DEAREST!

THERE'S DRUMMING...

VARIOUS FRIENDS OFFER AFFIRMING TESTIMONY...

THE VOWS HAVE BEEN CAREFULLY MEMORIZED...

BUT THE RING EXCHANGE IS EXTEMPORANEOUS.

A CEREMONIAL BROOMSTICK IS JUMPED, THEIR FATES ARE SEALED WITH A KISS... AND THE BARBECUE BEGINS!

AFTER THE LAST REVELERS DEPART, OUR NEWLYWEDS UNPLUG THE PHONE AND RETIRE TO THEIR MATRIMONIAL FUTON IN SEARCH OF NEW HEIGHTS IN **CONJUGAL RAPTURE**.

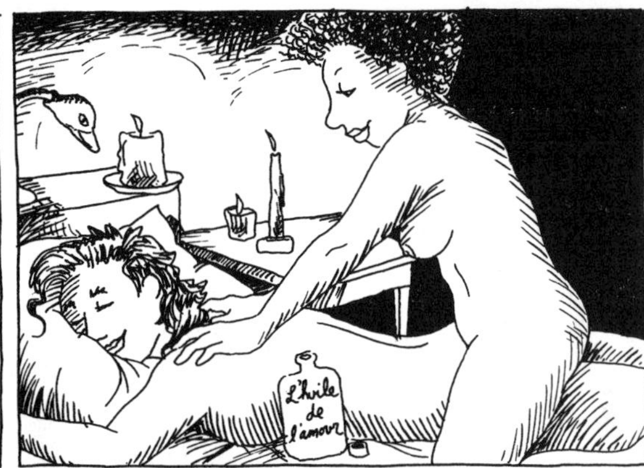

MEANWHILE... INSPIRED BY CLARICE & TONI'S ROMANTIC VOW OF COMMITMENT, MO & HARRIET ARE DETERMINED TO **FAN** THE **FALTERING FLAMES** OF THEIR OWN LACKLUSTER LOVE LIFE!

CLEAR THE DECKS! MO'S HAVING...
FEEL-INGS
89
©1990 BY ALISON BECHDEL
YEAH, CLARICE & TONI'S COMMITMENT CEREMONY WAS REALLY A TURNING POINT FOR ME. I REALIZED IT'S BEEN 3 YEARS SINCE PHYLLIS, AND DAMMIT, I WANT A GIRLFRIEND!
JEEZ, GINGER. WHAT A NEWS FLASH!
IF I WAITED 3 YEARS BETWEEN RELATIONSHIPS, I'D... I'D BE A HUNDRED AND TWO YEARS OLD.
DON'T LOOK NOW, BUT HERE COMES MO, AND IT LOOKS LIKE SHE'S GOT HER KNICKERS IN A TWIST.
MO! NICE TA SEE YA! COME ON IN AND VENT YOUR SPLEEN!
I DON'T KNOW WHAT THIS COUNTRY IS COMING TO! DID YOU SEE THE PAPER? THE CO-FOUNDER OF THE NATIONAL REVIEW JUST CAME OUT!
WOOF! ARF ARF!
YEAH, GREAT, HUH? ALL THAT HOOPLA ABOUT OUTING SEEMS TO BE HAVING AN EFFECT.
BUT WHAT KIND OF EFFECT? I MEAN, WHAT KIND OF MESSAGE DOES AN OPENLY GAY RIGHT-WING CONSERVATIVE SEND TO THE YOUTH OF AMERICA, LOIS?
WHAT'LL IT BE NEXT? GAY C.I.A. AGENTS? LESBIAN CORPORATE RAIDERS? QUEER FUNDAMENTALIST PREACHERS?! IT'S.. IT'S IMMORAL!
WELL... LIKE THE BUMPERSTICKER SAYS, WE ARE EVERYWHERE.
GROAN.
C'MON, MO. SURE, IT'S DISILLUSIONING, BUT WORSE THINGS COULD HAPPEN!
OH YEAH? LIKE THERE COULD BE A HUGE, NATIONWIDE SURGE IN ANTI-GAY AND ANTI-LESBIAN VIOLENCE, FOR EXAMPLE?
OR PERHAPS THE NUCLEAR REGULATORY COMMISSION COULD DECIDE TO RECYCLE LOW-LEVEL RADIOACTIVE WASTE INTO CONSUMER PRODUCTS?!
FACE IT! THE WORST IS ALREADY HAPPENING! LIFE ON THIS PLANET SUCKS!
AW, QUIT YOUR BELLYACHING AND GET OVER IT, MO. AT LEAST YOU HAVE A GIRLFRIEND.
AAUGH!
THUNK!
UH-OH.
LOOKS LIKE TROUBLE.
RIGHT HERE IN RIVER CITY.

CRISIS management
92
©1990 BY ALISON BECHDEL
MO HAS DROPPED IN ON HER PALS FOR A HIT OF NETWORK NEWS...
I CAN'T BELIEVE THIS COUNTRY! WE'RE ON THE BRINK OF WORLD WAR III JUST SO WE CAN KEEP DRIVING OUR BIG FUCKING CARS TO THE BIG FUCKING MALL!
..AND SO BUSH AND HIS BLOODTHIRSTY BUDDIES IN THE DEFENSE BIZ CAN PLAY 'WHOSE IS BIGGER' IN THE PERSIAN GULF, AND PROVE THAT WE NEED EVEN MORE MONEY FOR MILITARY SPENDING!
AND LOOKIT THIS! THE MEDIA DON'T EVEN QUESTION WHAT WE'RE DOING OVER THERE! THEY JUST WHIP EVERYONE INTO A FRENZY OVER 'PROTECTING THE AMERICAN WAY OF LIFE' AND CALL SADDAM HUSSEIN 'HITLER' TO BOOST THEIR RATINGS!
SUSIE SEXPERT'S
WHY DON'T YOU START CONSERVING ENERGY AND TURN THE TV OFF?
CLIK!
SUSIE SEXPERT'S GUIDE TO EXCRUCIATINGLY INCORRECT BEHAVIOR
I JUST DON'T GET IT! INSTEAD OF EXPLORING ENVIRONMENTALLY-SOUND ENERGY SOURCES, OR RAISING OUR PATHETIC FUEL-EFFICIENCY STANDARDS, WE'RE PREPARED TO KILL FOR THE LAST DROP OF OIL ON THE PLANET! IT'S INSANE!
JUST WAIT. NEXT THEY'LL START DRILLING UP THE WILDLIFE REFUGES.
IT'S TYPICAL ADDICTED BEHAVIOR. WE'RE A NATION OF OIL JUNKIES, TOTALLY SELF-DESTRUCTIVE AND WILLING TO DO ANYTHING FOR A FIX. WE'RE LIKE A HUGE DYSFUNCTIONAL FAMILY. IF YOU ASK ME, WHAT THIS COUNTRY NEEDS IS A GOOD 12-STEP PROGRAM!
PUH-LEEZE, SPARROW.
SAY, HAVE YOU GUYS ALL FOUND YOUR G-SPOT?
GINGER, HOW CAN YOU THINK ABOUT SEX AT A TIME LIKE THIS? MADMEN ARE ABOUT TO DESTROY THE EARTH!
CAN YOU THINK OF A BETTER TIME? I DON'T KNOW ABOUT YOU, GIRL, BUT I WANNA HAVE A G-SPOT ORGASM BEFORE ARMAGEDDON HITS.

MO'S BEEN STRANGELY **PEEVISH** EVER SINCE SHE PROPOSED COHABITATION TO HARRIET...

THUS TAUNTED, HARRIET, LIKE A SKILLED MARTIAL ARTIST, DEFTLY HONES IN ON HER OPPONENT'S WEAKEST POINT...

WILL OUR LACHRYMOSE HEROINES MANAGE TO **OVERCOME** THIS SOGGY STATE OF AFFAIRS? GODDESS KNOWS...UNTIL OUR **NEXT** POIGNANT EPISODE!

Outrageous Fortune
95
© 1990 BY ALISON BECHDEL

FOLLOWING THEIR FIERCE FEUD AND SUBSEQUENT SOB SESSION, OUR COURAGEOUS COUPLE SEEMS MORE DETERMINED THAN EVER TO ENTER INTO THAT RAPTUROUS CONDITION KNOWN AS DOMESTIC PARTNERSHIP!

NO KIDDING! WELL... CONGRATULATIONS! HOW, UH... EXCITING!
A TOAST! TO MO AND HARRIET! MAY THEY LIVE LONG AND HAPPILY TOGETHER, AND MAY THEY HIRE MOVERS SO I DON'T HAVE TO HAUL THEIR SHIT UP THREE FLIGHTS OF STAIRS!

HEAR, HEAR!
CLINK!

SO WHAT GIVES? LAST I HEARD, YOU TWO WEREN'T EVEN HAVING SEX!
MUST YOU SHOUT, CLARICE? WE, UH.. WE DID SOME PROCESSING.
AFTER WHICH WE HAD GREAT SEX. I THINK WE WERE JUST GOING THROUGH A PHASE.

HARRIET, JEEZ! D'YOU HAFTA SHARE OUR INTIMATE CONCERNS WITH DR. RUTH HERE?!
ANYHOW, WE WERE WONDERING IF YOU TWO COULD TELL US YOUR SECRET. I MEAN, YOU'VE BEEN INVOLVED FOR EIGHT YEARS, YOU'VE LIVED TOGETHER FOR SIX ... AND YOU'RE STILL IN LOVE!

YEAH. TELL US YOUR SECRET. YOU'RE OUR ROLE MODELS, YOU KNOW.
SPARE US! I DUNNO HOW WE DO IT... WE JUST LIKE BEING WITH EACH OTHER... WHICH ISN'T TO SAY IT'S ALWAYS BEEN EASY...

A-MEN. Y'KNOW, THERE'S TONS OF ADVICE WE COULD GIVE YOU. BUT THERE'S NO QUICK 'SECRET TO SUCCESS.' IF YOU WANT EASY ANSWERS, CHECK OUT YOUR COOKIES.
THANKS.

"MAKE NEW INVESTMENTS CAUTIOUSLY." OH, GREAT.
"YOU WILL DISCOVER AN EXOTIC NEW SEXUAL TECHNIQUE WITH THE HOT LESBIAN WHO JUST STARTED WORKING IN YOUR OFFICE."

LET ME SEE THAT!!

A CRISP AUTUMN AFTERNOON FINDS OUR HEROINES **OUTDOORS**, VIGOROUSLY EXERCISING THEIR FIRST AMENDMENT RIGHTS.

the Zealot
98
©1990 BY ALISON BECHDEL
EMMA, WE'VE BEEN GOING ALONG LIKE THIS FOR MONTHS AND MONTHS! I WANNA SEE YOU MORE OFTEN!
LOOK, LOIS. I TOLD YOU ABOUT DOROTHY WHEN THIS WHOLE THING STARTED. OUR AGREEMENT IS THAT I DON'T SPEND MORE THAN ONE NIGHT A WEEK WITH YOU, AND...
...IT'S NOT NEGOTIABLE.
YEAH, YEAH, YEAH. I KNOW. BUT HOW CAN YOU RESIST ME?
IT'S NOT EASY. THANK GOD I'M SO PRINCIPLED.
SPEND SATURDAY WITH ME! PLEASE? JUST THIS ONCE.
MMM... I REALLY CAN'T, HON. DOROTHY AND I HAVE PLANS TO GO SHOPPING.
SHOPPING?! YOU CAN DO THAT ANY OLD TIME! COME TO A DEMONSTRATION WITH ME, INSTEAD. IT'LL BE MUCH MORE PRINCIPLED.
WHAT DEMON-STRATION?
A QUEER NATION KISS-IN!
OH, PLEASE, LOIS. AREN'T WE BEYOND SHOCKING THE BOURGEOISIE?
NOT UNTIL THEY STOP BEING SHOCKED, WE'RE NOT! IT'S HIGH TIME PEOPLE JUST GOT USED TO US!
SO SHOVE IT IN THEIR FACES? I'M SORRY, BUT THAT'S JUST NOT THE MOST EFFECTIVE WAY TO WIN ACCEPTANCE.
AND SHOPPING IS? BESIDES, I WANT MORE THAN ACCEPTANCE! I WANT RESPECT!
YOU DON'T GET RESPECT BY PROVOKING PEOPLE!
IT'S NOT PROVOCATION! IT'S EDUCATION! A KISS-IN IS A VISIBLE, EMPOWERING, LIPS-ON FORM OF DIRECT ACTION AGAINST A SOCIETY THAT HATES US!
MMM... Y'KNOW, YOU'RE VERY SEXY WHEN YOU GET ZEALOUS!

LOIS AND HER QUEER NATION CRONIES HAVE DESCENDED ON A LOCAL MALL... AND THEY'RE **NOT GOING SHOPPING!**

Ménage à Deux
100
© 1990 BY ALISON BECHDEL
HAVE FUN UNPACK-ING!
MY CHIRO-PRACTOR WILL SEND YOU HER BILL.
THANKS FOR THE PIZZA!
SEE YA LATER.
THANKS YOU GUYS! BYE.
AHH!
PHEW!

CARRY ME OVER THE THRESH-OLD?
MO, I HAVE CARRIED THE ENTIRE CONTENTS OF BOTH OUR APARTMENTS OVER A DOZEN THRESHOLDS TODAY. I'M NOT LIFTING ONE MORE THING.

ISN'T IT EXCITING, HARRIET? OUR OWN PLACE! I'VE NEVER LIVED IN MY OWN PLACE WITH A LOVER BEFORE! LET'S PUT THE CATS' CHAIR OVER HERE...

...AND THE STEREO CAN GO HERE! I'LL SET IT UP. WHAT DO YOU WANT TO LISTEN TO?

LET'S SET THE BED UP FIRST, OKAY? I'M BEAT.
GOOD IDEA. MINE OR YOURS?

MO, YOU DON'T HAVE A BED. YOU HAVE AN ANCIENT PAD OF LUMPY COTTON BATTING WHICH I DON'T KNOW WHY YOU BOTHERED TO MOVE.
HEY, A NICE, FIRM FUTON BEATS THOSE LIMP, SAGGING OLD BEDSPRINGS OF YOURS ANY DAY OF THE WEEK!

AW, BUT IT'S OUR FIRST NIGHT TOGETHER! YOUR BED'LL BE OKAY.

AFTER A SHORT STRUGGLE..
HOW ROMANTIC! WHY DON'T YOU GET READY FOR BED AND I'LL DIG UP SOME CANDLES!

EVENTUALLY..
I'M JUST A HUNKA HUNKA BURNIN' LOVE!

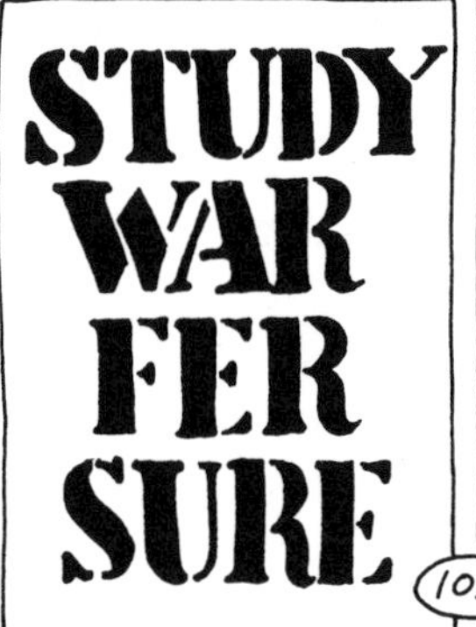

AS THE WORLD TEETERS ON THE BRINK OF WAR, IT'S **SUPPERTIME** IN NORTH AMERICA.

MEANWHILE, OUT ON THE STREETS...

Brief Encounter

Tired of playing **odd girl out** with Emma and Dorothy, Lois attempts to **distract** herself with an admirer from her Queer Nation focus group.

107

A tip o' the nib to Joan Benson!

ARMY OF LOVERS
©1991 BY ALISON BECHDEL
108
THE PREMENSTRUAL TENSION HAS REACHED **FEVER PITCH** AT GINGER'S HOUSE!
LOIS, I JUST CAN'T BELIEVE YOU'VE GOTTEN INVOLVED WITH ONE OF MY STUDENTS!
WILL YOU RELAX, GINGER? HOW WAS I SUPPOSED TO KNOW SHE WAS YOUR STUDENT? ANYWAY, YOSHI AND I AREN'T "INVOLVED." WE'RE JUST FUCK BUDDIES!
MAKE
EXCUSE ME? IT SOUNDED LIKE YOU JUST SAID 'FUCK BUDDIES.'
YEAH. YOU KNOW. WE JUST MESS AROUND. NO STRINGS ATTACHED.
MAKE LOVE NOT WAR
LISTEN, LOIS. I HAVE BEEN VERY PATIENT ALL THESE YEARS WITH YOUR ENDLESS PARADE OF GIRLFRIENDS. STRANGERS IN THE BATHROOM, MOANS OF ECSTASY AT 2 A.M., ALL THE PHONE CALLS AND DRAMAS! BUT I HAVE REACHED MY LIMIT!
I UNDERSTAND, GINGER. I'D PROBABLY BE FEELING JEALOUS TOO IF I WASN'T GETTING ANY.
JEALOUS?! DON'T MAKE ME LAUGH, YOU... YOU...
SLUT?
'SEX ADDICT' IS A MORE ACCURATE TERM, I THINK.
MAKE
WHO ASKED **YOU**?!
HEY, TEMPERS ARE RUNNING A LITTLE HIGH, GIRLS! I THOUGHT YOU MIGHT WANT ME TO MEDIATE!
THIS IS BETWEEN ME AND LOIS, SPARROW! AREN'T YOU LATE FOR A 12-STEP MEETING?
DON'T VENT YOUR RAGE AT **ME**! I CAN'T HELP IT IF YOU'RE SEXUALLY FRUSTRATED!
YOU'RE A FINE ONE TO TALK, SPARROW! WHEN WAS THE LAST TIME **YOU** HAD SEX WITH ANYBODY BESIDES YOURSELF?
SO? AT LEAST **I** DO IT WITH SOMEONE I **LOVE**, YOU **SLUT!**
OH, THAT'S SO ROMANTIC! DO YOU CRY OUT YOUR OWN NAME TENDERLY?
MAYBE I **DO** NEED A GIRLFRIEND. THEN I COULD GO OVER AND STAY AT **HER** HOUSE!

LIFE FORCE
110
©1991 BY ALISON BECHDEL

AS THE AMERICAN EMPIRE CONTINUES ITS INEXORABLE DECLINE BEHIND A FAÇADE OF YELLOW-BERIBBONED **DENIAL**, OUR PATIENT HEROINES CONTINUE, IN THEIR OWN INEXORABLE WAY, TO NOURISH THE **VITAL SPARK**.

MO AND HARRIET ARE GETTING DOWN AND DIRTY.

ISN'T THIS GREAT, HARRIET? JOINING WITH OUR NEIGHBORS TO FIGHT CITY HALL AND CLAIM THIS VACANT LOT FOR THE PEOPLE!
COMMUNITY GARDEN PROJECT

COUNTERACTING THE FEAR AND ALIENATION OF URBAN LIFE AS WE COME TOGETHER IN ALL OUR GRAND CULTURAL DIVERSITY TO TILL THE SOIL!

WORKING IN HARMONY WITH NATURE! RENEWING, IN OUR SMALL WAY, THE PLANET'S DAMAGED ECO-SYSTEMS! LAYING THE GROUNDWORK FOR A SUSTAINABLE COMMUNITY!
I'M GONNA PUT THE PEAS HERE. COULD YOU PICK THE ROCKS OUT?

JEEZ, HARRIET! I CAN'T **STAND** GETTING DIRT UNDER MY FINGERNAILS. DO WE HAVE ANY GLOVES?
COMM GARD PROJE

GINGER IS GIDDY WITH NEW AGENDAS.

NO, I WAS JUST VISITING ATLANTA FOR THE NATIONAL LESBIAN CONFERENCE.
OH. HOW NICE.

'NICE' IS NOT THE WORD I'D CHOOSE. GLORIOUS CHAOS IS MORE LIKE IT. CAN YOU IMAGINE 3,000 LESBIANS FROM NEARLY EVERY WAY OF LIFE HOLDING PLENARY SESSIONS IN THE CIVIC CENTER WHILE MERCURY IS IN RETROGRADE?
UM... NO, FRANKLY, I CAN'T.

IT WAS SOMETHING ELSE! OF COURSE, THE **NETWORKING** WAS THE MOST IMPORTANT PART.
Malika Barlowe
Call me!
STORYTELLING
VIDEOGRAPHY
HAIR BRAIDING
SMALL ENGINE REPAI

TONI AND CLARICE ARE STARTING FROM SCRATCH!

C'MON, HONEY, WAKE UP! IT'S TIME TO TAKE MY TEMPERATURE! IT'S IMPORTANT THAT WE DO THIS TOGETHER!

HUH? OH, RIGHT. OKAY, WHAT DO I DO?
YOU WRITE IT DOWN ON THIS CHART WHEN I'M DONE.

OKAY. ZNNNK!
CLAR-**EECE!**

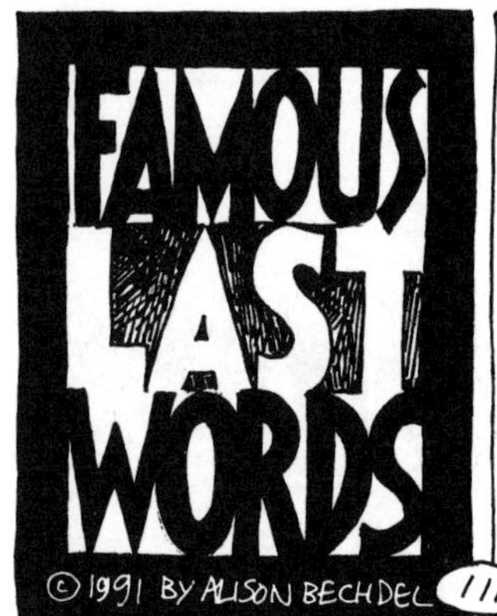

Ginger has confessed to indulging in flirtatious behavior at the National Lesbian Conference.

HAS SHE DONE THERAPY?

DID YOU GET HER RELATIONSHIP HISTORY?

IS SHE EMOTIONALLY AVAILABLE?

WHAT'S SHE LOOK LIKE?

HOW BUTCH IS SHE?

DID YOU SWIM NAKED TOGETHER IN THE HOTEL POOL?

IT DOESN'T MATTER BECAUSE NOTHING IS GOING TO HAPPEN.

DID I EVER TELL YOU ABOUT JASMINE? I MET HER AT A MEDITATION RETREAT WHERE NO ONE WAS ALLOWED TO TALK. AT THE END OF THE WEEK SHE GAVE ME HER ADDRESS AND WE EXCHANGED **REAMS** OF COSMIC LETTERS AND EROTIC POEMS. **SO** ROMANTIC!

I MET A WOMAN AT AN ANTI-RACISM CONFERENCE ONCE... WE HAD PHONE SEX LIKE YOU WOULDN'T BELIEVE FOR MONTHS AFTER, TILL HER BOSS FOUND OUT SHE WAS USING THE **WATS**-LINE.

BLACK/OUT

WELL THAT'S ALL VERY TOUCHING, BUT I DON'T WRITE POETRY AND I PREFER TO HAVE SEX IN PERSON.

Support Group
©1991 BY ALISON BECHDEL

113
ACME FLORAL
Dear Ginger,
The conference would've been a bust without you. I'm glad we met.
♡ Malika
Dear Malika
Thank you for the roses.

RIP!
SHIT.

GINGER, YOU'VE BEEN WORKING ON THAT FOR HOURS. AMERICAN EDUCATION IS IN EVEN SADDER SHAPE THAN I THOUGHT IF A PH. D. IN ENGLISH CAN'T WRITE A SIMPLE THANK-YOU NOTE.
CRUMPLE CRUMPLE
The Daily Distress
WELCOME HOME, TROOPS! MILITARY HARDWARE ON PARADE!
I CAN'T DECIDE WHAT TONE TO TAKE. I MEAN, WHAT DOES "GLAD WE MET" MEAN? IS THAT LIKE, "SO LONG, HAVE A NICE LIFE," OR "I'D LIKE TO GET TO KNOW YOU BETTER"? AND WHAT DOES THE LITTLE HEART MEAN? HER WHOLE MESSAGE IS SO OPEN TO INTERPRETATION.
ASSAULTS WIFE
TEACHER DENIES LEWD CONDUCT CHARGE
FRATERNITY PLEADS INNOCENT IN RAPE CASE

HERE. LET ME INTERPRET IT. "DEAR GINGER, I'D LIKE TO FUCK YOU. ARE YOU INTO IT? LOVE, MALIKA."
LOIS!

OH, COME OFF IT. YOU KNOW THAT'S WHAT YOU BOTH WANT. LIFE WOULD BE A LOT SIMPLER IF WE WERE ALL MORE UPFRONT ABOUT THIS STUFF.
LOIS, YOU ARE SO DYSFUNCTIONAL! THERE'S MORE TO A RELATIONSHIP THAN "FUCKING," AS YOU CALL IT. INTIMACY ISSUES, INTERNALIZED HOMOPHOBIA, ADDICTIONS, ABUSE HISTORIES... WE ALL HAVE HURT CHILDREN INSIDE US. IT'S NEVER SIMPLE!
NO SUSPECT IN MUTILATION SLAYINGS
MAN HELD IN GIRLFRIEND'S DEATH

LOOK, I JUST MET THE WOMAN. I DON'T KNOW IF I WANNA SLEEP WITH HER AND I SURE AS HELL DON'T KNOW IF I WANT TO GO INTO THERAPY WITH HER!

AHH, SHE LIVES TWO TIME ZONES AWAY ANYHOW. WHY DON'T YOU TRY FOR SOME LOCAL ACTION?
YEAH. DID YOU EVER WONDER WHY YOU ALWAYS FALL FOR WOMEN WHO ARE SOMEHOW UNAVAILABLE?
TOUCHY.
SHE DRINKS WAY TOO MUCH COFFEE.

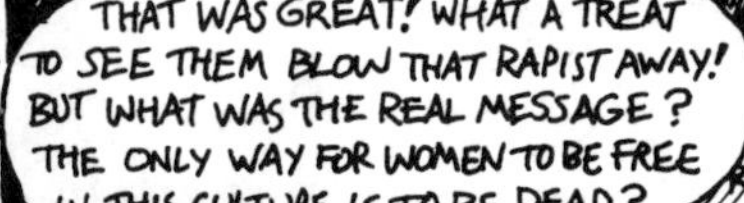

WHERE THEY WOULD CONSUMMATE THEIR LOVE FOR ONE ANOTHER, OPEN A GUERILLA TRAINING CAMP FOR WOMEN AND START FOMENTING ARMED RESISTANCE AGAINST RAPISTS.

HAVING AT LONG LAST GRADUATED FROM LAW SCHOOL, OUR FRIEND CLARICE IS PREPARING ASSIDUOUSLY FOR THE BAR EXAM.

WHY? WHY DID I EVER WANT TO BECOME A LAWYER? I SHOULDA GONE TO COSMETOLOGY SCHOOL LIKE MY MOTHER SAID.

HEY, COME ON! WHERE'S THAT FIERY RADICAL I FELL IN LOVE WITH? ARE YOU GONNA LET A FEW LITTLE SETBACKS GET YOU DOWN? SOON YOU'LL BE CLERKING FOR A DISTRICT COURT JUDGE! AREN'T YOU EXCITED?

UNNNH!

NO DANCING WITHOUT G-STRINGS, PASTIES

YEAH, RIGHT. THE WAY THINGS ARE GOING, **ARNOLD SCHWARZENEGGER** WILL BE PRESIDENT. I'M SURE HE'LL BE EAGER TO APPOINT AN EMBITTERED BLACK LESBIAN JUDGE.

the MARKET PLACE
116
©1991 BY ALISON BECHDEL

HEY, GINGER! YOU'RE LOOKING GOOD. I HEAR YOU HAVE A NEW LOVE INTEREST!
YEAH. HOW 'BOUT THAT?

GODDESS... A LONG-DISTANCE RELATIONSHIP. HOW ROMANTIC!
I KNOW. ALL I HAVE TO DO IS SEE HER HANDWRITING IN THE MAILBOX AND I FEEL LIKE I'M GONNA BURST, IT'S SO INTENSE.
MADWIMMIN BOOKS

JEEZ! AND YOU HAVEN'T EVEN KISSED YET!
NOPE. AND WE WON'T TILL ONE OF US FINDS THE TIME AND MONEY FOR A VISIT. LISTEN, I CAME IN TO GET A PRESENT TO SEND HER. YOU KNOW, SOME FUNKY LITTLE THING.

WELL YOU'VE COME TO THE RIGHT PLACE! 'FUNKY LITTLE THING' IS OUR MIDDLE NAME!
VENUS OF WILLENDORF COFFEE MUG? NOVELTY T-SHIRT? ECOLOGICALLY CORRECT CANVAS SHOPPING BAG WITH OUR LOGO ON IT?
CARDS $1.00
I'M NOT A LESBIAN BUT MY LOVER IS
MADWIMMIN BOOKS
MY MOM'S A DYKE AND ALL I GOT WAS THIS LOUSY T-SHIRT

UH...
EROTIC VIDEO? STAINED GLASS **VULVA** FOR YOUR KITCHEN WINDOW? VENUS OF WILLENDORF BOXER SHORTS?
NEUROTIC IN NATURE

WHERE DID YOU **GET** ALL THIS STUFF?
WE'VE BEEN EXPANDING! IN FACT, THE STORE IS DOING SO WELL, JEZANNA'S HIRING FOR A NEW POSITION!
CARDS $20.00
BOOKS

OH. LOIS MENTIONED THAT. SHE'S GONNA APPLY FOR IT.
YEAH. SO AM I. IT WOULD BE KIND OF A PROMOTION. I'D GET TO ORDER STUFF LIKE THIS, AND ALL THE ALBUMS AND TAPES AND C.D.'S.
I KNOW YOU KNOW
IMAGINE MY SURPRISE
DON'T DOUBT IT
LET'S FUCK!
2 NICE GIRLS

IS THAT A PROBLEM BETWEEN YOU AND LOIS? IT MUST BE A LITTLE UNCOMFORTABLE, COMPETING FOR THE SAME JOB.
OH, NO! WE'RE ABOVE ALL THAT. JEZANNA WILL HIRE THE MOST QUALIFIED WOMAN FOR THE JOB. I'LL FEEL FINE ABOUT WHOEVER SHE PICKS.

AS LONG AS IT'S **ME**.
S
P

ANTI-CIPA-TION
©1991 BY ALISON BECHDEL
117
ONE EVENING AT THE LOCAL CO-OP...
HI, MO!
HEY, GIRLS! I WAS GONNA CALL YOU TONIGHT TO TELL YOU ABOUT THIS GREAT NEW JOB I'M PROBABLY GONNA GET AT THE BOOKSTORE!
Sale! ORGANIC PARSNIP CHIPS 3.99
GOOD FOR YOU! HEY, GUESS WHAT! I OVULATED TODAY!
UH... JEEZ, THAT'S WONDERFUL, TONI. IS THERE SOMETHING UNUSUAL ABOUT THAT?
Sale! FROZEN KELP SHAKES .49
IGA
NO! THAT'S JUST IT! IT'S AMAZING, MO! WE'VE BEEN CHARTING HER TEMPERATURE FOR THE PAST 3 MONTHS, AND A PATTERN IS EMERGING!
YESTERDAY MY CERVICAL MUCUS WAS STICKY, THEN MY TEMPERATURE DROPPED THIS MORNING... THEN I FELT A SLIGHT CRAMP AFTER BREAKFAST. I'M SURE IT WAS THE EGG RELEASING!
Sale! BEET LOAF 7.95/LB.
YOU HAD EGGS FOR BREAKFAST AND GOT A CRAMP? SO? WHAT ARE YOU TWO TALKING ABOUT?!
NO PARKING 3PM-2PM THURSDAY THRU WEDNESDAY
THE BEGINNING OF A NEW LIFE, MO!
OH! WELL, IT'S NOT THAT DRAMATIC. BUT IT MIGHT INVOLVE A SMALL SALARY INCREASE!
MEANWHILE...
Guess that's all for now, sugar. I just can't wait to be with you! ♡ Malika
HEY GINGER! ARE YOU MASTURBATING IN THERE OR WHAT? I WANNA SHOW YOU SOMETHING!
KNOK KNOK!
IF I'M MASTURBATING, WILL YOU LEAVE ME ALONE?
NO! CHECK IT OUT. HOW DO I LOOK?
LIKE A WHITE GIRL IN A BLACK BRA. NOW CAN I HAVE SOME PRIVACY?
PRETTY HOT, HUH? I GOT IT IN HONOR OF MY NEW JOB AT THE BOOKSTORE.
BUT YOU DON'T HAVE IT YET! WHAT IF JEZ HIRES MO?
I BELIEVE IN THE POWER OF POSITIVE THINKING! CIAO! I'M GOING OUT DANCING TO CELEBRATE.
KISS MY BUTT
YOU'RE GOING OUT LIKE THAT? AREN'T YOU FORGETTING SOMETHING?
DUH! THE TAG! THANKS, GINGER. THAT WOULDA BEEN EMBARASSING!

The Blow
©1991 BY ALISON BECHDEL

IT'S MONDAY MORNING AT MO'S HOUSE,
ISN'T TODAY THE DAY JEZANNA SAID SHE'D LET YOU KNOW WHO SHE'S HIRING FOR THE NEW JOB?
YUP! LET'S HAVE DINNER AT THE TOPAZ TONIGHT TO CELEBRATE!
118
SALE
The Daily Distress
STRANGE CLUSTER OF BRAIN CELLS FOUND IN STRAIGHT MEN

AND AT LOIS'S TOO...
GOOD LUCK, LOIS! HOPE YOU GET THE JOB!
LUCK, SCHMUCK! IT'S IN THE BAG, BABE!

SQUEEK!
DAMN! WHAT ARE YOU TWO DOING HERE ON TIME?
MADWIMMIN BOOKS

WELL?
DIDJA DECIDE?
OKAY, OKAY. LET'S GET IT OVER WITH. LISTEN, I KNOW YOU WERE BOTH COUNTING ON THIS JOB...

POOR LOIS! SHE DIDN'T GET IT!
POOR MO! I HOPE SHE DOESN'T TAKE IT TOO HARD.

...BUT I HIRED SOMEONE ELSE.

YOU WHAT?
WHO?!

HER NAME'S THEA. SHE'S NEW IN TOWN. MAYBE YOU SAW HER WHEN SHE BROUGHT HER RESUMÉ IN LAST WEEK. SHE WALKS WITH CRUTCHES.

LOOK, I'M SORRY. I KNOW YOU'RE DISAPPOINTED. BUT IT'D BE A REALLY DUMB MOVE NOT TO HIRE HER.

SHE HAS YEARS OF EXPERIENCE AS A BUYER FOR A BOOKSTORE ON THE WEST COAST. SHE KNOWS THE JOB!

PLUS SHE'S AN ARTIST. SHE'S IN TOUCH WITH LOTS OF CRAFTSWOMEN AND HAS SOME GREAT IDEAS FOR SETTING UP A GALLERY IN THE STORE...

WHAT CAN I SAY? SHE'S SMART, FUNNY, HER REFERENCES ARE FANTASTIC!

JEZANNA, I CAN'T BELIEVE YOU PASSED UP ME AND LOIS FOR SOME STRANGER JUST BECAUSE SHE'S DISABLED!

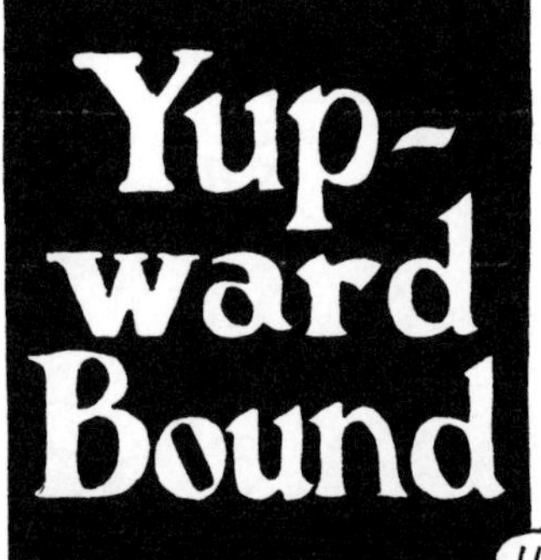

STAND BACK! MO'S IN A **MOOD!**

MO, LISTEN TO YOU! YOU SOUND LIKE THOSE WHITE MEN WHO WHINE ABOUT AFFIRMATIVE ACTION! YOU'RE JUST PISSED 'CAUSE YOU DIDN'T GET THE JOB!

YEAH, EASY FOR **YOU** TO SAY WITH YOUR FANCY NEW GIG. SO, IS THAT HOW CLERKS FOR JUDGES HAFTA DRESS?

A Pregnant Moment

MO AND HARRIET HAVE PREPARED A **ROBUST** LENTIL STEW FOR THEIR DINNER GUESTS.

123

...A ROLLING DONUT
124
©1991 BY ALISON BECHDEL

MORNING.
HI, MO.

LOIS, WHAT'S WITH THEA? I MEAN, WHY'S SHE IN A WHEELCHAIR?
I DUNNO. WHY DONCHA ASK HER?
MADWIMMIN BOOKS
BIG NEW BOOK!
BUY IT!

YEAH. I KNOW IT'S HARD TO BELIEVE, MO, BUT THE WHEELCHAIR DOESN'T IMPAIR MY HEARING AT ALL.
ECONOMIC FORECAST: DEEP DOO-DOO
DONUT HUT

UH... SORRY. I WAS JUST WONDERING WHY YOU'RE.. YOU KNOW... USING THAT IF NORMALLY YOU JUST USE CRUTCHES.
WELL THE CHAIR IS SO MUCH MORE DRAMATIC, DON'T YOU THINK? I USE IT WHEN I WANT PEOPLE TO FEEL EXTRA SORRY FOR ME.
PHEW! MAGIC JOHNSON ISN'T ONE OF THEM
A TIP O' THE NIB TO ZANA

UH...
HEY, I'M JUST KIDDING YOU. I'M REALLY USING THE CHAIR TODAY BECAUSE IT GOES SO GREAT WITH MY SHOES.

NO, SERIOUSLY. THE REAL REASON IS BECAUSE I TOOK MY CRUTCHES INTO THE SHOP FOR REPAIRS AND THEY WERE ALL OUT OF LOANERS! IT WAS THIS CHAIR OR A '76 HONDA!

THEA, I'M SORRY I...
NO! NO! THAT'S NOT IT! I'M USING THE CHAIR BECAUSE I TORE A HOLE IN THE SEAT OF MY PANTS THIS MORNING AND I DIDN'T HAVE TIME TO MEND IT! HA HA HAW!
HATE CRIMES UP
DAVID DUKE TO RUN FOR PREZ
DRUNKEN DONUTS
WOMEN'S GLIB
SLAP!

OKAY, OKAY—HEH HEH— FOR REAL NOW. I GET FATIGUED A LOT. ON BAD DAYS I USE THE CHAIR SO I HAVE MORE ENERGY FOR MY WORK AND STUFF.
YOU MUST BE EXHAUSTED AFTER THAT LITTLE ROUTINE. WANT A DONUT?

THEA, DON'T EAT THOSE! THEY'RE FULLA SUGAR AND GREASE! POISON!
OH, BUT IT'S OK FOR LOIS TO HAVE THEM? I JUST LOVE WHEN ABLE-BODIED WOMEN GIVE ME NUTRITIONAL ADVICE.

DON'T TAKE IT PERSONALLY, THEA. SHE SAID THE SAME THING TO ME 4,000 TIMES. IGNORE HER AND EVENTUALLY SHE GIVES UP.
D'YOU HAVE ANY OF THOSE ONES WITH TOXIC-LOOKING SPRINKLES?

PRIORITY MAIL
125
©1991 BY ALISON BECHDEL
OUR TRIBADIC TRIO HAS JUST RETURNED HOME FROM THEIR VARIOUS PLACES OF EMPLOY.

DID YOU SEE THE SUNSET? IT WAS SPECTACULAR!
UNH-UH.
THE BUS WAS SO JAMMED I COULDN'T SEE ANYTHING.
WHINE!

WANNA GO OUT, PUP?
ONE PHONE BILL, 6 NOT-FOR-PROFIT DONATION REQUESTS, AND 12 MAIL-ORDER CATALOGS FOR YOU...

ONE CREDIT CARD BILL, 2 AMAZING OFFERS, AND 12 IDENTICAL MAIL-ORDER CATALOGS FOR ME...

THICK, PATCHOULI-SCENTED ENVELOPE AND A HEFTY, CAREFULLY WRAPPED PACKAGE FOR **YOU.**
BE STILL MY HEART.

IT'S NOT FAIR, GINGER! YOU HAVEN'T HAD ONE PIECE OF JUNK MAIL IN MONTHS!
YEAH, OR ANY CAR TROUBLES, OR WORK CRISES OR **ZITS** EITHER! AND YOUR PMS HAS VIRTUALLY DISAPPEARED.
SHRED!
NEAT RITUAL OBJECTS FOR YOUR DEN!
CULTURAL APPROPRIATION INC.
GREENCO
save the RAINFOREST by BUYING OUR ECO-GADGETS!

I WISH I WAS IN LOVE.
WHAT'D SHE SEND THIS TIME? KIWI-FRUIT BATH GEL? GODDESS-SHAPED CHOCOLATES? CRYPTIC-LOOKING VIBRATOR ATTACHMENT?
LL BEAN
$45
SHOCKING BEIGE
THE GAY ~~MALE~~ MAIL ORDER CATALOG

STUFFED DATES, INDIVIDUALLY WRAPPED IN FUSCHIA TISSUE! AND A **PHOTO!**
OLIVIA RECORDS, DO-DADS & CRUISES
LESBIANS CAN MAKE MONEY TOO!
J. SCREW
XMAS CATALOG #37

SEE? HERE SHE IS! THIS IS MALIKA!

GINGER, WHAT A **BABE!** I MEAN, UM.. SHE LOOKS SO CALM AND CENTERED!
WHOA! SO WHEN'S SHE COMING?
SOON AFTER SHE GETS HERE, I HOPE.

MO ZONE
132
©1992 BY ALISON BECHDEL
MO, HOW COME YOU'RE NOT EATING?
HOW CAN I EAT? AN OZONE HOLE COULD OPEN UP OVER OUR HEADS ANY MINUTE NOW! LIFE AS WE KNOW IT IS ABOUT TO CHANGE FOREVER! AND I'M SUPPOSED TO EAT?
CAFE TOPAZ
Cafe Topaz
SKIN CANCER! CATARACTS! WEAKENED IMMUNE SYSTEMS! WITHERED CROPS! WHAT'S GONNA HAPPEN TO US?!
MO, CHILL! THE DAMAGE ISN'T IRREVERSIBLE YET.
OH, AND THAT'S SUPPOSED TO MAKE ME FEEL BETTER? JEEZ, CLARICE. YOU SHOULD BE DOING P.R. FOR THE DU PONT CORPORATION!
Cafe Topaz
EVEN IF WE STOP MAKING CHLORO-FLUOROCARBONS NOW, THE OZONE WILL CONTINUE TO DETERIORATE FOR DECADES! BUT GEORGE BUSH AND THE CHEMICAL INDUSTRY BALK AT EVEN GRADUAL PHASEOUT!
WHAT DO THEY CARE ABOUT THE PLANET? THEY'VE LIVED THEIR LIVES! THEY'RE ALL GONNA DIE BEFORE IT GETS REALLY BAD, SO THEY MIGHT AS WELL MAKE A BUCK!
HON, IT'S A REAL TREAT LISTENING TO YOU RANT, BUT COULD YOU SAVE IT FOR LATER? I'D LIKE TO HEAR HOW CLARICE & TONI ARE DOING, AND MAYBE HAVE AN ACTUAL CONVERSATION.
WE'RE DOING GREAT! WE GOT OUR FIRST SHIPMENT FROM THE SPERM BANK YESTERDAY!
IN FACT, WE COULD BE PREGNANT THIS VERY MOMENT!
WE? WHAT'D YOU DO, BOTH TAKE A HIT OF THAT STUFF?
IT'S JUST A FIGURE OF SPEECH, MO.
TONI, HOW EXCITING! WHEN WILL YOU KNOW FOR SURE?
IN A COUPLE WEEKS. I'LL SEE IF I GET MY PERIOD.
HARRIET! WE'LL HAVE TO GIVE THEM A BABY SHOWER!
WHAT A GREAT IDEA, HON!
THAT'S SWEET, MO!
I HAVE MY GIFT ALL PLANNED OUT! SOME MAXIMUM PROTECTION SUNBLOCK, A JUG OF DISTILLED WATER, AND AN EENSY WEENSY LITTLE LAVENDER GAS MASK!

SPRING FEVER
©1992 BY ALISON BECHDEL
133
LOVE'S IN BLOOM AT GINGER'S HOUSE... BUT SOME PEOPLE SEEM TO BE ALLERGIC!
HEY! GUESS WHAT! SHE'S COMING! IN TWO WEEKS, SHE'S GONNA BE HERE!
THUMP KA THUMP!
WHO?
WHO? MALIKA! MY BELOVED! WHO ELSE?
GINGER, WE HAVE TO TALK ABOUT YOUR PHONE HABITS. I HAD TO MAKE A CALL LAST NIGHT BUT YOU WERE STILL ON THE LINE WHEN I WENT TO BED AT TWELVE!
OH. SORRY! IT'S SO HARD TO KEEP TRACK OF TIME WHEN I'M TALKING TO HER. BUT AREN'T YOU EXCITED?
ARF!
WHY? IS SHE BRINGING SOMEONE FOR ME TOO?
IT'S A LITTLE EARLY IN THE DAY FOR EXCITEMENT.
YOU'D BOTH HAVE A LOT MORE ENERGY IF YOU EXERCISED IN THE MORNINGS. I FEEL SO ALIVE! LET'S GO, DIGGER!
WHY DO WE GIVE HER SUCH A HARD TIME, LOIS? SHE DESERVES TO BE HAPPY. ARE WE JEALOUS?
NAH. WE'RE JUST TRYING TO KEEP A LID ON HER ENTHUSIASM SO SHE WON'T BE QUITE SO DISAPPOINTED WHEN IT'S OVER.
YOU DON'T THINK THINGS ARE GONNA WORK OUT BETWEEN THEM?
OH, THEY MIGHT STAY TOGETHER TILL THEY'RE 80, BUT THAT "IN LOVE" STUPOR WON'T LAST MUCH LONGER.
WHY NOT? IF A COUPLE IS REALLY COMMITTED TO EXPLORING INTIMACY, THE "IN LOVE" FEELING CAN DEEPEN OVER TIME!
PUH-LEEZE! THAT'S JUST PROPAGANDA TO KEEP THERAPISTS IN BUSINESS. I'M A REALIST. IT DOESN'T LAST! WANNA BET GINGER AND MALIKA DON'T MAKE IT THROUGH THE WEEKEND WITHOUT HAVING TO PROCESS SOMETHING?
I HOPE THEY PROCESS! COPING CONSTRUCTIVELY WITH CONFLICT IS NECESSARY FOR AN ONGOING RELATIONSHIP!
CAMEL DENIES ITS "OLD JOE" ADS TARGET KIDS
SPARROW, I KNOW STRUGGLING FOR INTIMACY TURNS YOU ON. BUT I WANNA HAVE FUN.
FUN'S FINE, BUT SOONER OR LATER YOU HAVE TO DEAL WITH EACH OTHER'S ISSUES.
DESPITE 7,800% INCREASE IN SALES TO MINORS SINCE ADS BEGAN
AHH, ISSUES, ISSUES, ISSUES! I'M SICK OF ISSUES.
GESUNDHEIT.
"AND WE DON'T DRAW HIM TO LOOK LIKE A PENIS EITHER!" CHAIRMAN INSISTS

Alone at Last!
134
©1992 BY ALISON BECHDEL

GINGER ANXIOUSLY AWAITS THE ARRIVAL OF HER AIRBORNE AMOROSA!
GATE 14

GATE 14

BEEP BEEP BEEP

PREPARATION H
The Distress
N.O.T.A. LEADS IN POLLS

ARF! ARF ARF!
WHOA! IT'S GINGER AND HER LONG-DISTANCE BABE! DON'T JUST STAND THERE! COME ON IN!
CATHERINE DID IT

UM...THIS IS MY DOG, DIGGER. AND THESE ARE MY ROOMMATES.
ALL OF THEM?
NO, NO, JUST ME AND SPARROW OVER THERE ON THE PHONE. I'M LOIS AND THESE ARE MY FRIENDS MO AND YOSHI.

HI, NICE TO MEET YOU! GINGER'S MY LIT. PROFESSOR AT THE UNIVERSITY. SHE'S FAB!
NICE CATCH, MS. JORDAN!
HEY, MALIKA! I'VE HEARD SO MUCH ABOUT YOU!
OK... I GOTTA GO. TALK TO YOU LATER.
WOOF!

MALIKA! WELCOME!
LISTEN, DON'T WORRY. WE'RE GOING DOWNTOWN TO PROTEST THE LATEST CRAZED LESBIAN PSYCHO-KILLER FLICK. ARE YOU READY, SPARROW?
"BASIC INSTINCT" BASICALLY STINKS!

I'M NOT GOING! MY FAVORITE "STAR TREK" EPISODE IS ON TONIGHT, WHERE SPOCK GETS SPRAYED WITH ALIEN SPORES THAT MAKE HIM FALL IN LOVE!
THEY'LL TAPE IT. COME ON.
NICE TO MEET YOU!
ENJOY YOUR VISIT!

SLAM!

THE FUNDAMENTAL THINGS APPLY...
As Time Goes By...
135
©1992 BY ALISON BECHDEL

FINALLY FACE TO FACE WITH HER PASSIONATE PEN PAL, GINGER CHOKES!
6:05
SO. HERE'S OUR OPTIONS FOR TONIGHT. WE'LL GO HAVE DINNER FOR STARTERS, THEN SEE A MOVIE - HERE'S THE LISTINGS - OR THERE'S AN AFRICAN DANCE TROUPE IN TOWN, OR WE COULD GO TO THIS PLAY AT THE UNIVERSITY. THEN AFTER THAT WE CAN GO OUT DANCING, OR ELSE TO A PARTY SOME FRIENDS ARE HAVING. WHATEVER YOU PREFER.
CAN I GO TO THE BATHROOM FIRST?
MOVIE GUIDE
SNIFF

6:47
YOU'RE RIGHT. THIS IS MUCH BETTER THAN RUNNING ALL OVER TOWN. D'YOU PLAY SCRABBLE? OR MAYBE THERE'S AN OLD MOVIE ON CABLE. WE COULD MAKE POPCORN.
ZIPPY'S 'ZA

7:30
MMM. I GUESS I AM KINDA TENSE NOW THAT YOU MENTION IT.

7:58
HOW LONG HAVE YOU BEEN LIFTING WEIGHTS?

8:07

8:51

9:26
WHIMPER.

10:17
WHAT'S WRONG WITH YOUR DOG?
MMM? OH! SHE HAS TO GO OUT. DON'T MOVE! I'LL BE RIGHT BACK!
ARF!

11:10
SIGH

11:34
LOIS, I CAN'T BELIEVE YOU MADE ME SIT THROUGH THAT AWFUL MOVIE! WHY COULDN'T WE JUST STAY OUTSIDE PROTESTING?
"BASIC INSTINCT" PROMOTES RAPE
CLICK!
SOMEONE HAD TO GO IN THERE AND SET OFF THOSE STINK BOMBS, SPARROW! WHAT A THANKLESS LIFE US ACTIVISTS LEAD.
CATHERYNE DID IT

11:37
HEY, IT LOOKS LIKE GINGER & MALIKA MUST BE IN BED. WE SHOULD BE QUIET.
ZIPPY'S 'ZA

12:08

VIDEO DISPLAY
136

MALIKA'S VISIT IS COMING TO AN EXCITING ANTICLIMAX!
WHAT DO YOU MEAN, YOU DON'T HAVE ORGASMS WITH A PARTNER? MAYBE ALL YOUR OTHER PARTNERS WERE JUST BAD LOVERS! LEMME TRY AGAIN!
WHOA, BABE. RELAX. I'D BE VERY HAPPY TO MAKE LOVE SOME MORE, BUT NOT JUST SO YOU CAN "GIVE" ME AN ORGASM. I WISH EVERYONE DIDN'T MAKE SUCH A BIG DEAL OUT OF A FEW MUSCULAR CONTRACTIONS.

WELL, UH... D'YOU WANNA MAKE YOURSELF COME?
GINGER, IF THAT'S ALL I WANTED, I COULDA SAVED A COUPLA HUNDRED BUCKS AND STAYED IN SAN FRANCISCO. LOOK, DON'T WORRY ABOUT IT, OKAY?

OKAY, OKAY. NO PRESSURE. COME BACK TO BED AND I PROMISE I WON'T TRY TO MAKE YOU HAVE AN ORGASM. DEAL?
DEAL.

OH! WAIT A SECOND! I BROUGHT SOME-THING!
UH-OH. SOME KIND OF WILD SEX TOY FROM THE BIG BAD CITY?

YOU COULD CALL IT THAT. I WANTED TO HAVE SOMETHING TO REMEMBER YOU BY. I'LL SEND YOU A COPY.
VHS

MEANWHILE... MO & HARRIET ARE EXPERIENCING TECHNICAL DIFFICULTIES OF THEIR OWN.
BUT YOU DIDN'T EVEN ASK ME!
I KNEW YOU'D JUST TRY TO GUILT-TRIP ME! BESIDES, IT'S MY MONEY AND I'VE WANTED A VCR FOR A LONG TIME.
VCR INSTRUCTIONS

WHAT'S THE BIG DEAL? YOU'RE ALWAYS WATCHING MOVIES OVER ON LOIS & GINGER'S! ISN'T IT A LITTLE HYPOCRITICAL TO ACT LIKE YOU'RE TOO PURE TO HAVE ONE YOURSELF?

NO! SHARING THINGS WITH FRIENDS IS A GOOD WAY TO REDUCE THE RAMPANT JUNK PRODUCTION AND MINDLESS CONSUMERISM THAT'S KILLING OUR PLANET!
LOOK, I JUST WANNA FUCKING TAPE "ALL MY CHILDREN."
PANICSONIC VCR

RIGHT. NEXT YOU'LL NEED A BIGGER TV, THEN AN "ENTERTAINMENT CENTER" TO PUT IT IN AND A RECLINER TO WATCH IT FROM... THEN CABLE! IT'S AN ADDICTIVE SPIRAL! THE MORE YOU BUY, THE MORE YOU NEED! IT'S BETTER TO QUIT NOW, HARRIET!

OKAY, FINE. I'M MOVING OUT.

stunned

 138

I LOVE YOU A LOT MO, BUT I'M JUST NOT **IN LOVE** ANYMORE. I'M STARTING TO REALIZE THAT I'VE BEEN UNHAPPY FOR A LONG TIME NOW.
The Distress
"MURPHY BROWN" AFTERMATH:

THINGS HAVE GOTTEN SO... SO **STAGNANT** BETWEEN US. WE'VE STOPPED **GROWING.**
SINGLE MOMS RIOT: PELT QUAYLE WITH DIRTY DIAPERS

I NEED TO BE ALONE FOR A WHILE, SORT OUT MY FEELINGS, GET IN TOUCH WITH MYSELF.

MO, **TALK** TO ME!
WHAT'S LEFT TO **SAY** HARRIET? YOU USED UP ALL THE GOOD CLICHÉS! GOD, I FEEL LIKE I'M TRAPPED IN A **BAD SOAP OPERA!**

LEMME THINK A MINUTE....OH! I KNOW! HOW ABOUT THIS? "IS THERE **SOMEONE ELSE,** HARRIET?"

NO, NOBODY! I ALREADY TOLD YOU. NOBODY IN PARTICULAR ANYWAY.
JEEZIZ, HARRIET! I DON'T KNOW WHAT'S WORSE! BEING DUMPED FOR **NOBODY** OR FOR NOBODY IN **PARTICULAR!** YOU COULD AT LEAST HAVE HAD THE DECENCY TO HAVE AN AFFAIR!

IT'S JUST THAT I'VE BEEN MEETING A LOT OF NEW PEOPLE SINCE I STARTED VOLUNTEERING FOR THE MARCH ON WASHINGTON. I'M REALIZING THERE ARE THINGS I WANT THAT I'M NOT GETTING HERE.

LIKE **WHAT?** SOMEONE WHO MAKES LOTS OF MONEY AND LIKES TO SPEND IT ON ELECTRONIC GADGETS? SOMEONE WHO'LL EAT AT **BURGER KING** WITH YOU? **WHAT!**

LIKE SOMEONE WHO'S NOT SO NEGATIVE AND JUDGMENTAL! SOMEONE WHO CAN GIVE **ME** SOME SUPPORT INSTEAD OF **WHINING** ALL THE TIME! I'M TIRED OF THIS!

FINE! THEN LEAVE! GO GET SOME "SUPPORT" FROM YOUR NEW FRIENDS! GO ON! WHO'S STOPPING YOU?
FINE. I DON'T HAVE TO LISTEN TO THIS. I'M GOING TO A COMMITTEE MEETING.

WHAT TIME WILL YOU BE BACK? I'LL SAVE YOU SOME CURRIED SPINACH SURPRISE!

While Harriet packs to leave their apartment, Mo turns to her devoted friends for solace and understanding.

HARRIET BEDS DOWN ON THE COUCH FOR HER FINAL NIGHT AT THE APARTMENT.

I CAN'T BELIEVE YOU'RE JUST **LEAVING**. I MEAN, SHOULDN'T WE **PROCESS** THIS FOR SEVERAL MONTHS? AREN'T WE SUPPOSED TO PAY LOTS OF MONEY TO A **THERAPIST** BEFORE WE BREAK UP?

IT'S TOO LATE, MO. I'M SORRY. I SHOULDN'T HAVE LET THINGS SLIDE FOR SO LONG, BUT THERE'S NOTHING **LEFT** FOR ME TO PROCESS.

PANKSONIC

VODKA

JUST LIKE THAT, BANG! YOU DON'T LOVE ME ANY MORE. IT'S OVER.

SWEPT AWAY ON A RELENTLESS TIDE OF BODILY FLUIDS, OUR DISCONSOLATE HEROINES BID THEIR ULTIMATE ADIEUS!

EMOTIONS ARE **TURBULENT** AS CLARICE AND TONI BEGIN THEIR **FIFTH** ROUND OF INSEMINATION.

TIPS O' THE NIB TO JANE, DEB, KAT, SHEILA & BONNIE!

SURPRISE SURPRISE
143
©1992 BY ALISON BECHDEL

SPARROW, WHAT'S ON THIS TAPE IN THE VCR?
I DUNNO. IT'S NOT MINE. **DOWN,** DIGGER.
1001 AFFIRMATIONS

OH MY **GOD! LOOK** AT THIS!
REALLY, LOIS. I DON'T KNOW WHAT YOU SEE IN THOSE PORNO VIDEOS... **OH** MY **GOD!** THAT'S... THAT'S...

GINGER!
AND **MALIKA!**
WURF!

AAUGH!

MEANWHILE, IN CLARICE & TONI'S BATHROOM...
LET'S NOT GET TOO EXCITED. YOUR PERIOD MIGHT JUST BE LATE BECAUSE OF ALL THE STRESS WE'VE BEEN UNDER.
BUT I FEEL **DIFFERENT,** CLARICE. I THINK THIS MIGHT BE IT!

BUT MAYBE YOU'RE JUST **IMAGINING** THINGS BECAUSE YOU WANT IT SO BAD. DON'T BE DISAPPOINTED IF THE TESTER SHOWS NEGATIVE. WE'LL JUST TRY AGAIN!
RIP!

HON, I'M NERVOUS ENOUGH AS IT IS. I CAN'T PEE IF YOU'RE GONNA STAND THERE WATCHING ME LIKE THAT.
OKAY, OKAY. I'LL BE RIGHT OUTSIDE.

THERE. IN FOUR MINUTES, WE'LL KNOW.
I'LL SET MY **WRIST ALARM!**

BEEP BEEP BEEP

AAAUGH!

Mo is wallowing in her just-dumped status.

MO HAS MANAGED TO HEAVE HERSELF FAR ENOUGH FROM THE **SLOUGH** OF **DESPOND** TO MAKE IT TO HER WORKSHIFT AT THE CO-OP.

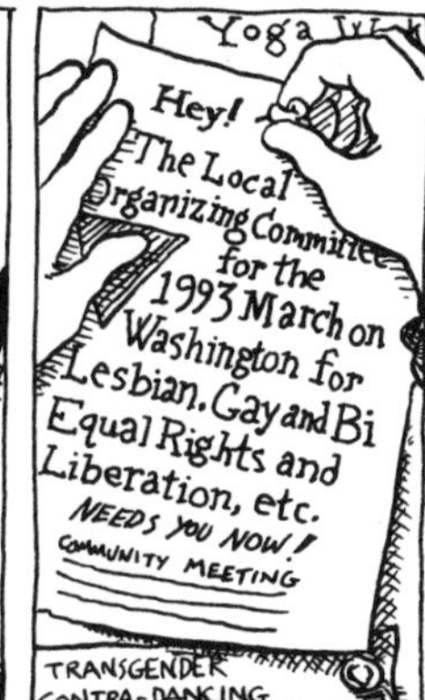

PLUS FOUR NEW WOMEN IN THE SENATE, ONE OF THEM THE ONLY **BLACK** SENATOR SINCE **RECONSTRUCTION!** THE ANTI-GAY INITIATIVE IN OREGON FAILED! THE PRO-CHOICE REFERENDUM IN MARYLAND PASSED! I FEEL **HOPEFUL!** I FEEL **YOUNG** AGAIN!

YEAH, WELL DON'T THROW OUT YOUR GERITOL YET! THE HOMOPHOBES WON IN COLORADO, IOWA DEFEATED AN EQUAL RIGHTS AMENDMENT, AND THE SENATE'S **STILL** 94 PERCENT BOYS!

NO PLACE LIKE HOME

152

©1992 BY ALISON BECHDEL

OUR VALIANT HEROINES HAVE VENTURED FORTH ON HOLIDAY VISITS TO THEIR **FAMILIES** OF **ORIGIN.**

LET'S JOIN THEM ON NEW YEAR'S EVE.

A TIP O' THE NIB TO MARCELLA PINO!

SAY THE RIGHT THING
153
©1992 BY ALISON BECHDEL

SORRY I'M LATE.
HI, BABE. WE ORDERED ALREADY.
TONI! GOD, YOU'RE LIKE... GROWING!
ONE EVENING AT CAFÉ TOPAZ...

YEAH, IT'S STARTING TO SHOW. CAN YOU BELIEVE IT? THERE'S A BABY IN HERE!
OH MY GOD! I CAN'T BELIEVE IT!

IT'S AMAZING!
IT'S HARRIET! AND THAT SHE-DEVIL SHE'S TAKEN UP WITH! HOW DARE THEY COME INTO THIS RESTAURANT?

UH-OH. SHE SEES YOU.
WHAT AM I GONNA DO? I CAN'T EAT WITH THEM HERE!

THEY'RE TURNING AROUND. THEY'RE LEAVING. GOOD MOVE, HARRIET.
YOU CAN LET GO OF MY ARM NOW. AND PUT DOWN THAT FORK

I CAN'T TAKE IT ANYMORE! EVERYWHERE I GO, THERE THEY ARE! IF SHE WANTS 'NO CONTACT' WHY'S SHE FOLLOWING ME AROUND?!

WHAT'S THIS NO CONTACT DEAL?
AHH, SHE SAYS SHE HAS TROUBLE KEEPING CLEAR BOUNDARIES WITH ME, SO SHE NEEDS A COUPLE MONTHS WHERE WE DON'T SEE EACH OTHER. THEN, SUPPOSEDLY, WE'LL BE ABLE TO BE FRIENDS. AS IF!

WELL, IT IS HARD TO JUST SWITCH GEARS FROM LOVERS TO FRIENDS WITH NO TRANSITION. TAKING A BREAK IS PROBABLY A GOOD IDEA.

THANK YOU, TONI, FOR THAT PEARL OF WISDOM. IT'S JUST WHAT I NEEDED TO HEAR.
BRAISED KOHLRABI AND OKRA GUMBO?
THAT'S FOR TONI.
Cafe Topaz

OH!
WHAT? DON'T TELL ME YOUR NAUSEA IS COMING BACK!

IT MOVED! I FELT IT MOVE, CLARICE! OH MY GOD! THERE REALLY IS A BABY IN HERE!!
EW, WEIRD. KINDA LIKE THAT SCENE IN 'ALIEN,' HUH?

SUGAR 'n SPICE
154
©1992 BY ALISON BECHDEL

LOIS STOPS IN AT THE HAIR PATROL ON HER LUNCH BREAK.
ARE YOU SERIOUS? AFTER YOU'VE GROWN IT ALL OUT SO NICE?
AHH, IT'S ONLY HAIR, MIKO! C'MON, DO ME! JUST LIKE THE PHOTO, OKAY?
TIME

MEANWHILE, BACK AT THE SHOP...
HERE YOU GO! GOTTA RUN...
THANKS, HON. SEE YOU TONIGHT.

WHO WAS THAT? YOUR LOVER?
YEAH. MAXINE. I FORGOT MY LUNCH THIS MORNING.

HUH. ME TOO, BUT NOBODY'S GONNA RUSH OVER AND DELIVER MINE WITH A KISS. MUST BE NICE.
YEAH, I GUESS IT IS.
VISA
NCR
jewelry 10% OFF

SPARE ME THE GORY DETAILS. I HEAR ENOUGH ABOUT DOMESTIC BLISS FROM CLARICE & TONI.
WILL THAT BE ALL?
YES.
HOTHEAD PAISAN

IT'S GETTING REALLY HARD TO TAKE! THEIR TENTH ANNIVERSARY, THEIR HOTSHOT CAREERS, A BABY COMING. NOW THEY'RE SHOPPING FOR A STATION WAGON.
I DON'T NEED A BAG, THANKS.
THANK YOU.
JINGLE

AND LOOKIT ME! BROKE, JILTED, DUSTING SHELVES ALL DAY AND GOING HOME TO MY CATS AT NIGHT. I'M A TRAGIC FIGURE!
OH, I DUNNO. PATHETIC, MAYBE. D'YOU EVER STOP AND LISTEN TO YOURSELF?

WH-WHADDAYA MEAN?
I MEAN YOU ARE A REAL PILL. I DON'T THINK I'VE EVER HEARD YOU SAY ANYTHING POSITIVE.

OH, COME ON. I SAY POSITIVE THINGS!
LET'S HEAR ONE.
MADWIMMIN BOOKS
OPEN

UM... YOUR HAIR LOOKS NICE LIKE THAT.
OH MY GOD!

TA DA! WHAT DO YOU THINK? IT'S THE FIRST "PEROT" IN TOWN!
UM... YOUR HAIR LOOKS NICE LIKE THAT.

Cultural Exchange
©1993 BY ALISON BECHDEL
155
THANKS, MO. DON'T WORK TOO HARD.
BYE, NAOMI. SEE YOU AT THE CO-OP.
MADWIMMIN BOOKS
MARY DALY
OUTERCOURSE A BEWILDERING TRIP

CAN YOU BELIEVE SHE'S SLEEPING WITH A **MAN?** I KNOW IT'S UNCOOL OF ME, BUT I CAN'T HELP FEELING ... I DUNNO... **BETRAYED.**
I KNOW WHAT YOU MEAN. YOU CAN JUST HEAR JERRY FALWELL GLOATING. "SEE? THAT'S ALL THEY REALLY WANT."

AND YOU KNOW WHAT ELSE? IT BUGS ME THAT SHE CAN COME IN HERE AND SOAK UP LESBIAN CULTURE, THEN GO HOME TO HER SAFE, SOCIETALLY APPROVED **BOYFRIEND.**
AAH, WHAT ARE YOU AFRAID OF, MO? THERE'S ROOM FOR EVERYBODY! **I** SAY THE MORE PEOPLE SOAKING UP LESBIAN CULTURE, THE BETTER!

OH, REALLY? LOOKS LIKE WE HAVE A CODE BLUE OVER AT THE PERIODICAL RACK.
I'LL HANDLE IT.
OFFICE
ACHÉ
COMMON LIVES LESBO LIVES
SOJOURNER
DA NOIVE
CUTE GIRLS ISSUE
BIKINI KILL
ON OUR BACKS
BLACK LACE
SCI-FI
NAIAD
WESTERN
NAIAD

CAN I HELP YOU FIND SOMETHING, SIR?
UM... JUST BROWSING.
CAUGHT LOOKING
ABSOLUT PORN
ON OUR RACKS
A TIP O' THE NIB TO JO DEN BOER!

HMM... I FIND THAT PUBLICATION RATHER **TAME** MYSELF. HAVE YOU EVER SEEN THIS ONE? THIS MONTH THERE'S A **HOT** PHOTO SPREAD OF THREE TOTALLY TATTOOED BABES WITH **STRAP-ONS** DOING AN **ARMPIT SHAVING** SCENE.
THE UNIVERSE ACCORDING TO SUSIE BRIGHT
AGAINST SADO-MASOCHISM
RAD ATTITUDE
ALL PURPOSE LUBRICANT
NEW TRENDS IN DILDO PIERCING
ON OUR RAG
SPONGE FUN

AND IF YOU'RE LOOKING FOR A **REAL** THRILL, CHECK OUT THE STORY, "SHE CAME IN WAVES," IN THIS NEW FEMALE EJACULATION ANTHOLOGY!
off our backs
CALYX
Ms
GETTING DRENCHED
QUIM

'SCUSE ME, I THINK I LEFT MY CAR AT A HYDRANT.

NICE WORK.
NOT REALLY. I'M LOSING MY TOUCH.
OH?

LAST WEEK I FLUSTERED A GUY SO BAD HE SPENT SIXTY BUCKS BEFORE HE LEFT.

WAGON HO
©1993 BY ALISON BECHDEL
156

NOT BAD, CLARICE. DID THE DEALER PAY YOU NOT TO TRADE IN THAT CLASSIC '77 PICKUP OF TONI'S?
DID I MENTION THAT THE RADIO EVEN DISPLAYS THE CALL LETTERS OF THE STATION YOU'RE TUNED TO?

GREAT. HAS MO SEEN IT?
VULVA
D2W04

YEAH. SHE SAID I WAS A SHAMELESSLY MATERIALISTIC, CARBON MONOXIDE-SPEWING MENACE, AND THAT IF I HAD ANY SENSE OF SOCIAL RESPONSIBILITY I'D RIDE THE BUS OR, BETTER YET, A BIKE.
GOD, I MISS HER.

HI, BABE! LOOK WHO I FOUND WHILE I WAS DRIVING AROUND AFTER WORK TRYING TO IMPRESS GIRLS IN OUR NEW STATION WAGON!
HARRIET! HI! CAN YOU STAY FOR SUPPER?
THE BIG BOOK O' BULGAR

I'D LOVE TO. WHOA, TONI! PUTTING ON A LITTLE WEIGHT THERE, HUH?
YEAH, ALMOST AS MUCH AS CLARICE.
IT'S REALLY WEIRD. SHE GETS PREGNANT AND I GAIN TEN POUNDS.

OUR MIDWIFE SAYS THAT'S NOT UNUSUAL. SOME PARTNERS EVEN GET SYMPATHETIC MORNING SICKNESS.
YEAH, WELL, LET'S JUST HOPE I DON'T GET SYMPATHETIC LABOR PAINS.

SO HARRIET! WE'VE BEEN SEEING YOU AROUND A LOT WITH ELLEN TUFEL. RUMOR HAS IT YOU'RE AN ITEM!

TONI!
NO, IT'S ALL RIGHT. IT'S TRUE. WE ARE.
REALLY! HOW'S IT GOING?

WELL, ACTUALLY IT'S WONDERFUL! I'M HAPPIER THAN I'VE BEEN IN A LONG TIME.
MMM! DINNER SMELLS GREAT, HON! WHAT'RE WE HAVING?

SO ARE YOU IN LOVE OR WHAT?
BIG TIME.
LENTIL STEW, MY FAVORITE! YOU SHOULDN'T HAVE!

Diversions
157
©1993 BY ALISON BECHDEL

SO THEA, I JUST READ ABOUT THIS COOL SHOW OF WEARABLE AGITPROP FIBER CONSTRUCTIONS OPENING AT THE FEMINIST ART CO-OP...
YEAH, MAXINE AND I ARE GONNA CHECK IT OUT TOMORROW. OH, HERE SHE IS NOW! CAN YOU LOCK UP?
WORKSHOP
PROTEST
DANCE
ORGY

SIGH.
MADWIMMIN BOOKS
CLOSED
CLIK!

SATURDAY NIGHT AND NO PLACE TO GO.
BUS STOP

UH... HI, SPARROW. I JUST STOPPED BY TO SAY HI. FOR A MINUTE.
OH, MO. I THOUGHT YOU WERE THE PIZZA.

HEY, MO! C'MON IN AND JOIN THE BURNOUT BRIGADE!
YEAH. WE HAVE A FABULOUS EVENING PLANNED. LOW-NUTRIENT FOODSTUFFS AND LIGHTWEIGHT ENTERTAINMENT, GUARANTEED TO TAKE OUR MINDS OFF OUR TROUBLES.
POPCORN CAJUN SEAWEED FLAVOR
VIDEO RAMA

OH, GREAT. ORDER A PIZZA, POP IN SISTER ACT, AND FORGET ALL ABOUT GENOCIDE, STARVATION, AND MASS RAPES IN BOSNIA! THE TRUE AMERICAN WAY.

LISTEN, MO. I HAVE BEEN DOING CRISIS INTERVENTION WITH BATTERED, HOMELESS WOMEN AND KIDS ALL WEEK LONG. TONIGHT, I AM GOING TO VEGETATE IN FRONT OF THE TV. IF YOU'RE SO WORRIED ABOUT BOSNIA, GO JOIN THE RED CROSS.

I'M SORRY. YOU'RE RIGHT. I'M PROJECTING MY OWN HOLLOW PURPOSELESSNESS ONTO EVERYONE ELSE. I NEED TO GET A LIFE.
POPKORN

HUH. YOU'RE LOOKING PRETTY FESTIVE FOR SUCH A LOST SOUL. NEW SHIRT? AND WHAT'S WITH THE EARRINGS?
NOTHING! JEEZ, IS IT SO UNUSUAL FOR ME TO LOOK NICE?

I KNOW WHAT'S WITH THE EARRINGS. MO'S HOT FOR SOMEONE. AREN'T YOU?
WHO?
I AM NOT! SHUT UP!
POPCORN NACHO CARAMEL FLAVOR
VIDEORAMA
VIDEORAMA

DON'T WORRY. YOUR SECRET'S SAFE WITH ME. ESPECIALLY SEEING AS SHE'S ALREADY SPOKEN FOR.
I DON'T KNOW WHAT YOU'RE TALKING ABOUT. WHAT'LL WE WATCH FIRST... TRUTH OR DARE, OR SHE'S GOTTA HAVE IT?
VIDEORAMA
VIDEORAMA

NO ONE IN CLARICE & TONI'S BABY GROUP HAS HAD AN ACTUAL BABY YET, SO OUR MOTHERS-TO-BE ARE VISITING A MORE ESTABLISHED GATHERING IN SEARCH OF GUIDANCE AND INSPIRATION.

ONE BIG HAPPY
©1993 BY ALISON BECHDEL
160

DUE TO AN INOPPORTUNELY BLOWN OIL PAN GASKET, OUR GALS HAVE FORSAKEN LOIS'S AGED VW FOR A MORE PUBLIC MEANS OF TRANSPORT TO THE MARCH ON WASHINGTON.
GREAT. THIS IS JUST GREAT, LOIS. THANKS TO YOU I'M GONNA BE TRAPPED OVERNIGHT ON A BUS WITH HARRIET AND THAT... THAT WOMAN.
TRY AND RISE ABOVE IT, MO. WE'RE LUCKY THEY HAD SEATS LEFT.
LIFT THE MILITARY BAN!
BAN THE MILITARY

MO, UM... HI. LISTEN, I'D LIKE YOU TO MEET ELLEN.
MO! AT LONG LAST! WELCOME ABOARD!
UH... HI.

YOU OKAY?
"WELCOME ABOARD." SHEESH! THE NERVE!

HEY, YOU TWO! SIT ACROSS FROM US!
THEA! I DIDN'T KNOW YOU WERE TAKING THE BUS!

YOU KNOW MY LOVER MAXINE.
SURE. GOOD TO SEE YOU.
UH... HI.

I'LL LET YOU HAVE THE AISLE SO YOU CAN FLIRT WITH THEA AFTER OL' MAXINE NODS OFF.

HEY GIRLS, ANYONE SITTING HERE?
NAOMI! NO, I WAS SAVING THESE SEATS ESPECIALLY FOR YOU.

HI!
THIS IS MY LOVER DAVID.
NICE T'MEETCHA, DAVE. RICECAKE?
BiNet USA
UH... HI.

AT LAST, THEY'RE OFF...
FROM THE HALLS OF SAM NUNN'S SENATE TO THE BUNKS IN SUB-MA-RINES WE WILL FIGHT OUR PEOPLE'S BATTLES IN THE COURTS AND ON THE STREETS...

BUT IT'S A LONG, STRANGE TRIP FOR OUR HEROINE.

AFTER-GLOW
©1993 BY ALISON BECHDEL
161

A BUS FULL OF WEARY BUT EXHILARATED MARCHERS WENDS ITS WAY HOMEWARD FROM OUR NATION'S MOMENTARILY QUEER CAPITAL.

SO WHERE'D YOU END UP STAYING, MO?
ON THE FLOOR WITH EIGHT OTHER PEOPLE AT MY COUSIN'S HOUSE IN THE BURBS. MY NECK IS DISLOCATED AND I HAVEN'T SLEPT IN SIXTY HOURS.

C'MERE. I'LL RUB YOUR NECK TILL MAXINE GETS BACK TO HER SEAT.
JEEZ, MO. WHO'D WANNA COME TO THE BABEFEST OF THE CENTURY AND **SLEEP?** I'M SO PUMPED ON ADRENALINE I DON'T THINK I'LL COME DOWN TILL NEXT WEEK.

DIDJA MAKE YOUR QUOTA, LOIS?
YUP. KISSED A WOMAN FROM EVERY STATE IN THE UNION. RHODE ISLAND WAS A DRAG QUEEN, THOUGH. DO YOU THINK THAT COUNTS?

A FEW SEATS BACK...
GINGER, WHAT DO YOU MEAN YOU DIDN'T LEAVE YOUR HOTEL? NOT EVEN FOR THE RALLY?

HEY, MALIKA AND I HADN'T SEEN EACH OTHER IN MONTHS. WE JUST LOST TRACK OF TIME.
WOW. I HOPE SHE GOT SOME OF THAT ON VIDEO.

AND UP FRONT...
YEAH, I'M COMPLETELY WIPED OUT, BUT IT WAS WORTH IT. I'M SO GLAD THE BABY GOT TO PICK UP THAT INCREDIBLE ENERGY.

WHAT ARE YOU TWO GONNA DO WITH YOURSELVES NOW THAT THE MARCH IS OVER?
GOSH, I DUNNO. NO MORE LATE-NIGHT MEETINGS, NO MORE PHONES RINGING OFF THE HOOK, NO MORE FRENZIED LAST-MINUTE ORGANIZING...

WELL, AS SOON AS I GET THREE MONTHS' WORTH OF LAUNDRY DONE, I'M GONNA RUN FOR CITY COUNCIL.

THANKS. THAT WAS GREAT.

LOIS! OMIGOD! YOU WERE RIGHT... I **DO** HAVE A CRUSH ON THEA! WHAT'M I GONNA **DO?!**

LEMME SEE... A COLD SPONGE BATH IN THE LAVATORY SOUNDS ABOUT YOUR SPEED.
Trailhound

Apple Pie Order
©1993 BY ALISON BECHDEL
162
HERE'S ANOTHER SHIPMENT, THEA. I, UH... I REALLY LIKE THAT SCENT YOU'RE WEARING.
COMPACT DISCS
BETTY GETS IT
GIRLS IN THE NOISE
LADY-SLIPPER
HUH? OH, YOU MUST SMELL THE FLEA AND TICK SHAMPOO I USED TO WASH THE DOG THIS MORNING. THANKS, I'LL PASS THAT ALONG TO REX.
HEY, LOOK! I JUST GOT BACK MY PICTURES OF D.C.!
THUNK
HERE'S ME AT THE DYKE MARCH WITH SOME COOL WOMEN I MET.
...AND HERE I AM GIVING A SAFE SEX DEMO AT THE LESBIANS AND AIDS ACTION.
...AND THIS IS ME BACK-STAGE AT THE RALLY. THAT'S MARTINA'S HEAD. AND THAT'S MELISSA ETHERIDGE'S HAND ON MY THIGH.
JEEZ, LOIS! I DIDN'T EVEN SEE THE RALLY, THE MARCH TOOK SO LONG TO GET THERE. AND HOW'D YOU GET TO DO ALL THIS STUFF? I SPENT THE ENTIRE WEEKEND LOST ON THE METRO OR STANDING AROUND GETTING SKIN CANCER.
THAT'S NOT TRUE, MO! YOU ALSO SPENT A LOT OF TIME OBSESSING ABOUT WHETHER YOU'D RUN INTO HARRIET AND ELLEN DOING A SPONTANEOUS KISS-IN SOMEWHERE.
OH, RIGHT. ⁂ SIGH ⁂ REMEMBER? THAT'S HOW HARRIET AND I FIRST KISSED, DOING C.D. TOGETHER AT THE '87 MARCH.
MARY CHAPIN-SHEET-ROCKER
JEEZ, THAT SEEMS LIKE AGES AGO. THINGS SURE HAVE CHANGED.
YEAH, AND NOT JUST MY LOVE LIFE. I KNOW THIS MARCH WAS EVEN BIGGER AND BETTER THAN THE LAST ONE, BUT I FELT KIND OF LOST, SOMEHOW. I MEAN, BASE-BALL, HOT DOGS, AND GAYS IN THE MILITARY IS NOT THE AGENDA I SIGNED UP FOR.
THE LESBIAN
YUP. THE CROWD CHEERING PATRIOTICALLY FOR A MILITARY COLOR GUARD IN FULL-DRESS UNIFORM WAS A LITTLE WEIRD.
WHY ARE WE SCRAMBLING FOR A PIECE OF THE PIE WHEN THE PIE IS ROTTEN? WE'VE GOTTA CHANGE THE SYSTEM, NOT GET CO-OPTED BY IT! AND I'M GONNA SCREAM IF I HEAR ONE MORE PERSON SAY WE'RE "JUST LIKE EVERYONE ELSE"!
MPACT DISCS
PHRANQUE
LUCIE BLUE TROMBONE
L7
HEY, LOOK AT THIS GREAT SHOT I GOT OF CLARICE AND TONI AT THE WEDDING.
DANG! I WAS SUPPOSED TO BE BEST WOMAN, BUT I GOT OFF AT THE WRONG METRO STOP.

In Their Dreams

163

NEWSFLASH! "A RECENT SEX SURVEY OF TWENTYSOMETHINGS REVEALS THAT AMONG MEN WHO FANTASIZE ABOUT CELEBRITIES, CINDY CRAWFORD AND DEMI MOORE RANK HIGH. WOMEN OPT FOR LUKE PERRY AND PRESIDENT CLINTON, WHILE GAY MEN TAPPED MARKY MARK AND TOM CRUISE." PERIOD. END OF PARAGRAPH.

FLUFF SECTION

D'YOU THINK THAT MEANS LESBIANS DON'T FANTASIZE ABOUT CELEBRITIES, OR DON'T ANSWER SURVEYS?

OH, COME NOW, GINGER! THERE ARE NO LESBIANS! AND IF THERE **ARE**, THEY **REALLY** JUST WANT TO SUCK COCK. I SAW IT ON **ROSEANNE**. SANDRA BERNHARD DUMPED MORGAN FAIRCHILD FOR TIM CURRY.

FILM

3 OF HEARTS

HOW COME MEN GET TO BE TOTALLY QUEER BUT WOMEN DON'T? I'M SICK OF BEING PORTRAYED AS SOME STRAIGHT SLOB'S PORNO FANTASY.

LOOK. COULD YOU TWO AT LEAST **TRY** TO CONCENTRATE? I'M NOT ORGANIZING THIS BABY SHOWER BY MYSELF.

SORRY, SPARROW. WHERE WERE WE?

THE GUEST LIST. WHAT DO WE DO ABOUT MO AND HARRIET?

WELL, WE'VE GOTTA INVITE THEM BOTH. WE'LL JUST WARN EACH OF THEM THE OTHER ONE'S GONNA BE HERE.

THEN WHAT IF **NEITHER** OF THEM COME? OR WHAT IF THEY **BOTH** COME AND THEIR TENSION SPOILS THE PARTY ATMOSPHERE?

WE COULD INVITE SO MANY PEOPLE THEY'D NEVER SEE EACH OTHER. YOU KNOW, ONE OF THOSE LOUD, ROCKIN' DANCE PARTY KINDS OF BABY SHOWERS.

MEANWHILE, ACROSS TOWN...

WASN'T THAT INCREDIBLE? I FIND THAT STARTING OFF THE FIRST CLASS WITH A VIDEO OF AN ACTUAL BIRTH HELPS TO CALM A LOT OF FOLKS' CONCERNS RIGHT AWAY.

CLIK

NATUREBORN BIRTHING CENTER

I ALSO THINK IT'S IMPORTANT FOR YOU DADS... ER, COACHES, TO SEE THE KIND OF SUPPORT YOU'LL BE PROVIDING DURING LABOR. NOW LET'S DISCUSS SOME OF OUR FANTASIES AND FEARS ABOUT CHILDBIRTH...

AND BACK AT THE RANCH...
HILLARY CLINTON AND QUEEN LATIFAH.
WHAT, IN THE SAME FANTASY, OR ONE AT A TIME?

...and baby makes three

164

HOW'D IT GO, MO? WASN'T THIS THE FIRST TIME YOU'VE ACTUALLY SOCIALIZED WITH HARRIET SINCE SHE LEFT YOU? I MEAN, SINCE SHE LEFT?

YEAH. IT WAS OKAY. WE TALKED A BIT. SOUNDS LIKE **YOU** TWO HAVE BEEN GETTING PRETTY CHUMMY WITH HER AND HER NEW **CONSORT**.

UH... WELL, WE HAD DINNER ONCE.

JEEZ, YOU GUYS! IS IT ASKING TOO MUCH THAT MY BEST FRIENDS HAVE THE DECENCY TO **OSTRACIZE** MY EX-LOVER?

MO, IT'S NOT LIKE SHE COMMITTED A CRIME. ANYWAY, HARRIET'S OUR FRIEND TOO. REMEMBER? WE INTRODUCED YOU TO HER.

YEAH. THANKS A **LOT**. SO HOW 'BOUT IF YOU JUST OSTRACIZE HER NEW GIRL-FRIEND?

SOME FRIENDS YOU ARE. WELL, AT LEAST YOU CAN GOSSIP TO ME ABOUT THEM. ARE THEY MAKING SCENES IN PUBLIC? NOT HAVING SEX? SEEKING PROFESSIONAL HELP?

MO, COME ON! IT'S BEEN A YEAR! STOP THINKING ABOUT HARRIET AND GET ON WITH YOUR LIFE.

Promises, Promises
165
©1993 BY ALISON BECHDEL

TONI, I'M HOME! I GOT IT! I GOT THE JOB!
WHICH ONE?

THE ONE AT THE ENVIRONMENTAL JUSTICE FUND! REMEMBER, THE ORGANIZATION THAT'S FIGHTING THE WAY POOR NEIGHBORHOODS END UP WITH ALL THE INDUSTRIAL POLLUTION AND WASTE DUMPS? I'M THE STAFF ATTORNEY!

THAT'S GREAT, SWEETHEART! I'M SO PROUD! UM... WHAT HAPPENED TO THE JOB WITH THAT FIRM, THE ONE THAT PAYS TWICE AS MUCH?
THIS WORK IS MUCH MORE IMPORTANT! PLUS I'LL HAVE WAY MORE RESPONSIBILITY. LET'S GO OUT AND CELEBRATE!

OH, CLARICE..I'M WORN OUT. I DIDN'T SLEEP WELL LAST NIGHT. MY ANKLES ARE SWOLLEN, MY BACK ACHES... WOULD YOU MIND JUST GOING AND GETTING SOME TAKEOUT FROM THE TOPAZ?
OH. OKAY. YOU PHONE THE ORDER IN AND I'LL BE RIGHT BACK.

VULVA
D2W04
VROOM!

HEY, CLARICE! PULL UP A CHAIR!
WE WERE JUST HOLDING AN INFORMAL REVIEW OF THE CLINTON ADMINISTRATION.
Topaz

OH, DON'T GET ME STARTED! IF THE GUY SAYS ONE THING, YOU CAN TRUST HE'LL DO THE OPPOSITE.
WE SHOULD'VE HAD A CLUE WHEN HE IMMEDIATELY ABANDONED HIS CAMPAIGN PLEDGE TO TAKE IN HAITIAN REFUGEES.
HOW ABOUT HIS LATEST BACK-OFF FROM LIFTING THE MILITARY BAN? SAYS IT'S A "LEGITIMATE CONCERN" THAT "OUR COUNTRY DOES NOT APPEAR TO BE ENDORSING A GAY LIFESTYLE."

AHH, ENDORSE MY BUTT, BILL.
NUCLEAR TESTING RESUMES

AND NOW LANI GUINIER! HE NOMINATES HER, THEN AS SOON AS THE RIGHT WING STARTS THEIR DISINFORMATION CAMPAIGN, HE LEAVES HER TWISTING IN THE WIND!
GOD FORBID HE SHOULD FIGHT FOR AN AFRICAN-AMERICAN WOMAN IN CHARGE OF CIVIL RIGHTS WHO MIGHT ACTUALLY CHANGE SOMETHING.

HEY! I'M GONNA CHANGE SOMETHING! LEMME TELL YOU ABOUT THE GREAT NEW JOB I GOT TODAY! GINA! A ROUND OF YOUR FINEST SPARKLING WATER FOR MY FRIENDS HERE!

the fairies' midwife
166
©1993 BY ALISON BECHDEL
BABE, LISTEN. I REALLY CAN'T GET AWAY THIS AFTERNOON. DO YOU MIND GOING TO SEE THE MIDWIFE WITHOUT ME, JUST THIS ONCE?
E.P.A.

WELL OF COURSE I MIND, CLARICE! BUT IF YOU CAN'T COME, YOU CAN'T COME. I JUST WISH YOU'D GET YOUR PRIORITIES STRAIGHT!
1001 LOOPHOLES
1993 TAX HANDBOOK
FEDERAL INCOME TAXATION OF CORPORATIONS
SPIRITUAL MIDWIFERY

SLAM

LATER, AT THE BIRTH CENTER...
TONI, WHEN YOU'RE DONE WEIGHING YOURSELF AND TESTING YOUR URINE, MIRIAM'S READY TO SEE YOU.
SEATTLE MIDWIFERY SCHOOL 1978-88
VISA
ACTIVE BIRTH
PULL YOUR OWN CHART

TONI! COME ON IN, HON. YOU LOOK RADIANT! WHERE'S CLARICE?
BUSTAGUT TRIATHLON

OH, MIRIAM. SHE'S TOTALLY WRAPPED UP IN THIS NEW JOB! LAST NIGHT SHE MISSED OUR PRENATAL CLASS. I FEEL LIKE SHE'S BACKING OUT ON ME.

HAVE YOU TALKED TO HER ABOUT IT?
YES, BUT SHE SAYS THERE'S NOTHING SHE CAN DO. IT'S A DEMANDING JOB AND SHE JUST NEEDS TO PUT IN A LOT OF TIME RIGHT NOW.
TREK

HM. SOUNDS A BIT LIKE MY EX-HUSBAND WHEN I WAS PREGNANT WITH ALEX. YOU CAN GO AHEAD AND GET ON THE TABLE.
WHAT DID YOU DO ABOUT IT?

LEFT HIM AND MOVED INTO A LESBIAN COMMUNE.
MIRIAM! I'M NOT GOING TO LEAVE HER! BESIDES, I DON'T THINK THEY HAVE LESBIAN COMMUNES ANYMORE.
MUDDYBUTT MOUNTAIN BIKE FESTIVAL

OH, DON'T WORRY, DARLIN'. I THINK CLARICE IS THERE FOR YOU. MAYBE SHE'S JUST UNSURE OF HER ROLE. SOMETIMES IT'S HARD FOR THE NONBIOLOGICAL MOM TO KNOW EXACTLY WHERE SHE FITS IN.

WE'VE GOT A LOVELY HEARTBEAT HERE. HAS THERE BEEN MUCH MOVEMENT GOING ON?
YES, A LOT! LAST NIGHT IN BED, I WAS HOLDING CLARICE, AND SHE FELT THE BABY KICK HER IN THE BUTT!
IRONBUNS MARATHON

MEANWHILE...
OUR COURT DATE IS WHEN?
AUGUST
BABY DUE!

one sultry summer evening
167
©1993 BY ALISON BECHDEL

BABE, I'M SORRY! I DON'T LIKE WORKING 18 HOURS A DAY. BUT MY FIRST TIME IN COURT IS GONNA BE AGAINST SOME HEAVY CORPORATE LAWYERS!
I KNOW, CLARICE. I JUST WISH YOU WERE AS CONCERNED ABOUT THE BABY AS YOU ARE ABOUT YOUR JOB.

I AM CONCERNED ABOUT THE BABY! IF I DON'T WIN THIS INJUNCTION AGAINST THE GARBAGE INCINERATOR, THE KID WILL HAVE LUNG CANCER BY THE TIME IT'S FIVE!
LOOK, I JUST NEED FOR YOU TO COMMIT TO THE REST OF OUR PRENATAL CLASSES OR ELSE I'M ASKING SOMEONE ELSE TO BE MY PRIMARY SUPPORT.

WHAT? WHO?!
I DON'T KNOW! SPARROW OR SOMEONE FROM OUR BABY GROUP. JESUS, MAYBE I'LL ASK THE PAPER GIRL! I SEE MORE OF HER LATELY THAN I DO OF YOU. AND AT LEAST SHE'S DEPENDABLE! SOB!

WAIL!
AW, TONI! I'M YOUR SUPPORT! I'M SORRY I HAVEN'T BEEN AROUND. FROM NOW ON I WILL BE, BABY. I GUESS I'VE BEEN KIND OF AN ASSHOLE.

A BIG ASSHOLE. - SNIFF -
YEAH, OKAY. A BIG, ROYAL ASSHOLE. C'MON, OR WE'LL MISS THE DANG CLASS.
KISS

MEANWHILE, MO IS PAYING A CALL OVER AT LOIS, GINGER, & SPARROW'S PLACE.

Y'KNOW, I THINK THEA IS ATTRACTED TO ME, TOO. I JUST SENSE THAT KIND OF ENERGY FROM HER.
MO, GIVE IT UP. SHE'S MARRIED. IF YOU WANNA GET LAID, COME WITH ME TO THE LOVE TUNNEL TONIGHT. IT'S MUCH SIMPLER.
OLD SPICE

WELL, CALL ME FUSSY, BUT I PREFER HAVING SEX IN A PLACE WHERE MY SHOES DON'T STICK TO THE FLOOR.
HEY, WANT A VIBRATOR? AN EX WHO WORKS AT THE PLEASURE PIT GAVE ME THIS, BUT I ALREADY HAVE ONE LIKE IT.

UH... YEAH, SURE. I COULD REALLY USE IT ON MY NECK.
YEAH, I BET.

HEY, LOIS. REMEMBER I WAS GONNA BORROW YOUR CAR? MALIKA'S FLIGHT GETS IN AT 7:10.
LIVE IT UP.
MALIKA'S COMING? THAT'S GREAT, GINGER!

YEAH! SHE'S GONNA STAY FOR A WHOLE MONTH THIS TIME. FOR ONCE, LOIS WON'T BE THE ONLY ONE GETTING ANY ACTION AROUND HERE.
DING DONG

HI.
HI. I'M JUNE. IS SPARROW READY?

IS IT IN THE STARS? OR JUST SOMETHING IN THE WATER? WHATEVER,... ON THIS NIGHT OUR LUSTY LASSES' FANCIES TURN TO ACTS OF **LOVE!**

MO'S CRUSH ON HER CO-WORKER REACHES A TURBO-CHARGED PITCH.

TONI'S HOT AND BOTHERED.

DOWN THE BLOCK, GINGER & MALIKA ARE LIVE AND IN-PERSON,...

... SPARROW GETS BACK IN THE SADDLE...

IT'S BEEN A LONG TIME, JUNE. I WANT TO GO SLOW. LET'S CONSULT THE **I CHING.**

WHAT-EVER.

"... A CAUTIOUS HALT HALFWAY BRINGS GOOD FORTUNE. GOING THROUGH TO THE END BRINGS MISFORTUNE."

I CHING OR BOOK OF CHANGES

... AND LOIS ADJUSTS HER VOLUME.

MOAN!

SIGH!

OH! OH! **OH!**

THUMP

VANITY FAIR

K.D.'S CLOSE SHAVE

CALVIN

Crushed
©1993 BY ALISON BECHDEL
169
LOOK, ANOTHER ONE. GOT IT AT THE CORNER STORE.
OH, GIMME A BREAK. ISN'T OUR FIFTEEN MINUTES UP YET?
SCIENTIFIC AMERICAN
LESBIANS: BETTER AT MATH?
kd lang ON FRACTAL THEORY, LAB ANIMAL RIGHTS

WHATSA MATTER, MO? CAN'T HANDLE THE SPOTLIGHT?
I JUST DON'T TRUST IT. I MEAN, WOULD SOMEONE PLEASE EXPLAIN TO ME WHAT'S SO REVOLUTIONARY ABOUT NEWSWEEK TELLING US WHAT WE DO IN BED?
STONE WASH BLUES
BOOBS OF RUBBER, ISOTONERS OF GOLD

LESBIANS ARE REPLACING STEP AEROBICS IN THE DEPRAVED CESSPIT OF MAINSTREAM AMERICAN CULTURE! LEMME TELL YA, WE DIDN'T KNOW WHEN WE HAD IT GOOD! MOVING INVISIBLY, BEING ON THE OUTSIDE-- THAT'S WHERE THE REAL, SUBVERSIVE POWER LIES! RIGHT, THEA?

NO WAY. SUBVERSIVE POWER IS LESBIANS IN BANANA REPUBLIC ADS.
OH.

Y'KNOW, YOU'RE ABSOLUTELY RIGHT! SHATTERING THE MYTH THAT LESBIANS AREN'T REAL PEOPLE IS OUR SINGLE MOST EFFECTIVE TOOL IN COUNTERING THE RAMPANT HOMOPHOBIA AND MISOGYNY IN SOCIETY TODAY.

MEANWHILE, ACROSS TOWN AT NATUREBORN...
39 CENTIMETERS, 39 WEEKS! BABY'S COMING ALONG BEAUTIFULLY!
SO NEXT MONDAY IS STILL THE DUE DATE? ANY WAY TO PUSH IT BACK A FEW DAYS?
GAY GAMES

OH, PLEASE, CLARICE! WHAT DO YOU WANT ME TO DO? STAND ON MY HEAD FOR A WEEK? IF THE BABY COMES, YOU'LL JUST HAVE TO RESCHEDULE YOUR BIG COURTROOM SCENE!
LOOK, DON'T FIXATE ON THE DUE DATE. IT'S JUST AN APPROXIMATION. ONLY 5 PERCENT OF BABIES ACTUALLY ARRIVE ON IT. MOST COME LATER, IN FACT.
BAREFOOT 15K

GREAT! HOW MUCH LATER? TWO DAYS? THREE?
LET ME GIVE YOU A FRIENDLY TIP, CLARICE. DON'T GET TOO HUNG UP ON KEEPING A TIGHT SCHEDULE FOR THE NEXT, SAY, EIGHTEEN YEARS OR SO.
MUD, SWEAT & GEARS BIKE TREK

BACK AT MADWIMMIN...
JEEZ, MO CHANGED HER POSITION SO FAST ON LESBIAN VISIBILITY OUT THERE, I THOUGHT SHE'D GET WHIPLASH. SHE HAS IT BAD FOR YOU, THEA.
OFFICE

YEAH, I KNOW. SHE REMINDS ME OF REX WHEN HE WAS A PUPPY. IT'S KIND OF CUTE ISN'T IT?
OFFICE

the Big Day
©1993 BY ALISON BECHDEL
170

MONDAY MORNING...
ARE YOU SURE? MAYBE WE SHOULD CALL THE MIDWIFE! MAYBE I SHOULD STAY HOME!
CLARICE, IT WAS JUST ONE CONTRACTION TWO HOURS AGO! I'M NOT IN LABOR! WHAT'S THE MATTER? YOU GETTING COLD FEET ABOUT GOING TO COURT TODAY?
NON-BIOLOGICAL MOMS SUPPORT GROUP
CLINTON'S POPULARITY SLIPS AGAIN

GOD, BABE! I'M SO NERVOUS! D'YOU THINK I CAN DO IT?
YEAH. I DO.
CLINTON READY TO USE FORCE IN BOSNIA

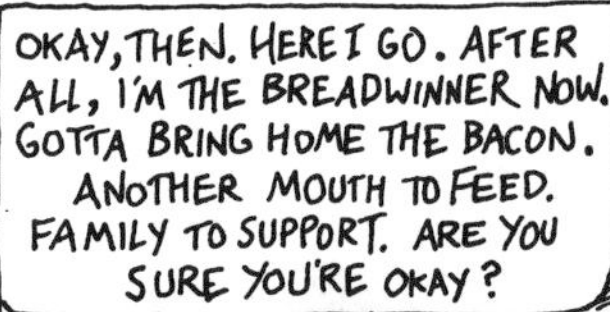
OKAY, THEN. HERE I GO. AFTER ALL, I'M THE BREADWINNER NOW. GOTTA BRING HOME THE BACON. ANOTHER MOUTH TO FEED. FAMILY TO SUPPORT. ARE YOU SURE YOU'RE OKAY?

I'M FINE! I'LL CALL YOU IF ANYTHING HAPPENS. NOW GET OUT OF HERE! I HAVE A MILLION THINGS TO DO TO GET READY.
LEZ DANCE

I LOVE YOU SO MUCH.
KISS
MMMM. BYE.

CLIK!
WHOA!

THAT AFTERNOON AT THE CO-OP...
...98 CENTS A POUND...
MO! HI! WHAT'RE YOU UP TO?
HI, TONI! I'M JUST RUNNING ERRANDS ON MY DAY OFF. WOW, YOU ARE REALLY BIG! YOU LOOK READY TO BLOW!
STOP THE INCINERATOR

OH, JEEZ! I'M SORRY! WHAT A STUPID THING TO SAY... I GUESS YOU'RE PROBABLY REALLY SICK OF COMMENTS LIKE THAT, HUH? HOW INSENSITIVE OF ME TO...
MO?
JUICE SALE

CAN YOU DO ME A FAVOR?
SURE, ANYTHING! WANT ME TO CARRY THIS STUFF TO YOUR CAR?
DONATE! SAVE OUR AIR
SPELT FLAKES

YEAH. AND THEN I'D LIKE YOU TO DRIVE ME HOME. I THINK I'M IN LABOR.
COOL.

HOLY SHIT! SHOULDN'T WE CALL AN AMBULANCE OR SOMETHING?
NAH. THAT'S JUST ON TV. THE BABY'S NOT COMING FOR A LONG, LONG TIME. JUST RELAX, AND DRIVE CAREFULLY.
Maple Avenue Co-Op

SQUEAL!

INFANT REPLAY
©1993 BY ALISON BECHDEL
171
MALIKA, I'M GONNA SMASH THAT FUCKING CAMCORDER!
YEAH, THIS IS RIGHT BEFORE THE BABY CROWNS.
SHE'S GETTING REALLY CLOSE NOW!
FONY
THERE'S THE HEAD! JEEZ, IT'S ALMOST AS INTENSE ON TV AS IN REAL LIFE!
LOOK HOW BEAUTIFUL TONI IS, POISED ON THE BRINK OF THIS MIRACULOUS RITE OF PASSAGE!
UNNGH!
OH MY GOD!
WHAT AN INCREDIBLE SHOT!
I STILL CAN'T BELIEVE IT.
MEANWHILE, OVER AT THE BIRTHING CENTER...
OH, WOW... IT FEELS WEIRD! I CAN'T BELIEVE THIS IS REALLY GONNA WORK.. ...AY!
MAKE SURE YOU'RE DEEP IN. HE NEEDS TO LATCH ONTO YOUR BREAST, NOT JUST THE NIPPLE. THERE, HE'S SUCKING!
IT'S WORKING! IT'S WARM! MY BREASTS ARE BUZZING!
AMAZING, ISN'T IT? SEE THE JAW MOVE, BY HIS EAR? HE'S SWALLOWING.
KID'S A GENIUS.
WELL! YOU CAN GO HOME IN A COUPLE HOURS IF YOU LIKE. YOU'RE COMING ALONG JUST GREAT--MUST BE DUE TO THAT WONDERFUL SUPPORT TEAM. WE DON'T OFTEN SEE THAT MANY PEOPLE AT A BIRTH.
YEAH... I'M GLAD EVERYONE COULD BE HERE, BUT IT WAS A LITTLE HECTIC. IT'LL BE NICE TO GET HOME AND SETTLE IN, JUST THE THREE OF US.
HELL ON WHEELS IN-LINE CRITERIUM
SMACK
I WONDER WHERE CLARICE AND TONI KEEP THEIR STAPLE GUN.
HAPPY BIRTHDAY, RAFAEL
SPARROW, I COULDN'T FIND ANY BUBBLEGUM CIGARS, SO I JUST GOT REAL ONES, OKAY?
NOW REWIND IT! I WANNA SEE HIM GET SUCKED BACK IN!
TANYA WANTS TO KNOW IF SHE CAN BRING SOME FRIENDS. THEY'RE DOING AN AVENGERS ACTION IN THE NEIGHBORHOOD LATER.
PARTY FAVORS

revelations
172
© 1993 BY ALISON BECHDEL
ONE RAINY MORNING AT MADWIMMIN BOOKS...
THEA, YOU SHOULDN'T DRINK COFFEE WHILE YOU'RE ON THE COMPUTER. WHAT IF IT SPILLS?
RELAX, MO. I'M VERY CAREFUL.
SHEESH! WHAT'S UP HER BUTT? SHE'S BEEN ACTING REALLY WEIRD TOWARD ME LATELY.
OKAY, YOU MIGHT AS WELL KNOW. THE OTHER DAY, SHE OVERHEARD YOU TELLING ME HOW **PUPPYLIKE** YOU FIND HER CRUSH ON YOU.
FEMINIST BOOKSTORE SCHMOOZE

SHIT! SHE MUST FEEL AWFUL! I'D BETTER TALK TO HER.
OFFICE
OH, JEEZ. I HATE LESBIAN HONESTY. LOOK, JUST DON'T TELL HER I TOLD YOU SHE HEARD WHAT YOU TOLD ME.

CLARICE! WHAT ARE YOU DOING HERE WITH A TWO-DAY-OLD KID AT HOME? STIR-CRAZY ALREADY?
I NEED SOME BOOKS ABOUT BABIES, FAST.
WHAT'S WRONG, CLARICE?

I DON'T KNOW! HE'S CRYING A LOT AND NOT NURSING. TONI'S NO HELP AT ALL – SHE KEEPS TELLING ME IT'S **NORMAL**. GOD, I SHOULD HAVE DONE MORE RESEARCH ON THIS!
CHILDREN & PARENTING
MR. SPOCK
The NEW FATHER

AND AS IF I DON'T HAVE ENOUGH TO DEAL WITH, HOW 'BOUT THAT JUDGE IN VIRGINIA?! HE SAYS A WOMAN IS UNFIT TO RAISE HER SON BECAUSE SHE'S A LESBIAN, THEN GIVES CUSTODY TO THE GRANDMOTHER!

WHAT IF **TONI'S** HOMOPHOBIC PARENTS TRIED SOMETHING LIKE THAT! D'YOU REALIZE HOW VULNERABLE WE ALL ARE TO THE LEGAL DECISIONS OF STUNTED, HATEFUL, PALEOZOIC **DICKHEADS** LIKE THIS GUY?!
PARENTS & CHILDING

YEAH, IT'S REALLY BAD NEWS. BUT WHEN WAS THE LAST TIME YOU GOT ANY SLEEP?
SLEEP? LIKE, LYING DOWN?

MAYBE YOU OUGHTA TAKE HER HOME.
I'LL GET MY JACKET.
A TIP O' THE NIB TO AMY RUBIN!

JUST GO EASY WHEN YOU TALK TO MO. YOU WOULDN'T THINK IT TO LOOK AT HER, BUT THERE'S A PASSIONATE BABE LURKING BENEATH THAT NEUROTIC EXTERIOR.
OH, BELIEVE ME, I'VE THOUGHT IT.
OFFICE

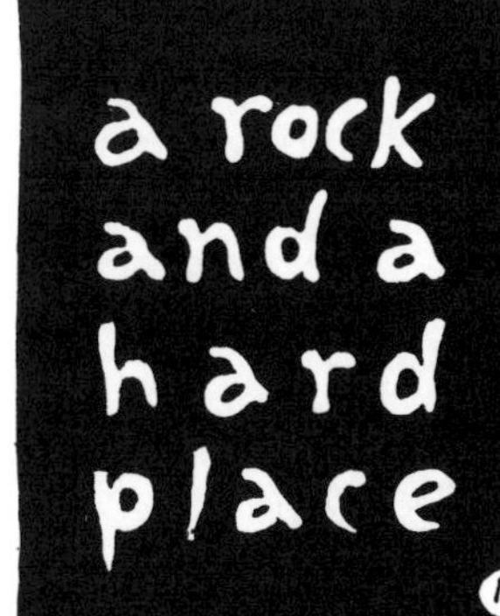
a rock and a hard place
173
©1993 BY ALISON BECHDEL

HEY, CLARICE! I THOUGHT I'D DROP IN AND RELIEVE THE BORE-DOM AND ISOLATION OF YOUR LIMITED LITTLE NUCLEAR FAM-ILY CIRCLE. HELLO, RAFAEL!
SAY HELLO TO AUNT MO! TELL HER SHE JUST MISSED YOUR FEEDING AND YOUR DIAPER CHANGE AND YOUR BURP!

BUT MAYBE YOU'RE BEYOND HELP.
AND WHAT A WORLD-CLASS BURP IT WAS, MY LITTLE SUGARTOES!

HI, TONI! HOW'RE THEY HANGING?
OH, GOD. MY NIPPLES ARE CRACKED, I'M CONSTANTLY LEAKING, HE EATS EVERY TWO HOURS 'ROUND THE CLOCK... I FEEL LIKE A FUCKING HOLSTEIN.
HONEY, NO MORE SWEARING, REMEMBER?
CHIPS
LA LECHE

MO, DID YOU SEE OUR BIRTH ANNOUNCEMENT IN THE LATEST TRIBUNE?
NOT YET. BUT ISN'T THIS PIECE ABOUT THE NATIONAL GAY AND LESBIAN TASK FORCE INTERESTING?
CHIPS
10% TRIBUNE
NGLTF HEAD QUITS

THE HIGH-POWERED EXECUTIVE DIRECTOR RESIGNS AFTER SIX MONTHS, IN A CLASH OVER STRATEGIES TO EXPAND THE ORGAN-IZATION. DON'T YOU LOVE THIS STUFF?

10% TRIBUNE

SOUNDS LIKE SHE WANTED TO TURN THE GRASSROOTS ACTIVIST-BASED TASK FORCE INTO A MORE CORPORATE, MAINSTREAM POLITICAL POWER, LIKE THE HUMAN RIGHTS CHAMPAGNE FUND.

IT'S AN INTERESTING DILEMMA, THOUGH. HOW DOES A NONPROFIT GAIN ENOUGH BUCKS AND INFLUENCE TO TAKE ON THE RELIGIOUS RIGHT, YET NOT LOSE THE PULSE OF THE QUEER ON THE STREET?
HEY, CHECK OUT THIS FACE HE MAKES WHEN HE HAS GAS!

READ OUR ANNOUNCEMENT, MO. IT'S ON PAGE 10.
OKAY, OKAY! HEY! ISN'T THIS HARRIET'S NEW GIRLFRIEND?!
WHIMPER...

YEAH! SHE'S RUNNING AGAINST SOME TRADITIONAL VALUES COALITION TYPE TO REPRESENT OUR WARD ON THE CITY COUNCIL!
VOTE!
ELLEN TUFEL
"HATE IS NOT A FAMILY VALUE."
CITY COUNCIL 3RD WARD
COMMUNITY
LEADERSHIP!
VOTE

OH, THAT'S JUST GREAT. WHO AM I GONNA VOTE FOR?
WAAA!

hot stuff
174
©1993 BY ALISON BECHDEL
IT'S SATURDAY EVENING...
OUCH! LOOKS LIKE YOU CLOSED YOUR MOUTH TOO CLOSE TO THE FLAME.
NO KIDDING.
WHAT?

LOIS BURNT HER LIP EATING FIRE WITH THE LESBIAN AVENGERS.
IT WAS SO COOL! YOU SHOULDA BEEN THERE! Y'KNOW DICK LILLY, THE TRADITIONAL VALUES COALITION GUY WHO'S RUNNING FOR CITY COUNCIL?

WE PICKETED HIS PANCAKE BREAKFAST FUND-RAISER DRESSED UP LIKE GIANT FLAMING CRÊPES SUZETTES!
Y'KNOW, THAT REMINDS ME OF ONE TIME BEFORE I GOT SOBER WHEN A BUDDY LIT MY APRICOT BRANDY ON FIRE AND SINGED ALL MY EYELASHES...
COME ON, JUNE, OR WE'LL MISS OUR MEETING.

MEANWHILE, OVER AT MADWIMMIN BOOKS...
I'M SORRY, WE'RE CLOSING.
OH... I JUST WANTED TO DROP OFF THIS CAMPAIGN POSTER FOR ELLEN TUFEL. COULD YOU PUT IT UP ON YOUR BULLETIN BOARD?
VOTE! ELLEN TUFEL
CITY COUNCIL
"HATE IS NOT A FAMILY VALUE"

GOT A BIG NIGHT PLANNED, MO?
OH, YEAH! I HAVE TO RUSH-LAST LOAD'S GOTTA BE IN BY 7:30 AT DUDS 'N SUDS! WHAT ABOUT YOU AND MAXINE? A QUIET EVENING AT HOME, ACTING OUT SCENES FROM 'CLAIRE OF THE MOON'?
T'AI CHI
Nintendo FOR SALE cheap
QUEER BINGO
PRE-MENSTRUAL SUPPORT

OKAY, THAT'S IT. WE HAVE TO TALK. YOU'VE BEEN MAKING LITTLE DIGS AT ME ALL WEEK. IF THIS IS BECAUSE YOU'RE FEELING HURT THAT I DON'T HAVE A CRUSH BACK ON YOU, ALL I CAN SAY IS I'M SORRY, AND I'M FLATTERED, BUT...

BUT YOU JUST DON'T THINK OF ME THAT WAY, AND BESIDES, YOU'RE IN A RELATIONSHIP ALREADY, AND YOU HOPE WE CAN STILL BE FRIENDS.
RITUAL DRUM FOR SALE
LUSCIOUS LESBOS LIVE LIVE LIVE
AVENGER LOFT PARTY
MARATHON 12-HOUR INNER CHILD WORKSHOP

WELL... YEAH.
OH, OKAY! SO THAT MUST HAVE BEEN MAXINE YOU WERE SUGGESTIVELY REFERRING TO AS A "BABE" WITH LOIS THE OTHER DAY. I THOUGHT IT WAS ME, BUT THE ACOUSTICS IN HERE AREN'T THE GREATEST.
BOOKS
CLOSED

JEEZIZ! WHAT ARE YOU DOING, SLINKING AROUND SPYING ON PEOPLE?
HAH! I KNEW IT!

OKAY. SO MAYBE I AM A LITTLE BIT ATTRACTED TO YOU. BUT IT DOESN'T MATTER BECAUSE ABSOLUTELY NOTHING'S GOING TO HAPPEN. GOT IT?
WOW! I NEVER SAW YOU BLUSH BEFORE! IT'S SO, UM... CUTE.

HI, SWEETIE! HI, MO! THEA, I'M DOUBLE-PARKED OUT FRONT. LOOKS LIKE YOU HAD A BIG DAY! THE WINDOWS ARE ALL STEAMED UP!

WHAT I LOVE BEST ABOUT NEW YEAR'S EVE IS THAT LITTLE WINDOW OF SEXUAL LAWLESSNESS AT MIDNIGHT WHEN YOU GET TO KISS EVERYONE. KIND OF LIKE GROWN-UP SPIN-THE-BOTTLE.

Y'KNOW, I'VE ALWAYS REGRETTED THAT I NEVER GOT TO PLAY SPIN-THE-BOTTLE WITH OTHER LITTLE DYKES WHEN I WAS A KID, INSTEAD OF BOYS.

I NEVER GOT TO PLAY SPIN-THE-BOTTLE WITH ANYONE.

IN THE WEE HOURS OF JANUARY FIRST...

on her back

180

BROKEN, ALONE, AND REFERRED TO IN THE THIRD PERSON WHILE STILL PRESENT . . . CAN OUR HEROINE POSSIBLY SINK ANY LOWER? DON'T MISS THE NEXT TAUT, WRENCHING EPISODE!

MEANWHILE, IT'S EVEN CHILLIER ACROSS TOWN

LOYALTY
©1994 BY ALISON BECHDEL
182
AMBER! CAN I HELP YOU FIND ANYTHING?
HI, JEZANNA. I'M LOOKING FOR "WOMEN WHO RUN WITH THE WOLVERINES."
MADWIMMIN BOOKS
Open

OH, SOMEONE JUST BOUGHT THE LAST COPY! WE'RE GETTING MORE IN ON TUESDAY. CAN I HOLD ONE FOR YOU?
NO, DON'T BOTHER. I HAVE TO GO OVER TO THE MALL ANYWAY. I'LL JUST PICK ONE UP AT BUNNS & NOODLE. THANKS!
THE NEUROMANTIC NAIAD

YOU'RE WELCOME! HAVE A NICE DAY!
SNAP!

CAREFUL, JEZ! YOUR BLOOD PRESSURE!
I SOLD THAT WOMAN HER FIRST LESBIAN SEX BOOK FIFTEEN YEARS AGO, AND NOW SHE'S TAKING HER BUSINESS TO THOSE CUTTHROATS!

HI, MO. HI, JEZ. SPEAKING OF CUTTHROATS, HERE'S YOUR COMPLETED TAX RETURN. TONI ASKED ME TO DROP IT OFF.
LORD HAVE MERCY! I SHOULD'VE STAYED IN THE DOG GROOMING BUSINESS WITH AUNT YOLANDA.

IS SHE OKAY?
OH, SHE'S UPSET ABOUT THAT NEW SUPERSTORE. SHE'S SPENT YEARS BUILDING UP OUR CUSTOMER BASE, THEN BUNNS & NOODLE WALTZES INTO TOWN AND STARTS LURING FOLKS AWAY WITH THEIR MASSIVE SELECTION AND BIG DISCOUNTS.
HEY! IT'S THE RAFSTER!

THEY SERVE GREAT CAPPUCCINO, TOO. ER... SO I'VE HEARD.
CLARICE! THAT PLACE IS OWNED BY A GIGANTIC CORPORATION! BOOKS ARE JUST A COMMODITY TO THEM, LIKE SMALL APPLIANCES, OR... OR HEALTH INSURANCE! THEY DON'T CARE ABOUT LITERATURE, OR IDEAS, OR COMMUNITY! HOW CAN YOU SHOP THERE?!
MO, YOU'RE SCARING THE KID.

RELAX! IT WAS ONLY A CUP OF COFFEE AND A NEWSPAPER. BUT YOUR POINT'S WELL TAKEN.
SO CLARICE! HOW'S FAMILY LIFE? CLAUSTROPHOBIC AND SUFFOCATING?
SQUEEEAL

WELL... A LITTLE. I REALLY MISS THE FREEDOM TO JUST GO DO SOMETHING. A CONFERENCE, A WEEKEND GETAWAY, EVEN A MOVIE.
HEY, DIDJA KNOW GINGER'S IN NEW JERSEY AT THE BLACK GAY AND LESBIAN CONFERENCE?
NGAH.

MEANWHILE, IN SECAUCUS...
EXCUSE ME... YOU MADE SOME VERY INTERESTING POINTS IN THAT LAST WORKSHOP. YOU'RE QUITE A SPEAKER!
7th BGLLF Conference
FROM SILENCE TO CELEBRATION
Beyond the 28 Days
WHY, THANK YOU! YOU WEREN'T HALF BAD YOURSELF! UH... I'M GINGER.
Schedule

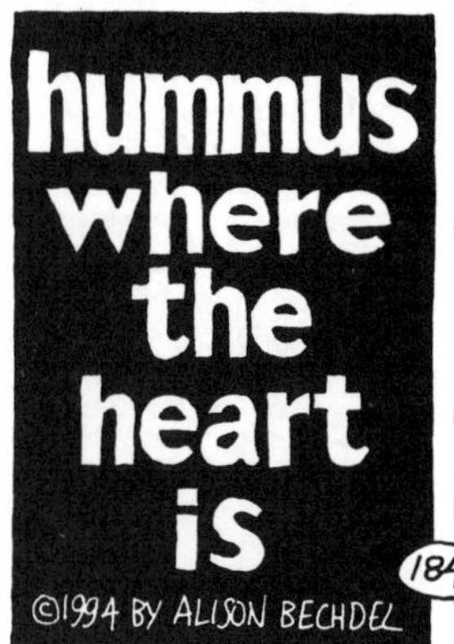
hummus where the heart is
184
©1994 BY ALISON BECHDEL

GINGER IS EXPECTED HOME IMMINENTLY FROM THE BLACK GAY AND LESBIAN LEADERSHIP FORUM CONFERENCE, AND MO HAS DROPPED BY FOR DINNER.
OKAY. I'M ALL DONE WITH MY FAMOUS HUMMUS À LA MO. AS SOON AS GINGER GETS HERE, WE CAN EAT.
INSTANT! JUST ADD H2O!

WHOA! CAN YOU BELIEVE ALL THESE SCI-FI RADIATION TESTS THE GOVERNMENT DID IN THE 40'S AND 50'S? DOCTORS DIDN'T EVEN TELL PEOPLE THEY WERE INJECTING THEM WITH PLUTONIUM!
YEAH. HOW CONVENIENT NO ONE'S ADMITTING IT UNTIL 50 YEARS AFTER THE FACT. MAYBE IN 2044, THEY'LL CONFESS TO ALL THE STUFF THEY'RE DOING NOW.
F.D.A. SEZ: MILK HORMONES ARE GOOD FOR YOU
The Distress
WHINE.

LIKE HOW THE ARMY FORCED SOLDIERS IN THE GULF WAR TO TAKE ALL KINDS OF EXPERIMENTAL ANTI-BOTULISM AND ANTI-NERVE GAS DRUGS. NOW THEY'VE GOT BIZARRE ILLNESSES, THEIR BABIES ARE DEFORMED, AND THE DEPARTMENT OF DEFENSE DOESN'T SEE A CONNECTION.
NO SHIT!
LOIS, YOU ARE SO NAIVE!
The Distress
ARF!

HELLO! I'M BACK! DIGGER! COME TO MAMA, YOU BIG WOLF-GIRL!
GINGER!

WELCOME HOME!
HOW WAS THE CONFERENCE?
OH, IT WAS GREAT! THE GRASSROOTS ORGANIZING WORKSHOP REALLY GOT ME ALL CHARGED UP! AND I GOT ME'SHELL NDEGEOCELLO'S AUTOGRAPH AFTER SHE PERFORMED SATURDAY.

NO KIDDING! I'VE SEEN HER ON MTV. PAIR OF ARMS, HUH?
RING RING
DON'T ANSWER THAT! UH... I MEAN, WE'RE TALKING! CAN'T WE LET THE MACHINE PICK UP?

BEEP! HI, IT'S MALIKA FOR GINGER. I MISS YOU, BABY! HOPE THE CONFERENCE WAS FUN... CALL ME AS SOON AS YOU GET IN, OKAY? I LOVE YOU, ANGEL LIPS! CLIK!
YOU DOG! YOU HAD AN AFFAIR, DIDN'T YOU?
GINGER! YOU DIDN'T!

DID YOU?
WELL, I WOULDN'T CALL IT AN AFFAIR. IT DIDN'T MEAN ANYTHING, IT JUST SORT OF HAPPENED. I HAVEN'T FIGURED OUT HOW TO TELL MALIKA YET.
TELL HER? WHY WOULD YOU WANT TO TELL HER?

LOIS, SHE TRUSTS ME!
SO WHY SPOIL IT? WHAT SHE DOESN'T KNOW WON'T HURT HER!
OH, GREAT! WHILE YOU'RE AT IT, WHY NOT SLIP SOME RADIOACTIVE IODINE INTO HER DECAF?

the best policy

© 1994 BY ALISON BECHDEL

188

MALIKA'S COMING FOR THE WEEKEND. I WAS THINKING MAYBE YOU AND I SHOULD CLEAR OUT TONIGHT SO SHE AND GINGER CAN HAVE SOME TIME ALONE.

HOW THOUGHTFUL, IF UNCHARACTERISTIC OF YOU, LOIS. SO, I GUESS IF MALIKA'S FLYING IN ALL THE WAY FROM SAN FRANCISCO, SHE MUST HAVE FORGIVEN GINGER'S LITTLE CONFERENCE TRYST.

190

MEANWHILE, MALIKA'S VISIT DRAWS TO A CLOSE...

A TIP O' THE NIB TO BARBARA SMITH

Au Courant
193
©1994 BY ALISON BECHDEL

HEY, COOL BOOTS, LOIS.
YEAH. I GOT 'EM FROM AN AUSTRALIAN SHOT-PUTTER AT THE GAMES.
TEAM HELSINKI

I SWAPPED HER MY DOC MARTENS. I WAS GLAD TO GET RID OF 'EM NOW THAT EVERY SUBURBAN MALL CRAWLER HAS A PAIR.
!
IGNITE THE RIOT

OH, JEEZ. HERE'S A SUBMISSION FOR "MADWIMMIN READ" FROM SOMEONE NAMED JILLIAN WHO IDENTIFIES AS A TRANSSEXUAL LESBIAN.
COOL.
GO HOMOS NY TEAM AQUATICS

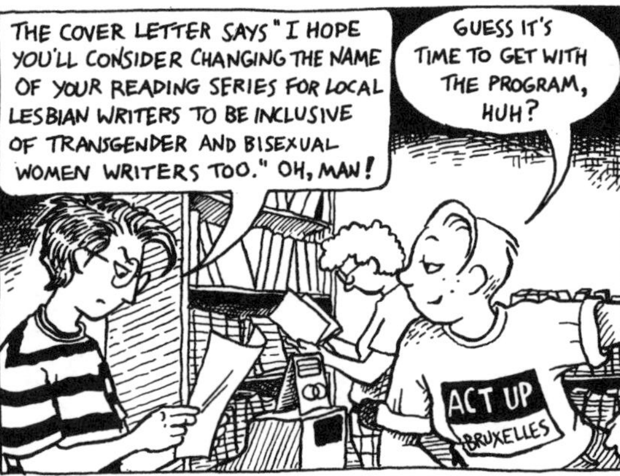
THE COVER LETTER SAYS "I HOPE YOU'LL CONSIDER CHANGING THE NAME OF YOUR READING SERIES FOR LOCAL LESBIAN WRITERS TO BE INCLUSIVE OF TRANSGENDER AND BISEXUAL WOMEN WRITERS TOO." OH, MAN!
GUESS IT'S TIME TO GET WITH THE PROGRAM, HUH?
ACT UP BRUXELLES

WHAT AM I SUPPOSED TO DO? HAVE BI WOMEN AND DRAG QUEENS COME IN HERE AND READ ABOUT SCHTUPPING THEIR BOYFRIENDS?

WHY NOT? I'M SURE THEY'D HAVE A UNIQUE PERSPECTIVE ON THE TOPIC.
LOIS, I'M STILL TRYING TO ADJUST TO LESBIANS USING DILDOS! WHAT AM I SUPPOSED TO MAKE OF A MAN WHO BECAME A WOMAN WHO'S ATTRACTED TO WOMEN?!

LOVE IS A MANY-GENDERED THING, PAL. GET USED TO IT.
WELL FINE. LET PEOPLE DO WHAT THEY WANT. BUT I'M NOT GONNA ADD THIS UNWIELDY "BISEXUAL AND TRANSGENDER" BUSINESS TO THE NAME OF MY READING SERIES. I DON'T EVEN KNOW WHAT TRANSGENDER MEANS!
SÃO PAOLO VOLLEYBALL
A TIP O' THE NIB TO JANIS WALWORTH!

IT'S SORT OF AN EVOLVING CONCEPT. I MEAN, WE HAVEN'T HAD ANY LANGUAGE FOR PEOPLE YOU CAN'T NEATLY PEG AS EITHER BOY OR GIRL.

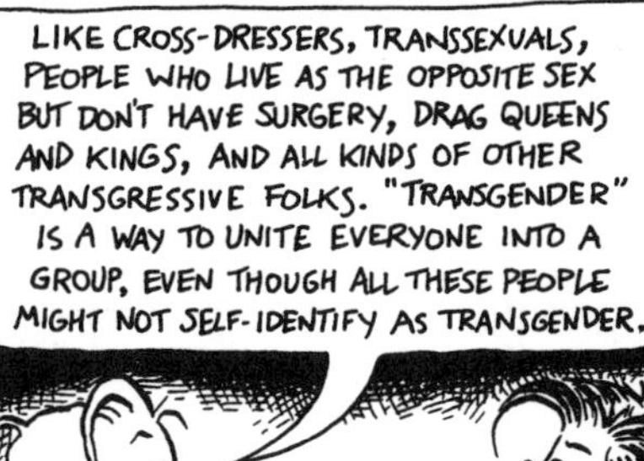
LIKE CROSS-DRESSERS, TRANSSEXUALS, PEOPLE WHO LIVE AS THE OPPOSITE SEX BUT DON'T HAVE SURGERY, DRAG QUEENS AND KINGS, AND ALL KINDS OF OTHER TRANSGRESSIVE FOLKS. "TRANSGENDER" IS A WAY TO UNITE EVERYONE INTO A GROUP, EVEN THOUGH ALL THESE PEOPLE MIGHT NOT SELF-IDENTIFY AS TRANSGENDER.

IN FACT, THE POINT IS THAT WE'RE ALL JUST OURSELVES, AND NOT CATEGORIES. INSTEAD OF TWO RIGID GENDERS, THERE'S AN INFINITE SEXUAL CONTINUUM! COOL, HUH?
HOW DO YOU KNOW ALL THIS STUFF?
GIRL JOCK

FROM HANGING OUT WITH JILLIAN AT LESBIAN AVENGERS MEETINGS. SHE TOLD ME SHE WAS GONNA SEND THIS TO YOU.
YOU LOVE TO WATCH ME SQUIRM, DON'T YOU?

LIME LIGHT
194
©1994 BY ALISON BECHDEL

THANK YOU, JILLIAN, FOR THAT FASCINATING, UH, TRANSSEXUAL VERSION OF THE OEDIPUS LEGEND, "OEDIPAL ComPLEX." THANKS ALSO TO MIKO TAKAGI AND DEIRDRE TRIVELPIECE FOR SHARING THEIR WORK WITH US TONIGHT, AND TO OUR ASL INTERPRETER, JO PALMER.
TRANSEXUAL MENACE

A TIP O' THE NIB TO LYNETTE REEP.
AND THANKS TO ALL OF YOU FOR COMING OUT TO SUPPORT OUR LOCAL AUTHORS, AND MAKING THIS FIRST EVENT IN OUR "MADWIMMIN READ" SERIES A SUCCESS. PLEASE STICK AROUND FOR REFRESHMENTS, AND COME BACK AGAIN NEXT MONTH.
CLAP
CLAP
CLAP

HUH! YOU PULLED IT OFF! NICE WORK, MO. AND LOOK AT ALL THESE PEOPLE! I BETTER GET UP TO THE REGISTER. YOU GO SCHMOOZE.
VERY IMPRESSIVE. NO ONE WOULD EVER SUSPECT YOU WERE A SHY PERSON, THE WAY YOU RAN THE SHOW.

EXCUSE ME. I JUST NEED TO SAY I WAS REALLY SHOCKED THAT YOU LET A MAN READ HERE TONIGHT. MEN HAVE ACCESS TO THE WHOLE WORLD. WHY SHOULD WE SHARE OUR MEAGER RESOURCES WITH THEM?
UH... WELL, FIRST OF ALL, HE'S NOT A MAN, HE'S A LESBIAN. I MEAN, SHE'S A LESBIAN. AND SECOND, I WANT THIS SERIES TO BE INCLUSIVE, AND NOT SOME PRIVATE CLUB. I MEAN, WHO AM I TO QUESTION SOMEONE ELSE'S IDENTITY?

HMPH. I SUPPOSE YOU THINK "LESBIANS" WHO SLEEP WITH MEN ARE DYKES TOO.
UH... WELL...
EXCUSE ME, MO. I'M MJ, THE ARTS EDITOR AT THE TEN PERCENT TRIBUNE. GREAT EVENT YOU PUT TOGETHER TONIGHT. LISTEN, WE'RE LOOKING FOR A NEW BOOK REVIEWER, AND I WONDER IF YOU'D BE AT ALL INTERESTED?
UH... ME? WRITE BOOK REVIEWS? FOR THE NEWSPAPER?!

MO, SORRY TO INTERRUPT. I'M FLORA, FROM THE QUEER VEGAN SOCIETY. WHEN YOU GET A CHANCE, LET'S TALK ABOUT SOME NON-ANIMAL PRODUCT ALTERNATIVES TO THE CHEESE YOU'RE SERVING HERE.
UH... OKAY.

HEY, THANKS FOR INCLUDING JILLIAN'S WORK TONIGHT. I'M GONNA TELL MY FRIEND BIFF TO SEND YOU SOME OF HIS POEMS. HE'S BEEN WRITING GREAT STUFF ABOUT HIS FEMALE-TO-MALE TRANSITIONING.
UH... BIFF?
MO, THIS WAS WONDERFUL. THANKS A LOT FOR MAKING IT HAPPEN. I NEVER READ IN PUBLIC BEFORE. COULD YOU TELL HOW NERVOUS I WAS?!
UH... NOT AT ALL, DEIRDRE. YOU WERE GREAT. I DON'T THINK ANYONE NOTICED YOU READ THAT ONE PAGE TWICE.

SO, I KNOW YOU'RE PROBABLY REALLY BUSY AND ALL, BUT WOULD YOU MAYBE LIKE TO DO SOMETHING SOMETIME? LIKE, I DUNNO. A MOVIE?
HERE YOU GO. CHECK OUT THESE RECIPES FOR MEAT, EGG, AND DAIRY-FREE HORS D'OEUVRES. THE PICKLED TOFU CHEESE IS MY PARTICULAR FAVORITE.

NO PICNIC
195
© 1994 BY ALISON BECHDEL

IS IT ALMOST DONE? I'VE GOTTA BE AT A MEETING IN AN HOUR.
JUST ABOUT. IS THIS FOR THE DOMESTIC PARTNERSHIP BENEFITS BILL?

YEAH. WE'VE GOT A PRETTY SOLID COALITION OF COMMUNITY GROUPS BEHIND US. NOW WE'RE GEARING UP FOR LOBBYING AND HEARINGS. YOU SHOULD THINK ABOUT TESTIFYING!
JEEZ, ELLEN. I CAN'T TAKE ANYTHING ELSE ON. I'M WORKING SIXTY HOUR WEEKS AS IT IS.

IT WOULD TAKE FIVE MINUTES! YOU COULD BRING RAFAEL UP TO THE PODIUM WITH YOU! IT'LL BE PERFECT!

COME ON! THE DOMESTIC PARTNERS REGISTRY IS A CRITICAL STEP TOWARDS GETTING OUR RELATIONSHIPS RECOGNIZED!
LOOK, I THINK IT'S GREAT YOU'RE DOING THIS, BUT GETTING THE GOVERNMENT INVOLVED IN MY PERSONAL LIFE IS NOT HIGH ON MY LIST OF PRIORITIES RIGHT NOW.

DID I TELL YOU I MIGHT BE GOING UP AGAINST THE UNION CARBUNCLE CHEMICAL CORPORATION? WE FOUND A L.U.S.T. AT THEIR SOUTH END PLANT, AND I THINK IT'S CONNECTED TO THE HIGH CANCER RATE OVER THERE.
A LUST?

LEAKY UNDERGROUND STORAGE TANK. IT'S CONTAMINATING THE GROUND WATER.
HEY, IF YOU'RE SO WORRIED ABOUT CONTAMINATION, QUIT POKING MY TOFU WITH THAT CHICKEN FORK.

I KNOW HER JOB'S IMPORTANT, BUT I'M NOT SURE I CAN GO ON LIKE THIS! SHE'S HARDLY EVER HOME! I MIGHT AS WELL BE A SINGLE PARENT!
HUH. JUST BE GLAD YOU'RE NOT MARRIED TO MS. PUBLIC SERVANT OVER THERE.

WHAT'S GOING ON? I THOUGHT YOU TWO WERE SO HAPPY!
I DUNNO. FOR A LONG TIME I FELT REALLY ATTRACTED TO HOW DRIVEN AND HIGH-POWERED SHE IS. I MEAN, SHE'S THE EXACT OPPOSITE OF MO!
RRRM RRRRM

BUT POLITICS IS HER LIFE. THE CITY COUNCIL, COMMUNITY PROJECTS, BOARD MEETINGS, FUNDRAISING... I FEEL LIKE I'M JUST ANOTHER COMMITMENT SHE HAS TO FIND TIME FOR.

WOW. SHE JUST TOLD US YOU WERE TALKING ABOUT LIVING TOGETHER.
I KNOW. SHE'S SO EXCITED ABOUT THIS DOMESTIC PARTNERSHIP BILL. I HAVEN'T HAD THE HEART TO TELL HER I DON'T WANT TO BE HER DAMN DOMESTIC PARTNER.
COME AND GET IT!

THERE'S MY TIGER BOY! ARE YOU READY FOR YOUR CHICKEN?
CLARICE, HE HASN'T EATEN CHICKEN FOR WEEKS NOW. THE ONLY THING HE'LL TOUCH IS BEETS WITH PEANUT BUTTER.
HARRIET, I HAVE TO LEAVE IN TWENTY MINUTES, OKAY?
DON'T ASK ME. I DIDN'T SPEND ALL DAY BARBECUING THIS NICE MEAL FOR YOU.

NO... I WAS ALL READY TO, BUT THEN THE VATICAN MADE THEIR LITTLE PRONOUNCEMENT ABOUT HOW SAME SEX COUPLES SHOULDN'T BE ALLOWED TO ADOPT OR USE ALTERNATIVE INSEMINATION. MY MOM'S SO POPE-CRAZY, I THOUGHT I'D WAIT TILL THINGS QUIETED DOWN.

HAVE A NICE WAIT.

A CHECK FOR RAFFI, A PHOTO OF THE NEIGHBORS' SON, JULIO, FOR YOU.

HUH. JULIO LOOKS A LITTLE LIGHT IN THE LOAFERS TO ME.

THE KITCHEN CREW IS STARTING TO CRASH...

SO WHAT MAKES SOME GAY PEOPLE TURN OUT TO BE REVOLUTIONARY ACTIVISTS, AND OTHERS TURN OUT TO BE SNIVELING COLLABORATIONISTS?

THE AMOUNT OF REFINED SUGAR THEIR MOTHERS ATE WHILE THEY WERE IN THE WOMB?

SOMEONE STOP ME. I CAN SEE BOB DOLE'S FACE IN THE BUTTER PECAN.

virtual interface

©1994 BY ALISON BECHDEL

197

OUR HEROINE VENTURES INTO A LOCAL CAFFEINE DEN.

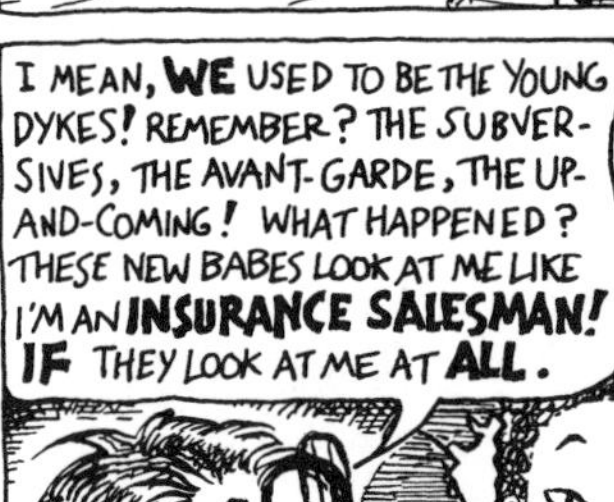

BUFFED
©1994 BY ALISON BECHDEL
198

ALL READY FOR YOUR BIG NIGHT, MO? D'YOU NEED ANY POINTERS? WANT ME TO COME OVER AND TAKE A PICTURE OF YOU TWO BEFORE YOU GO OUT?
OH, MY GOD! YOU HAVE A DATE?
NO, I DO NOT HAVE A DATE. UH... AND IF I DID, I WOULD RESENT THAT TONE OF VOICE.
ALL FREEDOM RINGS 80% OFF!

SHE'S GOING TO THE MOVIES WITH DEIRDRE, ONE OF THE WRITERS WHO READ HERE LAST MONTH.
REALLY! I LIKED HER. SHE WAS SMART. AND NOT UN-ATTRACTIVE, AS I RECALL.

SO MO, ARE YOU GONNA PUT OUT?
LOIS! THIS ISN'T A DATE! SHE JUST WANTS TO MEET MORE PEOPLE. AND IF IT WAS A DATE, I WOULD CERTAINLY NOT HAVE SEX WITH HER THE FIRST TIME WE WENT OUT!
MADWIMMIN BOOKS
CHLOE PLUS MIL-DRED
THE BOOK OF SHORT LESBIAN PENGUIN STORIES

WHOA! HAVE YOU SIGNED THE YOUTH FOR CHRIST "TRUE LOVE WAITS" CHASTITY PLEDGE?
NO, IT'S JUST... I'VE DONE THE U-HAUL SCENE, Y'KNOW? I'M TIRED OF GOING TO BED WITH A DATE AND WAKING UP WITH A DOMESTIC PARTNER. FROM NOW ON I'M GONNA WAIT UNTIL I KNOW THIS IS WHO I WANT TO BE WITH BEFORE I SLEEP WITH HER.

WHAT KIND OF TWISTED LOGIC IS THAT? HOW D'YOU KNOW YOU WANNA BE WITH HER UNLESS YOU DO HER?
LOIS, I'M NOT LIKE YOU. IF I HAVE SEX, I FALL IN LOVE. IT'S A GENETIC DEFECT.

MO, WHY ARE YOU SO SURE TONIGHT ISN'T A DATE?
OH, IT'S A DATE! THIS BABE DEIRDRE WAS CREAMING HER JEANS WHEN MO SAID SHE'D GO OUT WITH HER.
LOIS!

GO ON. GIVE HER A TUMBLE. SHE WANTS YOU.
LOOK. EVEN IF I WAS INTERESTED, I'D WANNA GO REALLY SLOW. I THINK IT WOULD BE EXCITING.
I WISH MAXINE AND I HAD DONE THAT. ONCE YOU GO ALL THE WAY, YOU CAN NEVER GET BACK THAT SUBLIME, TORTURED TENSION OF JUST HOLDING HANDS, OR THE FIRST TIME YOU UNBUTTON HER SHIRT.

YEAH. MY NEW GUIDE-LINE IS, YOU SHOULDN'T BE NAKED WITH SOME-ONE TILL YOU KNOW WHAT HER RELATIONSHIP WITH HER MOTHER IS LIKE.

GOOD POINT. IF I'D DONE THAT, I NEVER WOULD'VE TAKEN MY COAT OFF WITH MAXINE.
OKAY. I'M OUTTA HERE. I HAVE TO GO TO THE GYM BEFORE MY, UH... APPOINTMENT.

GO GIRL! WORK IT!
PUMP IT UP!

SHORTLY THEREAFTER...
MO! I DIDN'T KNOW YOU WORKED OUT HERE! THIS IS MY MOM, BETTY. MOM, THIS IS WHO I'M GOING OUT WITH TONIGHT!
YMCA MOTHER-DAUGHTER SWIM MEET THIS SATURDAY!
NICE TO MEET YOU, MO. DEIRDRE'S SO LOOKING FORWARD TO YOUR DATE!

from the sublimation to the ridiculous

200

AFTER AN EVENING OF EXPERIMENTAL LESBIAN FILM, MO AND DEIRDRE'S QUASI-DATE CONTINUES OVER COFFEE.

I DIDN'T QUITE GET WHY THEY KEPT INTERCUTTING THE SEX SCENE WITH THAT FOOTAGE OF CHERNOBYL AFTER THE ACCIDENT, BUT IT WAS STILL PRETTY HOT.
UH... DOESN'T THAT STUFF KEEP YOU AWAKE?
JAVA JONES

THIS? I GUESS. BUT I'M NOT PLANNING ON GOING TO SLEEP ANYTIME SOON.
OH. UM... I GUESS YOU PROBABLY DO YOUR WRITING AT NIGHT, HUH?
DINK DINK

EFTSOONS, AT MO'S BACHELOR DIGS...

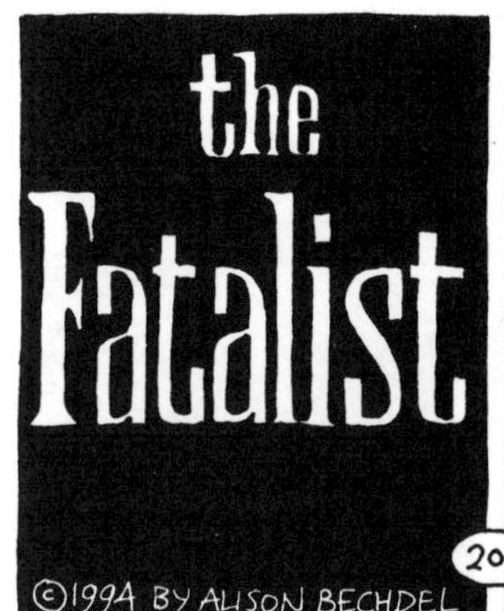

I'M LOOKING AT HOW THE HYPERSEXUALIZED PERSONAE OF BLACK WOMEN AND LESBIANS IN THE MALE LITERARY CANON CONTRAST WITH OUR ACTUAL EXPERIENCES OF DESIRE, FOCUSING ON INTERSUBJECTIVE MODALITIES OF **LESBIAN IMPOTENCE**.

YOU KNOW WHAT'S WRONG WITH YOU, MO? YOU'RE AFRAID OF LETTING ANYTHING **GOOD** HAPPEN.

RING

NO. SHE SOUNDED PRETTY UPSET, THOUGH.

MAYBE I SHOULD COME WITH YOU, IN CASE SHE NEEDS TO TALK. I MEAN, MY MOM'S BEEN SICK A LOT. DO YOU THINK SHE'D MIND?

PROBABLY. BUT IT'S WORTH A TRY. LET'S GO.

the rock
202
©1994 BY ALISON BECHDEL
... SO ARE YOU TWO CLEAR ON WHAT YOUR JOBS ARE WHILE I'M GONE?
YEAH.
GOT IT.

I'M GONNA HAVE TONI COME IN AND DO THE BOOKKEEPING AND PAYROLL, BUT MO IS RESPONSIBLE FOR EVERYTHING ELSE: MEETING WITH SALES REPS, ORDERING, PAYING BILLS, MAKING DEPOSITS, DOING THE SCHEDULE, ALL THAT. I WANT THE THREE OF YOU TO WORK TOGETHER, BUT IF YOU CAN'T, MO'S THE BOSS. OKAY?
GULP!

JEZANNA, YOU SOUND LIKE YOU'RE NEVER COMING BACK! THIS IS JUST FOR A LITTLE WHILE, RIGHT?
OH! AND WE'RE OUT OF TOILET PAPER, AND THE SPIRITUALITY SECTION NEEDS RE-ALPHABETIZING. Y'KNOW, MAYBE I SHOULD WRITE UP A DETAILED LIST OF ALL THE THINGS YOU'LL HAVE TO...
JEZ, WE'LL FIGURE IT OUT! DESPITE THE FACT THAT YOU'RE A TOTAL CONTROL FREAK, AND DO ALL THE IMPORTANT STUFF AROUND HERE YOURSELF, I THINK WE'VE MANAGED TO PICK UP A THING OR TWO BY OSMOSIS.
DON'T WORRY ABOUT THE STORE! YOU NEED TO TAKE CARE OF **YOURSELF** IF YOU'RE GONNA BE ANY USE TO YOUR MOTHER. NOW, ARE YOU OKAY?

JEZANNA! I CAME RIGHT OVER! ARE YOU OKAY? WHAT HAPPENED?
HI, TONI. I JUST FOUND OUT MY MOTHER HAS BREAST CANCER, AND I'M FLYING OUT TO BE WITH HER TOMORROW. COME ON, LET'S GO OVER THE BOOKS. I HAVE A LOT TO DO TONIGHT.
BREAST CANCER?! HOLD ON, JEZ! LET'S TALK ABOUT THIS! ARE YOU OKAY?

YES, I AM **OKAY!** I'M NOT THE ONE WHO'S **SICK.** WHY ARE YOU ALL UP IN MY FACE? AND WHAT ARE YOU TWO EVEN **DOING** HERE? YOU DON'T WORK FOR ME!
WE'RE YOUR **FRIENDS.** THIS IS WHAT FRIENDS **DO.**
LISTEN. MY MOM'S HAD CANCER FOR FIVE YEARS NOW. I CAN HELP YOU DEAL WITH THIS IF YOU WANT TO TALK.

THERE'S NOTHING LEFT TO SAY! I TOLD HER A THOUSAND TIMES, "**MAMA!** YOU NEED TO GET A **MAMMOGRAM!**" I EVEN MADE APPOINTMENTS! DID SHE KEEP THEM? NO, SHE DID NOT!

ONE DAY SHE NOTICED A LUMP! DID SHE **TELL** ANYONE? NO, SHE DID NOT! DIDN'T WANT TO BE ANY **TROUBLE!** THEY ONLY FOUND IT SIX MONTHS LATER WHEN MY COUSIN DRAGGED HER IN FOR A PHYSICAL!
YOU'RE ANGRY. THAT'S GOOD. STAY WITH YOUR FEELINGS.
HEY! IF YOU THINK I'M GONNA BREAK DOWN BAWLING SO YOU CAN ALL MAKE A FUSS, YOU GOT ANOTHER THINK COMING. LET'S GO, TONI!

HOW BAD IS IT?
THEY DON'T KNOW YET. OR SHE JUST WON'T SAY.
UNDERNEATH THE ATTITUDE, SHE'S REALLY SCARED.

YEAH, SHE IS IN SO MUCH **DENIAL.** COME ON, LET'S GET THESE BOOKS RE-ALPHABETIZED!
THE BLACK WOMEN'S HEALTH BOOK
MY MOTHER MY SELF

YIKES! MO'S...
minding the store
203
©1994 BY ALISON BECHDEL

RIGHT.... OKAY.... WELL LISTEN, I'M REALLY GLAD YOUR MOM MADE IT THROUGH THE SURGERY ALL RIGHT. HANG IN THERE, JEZ, AND I'LL TALK TO YOU TOMORROW.... YES, THE STORE IS FINE. I'VE GOT EVERYTHING UNDER CONTROL. DON'T WORRY! OKAY, BYE.

EXCUSE ME. I'M LOOKING FOR A COPY OF THAT NEW BOOK, "STRANGE JUSTICE: THE SELLING OF CLARENCE THOMAS."
SURE! WE JUST GOT A SHIPMENT IN THIS MORNING. LEMME GET YOU ONE.
MADWIMMIN BOOKS

HEY, MO. CHECK IT OUT. THEY SENT US THE WRONG NEW CLARENCE THOMAS BOOK. WE HAVE THIRTY COPIES HERE OF THE WACKO ONE BY SENATOR DANFORTH!
HOW'D THAT HAPPEN? SHIT! I'VE GOT A CUSTOMER OUT THERE WAITING FOR THE RIGHT ONE!
RESURRECTION
JOHN DANFORTH

ISN'T THERE A DISPLAY COPY IN THE WINDOW? SELL THAT.
GOOD THINKING!
RESURRECTION

AAUGH!
HEATHER'S MOMMIES WEAR ARMY BOOTS
CAMILLE FAGLIA
SIMPS 'N PIMPS
(TIP O' THE NIB TO KATHLEEN DE BOLD)

WHAT IS THIS BABY DOING UNSUPERVISED?!
UH... I'M WATCHING HIM WHILE TONI'S ON THE COMPUTER.
WAA!
LOIS! WATCHING MEANS WATCHING! YOU CAN'T TAKE YOUR EYES OFF A TODDLER! HE COULD'VE GOTTEN HURT!

DID PUMPKIN GET A BOO-BOO?
LET'S KEEP A LID ON THE CHAOS, OKAY? WE HAVE CUSTOMERS.
AAAH!

HERE, RAFFI. ARE YOU HUNGRY?
HEY, MO, WAS THAT JEZANNA ON THE PHONE? HOW'S HER MOTHER?
SHE GOT THROUGH THE MASTECTOMY OKAY, BUT JEZ SOUNDED PRETTY FRIED. I MEAN, ON TOP OF EVERYTHING ELSE, SHE'S GOTTA DEAL WITH HER FAMILY AND THE DOCTORS.
AAAA

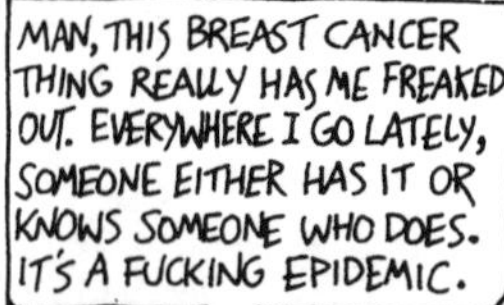

MAN, THIS BREAST CANCER THING REALLY HAS ME FREAKED OUT. EVERYWHERE I GO LATELY, SOMEONE EITHER HAS IT OR KNOWS SOMEONE WHO DOES. IT'S A FUCKING EPIDEMIC.
YEAH. AND THE SCARIEST THING IS, THERE'S NOTHING YOU CAN DO TO PREVENT IT. SOMETIMES MY BREASTS FEEL LIKE TICKING TIME BOMBS.
MF

THEY SAY CHILDBIRTH REDUCES YOUR RISK FACTOR A LITTLE. YOU COULD GET PREGNANT.
NOW THERE'S A TEMPTING OPTION.
UH... I THINK I'LL TRY LIVING SOLELY ON ORGANIC WHEAT GRASS JUICE INSIDE A LARGE, TOXIN-FREE BUBBLE FIRST.
NGA.

LISTEN, IF YOU'VE GOT YOUR HANDS FULL HERE, I'M SURE I CAN GET A COPY OF THAT BOOK OVER AT THE BUNNS AND NOODLE SUPERSTORE.
MABEL MANIC
CHERRY AIMLESS: MARDI GRAS NURSE
HER TONGUE ON MY DISSERTATION

Trouble

Trouble
204
©1994 BY ALISON BECHDEL

HEY, LOIS. ARE YOU CLOSING? I THOUGHT YOU GUYS WERE OPEN TILL EIGHT TONIGHT.
NO, SORRY. BUT GO ON IN, MO'S STILL HERE. I GOTTA RUN. THE AVENGERS ARE PLANNING AN ACTION AGAINST THE REPUBLICANS' CONTRACT "ON" AMERICA.
MADWIMMIN BOOKS

JILLIAN'S GONNA PUT ON A NEWT GINGRICH MASK, DRIVE BY IN A LIMO, AND MOW US ALL DOWN WITH A TOY UZI. WE HAVE FAKE BLOOD AND EVERYTHING.

HI, MO. I WAS IN THE NEIGHBORHOOD. I THOUGHT I'D SEE IF YOU WANTED TO GO GET SOMETHING TO EAT.

UH... HI, DEIRDRE. JEEZ, I CAN'T. I HAFTA WRITE A BOOK REVIEW FOR THE TRIBUNE TONIGHT, AND I HAVEN'T EVEN STARTED IT YET.
WHAT BOOK? WE CAN TALK ABOUT IT OVER DINNER. YOU GOTTA EAT, RIGHT?
ZIP
CO-OP CREDIT UNION

NO, I REALLY HAVE TO GO HOME AND GET TO WORK. IT'S A NEW LESBIAN EROTICA COLLECTION. I'M GONNA DISCUSS IT IN THE CONTEXT OF OUR EROTOPHOBIC SOCIETY AND CLINTON'S FIRING OF JOYCELYN ELDERS FOR MENTIONING MASTURBATION.
CREDIT UNION

THAT GUY IS SO GUTLESS! I MEAN, WHAT'S HE TRYING TO PROVE BY CANNING THE ONLY PERSON IN WASHINGTON WITH ANY INTEGRITY? DOES HE THINK THAT'S GONNA WIN BACK ALL THE ANGRY WHITE MEN WHO VOTED REPUBLICAN THIS FALL?
OFFICE

HE'D DO A LOT BETTER BY TAKING A STAND FOR ONCE. IF PEOPLE WANT A CONSERVATIVE PRESIDENT IN '96, THEY'LL VOTE FOR A REAL ONE.

CLINTON'S ALREADY LOST VOTES OVER THE MILITARY FIASCO. ONE IN THREE GAY VOTERS PICKED REPUBLICANS IN THE LAST ELECTION!
THE FOOLS! YOU CAN BET YOUR BUMPERSTICKERS THEY'RE MOSTLY WHITE GAY MEN WITH BUCKS, HAPPY TO SELL OUT IMMIGRANTS AND SINGLE MOTHERS ON WELFARE FOR A CHANCE AT A FUCKING TAX BREAK.

WHEN ARE PEOPLE GONNA LEARN? WE'VE GOTTA STICK TOGETHER IF WE EVER HOPE TO HAVE ANY REAL POWER IN THIS COUNTRY!
OFFICE

SO LIKE, WHAT'D YOU THINK OF THE BOOK?
I, UM... HAVEN'T READ IT YET.

MAYBE I CAN HELP YOU WITH YOUR RESEARCH. THOSE BOOKS ALWAYS INCLUDE A STORY ABOUT WOMEN HAVING SEX AT THE OFFICE.
UH... YES, I THINK YOU'RE RIGHT.

GASP.

OOF.
MOAN.
CRASH!

MEANWHILE, AT THE BOOKSTORE...

A BLEAK WINTER'S EVE FINDS OUR VARIOUS HEROINES ENGAGED IN AN EVEN **BLEAKER** COMMON PURSUIT.

post coitum tristis[1]

[1] a certain melancholy sometimes experienced after sex.

Family Hour
©1995 BY ALISON BECHDEL
210
I DUNNO. IT'S NOT LIKE I DIDN'T ENJOY IT. I JUST WISH WE'D WAITED A LITTLE LONGER.
SO GINGER, WHY WAS MALIKA CALLING LAST NIGHT? CAN'T LIVE WITHOUT YOU?
NO. SHE JUST WANTED TO GIVE ME HER NEW ADDRESS. SHE MOVED IN WITH THE WOMAN SHE MET A WEEK AFTER WE BROKE UP.
J. SCREW
I MEAN, I KNOW IT SOUNDS VICTORIAN, BUT DON'T YOU THINK THERE'S SOMETHING TO BE SAID FOR HOLDING OUT?
OH, GINGER. THAT MUST'VE HURT!
ACTUALLY, IT KIND OF HELPED. I DECIDED TO QUIT MAKING EXCUSES. THIS SUMMER I FINISH MY DISSERTATION OR ELSE.
THAT'LL SHOW HER. I BET THE NEW BABE ONLY HAS A MASTER'S DEGREE.
DING DONG!
THERE'S THE FOOD! I'LL GET IT.
WURF!
SO WHY DIDN'T I HOLD OUT? AM I SABOTAGING MYSELF? DO I REALLY FEAR INTIMACY?
Y'KNOW, I'M TIRED OF THIS LIMBO! I WANNA BE AN ADULT, GET ON WITH MY LIFE, MY CAREER.
YEAH. IT'D BE NICE TO HAVE A LITTLE POWER, TOO. DID I TELL YOU THE SHELTER DIRECTOR IS FINALLY LEAVING? I'M GONNA APPLY FOR HER JOB.
ARF! arararf WOOF!
J. SCREW
ON THE OTHER HAND, HAVING ORGASMS WITH SOMEONE IS A FAIRLY INTIMATE UNDERTAKING. BUT ON THE OTHER HAND, I HARDLY KNOW HER!
I'M STARVING!
CHANNA MASALA...SAAG PANEER...
WHERE'S MY ALOO PARATHA?
ARE YOU GUYS LISTENING TO ME?!
YEAH, YEAH. YOU SLEPT WITH SOMEONE YOU BARELY KNOW...
...AND NOW YOU REGRET IT. BUT NOT AS MUCH AS WE DO.
LISTEN, MO. YOU WANNA KNOW MORE ABOUT DEIRDRE? IF YOU PROMISE TO QUIT WHINING ABOUT HOW SORRY YOU ARE YOU GOT LAID, I'LL RUN A CHECK ON HER FOR YOU.
MEANWHILE, ACROSS TOWN...
THANKS FOR ASKING US TO STAY, TONI. IT GETS KINDA LONELY THE NIGHTS ANA WORKS LATE.
TELL ME ABOUT IT. IT'S SUCH A TREAT TO HAVE ANOTHER ADULT AT THE DINNER TABLE.
BAP.
MORE BIZZA!
ANIMAL CRACKERS
HERE, HONEY. I MADE YOU A SPECIAL RAFFI SIZED PIECE OF PIZZA.
JU-UNE! I'M HO-O--
OH! GLORIA, HI!
CLARICE! WHAT ARE YOU DOING HERE? IT'S EARLY!

Lois has promised to do a background check on Deirdre for Mo.

business as usual

212

©1995 BY ALISON BECHDEL

BRIGHT AND EARLY ONE SPRING DAY...

TO-NI...
UNH. WHAT TIME IS IT?
TIME FOR LOVE, SLEEPING BEAUTY.
DEET! DEET! DEET!
DEET! DEET! DEET!
DEET! DEET!...
SMEK!
CLARICE, ARE YOU NUTS? RAFFI WILL BE UP ANY MINUTE, YOU HAVE TO GO TO WORK, AND I HAVE A MILLION THINGS TO DO THIS MORNING!
EXCUSE **ME**! YOU'RE THE ONE WHO'S BEEN COMPLAINING WE DON'T HAVE ENOUGH **SEX**.

YOU DID THIS ON PURPOSE, DIDN'T YOU?
WHAT?
YOU SUDDENLY FEEL LIKE MAKING LOVE ON A BUSY MORNING, THEN IT'S **MY** FAULT FOR SAYING NO! DO YOU HAVE ANY IDEA WHAT MY DAY IS LIKE?
YEAH! YOU HANG OUT WITH **GLORIA** DRINKING COFFEE AND WATCHING THE KIDS PLAY.
WHAT?!
OH MY GOD! IT'S THURSDAY! WHAT WAS I THINKING?! I HAVE A BREAKFAST MEETING DOWNTOWN IN TWENTY MINUTES! I HAVE TO GET **OUT** OF HERE!

I WON'T BE HOME TILL LATE! TONIGHT'S THE SOUTH END CITIZEN ACTION GROUP MEETING, AND I HAVE TO BE THERE.
OH, WELL, IF YOU **HAVE** TO BE THERE. A PRIORITY'S A PRIORITY!
WHAT?
I SAID MAYBE **GLORIA** WILL WANT TO COME OVER FOR DINNER AGAIN TONIGHT.

LATER THAT MORNING...

WHAT?!
MADWIMMIN BOOKS
OPEN
RIF!
I SAW HER AT THIS PARTY MAKING OUT WITH HER EX-LOVER WHO IT TURNS OUT ISN'T HER EX AT ALL BUT HER **CURRENT**. THEY'VE JUST DECIDED TO SEE OTHER PEOPLE.

The
TANGO
of
ANGER
214
©1995 BY ALISON BECHDEL

THE BOSS IS BACK.
I SEE YOU DECIDED TO EXPAND OUR SELECTION OF GAY MEN'S EROTICA WHILE I WAS GONE, MO.
WHAT?! WE DON'T HAVE A MEN'S EROTICA SECTION!
BOOKS
PAGETURNERS
POTBOILERS

MO, WHY AM I LOOKING AT A BOX FULL OF VERY EXPENSIVE GYM QUEENS?
OH! I MADE A MISTAKE ON AN ORDER... I KEEP MEANING TO SEND THOSE BACK, BUT WE DON'T HAVE ANY PACKING TAPE.
BOB 'N ROD
$60

GIVE ME STRENGTH.
I'LL GET RIGHT ON IT, AS SOON AS I UNPACK THIS STUFF.

AND WHAT ARE ALL THESE RUGRATS DOING HERE? ARE WE OFFERING DAYCARE NOW?
NO, TONI AND HER FRIEND GLORIA BRING THEIR KIDS OVER WHILE TONI DOES THE PAYROLL. STELLA JUST STARTED WALKING.

SORRY, JEZ. THEY'RE A LITTLE WOUND UP. ARE YOU READY TO GO OVER THE BOOKS?
OKAY, LET'S SEE HOW YOU MANAGED.

TONI, WHAT IS ALL THIS? YOU CHANGED MY SYSTEM!
WELL, YEAH... I HAD A HARD TIME FOLLOWING IT, SO I SET UP A MORE, UH... CONVENTIONAL ONE. THIS WAY IT'LL BE EASIER TO PUT IT ON THE COMPUTER.

EXCUSE ME? DID I ASK YOU TO COMPUTERIZE MY BUSINESS? I LIKED THE OLD SYSTEM!
Y'KNOW, JEZANNA, MAYBE YOU SHOULD TAKE A FEW DAYS TO UNWIND BEFORE YOU JUMP BACK INTO THINGS HERE.

I'M NEVER LEAVING THIS STORE AGAIN! GOD KNOWS WHAT I'D COME BACK TO! DILDOES IN THE WINDOW DISPLAY, PROBABLY, AND ALTERNATIVE INSEMINATION CLINICS IN THE BACK ROOM!

LISTEN, I KNOW YOU'RE UPSET ABOUT YOUR MOTHER. DO YOU WANT TO TALK ABOUT IT? HOW'S SHE DOING?
MY MOTHER IS AN UNREPENTANT OLD HARRIDAN. AT HER WEAKEST WITH THE CHEMO, SHE MANAGED TO REMIND ME THAT IF I LOST WEIGHT, I MIGHT STILL BE ABLE TO FIND A HUSBAND.

SOUNDS LIKE SHE'S PROBABLY SCARED, AND JUST LASHING OUT AT WHOEVER'S HANDY.
TONI, IS RAFFI WITH YOU? I LOST SIGHT OF HIM!

RAFAEL!
RIP!
DAMMIT, MO! I HOPE YOU LIKE BEEFCAKE, GIRL, BECAUSE YOU JUST BOUGHT YOURSELF A COFFEE TABLE BOOK.

their brilliant careers

216

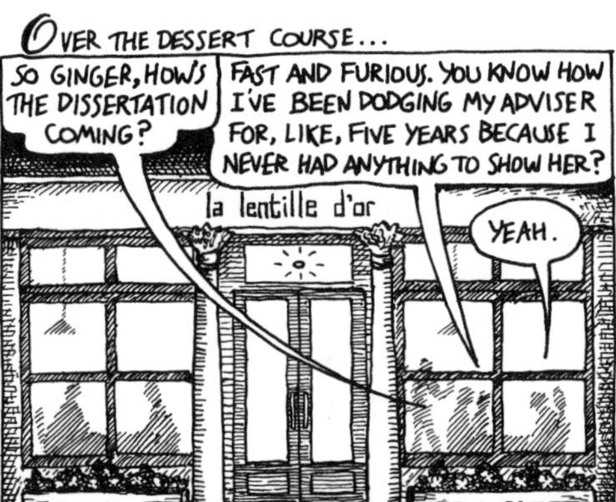

an
entrance
and an
exit
217
©1995 BY ALISON BECHDEL

...SO I SAID TO HER, "I WON'T BE TOYED WITH, DEIRDRE. FIND SOMEONE ELSE TO BE YOUR SEXUAL PLAYTHING!"
SPEAKING OF WHICH...DID I MENTION THE SUCCULENT DETAILS OF MY NIGHT WITH BABETTE THE WAITRESS? TALK ABOUT A FEAST.
OFFICE
EXCUSE ME. I HATE TO INTERRUPT, BUT...
SNATCH THE POWER

WOULD ONE OF YOU GO WORK THE REGISTER? THIS IS A PLACE OF BUSINESS! KEEP YOUR LOVE LIVES OUT OF IT!

PRESENTLY...
HI! IS JEZANNA IN?
YEAH. I'LL BUZZ HER. WHO SHOULD I SAY IS HERE?
MADWIMMIN BOOKS

AUDREY?
HI, BABY! I GOT THE WEEKEND OFF! I THOUGHT I'D COME UP AND GIVE YOU A THRILL!

MEANWHILE...
THANK YOU, CLARENCE THOMAS AND SANDRA DAY O'CONNOR.
The Distress
SUPREME COURT NEGATIVE ON AFFIRMATIVE ACTION

LEMME SEE... I THINK MY FAVORITE ARGUMENT AGAINST AFFIRMATIVE ACTION IS THAT "SPECIAL TREATMENT" IS INSULTING TO AFRICAN AMERICANS. I MEAN, HOW MANY WHITE GUYS DO YOU KNOW WHO FEEL "INSULTED" BY THE SPECIAL TREATMENT THEY'VE GOTTEN FOR CENTURIES?
CLARICE, WILL YOU PUT DOWN THE PAPER? WE ONLY SEE EACH OTHER FOR AN HOUR A DAY. COULD WE AT LEAST TRY TO HAVE A CONVERSATION?

I'M HAVING A CONVERSATION!
WITH WHO? I WAS TALKING TO YOU ABOUT HOW TO COME OUT TO MY PARENTS, WHEN YOU PICKED UP THE NEWSPAPER AND STARTED RANTING!

TONI, I'VE HEARD YOUR PLANS TO COME OUT TO YOUR FOLKS NINE MILLION TIMES SINCE WE FIRST MET. EXCUSE ME IF EVERY ONCE IN A WHILE MY MIND WANDERS.
OKAY, CLARICE! I HAVE HAD IT WITH YOU! I DESERVE BETTER THAN THIS! I'M GOING OVER TO GLORIA'S, WHERE SOMEONE WILL LISTEN TO ME!

OH YEAH? AND WHAT ELSE WILL SHE DO TO YOU?
SHUT UP! DON'T YOU EVER TALK ABOUT HER LIKE THAT! YOU ARE SO FULL OF... OF POOP!
WAHAA!

SLAM!
POOP.

another Saturday night
218
©1995 BY ALISON BECHDEL

THANKS FOR DOING THIS, MO. TONI AND I REALLY NEED TO GET A BREAK.
WHERE ARE THOSE TWO?
WHAT TWO?

UH... I FORGOT TO TELL YOU. HARRIET AND ELLEN ARE GOING OUT WITH US.
YOU'RE DOUBLE DATING WITH MY EX AND HER LOVER, THE HUMAN DYNAMO? WELL DON'T I FEEL LIKE THE PATHETIC MAIDEN AUNT!
BZZT!
HERE THEY ARE.

HI, GIRLS.
HI! EXCUSE MY SUIT. I HAD TO GO RIGHT FROM A VICTORY FUND RECEPTION TO A MEETING OF THE WOMEN I'M GOING TO BEIJING WITH.
YOU'RE GOING TO THE U.N. CONFERENCE ON WOMEN? HOW EXCITING!

HI, MO. HI, RAFAEL!
NICE TO SEE YOU, MO. ARE YOU THE BABYSITTER?
NO. I'M THE FRENCH TUTOR.
C'MON, LET'S GO! IF WE DON'T LEAVE THIS SECOND, WE'LL MISS THE BEGINNING! I HATE THAT!

BYE-BYE! BE GOOD.
DO I HAVE A CHOICE?
WAAAH!

LATER THAT EVENING...
I WONDER IF WOMEN ARE HAVING MORE AFFAIRS SINCE THIS MOVIE?
THALIA
THE BRIDGES OF MADISON COUNTY 7 & 9:30
WHY SHOULD THEY? THE ULTIMATE MESSAGE IS TO STAY ON THE FARM AND BE A MARTYR.

YEAH, BUT STILL... THE AUDIENCE REALLY WANTED HER TO GO OFF WITH CLINT EASTWOOD. DIDN'T YOU?
I DUNNO. I FELL ASLEEP IN THE MIDDLE. WHY D'YOU CARE? THINKING OF LEAVING CLARICE AND RAFFI FOR A STRAY PHOTOJOURNALIST?
CAFE

UM... NO. BUT I AM KIND OF... UH.. ATTRACTED TO SOMEONE. GOD! I ACTUALLY SAID IT! I'M NERVOUS, HARRIET! I NEVER FELT LIKE THIS BEFORE!
TONI, ARE YOU SERIOUS? IT'S GLORIA, ISN'T IT? HAVE YOU TOLD HER? DOES CLARICE KNOW?

CLARICE, D'YOU EVER WONDER IF YOU'RE IN THE RIGHT RELATIONSHIP? LIKE, MAYBE THERE'S SOME MYSTERIOUS STRANGER OUT THERE WHO'S GONNA COME ALONG AND CHANGE YOUR LIFE?
I KNOW TONI'S THE RIGHT ONE FOR ME. BUT I STILL FANTASIZE. DOESN'T EVERYONE CARRY AROUND A MYSTERIOUS STRANGER IN THEIR HEAD?

MAYBE. BUT.. UH... WHAT DO YOU DO WHEN THEY SHOW UP IN YOUR BED?
ELLEN! WHAT ARE YOU SAYING? NO, DON'T TELL ME! OH, MAN! DOES HARRIET KNOW?

MEANWHILE, MO HAS A FEW QUESTIONS TOO.
IS THIS EERILY REMINISCENT OF TENTH GRADE, OR WHAT?
WILL I EVER HAVE A LIFE?
ARE MY FRIENDS THAT MUCH MORE STABLE AND MATURE THAN I AM?

AFTER A MOST INTERESTING DOUBLE DATE, OUR DOTING COUPLES FIND THEMSELVES ALONE AT LAST.

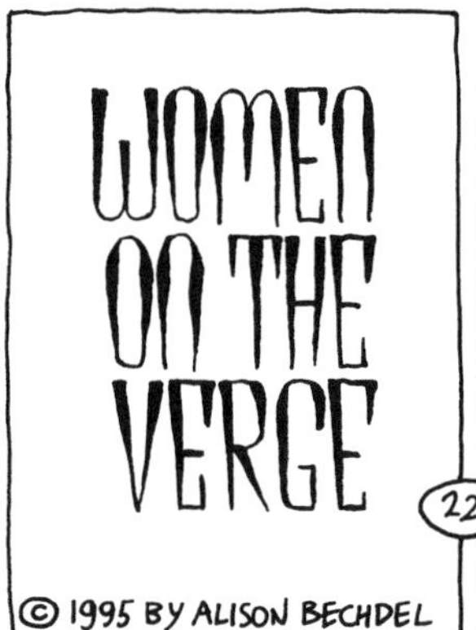
WOMEN ON THE VERGE
© 1995 BY ALISON BECHDEL

WHILE RAFAEL AND STELLA RECHARGE . . .
TONI, D'YOU MIND IF I TURN THE RINGER OFF ON YOUR PHONE? SOMETIMES IT WAKES STELLA.
NO, GO AHEAD. IF ANYONE CALLS, WE'LL HEAR THEM WHEN THE MACHINE PICKS UP.
221

SO. HAVE YOU HAD THE BIG COMING OUT TALK WITH YOUR FOLKS YET?
NO. I CAN'T TELL THEM WHEN CLARICE AND I ARE GETTING ALONG SO BADLY. I REALLY NEED HER TO BE THERE FOR ME WHEN THEY FLIP OUT.
RICE MILK

WHY DO YOU THINK YOU TWO ARE HAVING SUCH A HARD TIME?
OH, I DON'T KNOW, GLORIA. MAYBE SHE FEELS JEALOUS OF HAVING TO SHARE ME WITH RAFFI...

...OR MAYBE SHE'S JEALOUS OF YOU.
ME?

WELL, WE DO SPEND A LOT OF TIME TOGETHER. SHE'S MADE A COUPLE OF REMARKS.
SO HAS ANA. SHE ACTUALLY ASKED ME IF... IF WE WERE SLEEPING TOGETHER.

SLEEPING TOGETHER? WHAT DO THEY THINK WE DO ALL DAY?! WITH TWO TODDLERS, WE'RE LUCKY IF WE MANAGE LUNCH!
I KNOW. IT'S KINDA FUNNY.

UM... I WON'T SAY I HAVEN'T THOUGHT ABOUT IT, THOUGH.
REALLY?

OH, GOD! I'M SORRY! FORGET I SAID THAT!
I'VE THOUGHT ABOUT IT TOO. I DON'T KNOW WHY CLARICE DOESN'T TREAT YOU BETTER. YOU'RE SO SWEET AND SO BEAUTIFUL.

OH, NO.
TONI, WE CAN'T!

I KNOW. WE CAN'T.

≥CLIK!≤ HI. WE CAN'T COME TO THE PHONE RIGHT NOW, SO LEAVE A MESSAGE! ≥BEEEP!≤
ANTONIA! ESTA ES TU MADRE! I AM VERY UPSET! I WAS JUST BABYSITTING AT YOUR COUSIN CARMEN'S, AND FOUND A STRANGE LETTER YOU WROTE HER ABOUT RAFAEL AND YOUR...YOUR FRIEND. YOU SAY YOU ARE "UNA FAMILIA LESBIANA". ¡I AM SICK! ¡I CAN'T SPEAK TO YOU! ¡CALL ME IMMEDIATAMENTE!

INDISCREET

222

THEIR INCIPIENT KISS QUASHED BY A HYSTERICAL PHONE MESSAGE FROM TONI'S MOTHER, OUR HEROINES APPEAR TO BE MOMENTARILY **NONPLUSSED.**

WHOA.

YEAH. GUESS I WON'T BE NEEDING THE JUDICIOUSLY PHRASED COMING OUT SPEECH I'VE BEEN FINE-TUNING FOR THE PAST FIFTEEN YEARS.

I GUESS NOT.
UH... LISTEN. I'M SORRY ABOUT WHAT ALMOST HAPPENED BEFORE YOUR MOM CALLED.
YOU ARE?

WELL, I MEAN... HAVING AN AFFAIR WOULD KIND OF WRECK OUR LIVES, DON'T YOU THINK?
MY LIFE IS **ALREADY** WRECKED! MY MOTHER IS PROBABLY BOARDING A PLANE THIS MINUTE TO COME RESCUE MY BABY FROM THE "UNHEALTHY INFLUENCE OF MY DEPRAVED LIFESTYLE."

WITHOUT RAFFI TO SUPPORT, CLARICE WILL BE FREE TO **DUMP ME** SO SHE CAN SPEND **ALL** HER TIME AT THE OFFICE!

IN THIS JOB MARKET I'LL BE LUCKY TO FIND WORK AS A TELEMARKETER! I'LL PROBABLY END UP **HOMELESS** AND GO MAD WITH **GRIEF!**

I HAVE NOTHING TO LOSE, GLORIA! KISS ME!

shlurp

TONI, NO! COME ON. THIS IS CRAZY. YOU'RE UPSET. THE KIDS'LL BE UP ANY MINUTE! WE CAN'T!
I KNOW, I KNOW. YOU'RE RIGHT.

I DON'T WANNA RUIN OUR FRIENDSHIP. YOU'RE THE ONLY PERSON I CAN COUNT ON.
RELAX! IT'S OKAY!

MY LIFE IS SUCH A MESS. SNIFF!
YOU'LL FIGURE IT OUT! YOU CAN HANDLE YOUR MOTHER! YOU'LL FIND A GOOD JOB AGAIN! AND THINGS WITH CLARICE WILL GET BETTER, I PROMISE.

D'YOU REALLY THINK SO?
MOMMY! HAFTO GO POTTY WIKE BIG BOY!
KA-CLICK

mouths o' babes

224

Pajama Party
226
©1995 BY ALISON BECHDEL

ARE YOU SURE THIS IS OKAY? WE COULD STOP BY AFTER DINNER AND PICK HIM UP.
NO WAY! THE WHOLE POINT IS FOR YOU GUYS TO HAVE A NIGHT ALONE. NOW GET OUTTA HERE!
HEY, RAFSTER!

I DUNNO, TONI. HE'S NEVER SLEPT AWAY FROM HOME BEFORE. D'YOU THINK HE'LL BE ALL RIGHT?
HE'LL BE FINE. I'M MORE WORRIED ABOUT SPARROW, GINGER, AND LOIS. AT LEAST THERE'S THREE OF THEM.

GOOD! NOW CLICK ON THE HYPER-TEXT LINK TO THE MUPPET PAGE AND WE'LL FIND YOU A NICE BEDTIME STORY.

ANY NEWS FROM HOMOPHOBIA CEN-TRAL? OR IS YOUR MOTHER STILL NOT SPEAKING TO YOU?
CARMEN WENT OVER LAST NIGHT TO RUN INTER-FERENCE. SHE SAYS MOM'S MOUTH HAS STOPPED FOAMING.

SHOULDN'T HE BE WINDING DOWN ABOUT NOW?
WOOF! DOGGY EAT!
YIP!

CLARICE, WHAT HAPPENED WITH GLORIA WAS TOTALLY CRAZY. I DIDN'T MEAN TO HURT YOU.
IT'S MY OWN FAULT. I'VE BEEN SO DISTANT AND WRAPPED UP IN MY WORK. I'M SURPRISED YOU DIDN'T LEAVE ME MONTHS AGO.

LOIS!
RELAX! IT'S NON-TOXIC, NON-STAINING, AND CON-TAINS NATURAL FLAVORING.
FORPLAY
ECONO SIZE

GOD, IT'S WEIRD NOT HAVING RAFFI HERE. UH... I FEEL AWKWARD, PLANNING TO HAVE SEX LIKE THIS. MAYBE WE SHOULD RELAX WITH SOME TV FIRST...
CLARICE, IT'S BEEN FIVE MONTHS! I'M NOT WASTING ONE MORE SECOND ON MARY TYLER MOORE.

HOW ARE WE GOING TO EXPLAIN THE DRIED LUBE IN HIS HAIR?
EEK! NO THAMPOO!
JESUS. NO WONDER CLARICE AND TONI ARE ON THE SKIDS.

CLARICE! WHAT IS THIS?!
IT'S... YOU KNOW... KIND OF A NIGHTGOWN, I GUESS. I THOUGHT IT MIGHT HELP. D'YOU LIKE IT?

RHODA! WHY DID YOU REPLACE MY FLANNEL NIGHTIE WITH THIS FLIMSY NEGLIGÉE FOR MY TRIP TO THE HOSPITAL?
HEY, KID. YOU WEREN'T GONNA MEET ANY DOCTORS IN THAT OLD THING.

Poetic Justice
228
©1995 BY ALISON BECHDEL

SOMEWHERE IN A RENOVATED DOWNTOWN WAREHOUSE...
MO'S PULCHRITUDINOUS PAL PERFORMS HER PUERILE POETRY.
HER PUSSY SUCKED ME IN LIKE A CARLETON SHEETS REAL ESTATE INFOMERCIAL...

AFTERWARDS...
GINGER! WHAT ARE YOU DOING HERE?
HI, MO! ONE OF MY OLD STUDENTS READ TONIGHT. THE ONE WEARING THE RHINE-STONE-STUDDED DILDO.

RATHER A HACK-NEYED TAKE ON THE PHALLIC PRE-TENSIONS OF THE PENIS, DIDN'T YOU THINK?
OH. THIS IS SYDNEY. SHE'S THE NEW ASSISTANT PROF IN THE WOMEN'S STUDIES DEPARTMENT. MO WORKS AT MADWIMMIN BOOKS.

YES, I'VE SEEN YOU THERE. NOT A BAD BOOK-STORE FOR THE PROVINCES.
BUT YOU KNOW, GINGER, YOUR STUDENT WAS POSI-TIVELY INSPIRED NEXT TO THAT VAPID BLONDE BUTCH WITH THE INFO-MERCIAL SIMILES.

OH, COME ON! JUST BE-CAUSE BEATRICE IS GOOD-LOOKING, PEOPLE THINK SHE MUST BE STUPID. HER POETRY WORKS ON LOTS OF LEVELS! LOOK BE-LOW THE SURFACE!
IF I LOOKED BE-LOW HER SURFACE, YOU KNOW WHAT I'D SEE? NOTHING. ZIP. THE VOID. ONE BIG FOUCAULDIAN LACUNA.

UH... WE WERE GONNA GO GET SOME COFFEE. CARE TO JOIN US?
THANKS, BUT BEATRICE AND I ARE GOING OUT.

UH... BEATRICE?
'SCUSE ME...

OH HI, MO. LISTEN, A BUNCH OF US ARE GOING OVER TO SYLVIA'S FOR MARTINIS AND FAG PORN. WANNA COME?
OH.

UM... I THINK I'LL TAKE A RAIN CHECK.

HEY, MO! DID YOU CHANGE YOUR MIND?
YEAH. SHE'S JUST A BIG LACUNA AFTER ALL. LET'S GO GET SOME HIGH-TEST.

DOUBLE NEGATIVE

229

©1995 BY ALISON BECHDEL

writer's blockade

230

face to face

231

IN THE OFFICE OF MADWIMMIN BOOKS...

HEY, NICE TO HEAR YOUR VOICE! YEAH, SHE'S HERE. HANG ON.

JEZ, IT'S YOUR BABE.

HER NAME'S **AUDREY** IF YOU DON'T MIND.

MEANWHILE, UP AT THE REGISTER.

OH, NO! LOIS, HERE COMES THAT INSUFFERABLE SNOB I WAS TELLING YOU ABOUT! I GOTTA **HIDE**!

MADWIMMIN BOOKS

HI. HOWYA DOIN'?

HEY, WEREN'T YOU SECOND RUNNER-UP IN THE DRAG KING CONTEST LAST WEEKEND?

YEAH! PRETTY GOOD SHOW, HUH?

WELL, LET'S JUST SAY I'VE SEEN AVON LADIES WITH MORE BALLS. BUT THEN I'M USED TO THE CULTURE OF A MUCH LARGER CITY. YOU'LL CATCH UP IN A FEW YEARS, I EXPECT.

THE NEW FUCK YOU

YEAH, WELL. I DIDN'T SEE YOU UP ON THE STAGE.

OH, I'M PURELY AN OBSERVER. I'M RESEARCHING AN ARTICLE ON GENDER TRANSGRESSION UNDER ADVANCED CAPITALISM. PERHAPS I COULD INTERVIEW YOU!

SMEK!

UH... I DON'T THINK SO. THEORY GIVES ME HIVES.

OH, REALLY. WELL, I'D LIKE TO TALK TO SOMEONE ABOUT ORDERING TEXTBOOKS FOR THE COURSES I TEACH AT THE UNIVERSITY. I THOUGHT YOU COULD USE THE BUSINESS MORE THAN THE CAMPUS BOOKSTORE.

SURE. HEY, JEZANNA. THIS WOMAN HAS A BIG ORDER.

HAVE MO TAKE IT. I HAVE TO FLY TO ST. LOUIS. MY MOTHER'S NOT DOING WELL.

JEEZ, I'M SORRY.

WELL, AUDREY'S THERE, THANK GOD. DATING AN ONCOLOGY NURSE WAS THE BEST MOVE I EVER MADE. WHERE **IS** MO? I THOUGHT...

MO?

UH... I WAS JUST GETTING THESE STAPLES OUT OF THE CARPET. VERY HAZARDOUS.

TAKE THIS WOMAN'S ORDER, WILL YOU?

REALLY, MO. IT'S NOT NECESSARY TO GENUFLECT IN MY PRESENCE.

SYDNEY?

THEA?

WELL! IT'S BEEN A LONG **TIME**, HASN'T IT?

ZOUNDS! **HEREBY** HANGS A TALE! STAY TUNED!

A Smidge Too Far
232
©1996 BY ALISON BECHDEL

IN OUR LAST TEMPESTUOUS EPISODE, THEA APPEARED TO HAVE HAD A PRIOR ACQUAINTANCE WITH A PARTICULAR POMPOUS PROFESSOR.
SYDNEY?
THEA?

BUT AFTER SYDNEY LEAVES, THEA IS A TAD RETICENT WITH THE DETAILS.
MO, I SAID DROP IT! I DON'T WANT TO TALK ABOUT IT!
LOIS! THEA KNOWS SYDNEY AND WON'T TELL ME HOW!
REALLY? MUST BE SOMETHING PRETTY SEAMY.

YEAH! MAYBE THEY MET IN ONE OF THOSE "EX-GAY" MINISTRIES, TRYING TO OVERCOME THEIR UNWHOLESOME DESIRES!
MAYBE SYDNEY HOSTED A FUCKERWARE PARTY WHERE THEA BOUGHT A MARITAL AID THAT SHORT-CIRCUITED AND ELECTROLYSIZED ALL HER LOVER'S PUBIC HAIR.
THE NADIR OF DESIRE
DOUBLE MUFF
MY LOVER USED TO BE A WOMAN

NO, I KNOW! THEY USED TO BE LOVERS UNTIL ONE DAY THEA CAME HOME EARLY AND DISCOVERED SYDNEY'S PENCHANT FOR CROSS-DRESSING AS BEVERLY LA HAYE!
GROW UP, ASSHOLES!
SNARK.

THAT EVENING...
MAYBE TONI HAS THE SKINNY ON SYDNEY'S SORDID SECRET.
NOK NOK
'95 TAX

HI.
UH... ARE CLARICE AND TONI HERE? I, UM... HAVE SOMETHING TO DROP OFF.
?
'95 TAX

COME ON IN! THEY'RE OUT TO DINNER. I'M CARLOS, THE MALE ROLE MODEL.
OH, RIGHT! NICE T'MEET YOU. I'M MO. SO HOW'S IT GOING?
TÍO CA-WOSE! UP!

IT'S GOING GREAT! TODAY WE PRACTICED STANDING UP TO PEE, AND THEN WE REDID THE DOLLHOUSE DRAPES! RIGHT, RAFFLES?

RING!
OH, THAT'S PROBABLY TONI NOW. HANG ON.

MANLY-MAN TRAINING ACADEMY, BUTCH SPEAKING!
¿!?

OH! SEÑOR ORTÍZ! SÍ, THIS IS TONI'S NUMBER. ... ¿I DE QUÉ ESTÁS HABLANDO?! ¡NO! I'M NOT THE FATHER! I'M JUST THE BABYSITTER, I SWEAR!

¿QUÉ?! YOU WANT ME TO MARRY YOUR DAUGHTER? WELL OKAY, BUT I'M KEEPING MY OWN NAME!
A TIP O' THE NIB TO MARIO MARTINEZ

CLIK!
SOMEHOW, I DON'T THINK THAT HELPED TONI'S CHANCES FOR A MOVING RECONCILIATION WITH HER PARENTS.

Seeing Pink
©1996 BY ALISON BECHDEL 234

THANKS FOR THE RIDE. SURE YOU DON'T WANT TO COME TO THE READING? EVEN IF YOU DON'T LIKE MIKO'S BOOK, YOU'LL MEET A LOT OF NEW PEOPLE.
NAH. I HAVE A TON OF PAPERS TO GRADE.
MADWIMMIN BOOKS
BOOK PARTY TONITE

SINCE WHEN HAVE A FEW PAPERS STOPPED YOU FROM... OH, I GET IT! YOU'RE AFRAID OF RUNNING INTO THEA, AREN'T YOU?! WELL, LOOK. SHE'S LEAVING. YOU DON'T HAVE TO WORRY.
WHAT DO YOU KNOW ABOUT THEA AND ME?
MADWIMMIN BOOKS

NOTHING! LOIS WAS PUMPING ME FOR INFORMATION THE OTHER NIGHT ABOUT HOW YOU TWO KNOW EACH OTHER. IS IT SOME BIG SECRET?
WHAT'D YOU TELL HER?!

WHAT COULD I TELL HER? I DON'T KNOW ANYTHING!
LOOK, IT'S PRIVATE, OKAY?! Y'KNOW, IF LESBIANS WEREN'T SO BUSY OBSESSING ON THE DETAILS OF EACH OTHER'S **LOVE LIVES** LIKE A PACK OF PUBESCENT **POM-POM** GIRLS,
CAFé

...MAYBE WE'D BE MAKING A LITTLE MORE HEADWAY AGAINST ALL THE WHITE-SUPREMACIST, BIOCHIP-IMPLANT-CONSPIRACY-THEORISTS WHO WANT **PAT BUCHANAN** TO MAKE THE TRAINS RUN ON TIME!
LOVE LIVES? SO WERE YOU AND THEA AN **ITEM?**

A BIT LATER...
CONGRATULATIONS, MIKO! I HOPE THE BOOK DOESN'T DO **TOO** WELL. I DON'T KNOW **WHAT** I'D DO IF YOU EVER QUIT CUTTING HAIR!
UH...THANKS, JOSIE.
HAIR STORIES
HAIR STORIES
HAIR STORIES MIKO TAKAGAWA

SO FAR TONIGHT, TEN CLIENTS HAVE TOLD ME THAT.
KEEP SMILING. I'LL GO FRESHEN UP YOUR SELTZER.
"A TONSORIAL TOUR DE FORCE" — GORE VIDAL SASSOON

ACTUALLY, I'M GLAD TO SEE BUCHANAN GETTING A GOOD TURNOUT. HE KEEPS THE REPUBLICANS OFF-BALANCE, AND HE'S SUCH A **LUNATIC**, HE'LL NEVER GET ELECTED.
HEY, MO! HOW'S IT GOING?
Chardonnay IN-A-JUG

DID YOU HEAR THAT? IT IS **SO** IRRESPONSIBLE TO DISMISS THAT FASCIST AS 'FRINGE.' NEXT THING YOU KNOW, HE'LL BE GOOSESTEPPING INTO THE **OVAL OFFICE!**

IF PROGRESSIVES WEREN'T SO BUSY **RATIONALIZING** OVER WINE AND CHEESE, MAYBE WE'D ACTUALLY BE MAKING SOME HEADWAY AGAINST THE SWELLING RANKS OF ARYAN NATION **UZI FREAKS** WHO WANT **PAT BUCHANAN** TO BE THEIR GENERALISSIMO!

WELL, YOU HAVE TO ADMIT, HIS ATTACK ON BIG BUSINESS HAS TOUCHED A POPULIST NERVE.
OH, PLEASE! HE DOESN'T CARE ABOUT WORKERS! HE'S JUST PREYING ON PEOPLE'S FINANCIAL INSECURITY TO FUEL HIS BIGOTED, IMMIGRANT-BASHING AGENDA! BUCHANAN'S HATE-MONGERING SERVES CORPORATE INTERESTS MORE THAN STEVE FORBES COULD EVER **HOPE** TO WITH HIS FLATULENT **FLAT TAX!**

WHY'D YOU BAIT HER LIKE THAT?
DON'T HER EARS TURN AN ENTRANCING SALMON HUE WHEN SHE'S APOPLECTIC?

the ties that chafe
©1996 By Alison Bechdel
235
Jezanna ("Alberta" to her folks) is at the hospital.
Looks like I'll be votin' for that sorry-ass Clinton again. These Spam-head Republicans are even more worthless than he is.
Yeah. Painful as it is, I have to agree with you.
What's so painful? Voting for Clinton, or agreeing with your father?
G.O.P. race down to Dole, Buchanan

Both, most likely. She's just that contrary.
I like a little contrariness in a woman. She takes after you.

Well, maybe. But just you watch out for her temper.
Mama, Mother Theresa would lose her temper around you. Will you stop running me down to Audrey?

You see how she talks to me?

Y'know, if these Spam-heads ever tried solving the country's problems instead of messing with matters that don't concern them, maybe you two could get married good and proper some day.
All I know is, you're lucky you found this girl, Alberta. No man would put up with you.
21 States introduce bills blocking recognition of gay marriage
"Most important issue on our docket," says radical right
Soak it up, babe. I think this is the closest we get to an actual blessing.

Meanwhile, back in River City...
So did you find out why your dad called last night?
I'm sure he just wanted to browbeat me into going straight to appease my mother.

Are you gonna call them back or what?
I tried earlier and no one was home. They're probably out hiring a deprogrammer to come rescue me from my wicked surroundings.

You make them out to be these rabid fanatics, Toni. They're just regular people, a little wigged out by their dyke daughter, is all.

Clarice, my own mother, flesh of my flesh, thinks I'm the **ANTICHRIST!** Well, you know what? I don't need that kind of meanness in my life, and I don't want my child exposed to it!

Babe, I know it's really painful for you, but...
Damn right it is! Why should I keep reaching out, only to get rejected again and again? I've had it! She doesn't want to talk to me? Fine! I'll never speak to her again!
Heh-wo? Hi!

Raffi, please don't play with the phone. It's not a toy.
Toni, can you grab it from him?
Raffi! Are you **TALKING** to someone?
Annh!

Hello?
¿¡Hola?! Antonia?!

MAMÁ?! What are **YOU** doing on the line?
Something tells me our little hellion just discovered the 'redial' button.

THROUGH AN UNFORTUNATE INCIDENT INVOLVING RAFAEL AND THE REDIAL BUTTON, TONI IS STARTLED TO FIND HERSELF ON THE PHONE WITH THE VERY MOTHER SHE ONLY MOMENTS AGO VOWED NEVER TO SPEAK TO AGAIN.

YEAH, IT'S AMAZING. HE'S GROWING SO FAST! EVERY DAY HE DOES SOMETHING HE COULDN'T JUST THE DAY BEFORE.

COME, MY LITTLE HELLSPAWN. IT'S TIME FOR YOUR HOSE-DOWN.

NO!

MEANWHILE, OVER AT THE OLDEST EXTANT GROUP HOUSEHOLD IN LESBIANDOM...

NO, BUT I COULD TELL BY THE LOOK IN HER EYES AS SHE WAS DENYING IT. SEE FOR YOURSELF. SHE'S COMING OVER FOR DINNER.

REALLY! WELL, THIS SHOULD BE AN INTERESTING MEAL...

SHALL WE SLIP SPANISH FLY INTO THE STUFFED SQUASH, OR SALTPETER INTO THE SOY SAUCE?

BACK AT TH' RANCH, TONI'S OFF THE PHONE...

legal beagle
A TIP O' THE NIB TO DEB LASHMAN!
237
©1996 BY ALISON BECHDEL

THANKS FOR DOING THIS, CARLOS. WE SHOULD BE DONE WITH THE LAWYER BY EIGHT.
HEY, DE NADA! I GOT A VERY EXCITING EVENING PLANNED. FIRST, A QUIET DINNER FOR TWO CHÉZ COLONEL SANDERS...
ZIP!

...THEN ON TO BABY GAP WHERE WE'LL TRY ON OVER-PRICED OUTFITS WE HAVE NO INTENTION OF BUYING.
BZZT!

HI THERE. TONI? I'M ALEXIS. I HOPE YOU LIKE DOGS. BRUCE IS ALONE ALL DAY, SO I THOUGHT I'D BRING HIM ALONG.
OH... FINE. HE'S, UH.. VERY SWEET.
M-MOMMY?
LAWYERS DO IT IN THEIR BRIEFS

IT'S OKAY, RAFFI. IT'S JUST A... A PUPPY DOG. HE WON'T HURT YOU.
THIS THE ADOPTEE?
UH... YES. THIS IS RAFAEL. AND THIS IS OUR FRIEND CARLOS. CARLOS, THIS IS ALEXIS, THE LAWYER WHO'S HANDLING THE ADOPTION.
AANH!
SNIFF?

CHARMED, CARLOS.
I THINK WE'LL BE OFF.
GOOD IDEA. BYE-BYE, PUMPKIN! I LOVE YOU!

CLARICE MENTIONED ORDERING IN SOME CHINESE FOOD. MIND IF I CALL NOW? WE'RE STARVING!
NO, GO AHEAD. HERE'S THE MENU. ORDER ANYTHING THAT'S CIRCLED FOR CLARICE AND ME. UH.. WILL YOU EXCUSE ME A MINUTE?
WUF.
LAWYERS DO IT IN THEIR BRIEFS
PANDA GARDEN

CLARICE, WILL YOU GET OUT HERE? YOUR LAW SCHOOL CRONY AND HER STALLION ARE ORDERING DINNER. I CAN'T BELIEVE YOU'RE HIRING THIS WOMAN TO REPRESENT US! SHE'S GOT THE SOCIAL SKILLS OF A RHINOCEROS.
HON, RELAX! ALEXIS HAS A HIGHLY RESPECTED FAMILY LAW PRACTICE! SHE KNOWS WHAT SHE'S DOING!

LATER...
WHOOPS! THIS IS THE FORM FOR ANNULMENT! I WONDERED WHY THEY WANTED TO KNOW IF THE MARRIAGE HAD BEEN CONSUMMATED. CLARICE, IF YOU'RE DONE WITH THAT CRAB RANGOON, I KNOW BRUCE WOULD JUST LOVE SOME.

HERE WE GO. NOW WHAT THESE PAPERS WILL SAY, TONI, IS THAT AS RAFFI'S ONLY LEGAL PARENT, YOU CONSENT TO CLARICE ADOPTING HIM WITHOUT GIVING UP YOUR OWN PARENTAL RIGHTS.
IGNORE THIS DUCK SAUCE ON PARAGRAPH TWO.

HERE'S A TRICKY QUESTION. "THE PETITIONER..." THAT'S CLARICE... "IS RELATED TO THE PERSON TO BE ADOPTED AS FOLLOWS: STEPMOTHER, STEPFATHER, UNRELATED, OTHER RELATIONSHIP." I'D SAY THIS IS PROBABLY A CASE OF "OTHER," WOULDN'T YOU?

UM... ALEXIS? PARDON MY ASKING, BUT HAVE YOU EVER DONE THIS BEFORE?
OH, SURE! I'VE DONE LOTS OF ADOPTIONS!

REALLY? FOR LESBIANS?
NO, YOU'LL BE MY FIRST! ISN'T IT EXCITING?

GAK! THEA? WHAT'S SHE - **KOFF**- SAYING ABOUT ME?
ACK!
WHOA, TAKE IT EASY. THOSE SEVERED BIRD LIMBS HAVE BONES IN 'EM, Y'KNOW.

241

© 1996 BY ALISON BECHDEL

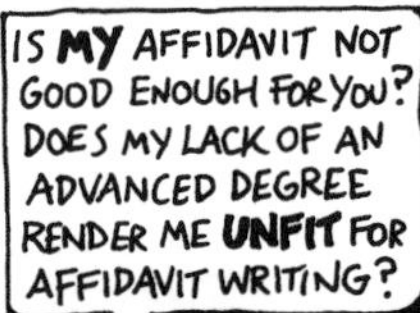

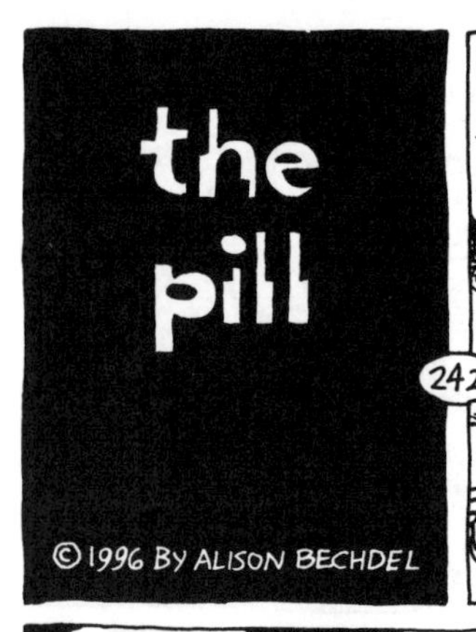

the pill
242
©1996 BY ALISON BECHDEL

MO, WHICH OF THESE MID-RANGE DILDOES DO YOU THINK WOULD SELL BETTER? THE ONE SHAPED LIKE A MANATEE, OR THE "BALLISTIC REALISTIC III"?
I'M SURE I DON'T KNOW.
DICKS FOR CHICKS WHOLESALE CATALOG

JEEZ, IT'S A FRICKIN' SAUNA IN HERE. FIRST JEZANNA JACKS UP OUR HEALTH INSURANCE, THEN SHE TURNS OFF THE A/C.
UH HUH.

HEY, GINGER HAD PROFESSOR SYDNEY OVER AGAIN LAST NIGHT. SHE ASKED ABOUT YOU.
OFFICE
REALLY.

Y'KNOW, I THINK SHE LIKES YOU.
DO I HEAR THE GUILELESS TONES OF GIRLISH GOSSIP?
OFFICE
SLAM!

SYDNEY'S GOT A THING FOR MO.
SYDNEY? I DIDN'T KNOW YOU WERE SEEING HER.
I'M NOT! I CAN'T STAND THAT POINTY-HEADED PRIMA DONNA. BESIDES, I'D NEVER GO OUT WITH ANYONE WHO DID WHATEVER IT WAS SHE DID TO YOU.

WHAT MAKES YOU THINK SHE EVER DID ANYTHING TO ME?
OH, GIVE IT UP, THEA! EVERYONE KNOWS YOU WERE LOVERS ONCE. AND YOU'RE SO EVASIVE ABOUT HER, IT'S NOT HARD TO GUESS SHE FUCKED YOU OVER.

YOU DON'T KNOW ANYTHING ABOUT IT, LOIS! GOD! GET A LIFE AND STAY OUT OF MINE!

GREAT. NOW THEA'S MAD AT ME TOO. YOU CAN FORM A CLUB.
I'M NOT MAD AT YOU.

MO, YOU'VE BEEN TREATING ME LIKE A JEHOVAH'S WITNESS ALL DAY! IS IT MY BREATH? WHAT?
I'M JUST CONFUSED. I GUESS I THOUGHT YOU AND I WERE CLOSER THAN IT TURNS OUT WE REALLY ARE.

WHAT ARE YOU TALKING ABOUT?

I FOUND THE PROZAC IN YOUR BACKPACK, LOIS. WHY DIDN'T YOU TELL ME?
WHAT WERE YOU DOING IN MY BACKPACK?

IT WAS AN ACCIDENT. HOW LONG HAVE YOU BEEN TAKING THAT STUFF? I JUST DON'T UNDERSTAND WHY YOU WOULDN'T TELL ME!
OH NO? TAKE A WILD GUESS!

BECAUSE YOU'RE ASHAMED OF BUYING INTO AN INSIDIOUS CORPORATE PLOT TO TURN US ALL INTO NUMBED-OUT EMOTIONAL ZOMBIES?!
NO! BECAUSE I DIDN'T WANT TO LISTEN TO THIS BULLSHIT!

TALK ABOUT EMOTIONAL ZOMBIES! YOU HAVE ALL THE SENSITIVITY OF A... OF A BALLISTIC REALISTIC III!

non compos mentis
©1996 BY ALISON BECHDEL
243
BZZT!
¡MIERDA! SHE'S EARLY!
CLUNK!
TONI, RELAX! I'LL GET THE DOOR. YOU BETTER GET HIM IN B-E-D FAST SO THE D-O-G DOESN'T WIG HIM OUT.
EVERYONE POOPS

HEY! HOW'RE MY FAVORITE PETITIONERS TO ADOPT?
IS THAT PASTA SALAD?
HI, ALEXIS. HI, BRUCE.

SHORTLY...
TONI! PULL UP A CHAIR!

SO WHAT'S THE NEWS, ALEXIS?
EVERYTHING'S GOING VERY WELL. THERE IS THIS ONE SMALL MATTER OF YOUR CRIMINAL RECORD, THOUGH, CLARICE.
WHAT?

MARCH 2, 1981. DISORDERLY PERSON. JUNE 3, 1981. CRIMINAL TRESPASS. JULY 19,...
OH, THOSE ARE ALL CIVIL DISOBEDIENCE ACTIONS. THEY DON'T COUNT, DO THEY?

WHO KNOWS? YOU'LL HAVE TO PROVIDE A WRITTEN EXPLANATION TO THE JUDGE. OH, DID I MENTION JUDGE BOOKER DENIED OUR MOTION TO WAIVE THE HOME STUDY?
BOOKER? SHE'S A CONSERVATIVE GORGON! YOU TOLD ME WE HAD JUDGE FAIRCHILD!

THERE WAS A SCHEDULING ERROR. DIDN'T I CALL YOU?
OH, NO! I THOUGHT WE'D HAVE EVERYTHING SETTLED BY THE TIME MY PARENTS CAME TO VISIT! THIS IS TURNING INTO A NIGHTMARE!
TONI, TRUST ME. YOUR FOLKS AREN'T GONNA ABSCOND WITH RAFFI. YOU'VE BEEN WATCHING TOO MANY MOVIES OF THE WEEK.

LISTEN, THE HOME STUDY WILL BE A SNAP. THEY'LL LOOK AROUND, ASK A FEW QUESTIONS. YOU CAN EVEN HIRE A LESBIAN SOCIAL WORKER, IF YOU CAN FIND ONE.
UH... I DIDN'T KNOW THERE WAS ANY OTHER KIND.

WUF.
'SCUSE US A MINUTE. BRUCE HAS TO TAKE A DUMP.

CLARICE! THIS WOMAN'S AN IDIOT! GET RID OF HER!
HONEY, SHE'S AN OLD FRIEND. I CAN'T FIRE HER! IT'LL BE OKAY. SHE'S JUST A LITTLE QUIRKY, IS ALL.

POOR BRUCIE! DID THAT PASTA SALAD GIVE YOU THE SQUIRTS? I'LL HAVE TO TELL CLARICE AND TONI TO HOLD THE RAW ONIONS NEXT TIME.
OH, BRUCE! NOT IN THE HERB GARDEN!
THUNK

in
LOCO
parentis
245
©1996 BY ALISON BECHDEL

I'M SO NERVOUS! I WISH WE'D BEEN ABLE TO FINALIZE THE ADOPTION BEFORE THEY GOT HERE.
HON, YOUR PARENTS LOVE YOU. I'M THE ONE WHO SHOULD BE WORRIED. AFTER ALL, I'M THE WANTON SHE-DEVIL WHO PERFORMS UNSPEAKABLE ACTS WITH THEIR DAUGHTER.
Gate 29
HOWEVER INFREQUENTLY.

ALL TOO SOON...
PAPÁ! MAMÁ!
¡AY! THERE HE IS!
¡VEN PARA ACÁ, RAFAEL! GIVE UN BESO GRANDE TO YOUR ABUELA!
26

I THOUGHT WE'D GO BY THE MOTEL FIRST SO YOU CAN CHECK IN, THEN WE'LL ALL GO BACK TO OUR PLACE TO EAT.
OH, NO! LET'S GO TO A RESTAURANT. WE DON'T WANT TO... TO IMPOSE ON YOU.

MAMÁ, WHAT'S THE POINT OF FLYING TWO THOUSAND MILES IF YOU WON'T COME TO OUR HOUSE? I HAVE A MEAL ALL PREPARED.
¡E'TA BIEN! I DON'T WANT A FIGHT!
Hertz

OVER THE ARROZ CON TOFU...
GO ON, JORGE!
HRRM! ANTONIA, WE HAVE SOMETHING TO TELL YOU.

WE HAVEN'T COME ALL THIS WAY JUST TO VISIT. WE WANT YOU TO KNOW THAT WE CANNOT CONDONE YOUR LIFESTYLE, AND WE'RE HOPING TO PERSUADE YOU TO COME HOME WITH US SO RAFAEL CAN GROW UP IN A REAL FAMILY.
MORE DOOS PEEZ.

WHOA! MR. ORTIZ, EXCUSE ME, BUT YOU ARE WAY OUTTA LINE HERE!
CLARICE, THIS IS NOT ABOUT YOU. IT'S JUST NOT RIGHT TO BRING A YOUNG BOY UP IN THIS TYPE OF SITUATION.
RAFFI, COME HERE, SWEETHEART! TIME FOR BED. ¡PRONTO!

HOW DARE YOU?! DON'T YOU TELL ME WHAT KIND OF "SITUATION" IS RIGHT FOR MY CHILD!
YOUR CHILD? WHAT MAKES HIM YOURS, I'D LIKE TO KNOW?

BZZZT!

HI THERE! I'M GWYNNE, FROM SYNERGY ADOPTION SERVICES. I'M HERE FOR THE HOME STUDY!
WHAT? OUR APPOINTMENT WAS FOR NEXT TUESDAY!

OH, NO. COULDN'T BE! I'LL BE IN PROVINCETOWN NEXT WEEK. THIS IS THE ONLY TIME I HAVE TILL AFTER LABOR DAY. IS NOW A PROBLEM?
UH... WELL, ACTUALLY, TONI'S FOLKS JUST FLEW IN FROM PUERTO RICO, AND WE'RE IN THE MIDDLE OF DINNER...

THAT'S PERFECT! SUPPORTIVE GRANDPARENTS ARE A BIG PLUS IN THESE CASES. DON'T MIND ME. I'LL WAIT TILL YOU'RE DONE EATING.
BARGE!

the Converts

246

CLARICE AND TONI'S ADOPTION CASEWORKER HAS SHOWN UP AT A RATHER INOPPORTUNE JUNCTURE.

A TIP O' LA PLUMA TO MARIO VILLALOBOS!

* MOM, DAD... GWYNNE IS... FROM THE **CHURCH**! YEAH! AND SHE'S HERE TO TALK ABOUT, UH... RAFAEL'S **CHRISTENING**! WE'VE DECIDED TO GET HIM BAPTIZED!

The Line
247
©1996 BY ALISON BECHDEL

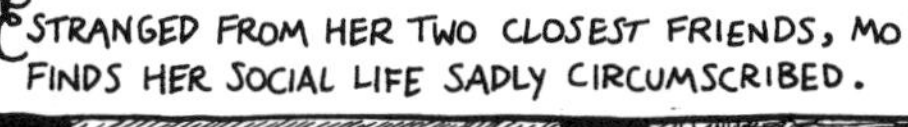
ESTRANGED FROM HER TWO CLOSEST FRIENDS, MO FINDS HER SOCIAL LIFE SADLY CIRCUMSCRIBED.

THE 7 HABITS OF HIGHLY EFFECTIVE PEOPLE

AMAZING! THAT RESOLUTE GAZE, THAT FIRMLY SET JAW! YOU LOOK LESS INEFFECTUAL ALREADY!
HELLO, SYDNEY.
7 HABITS OF BALD MOTIVATIONAL SPEAKERS

DO YOU KNOW WHY PEOPLE READ SELF-IMPROVEMENT BOOKS?
OH, RAPTURE! YOU'RE GOING TO TELL ME.
7 HABITS OF HIGHLY ANAL

BECAUSE THEY CAN'T ACCEPT THAT REAL CHANGE IS FUTILE! HOPELESS! NON POSSUMUS! READ ALL THE BOOKS YOU WANT, YOU'LL STILL BE THE SAME WEAK-WILLED WRETCH TILL THE DAY YOU DIE!
HEY!

WHAT A SCAM. I SHOULD WRITE ONE OF THESE THINGS.
YEAH. "HOW TO LOSE FRIENDS AND ANTAGONIZE PEOPLE."
FLIP

FROM WHAT MY SOURCES TELL ME, THAT'S YOUR BEAT.
WHAT DO YOUR "SOURCES" TELL YOU?

OH, JUST THAT NEITHER LOIS NOR YOUR FRIEND CLARICE IS SPEAKING TO YOU BECAUSE YOU'RE SUCH A RIGID, SELF-RIGHTEOUS PRIG.
IS THAT RIGHT? WELL IF I HAD A SUPERIORITY COMPLEX THE SIZE OF YOURS, I WOULDN'T THROW STONES.

SOUNDS LIKE MY SOURCES WERE RIGHT.
SYDNEY, IF YOU DON'T LIKE MY PERSONALITY, FEEL FREE TO GO PESTER SOMEONE ELSE.

BUT THAT'S JUST IT! I DO LIKE YOUR PERSONALITY, MO! I ADMIRE YOU FOR PUTTING PRINCIPLES BEFORE PEOPLE-PLEASING.
WELL! AS LONG AS YOU ADMIRE ME, WHAT DO I NEED WITH FRIENDS?

SEE? YOU'RE CRUSTY. THAT'S GOOD. BUT I BET PEOPLE MISUNDERSTAND YOU A LOT.
WELL...

YOU DON'T NEED TO BECOME A BETTER PERSON, MO. YOU'RE PERFECT JUST THE WAY YOU ARE!
THANKS, SYDNEY, BUT YOU MAKE A REALLY GHOULISH MISTER RODGERS.
HUH. HAS SHE ALWAYS HAD SUCH LONG FINGERS?

false moderation

248

THE FATEFUL VISIT DRAWS TO A CLOSE.

FINAL BOARDING FOR FLIGHT 1453...
WELL, THANKS AGAIN FOR THE CAR YOU BOUGHT RAFFI. AND, UH... FOR NOT PRESSURING ME ABOUT MOVING BACK TO SAN JUAN WITH HIM AFTER I SAID NO.
WE CAN'T FORCE YOU. IF YOU CHANGE YOUR MIND, YOU'RE ALWAYS WELCOME.
USAir

Ph. D. & Sympathy
250
©1996 BY ALISON BECHDEL

I'LL BE THE LEXUS LESBIAN WITH A FLAT TIRE, AND YOU BE THE SURLY BIKER WHO STOPS TO HELP.
GEE, I DUNNO, BABETTE. I'M KINDA TIRED.

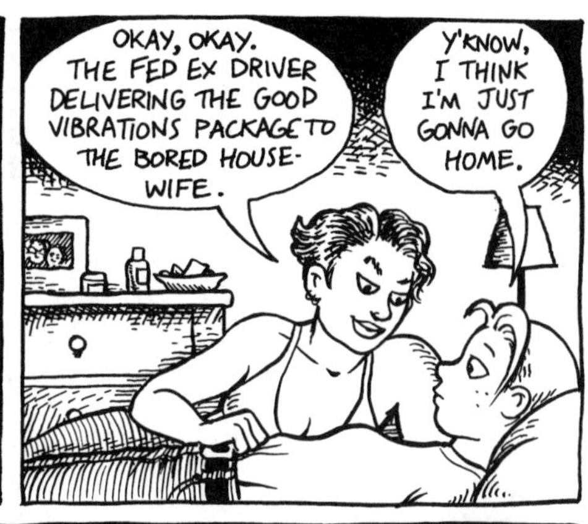
OKAY, OKAY. THE FED EX DRIVER DELIVERING THE GOOD VIBRATIONS PACKAGE TO THE BORED HOUSE-WIFE.
Y'KNOW, I THINK I'M JUST GONNA GO HOME.

MEANWHILE...
... SO THIS WOMAN'S HUS-BAND SHOWS UP AT THE SHEL-TER TODAY WITH A DOZEN ROSES AND A HUNTING RIFLE.
LONG-STEMMED?
TIP O' THE NIB TO PATTI McMANAMY

GINGER!
SPARROW, EVERY DAY YOU HAVE SOME NEW HORROR STORY! I CAN'T LET IT IN ANYMORE. HOW DO YOU DO THAT JOB?

WELL, WE CAN'T ALL SIT AROUND NOT WRITING OUR DISSERTATIONS.
KA-KLICK
WUF!

WE'VE GOTTA TALK TO HER.
YEAH. GENTLY, THOUGH, OR SHE'LL FREAK.
CLOMP CLOMP CLOMP

NOK NOK
LOIS? CAN WE COME IN?
DEPRES-SION IS A BUMMER

LOIS, IS THERE SOME-THING...
WHAT IS UP WITH YOU, GIRL? MO SAYS YOU'RE POPPING PROZAC! WHAT ARE YOU DEPRESSED ABOUT?
THAT WORM! SHE TOLD YOU? WITH A FRIEND LIKE MO, WHO WOULDN'T BE DEPRESSED?

IT WAS AN ACCIDENT. SHE THOUGHT WE KNEW.
YEAH. SO HOW COME WE DIDN'T?
OH, YOU GUYS HAVE ENOUGH TO WORRY ABOUT WITH YOUR CAREERS AND ALL. YOU DON'T NEED TO HEAR ABOUT MY PROBLEMS.

ARE YOU KIDDING? I'D MUCH RATHER HEAR ABOUT YOUR PROBLEMS THAN WORK ON MY DISSERTATION.
THANK YOU, GINGER. CONSIDERING YOU'D RATHER FELLATE BILL CLINTON THAN WORK ON YOUR DISSERTA-TION, THAT'S VERY GENEROUS.

DESPERATE MEASURES
©1996 BY ALISON BECHDEL

251
HONEY! I'M HOME!

HELLO, DARLING! LET ME GET YOU A MARTINI AND YOUR SLIPPERS.
MY, WHAT A HEAVY BEARD YOU'VE GROWN SINCE THIS MORNING, MOMMY!
KISS KISS
THAT'S NOT MOMMY! THAT'S CARLOS!

OH, SUGAR, I KNOW IT'S CARLOS! I WAS JUST BEING SILLY!
SOUNDS LIKE TIME FOR ANOTHER DEPOSIT INTO HIS THERAPY FUND.

WHERE'S TONI?
OUT FOR A WALK. SHE WAS ALL UPSET OVER SOMETHING HER MOM SENT IN THE MAIL.

JESUS CHRIST!
EXODUS INTERNATIONAL
FREEDOM FROM HOMOSEXUALITY IS POSSIBLE THROUGH THE POWER OF JESUS CHRIST

MEANWHILE...
OKAY. "GENDER, DEVIANCE, AND THE INFOMERCIAL" SHOULD BE IN ON THURSDAY. ANYTHING ELSE?
DINNER, MAYHAP?
MADWIMMIN BOOKS

OH, PLEASE! I CAN'T HAVE DINNER WITH YOU, SYDNEY!
WHY NOT? BECAUSE I'M A FLESH-EATER?

NO. BECAUSE YOU'RE ARROGANT, CONDESCENDING, AND COMPLETELY OB-NOXIOUS.
YET STRANGELY COMPELLING.

THAT WEASEL! DOES SHE HAVE TO DO HER FLIRTING WHERE I WORK?
FRANKLY, I DON'T SEE THE ATTRACTION. DOES SYDNEY HAVE SOME KIND OF ILL-DRESSED IDEOLOGUE FETISH?
TIP O' THE NIB TO FARAR ELLIOTT!

OH, COME ON! MO'S A CATCH. WELL... IN A REPRESSED, BUTCH BOTTOM KIND OF WAY. I'VE GOTTA WARN HER ABOUT SYDNEY!
DOES THIS MEAN WE'RE FINALLY GONNA FIND OUT WHAT SHE DID TO YOU?

IF THAT'S WHAT IT TAKES.
TILL FRIDAY, THEN.
CIAO, BELLA.

252

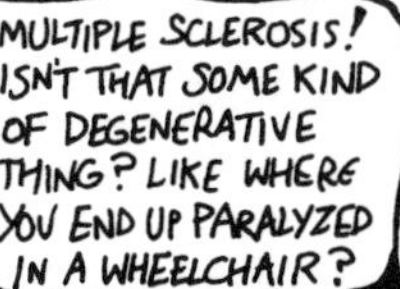

A TIP O' THE NIB TO LINNEA STENSON!

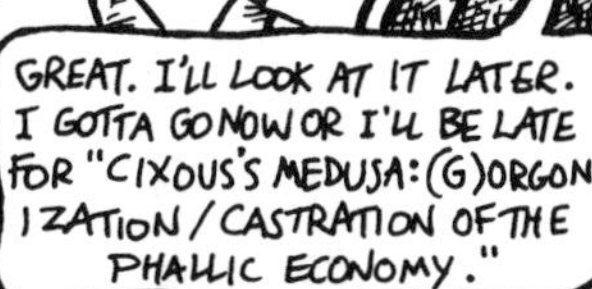

SHE DIDN'T COME HOME THAT NIGHT.

AT THE ANNUAL HOLIDAY CRAFT BAZAAR, OUR HEROINE IS EXHIBITING SOME BIZARRE AND CRAFTY BEHAVIOR.

the retraction
254
©1996 BY ALISON BECHDEL

AFTER WORK, MO BRINGS THE NEW INTERN UP TO SPEED.
I DON'T WANT TO DISILLUSION YOU, BUT THIS IS NOT A GLAMOROUS JOB. IT'LL BE A LOT OF GRUNT WORK. SHELVING BOOKS, KEEPING THEM DUSTED...
OMIGOD! HANDLING BOOKS? CARESSING THEIR SPINES, SMELLING THEIR NEW BOOK SMELL?! IT'LL BE LIKE, TOTALLY ORGIASTIC!
Closed
free THE WEEKLY WHINE

YEAH, RIGHT. SO, JEZANNA TELLS ME YOU'RE IN HIGH SCHOOL.
WHATEVER. MAINLY, I'M A POET. WANNA READ THE SESTINA I WROTE AT LUNCH?

IT'S CALLED "SUCK MY LEFT ONE, SLOBODAN MILOSEVIC."
UH...
THE HAIL MARYS
ANJI'S ZINE
MY LIFE EMMA GOLDMAN
KAMEL MENTHE

WELL HELLO THERE, MO! IS THIS WHY YOU LEFT ME THAT TERSE LITTLE MESSAGE CANCELLING OUR DINNER DATE? IF YOU DON'T MIND MY SAYING SO, YOU COULD BE HER MOTHER.
OH, LIKE THAT WOULD STOP YOU.
ACTUALLY, MY MOM'S MORE THE BUFFED AND COIFFED TYPE.

AND ANYWAY, IT'S NOT WHAT YOU THINK. SHE'S OUR NEW INTERN AT THE STORE. ANJALI, SYDNEY.

DE-LIGHTED.
SO, DO YOU WANT TO RESCHEDULE, OR DID YOU MEAN "FRY IN HELL" LITERALLY?
UH... I'M GONNA GO GRAB A SMOKE.
KAMEL

THEA JUST TOLD ME HOW YOU DITCHED HER WHEN SHE GOT DIAGNOSED WITH MS.
OH. UH... YOU DIDN'T ALREADY KNOW?

ARE YOU NUTS? DO YOU THINK I'D AGREE TO GO OUT WITH THE POND SCUM WHO'D DO A THING LIKE THAT?
UH...

"UH"? SURELY YOU CAN DO BETTER THAN THAT! WHERE'S YOUR SCATHING RIPOSTE? YOUR TWISTED INTELLECTUALIZATION?
I...

OH, JEEZ! DON'T CRY SYDNEY!

SHORTLY...
HONK.
ANJALI, I'M SORRY, BUT I HAVE TO GO TO DINNER. I'LL FINISH EXPLAINING THINGS TO YOU TOMORROW.
Open
'KAY, WHATEVER. SHOULD BE INTERESTING.

DATE by default
255
© 1996 BY ALISON BECHDEL

FOLLOWING SOME MILD MELODRAMA AT THE COFFEE SHOP, MO HAS PACIFICALLY AGREED TO DINE WITH SYDNEY.

ARE YOU OKAY? D'YOU WANT TO TALK ABOUT IT?
YEAH. JEEZ, I GUESS A GIRL HAS TO BREAK DOWN IN TEARS TO GET A DATE WITH YOU.

SYDNEY, IF THAT LITTLE OUTBURST WAS SOME KIND OF SCAM...
IT WASN'T! I WAS GENUINELY UPSET!
Pastafazool
Pasta
fazool

AND THIS IS NOT A DATE, OKAY? I JUST WANTED TO APOLOGIZE FOR HURTING YOU.

IT'S ODD. BEING CALLED POND SCUM NEVER BOTHERED ME BEFORE. BUT SOMEHOW, WHEN YOU SAID IT, IT REALLY GOT IN!
I SAID I WAS SORRY.

IN THAT INSTANT, YOU MADE ME REALLY UNDERSTAND WHAT A SHIT I'D BEEN TO THEA ALL THOSE YEARS AGO. YOU HAVE A CERTAIN MORAL AUTHORITY ABOUT YOU, MO. A KANTIAN CATEGORICAL IMPERATIVE KIND OF THING. VERY SEXY.

PASTA PUTANESCA...
...AND VERMICELLI WITH CHARD STEMS. DO EITHER OF YOU LADIES WANT SOME FR...
NO!

SYDNEY, I'M TRYING TO HAVE A SERIOUS DISCUSSION HERE. COULD YOU QUIT TEASING ME FOR A SECOND?
TEASING YOU IS A RARE PLEASURE, BUT AT THE MOMENT I'M PERFECTLY SERIOUS.

COMPLETELY?
MM-HMMM.
SLURP

HUH. Y'KNOW, YOU HAVE A RAKISH, DEBAUCHED SORT OF CHARM YOURSELF.
WATCH OUT. I MIGHT CORRUPT YOU.
HELLO, MO. HELLO, SYDNEY.
Menu

H-HI, THEA. MAXINE.

SHIT! I TOLD HER I WASN'T GONNA GO OUT WITH YOU.
LOOKS LIKE I'M HAVING A DELETERIOUS EFFECT ON YOUR MORALS ALREADY. SHALL WE KNOCK OVER A PASTRY SHOP FOR DESSERT?
URP.

Futures Trading

©1997 BY ALISON BECHDEL

256

the EX factor

GOD! YOU KNOW SO MUCH, YOU TELL ME! EXCEPT I HAVEN'T "TAKEN UP" WITH HER. THERE WAS FLIRTING, I ADMIT, BUT I DON'T REALLY TRUST HER.

metamorphosis
258
©1997 BY ALISON BECHDEL
SYDNEY APOLOGIZED TO YOU? WHAT'D YOU DO?
WELL, LET'S JUST SAY IT WASN'T A HALLMARK MOMENT.
OFFICE

SHE HAS A PAIR OF BALLS, WALTZING IN WITH AN "I'M SORRY" ALL THESE YEARS AFTER DEEP-SIXING YOU.

EXCUSE ME. A CUSTOMER NEEDS HELP WITH THE VIBRATOR ATTACHMENTS.
THANK YOU. I'LL TAKE CARE OF IT.
OFFICE

WHEN ARE YOU TWO GONNA STOP THIS ABSURD LITTLE FEUD?
WHENEVER SHE WANTS. SHE STARTED IT. WHO HAS A PAIR OF BALLS?

YOU SHOULD KNOW, FROM WHAT I SAW AT THE RESTAURANT THE OTHER NIGHT.
SYDNEY? LISTEN, THEA. THAT WASN'T WHAT IT LOOKED LIKE.

OH, MO. I KNOW WHAT IT WAS. LOOK, DON'T FEEL LIKE YOU HAVE TO PROTECT MY FEELINGS. SYDNEY CAN BE VERY CHARMING, AS I RECALL.
BUT... BUT SHE WAS SO CRUEL TO YOU.

YEAH, WELL WHO KNOWS. MAYBE SHE'S CHANGED. SHE ACTUALLY APOLOGIZED TO ME LAST NIGHT.
SHE DID? SO... DID YOU MAKE UP?

NO! SHE'S A JERK! I'M JUST SAYING, DON'T TAKE MY WORD FOR IT. FIND OUT FOR YOURSELF.
REALLY?

WHAT DO YOU WANT, MY BLESSING? KNOCK YOURSELF OUT.

THANKS. ENJOY IT.
ACTUALLY, IT'S FOR MY MOTHER, BUT I'M SURE SHE WILL.

UH... LOIS? CAN I ASK YOU A QUESTION?
BESIDES THAT ONE?
BODY ALCHEMY: TRANSSEXUAL PORTRAITS

DO... DO YOU BELIEVE PEOPLE CAN REALLY CHANGE?
WELL, OF COURSE! SOME HORMONES, SOME SURGERY... WHY? ARE YOU CONSIDERING IT?

NO, I MEAN LIKE, ESSENTIALLY. SAY A PERSON USED TO BE A JERK. D'YOU THINK THEY CAN EVER BECOME A PERSON WHO'S NOT A JERK?

AW, MO! YOU WEREN'T THAT MUCH OF A JERK! DON'T WORRY, I FORGIVE YOU! I KNEW YOU'D COME AROUND EVENTUALLY.

overbooked
260
©1997 BY ALISON BECHDEL
SO MO, ARE YOU GONNA GIVE IT UP FOR SYDNEY TOMORROW NIGHT?
NOW THAT WE'RE FRIENDS AGAIN, LOIS, I CAN ANSWER THAT HONESTLY. **GET STUFFED.**
OFFICE

BUT JEZANNA, A MADWIMMIN WEB SITE WOULD BE THE **BOMB!**
THAT'S EXACTLY WHAT I'M AFRAID OF. LISTEN, I HAVE **ZERO** MONEY TO DO ANYTHING EXTRA RIGHT NOW.

YOU COULD PUT IT UP FOR TWENTY BUCKS A MONTH! I CAN GET YOU A DEAL AT MY FRIEND'S ISP!
HEY, JEZ. D'YOU MIND IF I LEAVE A LITTLE EARLY? I HAFTA GET THESE VIDEOS BACK BY SIX.
GO AHEAD! RETURN YOUR VIDEOS! LAUNCH A WEB SITE! AND I WONDER WHY I'M NOT SELLING ANY @#*☹! BOOKS.
A TIP O' THE NIB TO MY FAVORITE GEEK, CARYL SHAW

UH... SEE YOU TOMORROW, THEN.
I ALREADY DID A MOCK-UP! LEMME SHOW YOU!

SOON...
VIDEO
NO ESCAPE

UM... HI, CLARICE.
MO!
THE LION KING
THE LION KING
THE LION KING

JEEZ, IT'S BEEN A WHILE. UH... HOW'S THE ADOPTION COMING?
OKAY. OUR HEARING IS ON MONDAY.
CINDERELLA
THE LITTLE MERMAID
TRIUMPH OF THE WILL

HOW'S RAFFI? GOD, I MISS HIM.
NO ONE'S FORCING YOU TO STAY AWAY, YOU KNOW.
101 DALMATIANS
HAYLEY MILLS
BEAUTY & THE BEAST

LOOK, I'M SORRY. I KNOW I'VE BEEN A PILL LATELY.
A LITTLE.

BUT NOBODY'S PERFECT, RIGHT? AND JUST BECAUSE YOU'RE A TOTAL YUPPIE ASSIMILATIONIST DOESN'T MEAN I DON'T STILL, YOU KNOW, **LOVE** YOU.

...SO IF YOU EVER NEED A SITTER OR ANYTHING, CALL ME, OKAY?
REALLY?

AS A MATTER OF FACT, WE HAVE TO GO TO THIS BIG AWARDS DINNER TOMORROW NIGHT, AND CARLOS JUST CANCELLED ON US.
SAY NO MORE! I'LL BE THERE!
OLD YELLER
FAMILY

THANKS SO MUCH, MO! SEE YOU TOMORROW AT SIX.
SO I'LL COME BY AROUND SIX!
VIDEO
MI VIDA LOCA

Pierce the Veil
261
©1997 BY ALISON BECHDEL
NICE TO MEET YOU, SYDNEY. IT WAS SO SWEET OF YOU TWO TO CANCEL YOUR DATE AND HELP US OUT.
NOT A PROBLEM. WHAT A GORGEOUS DRESS!
SO WHAT'S THIS FANCY SHINDIG YOU'RE OFF TO?
OH, IT'S ONLY THE COMMUNITY CENTER'S ANNUAL FUNDRAISING DINNER.
AND CLARICE IS ONLY RECEIVING THE NEW LEADERSHIP AWARD.
WELL CONGRATULATIONS, CLARICE! THE ABILITY TO TRULY LEAD IS A RARE GIFT.
WHY THANKS!

HERE HE IS! HI, RAFFI! HOW BIG YOU ARE! REMEMBER ME?
UH...HE SEEMS TO BE GOING THROUGH A SHY PHASE.

SO RAFFI, WHERE ARE THE TOYS?

NOT BAD, MO.
SHE SEEMS LIKE A REAL CATCH. BEHAVE YOURSELVES, OKAY?

SOON...
WATCH OUT! PRINCESS LEIA'S PACKING AN IMPERIAL BLASTER, AND SHE'S PREMENSTRUAL!
SHRIEK!
The Nation

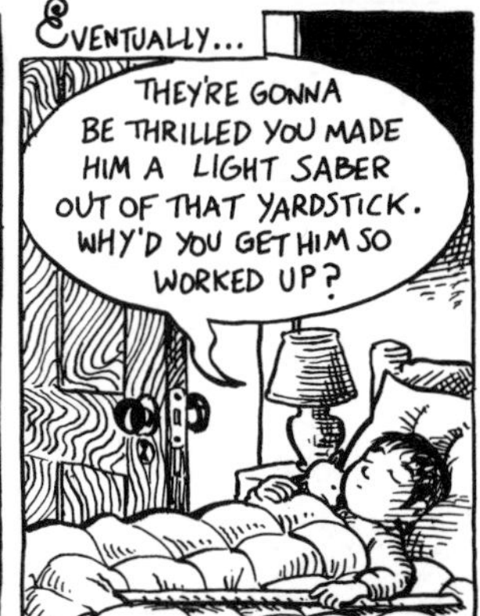
EVENTUALLY...
THEY'RE GONNA BE THRILLED YOU MADE HIM A LIGHT SABER OUT OF THAT YARDSTICK. WHY'D YOU GET HIM SO WORKED UP?
A TIP O' THE SABER TO BEN LASHMAN-VAN BUREN

SO HE'D CRASH! NOW WE HAVE THE WHOLE EVENING TO OURSELVES.
UH...SAY, KATHA POLLITT'S COLUMN THIS WEEK IS ABSOLUTELY WITHERING.
The Nation
THE CORPORATIZATION OF MACRAMÉ

I'M SURE IT IS. I'D REALLY LIKE TO KISS YOU NOW.
UH... JEEZ, SYDNEY.

WHAT? IS IT MY FEMME AGGRESSIVENESS? DO I INTIMIDATE YOU?
NO! IT'S JUST... YOU'RE TRYING SO HARD! YOU'VE BEEN TRYING HARD ALL NIGHT.

YOU'RE NERVOUS! AREN'T YOU?

I AM NOT! I JUST TEND TO BE SOMEWHAT HIGH STRUNG!
Y'KNOW, YOU'RE SORT OF ADORABLE WHEN YOU BREAK OUT IN A FLOP SWEAT.

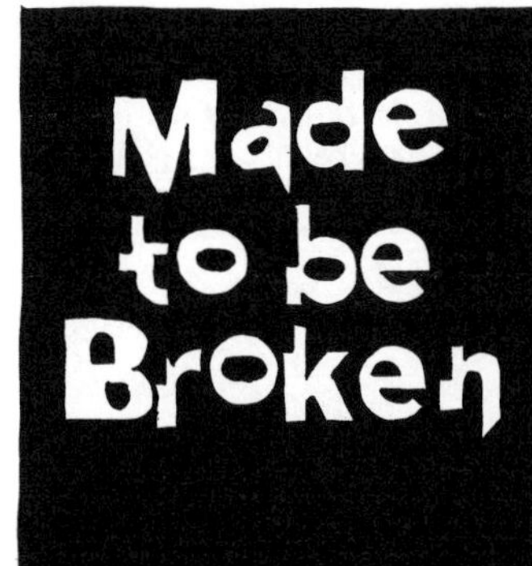
Made to be Broken
©1997 BY ALISON BECHDEL
262

I HOPE WE DIDN'T USE UP ALL OUR LUCK ON THIS PARKING SPACE.
RAFFI, LET'S LEAVE YOUR LIGHT SABER IN THE CAR, OKAY?
NO!
COURTHOUSE
U.S. MAI

LET HIM BRING IT, TONE. IT'LL KEEP HIM QUIET.
NO WANOO BE QUIET.
OH MY GOD! I SWEAR, CLARICE. THIS IS THE LAST STRAW!
TOO GOOD TO BE LEGAL

CLARICE! TONI! WHY ARE YOU HERE SO EARLY? I KNOW YOU'RE ANXIOUS ABOUT THE ADOPTION, BUT...
ALEXIS! IT'S FIVE OF NINE! WHY ARE YOU OUT JOGGING?!
TOO GOOD TO BE LEGAL

FIVE OF NINE? WHOA! GUESS I FORGOT TO SET MY WATCH AHEAD FOR DAYLIGHT SAVINGS! SO THAT'S WHY THE ELEVEN O'CLOCK NEWS WAS ON AT TEN LAST NIGHT!
WILL YOU GO HOME AND CHANGE? THE JUDGE IS WAITING!
TOO GOOD

I KNEW SHE WAS GONNA SCREW THIS UP.
RAFFI! IF YOU CAN'T SIT QUIETLY I'M GONNA TAKE THAT FROM YOU!
WHAP! WHAP!

THE FIRST CASE WILL BE IN RE: R.C. THE JUDGE IS READY FOR YOU IN HER CHAMBERS.

HI, DENNIS. UM... OUR LAWYER HAS HAD A SLIGHT DELAY... SHE'LL BE HERE ANY MINUTE NOW.
IN FIVE, OR YOU'LL HAVE TO RESCHEDULE. JUDGE BOOKER'S POLICY.
STACK STACK

I WONDER IF JUDGE BOOKER KNOWS HER CLERK IS TREASURER OF THE LOCAL LOG CABIN CHAPTER.
IF WE RESCHEDULE, COULD WE GET JUDGE FAIRCHILD? C'MON, LET'S GET OUTTA HERE BEFORE THAT FRUITCAKE GETS BACK!
I'M HERE! I SKIPPED THE SHOWER!

MORNING, YOUR HONOR! MAY I PRESENT CLARICE CLIFFORD, ANTONIA ORTIZ, AND RAFAEL CLIFFORD-ORTIZ.
HOW DO YOU DO. PLEASE SIT DOWN. MY, WHAT AN INTERESTING BLOUSE, COUNSELOR.
TOO GOOD TO BE LEGAL

WELL, LADIES. I'VE REVIEWED YOUR FILE. AS I'M SURE YOU KNOW, I TEND TO BE RATHER A TRADITIONALIST WHEN IT COMES TO FAMILY LAW...
RAFFI! GIVE MOMMY THE-

NO!
CRASH!

Moment of Truth
©1997 By Alison Bechdel
263

Judge Booker is surprisingly calm following Raffi's demolition of her Tiffany lamp.
Well, boys will be boys, will they not?
Heh heh. Isn't that the truth, your honor? Why, just the other day my dog Bruce...
Clink!
Too good to be legal

Therefore, considering that a clear legal precedent has been established...

...And that your son seems perfectly normal and healthy, I can find no legitimate reason to deny this adoption.
Too good to be legal

That night at the party...
Mo, you can tell Sydney we forgive her for turning our sweet little angel into a saber-wielding commando. That ole Phyllis Schlafly clone ate it up.
Speaking of Sydney, what's going on with you two?
Congratulations!

Yeah! What happened after you two babysat for us Saturday night?
Have you done it yet?

I bet not. I bet Sydney took her home and read lurid post-modern essays on the ontology of the dildo to her until they both saw God.

Hey, girls! I hate to tear myself away from your state-sanctioned two-parent household, but I have to get back to my dissertation.

Ginger, that's great! So you're finally doing it!

Yeah. Unlike you and Sydney. She says you discussed your mutual attraction till 5 A.M. the other night, then you sent her home! What're you waiting for?

God! What is **with** you people?! I never **met** such a bunch of vicarious thrillseekers! You'd think you didn't have sex lives of your own!

Where'd that jacket get to?
Say, are there any more of these kelp balls left?
I'll go check!
Jezanna! So glad you could make it!

let the lover beware

©1997 BY ALISON BECHDEL

265

MO'S HAVING A COFFEE BREAK WITH EVERYBODY'S FAVORITE CONFIDANTE.

IT'S THE BEST SEX I EVER HAD.

NOT NECESSARILY A GLOWING TESTIMONIAL IN YOUR CASE. SO, HOW'D YOU LIKE THE "CYBORGASM"?

MEANWHILE, OVER AT THE UNIVERSITY...

HOW NICE TO KNOW THIS DELIGHTFUL STRESS WON'T END AFTER I DEFEND MY DISSERTATION NEXT WEEK.

Dole PESTICIDES FOR THE THIRD WORLD

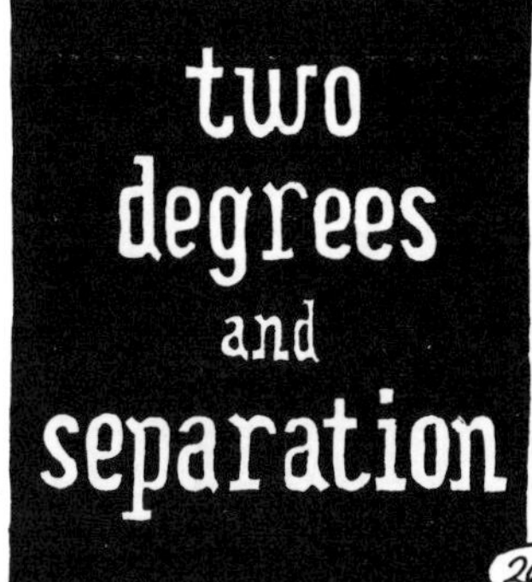
two degrees and separation
266
©1997 BY ALISON BECHDEL

Conventional
Organic
HEY, SPARROW. AM I INTERRUPTING A PRIVATE MOMENT WITH THOSE PEACHES?
89¢

OH, HI, MO. HEY, I LEFT A MESSAGE FOR YOU. I KNOW IT'S TOTALLY LAST MINUTE, BUT WE'RE HAVING A LITTLE DINNER TONIGHT TO CELEBRATE GINGER GETTING HER PH.D. CAN YOU COME?
JEEZ, I'D LOVE TO, BUT SYDNEY'S COMING OVER. I'M MAKING CURRIED ARTICHOKE AND MUNG BEAN GUMBO. IT'S SUPPOSED TO BE SOME KINDA **APHRODISIAC**. NOT THAT WE NEED ANY HELP.
1.39
PEARS
$6.98

OH, OKAY. MAYBE SOME OTHER TIME.
YEAH. ARE YOU OKAY? YOU LOOK KINDA TIRED.
DRIED STUFF on sale

OH. UH... THINGS ARE REALLY HARD AT THE SHELTER. WE JUST LOST HALF OUR FEDERAL FUNDING, AND WE'VE GOT MORE WOMEN THAN EVER WHO NEED HELP.
SPARROW, IF YOU'RE GONNA STAND HERE YAKKING, GIVE ME THE LIST.

UH... HI, JUNE.
THAT'S AWFUL! WHAT'RE YOU GONNA DO?
WELL, I HAVE THIS NEW PLAN. WHEN REPUBLICAN POLITICIANS FINISH A TERM IN OFFICE, THEY HAVE TO SPEND THE REST OF THEIR CAREERS PROVIDING DIRECT SOCIAL SERVICES. SORT OF AN INCENTIVE PROGRAM.

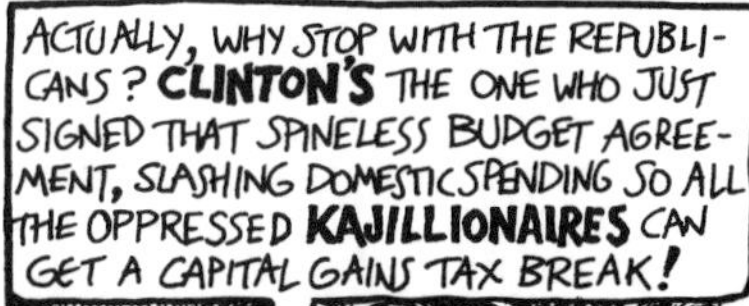

ACTUALLY, WHY STOP WITH THE REPUBLICANS? **CLINTON'S** THE ONE WHO JUST SIGNED THAT SPINELESS BUDGET AGREEMENT, SLASHING DOMESTIC SPENDING SO ALL THE OPPRESSED **KAJILLIONAIRES** CAN GET A CAPITAL GAINS TAX BREAK!
THREE SEVENTY-NINE FOR A LOAF OF BREAD! I TOLD YOU WE SHOULD'VE GONE TO SHOP 'N DROP!
THUNK!

AND THE THING IS, IT'S A **VICIOUS CIRCLE!** THE MORE MONEY BIG CORPORATIONS MAKE, THE MORE LEVERAGE THEY HAVE TO GET BUSINESS-FRIENDLY LAWS PASSED, LIKE "WORKFARE" BILLS THAT SUPPLY THEM WITH DIRT-CHEAP LABOR. **THEY'RE** RAKING IN MORE THAN EVER WHILE **OUR** TAXES GO UP AND REAL WAGES GO DOWN.
SPARROW, TAKE IT EASY! THOSE ARE ORGANIC!
SPLORT!

LATER...
FINE. MOVE AWAY IF YOU HAVE TO. BUT FOR **BUSINESS SCHOOL?**
GOD! WILL YOU STOP ACTING LIKE I'VE MADE A PACT WITH THE DEVIL? GETTING AN M.B.A. IS NOT A CRIME!

AT THE UNIVERSITY...
SYDNEY! EVERYONE FINALLY SIGNED OFF ON THIS THING! COME FILE IT WITH ME AND THEN WE'LL GO TO MY PLACE. SPARROW'S MAKING A CELEBRATION DINNER.
GREAT! MO AND I WERE GONNA DO SOMETHING, BUT I'LL CALL AND GET A RAIN CHECK.
SYDNEY
OWSKI

RING!

IT'S THE EVENT O' THE SEASON!
BLUE PARTY
267
©1997 BY ALISON BECHDEL

YOU'RE GOING TO GINGER'S PARTY? ...YEAH, I KNOW IT'S A BIG DEAL SHE FINALLY GOT HER DOCTORATE. I MEAN, I WAS INVITED TOO, BUT I TOLD SPARROW WE ALREADY HAD PLANS. I'M MAKING MY SPECIAL MUNG BEAN GUMBO!

WELL, WHY DON'T GINGER AND I PICK YOU UP? THAT WAY WE'LL SEE EACH OTHER AND GO TO THE PARTY! KILL TWO BIRDS WITH ONE STONE.
SUCH A ROMANTIC.
SHH!

MEANWHILE...

WHAT AM I SUPPOSED TO DO WHILE YOU'RE OFF IN BOSTON AT BUSINESS SCHOOL? SIT HOME KNITTING YOU POWER TIES?
WELL... I DUNNO. MAYBE WE SHOULD TAKE A BREAK, SEE OTHER PEOPLE FOR A WHILE.
CHOP CHOP!

WHAT?
IT'S A TWO YEAR PROGRAM. I DON'T EXPECT YOU TO JUST WAIT AROUND.
URF.
CLIK

HI! I PICKED UP THE CAKE. NEED HELP WITH DINNER?
SOB!
SWEETIE, I'M JUST THINKING OF YOU!

UH...I'LL GO PUT THIS ON A PLATE.
CAN'T WE DISCUSS THIS LIKE ADULTS? YOU ALWAYS GET SO EMOTIONAL!
I THINK YOU'D BETTER LEAVE RIGHT NOW!

JUNE! WHERE ARE YOU GOING?
BOSTON.

YOU'RE NOT STILL MAD, ARE YOU? I'LL EAT YOUR GUMBO LATER!
I DON'T THINK SO.
WHAT'S GOING ON IN HERE?
UH... THERE'S A SMALL PROBLEM WITH DINNER.

SNIFF! I'M SORRY, GINGER!
OH, SPARROW! DON'T WORRY ABOUT THE FOOD!

THE IMPORTANT THING IS SHARING THIS... UH... HAPPY MOMENT WITH ALL OF YOU!
BAW!

MAYBE FOR APPETIZERS WE SHOULD HAVE SOME OF THESE NEW ANTIDEPRESSANTS I'M TAKING.
"CONGRATULATIONS ON YOUR RETIREMENT?" LOIS, THIS ISN'T THE CAKE I ORDERED!
SHIK SHIK

the mythology of everyday life
270
©1997 BY ALISON BECHDEL

OUR HEROINE RETURNS HOME FROM HER LABORS.
YOU LOOK LIKE YOU'VE BEEN PARBOILED, SWEET-HEART.
HI, MEEMA.
UNH. OUR AIR CONDITIONER DIED, AND THE ONLY THING I HAD TIME TO EAT ALL DAY WAS A SNO-CONE.
OH, CLARICE. I HAVEN'T EVEN THOUGHT ABOUT DINNER YET! WE JUST GOT BACK FROM THE MOVIES.

HERCULES. IN DIGITAL STEREO AIR CONDITIONING.

HOW NICE FOR YOU. IN CASE YOU'RE WONDERING WHAT **I** DID TODAY, I WON AN INJUNCTION AGAINST A NITRIC ACID PLANT, THEN I FAILED TO PREVENT 300 ACRES OF WETLANDS FROM BEING TURNED INTO A **LANDFILL**, THEN MY CASE AGAINST A PESTICIDE COMPANY GOT **DISMISSED** ON PROCEDURAL GROUNDS.
MEEMA! IN DA MOVIE, HEWKUWEES, HE, HE, HE CUT OFF DA MONSTOW'S HEAD AN' DEN IT GWEW MOW HEADS!
THAI PLACE
PASTA HUT

IT GREW MORE HEADS? HUH. THINGS HAVEN'T CHANGED MUCH IN THREE MILLENNIA.
HEY, THAT BEER LOOKS GOOD.
OOPS.
SWEETIE, THAT WAS THE LAST ONE. HOW ABOUT SOME NICE, COLD APPLE JUICE?

OKAY. HERE'S A THOUGHT. MAYBE IF I GO OUT AND COME BACK IN, YOU'LL TELL ME YOU FOUND A **JOB** TODAY, THERE'LL BE SOMETHING TO **EAT**, AND STANLEY **KOWALSKI** HERE WILL BE GONE.
CLARICE, I'M SORRY YOU HAD A BAD DAY, BUT YOU DON'T NEED TO BE RUDE.
I SHOULD BE GOING ANYWAY. BLANCHE AND STELLA WILL BE WANTING THEIR DINNER.
PIZZA

AN' MEEMA, DERE WAS DIS GUY DEUCE.
DEUCE?
ZEUS, RAFFI.

YEAH. I WIKED HIM. HE HAD A BIG BEARD AN' HE WAS HEWKUWEESES FATHOW.

HIS FATHER?
YEAH. CAN I HAVE A FATHOW?
I AM DEFINITELY LEAVING. ENJOY THIS PRECIOUS FAMILY MOMENT.

UM... WELL, YOU SEE, RAFFI... WHEN MOMMY AND I DECIDED WE WANTED YOU, WE... UH... WENT TO A PLACE CALLED THE **SPERM BANK**...
CLARICE, RELAX! NO, RAFFI, YOU CAN'T HAVE A FATHER. YOU HAVE TWO MOTHERS.
SLAM!

DEN, CAN I HAVE A GIANT DOG WIF THWEE HEADS WIKE IN DA MOVIE?
A DOG? **OKAY!**
NICE WORK, COUNSELOR. ARE YOU THIS COOL-HEADED IN COURT?

OUR PREOCCUPIED PALS HAVE PACKED UP ALL THEIR CARES AND WOES AND BROUGHT THEM TO THE BEACH.

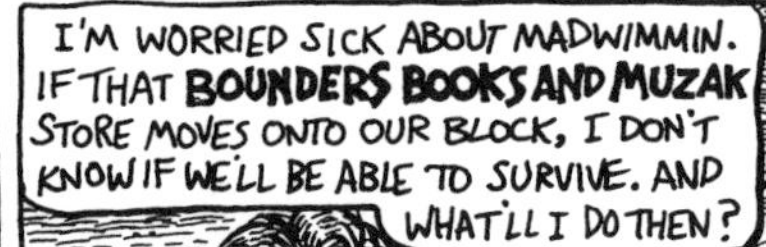

one day
©1997 BY ALISON BECHDEL
272
I'M BA-ACK!
HEY, STANLEY! WAY TO GO! TEAMSTERS RULE!
BOOKS
BOOKS
BOOKS
CELEBRITY BIOS
UPS

I'M TELLIN' YA, MO, **YOU** OTTA STAGE A WALKOUT. GET MAN-AGEMENT TO PAY YOU ENOUGH TO BUY ANOTHER SHIRT.
YEAH, YEAH. AT LEAST **MY** SHIRT'S NOT AN INDUSTRIAL SHADE OF GREEN-ISH BROWN.
UPS

MEANWHILE, IN THE BACK OFFICE...
MAD-WIMMIN BOOKS. CAN I HELP YOU?
JEZ, IF WE JUST RETURN A FEW DOZEN TITLES THAT AREN'T MOVING, WE CAN AFFORD A SHIPMENT OF COOL NEW VIBRATORS THAT ATTACH TO YOUR FINGER.

OH, OKAY. AND WHEN A CUSTO-MER COMES IN LOOKING FOR "STEPPE SISTERS: FEMALE HOMOEROTICISM DURING THE MONGOL EMPIRE," I'LL JUST SELL HER A **FIDGETY DIGIT** INSTEAD!
MONGOL STUDIES

ANYONE WHO'D WANT TO READ THAT ARID TOME NEEDS A VIBRATOR.
DAMMIT, LOIS! WE'RE NOT RETURNING ANY BOOKS! I DON'T CARE HOW DEAD BUSINESS IS!
JEZ, I THINK IT'S YOUR MOM ON LINE ONE.
OFFICE
THWUNK
STEPPE

MAMA?!

YOU'D BEST GET YOURSELF ON A PLANE, GIRL. I'M NOT LONG FOR THIS WORLD.
MAMA! WHAT'S GOING ON? DID SOMETHING HAPPEN? ARE YOU STILL AT HOME?
OXYGEN
ENSURE

HI, BABY. IT'S ME. SHE JUST NODDED OFF. THE PAIN WAS REALLY BAD THIS MORNING AND SHE NEEDED A LOT MORE MORPHINE.... HOW CLOSE IS SHE? I CAN'T PREDICT THAT, HON. BUT SHE WON'T TOUCH YOUR COUSIN ETTA'S POT ROAST, AND SHE REALLY WANTS TO SEE YOU.
XENA

MEANWHILE...
WHAT AM I WEAR-ING? YOU MEAN RIGHT NOW? A STRIPED SHIRT AND A PAIR OF JEANS. WHY?
MO!
BEST LESBIAN EROTICA OF AUG. 1997
CLEAVAGE PRESS

GOTTA GO, SYDNEY!
I'M CATCHING A 3:30 FLIGHT. MY MOTHER'S WORSE. I'LL CALL EVERY DAY TO CHECK IN. TRY NOT TO BANKRUPT US, OKAY?

UH...**RIGHT**. HEY, JEZ...I HOPE SHE'LL BE...YOU KNOW, OKAY.
UM... TAKE CARE.

Change to Spare
©1997 BY ALISON BECHDEL
273
YES, I'M SURE! I NEED A CHANGE! MY LIFE IS TOTALLY STALLED.
I DUNNO IF THIS WILL CHANGE YOUR LIFE. BUT I WISH YOU AND JUNE HAD BROKEN UP YEARS AGO IF THAT'S WHAT IT TOOK TO MAKE YOU CHANGE THIS WASHED-UP 'DO.

The Chop Shop

OH, REALLY. SPEAKING OF WASHED-UP, I HEAR YOU'RE NOT HAVING MUCH LUCK SELLING YOUR SECOND BOOK.
HEY, I CAN'T HELP IT IF ALL PUBLISHERS WANT IS "BILLY GRAHAM'S FAVORITE LOW-FAT CHICKEN SOUP FOR THE SPIRIT RECIPES."
VITA SINE LITTERIS MORS EST
GEL

LATER...
GRRR!
DIGGER, RELAX! IT'S ONLY ME.

...AND CYNTHIA COOPER GETS INSIDE FOR TWO!
SNIFF SNIFF
GO, COOP!

GINGER! WHAT'S BURNING?
AAA!
...CHARLOTTE LEADS HOUSTON 54-39. YOU'RE WATCHING THE WNBA ON NBC.

SPARROW, I DIDN'T RECOGNIZE YOU!
IT'S COMING FROM UPSTAIRS. COULD YOU PLEASE TURN THE TV DOWN?
RING!
TWICE AS MANY WOMEN SAY O.B.'S APPLICATOR IS MORE COMFORTABLE TO INSERT THAN TAMPAX!

BAM! BAM! BAM!
LOIS! WHAT'S THAT SMELL?
SHIT!
SKREEK!
IT'S OKAY! I'VE GOT THE WINDOW OPEN!

A CIGAR? OH, THIS IS THE LAST STRAW!
HEY, NICE HAIRCUT! HOW ABOUT YOU AND I PASSING OUT ON THE VERANDA? OR WOULD YOU RATHER PASS OUT HERE?

WILL YOU PUT THAT OUT! I HAVE HAD IT WITH YOU AND YOUR ARRESTED DEVELOPMENT!
WHY THANK YOU! I LIKE TO THINK MY DEVELOPMENT IS ARRESTING.
STOMP STOMP

GOD! I AM TOO OLD TO BE LIVING IN A SWINGING BACHELOR PAD!
YEAH, WELL, YOU MIGHT NOT HAVE TO MUCH LONGER.
CLUNK!

THAT WAS THE LANDLORD. HE'S PUTTING THE HOUSE ON THE MARKET.

all for one
274
©1997 BY ALISON BECHDEL
THE FIRST PROSPECTIVE BUYERS HAVE JUST FINISHED TOURING OUR HAPLESS HOUSEMATES' HOME.
I DON'T KNOW... IT'S NOT THE GREATEST NEIGHBORHOOD.
BUT THE PRICE IS RIGHT. AND ONCE WE FIXED THE PLACE UP, IT'D REALLY IMPROVE THE WHOLE BLOCK.
THANKS, HON. WE'LL TRY AND GIVE YOU MORE NOTICE NEXT TIME.
YOU DO THAT.
I BET THE WIFE HYPHENATES THEIR LAST NAMES AND THE HUSBAND JUST USES HIS OWN.
NICE TOUCH, LOIS, THE DILDOS ALL TUCKED UNDER YOUR COVERS LIKE THEY WERE GOING TO SLEEP. I'D SWEAR BRAD AND JANET BLANCHED, IF THEY WEREN'T SO COLORLESS TO BEGIN WITH.
I CAN'T LIVE LIKE THIS! STRANGERS TRAIPSING THROUGH THE HOUSE, NOT KNOWING WHERE WE'LL BE IN TWO MONTHS... WE'VE GOTTA DO SOMETHING!
MAYBE ANOTHER LANDLORD'LL BUY THE PLACE AND WE WON'T HAVE TO DO ANYTHING.
MORE LIKELY, MS. MINIVAN-HYPHEN WILL BE MOVING IN WITH HER LAURA ASHLEY TOILET PAPER.
EVEN IF ANOTHER LANDLORD BUYS THE PLACE, HE COULD BE A CREEP, OR JACK UP THE RENT, OR SUBDIVIDE. LET'S FACE IT. IT'S TIME TO MOVE ON.
MOVE ON TOGETHER? OR MOVE ON APART?
LOOK, LIVING COOPERATIVELY IS A GREAT THEORY, BUT THE ACTUALITY'S REALLY WEARING ON ME. I NEED TO COME HOME TO A CALM ENVIRONMENT. NO BARKING, OR TV, OR SCREAMING FROM OTHER PEOPLE'S BEDROOMS.
YEAH, WELL... IT WOULD CERTAINLY BE A RELIEF TO CONDUCT MY PERSONAL LIFE FREE FROM OTHER PEOPLE'S SCRUTINY.
MMM. AND WHAT I'D GIVE TO FIND THE GARLIC PRESS OR THE REMOTE EXACTLY WHERE IT'S SUPPOSED TO BE.
"PACHELBEL BY THE SEA"
NEGATIVE IONS
PEACE.
SHELVED IN LIBRARY OF CONGRESS ORDER
BURLED WALNUT REMOTE RACK
ORGANIZATION.
RETRO LOUNGE COMPILATION
BABALU!
THINKS A LEFTIST IS A SOUTHPAW FISTER
FREEDOM.
LIVING ALONE CAN BE VERY GROWTHFUL.
UNGRAMMATICAL, BUT NO DOUBT TRUE.
YEAH. I'M FEELING EXCITED ALREADY.

handling it
275
©1997 BY ALISON BECHDEL

IT'S BEEN A LONG DAY AT THE HELM FOR OUR HEROINE...
MO, REMEMBER, I'LL BE OUT TOMORROW AND FRIDAY FOR ROSH HASHANAH.
MADWIMMIN BOOKS
SKREE
Closed

OH, RIGHT. DAMN! I'LL HAVE TO CANCEL MY CHIROPRACTOR APPOINTMENT.
DON'T GIVE ME ANY GRIEF. YOU HAD PLENTY OF WARNING. NOT THAT YOU SHOULD NEED IT.

I KNOW, I KNOW. IT'S FINE. HAPPY NEW YEAR.
THANKS.
SHANAH TOVAH, BABE.

Y'KNOW, THERE'S NOT MUCH POINT IN GOING OUTSIDE TO SMOKE IF YOU'RE JUST GONNA STAND IN FRONT OF THE DOOR.

WHY ARE YOU SMOKING WITH HER, ANYWAY? YOU SHOULD BE SETTING AN EXAMPLE!
AND YOU! FOR ALL YOUR SOPHISTICATED POLITICAL ANALYSIS, YOU'RE PLAYING RIGHT INTO THE TOBACCO INDUSTRY'S HANDS! THE YOUNGER THEY HOOK YOU, THE BIGGER THEIR PROFITS!
Lilith Fair

DON'T YOU "WHATEVER" ME, YOU POSTMODERN PREPUBESCENT!

KEEPING UP MORALE, I SEE.
SYDNEY, HI! DIDN'T YOU GET MY MESSAGE? I CAN'T AFFORD TO GO OUT TONIGHT. I CAN'T EVEN FIGURE OUT HOW EVERYBODY'S GONNA GET PAID THIS WEEK.

MY TREAT! I SENT OFF MY MANUSCRIPT TODAY. LET'S CELEBRATE.
YOU ALWAYS TREAT. IT DOESN'T FEEL RIGHT.

WE CAN PRETEND I'M MARTHA STEWART AND YOU'RE MY POOL GIRL.

MEANWHILE...
THAT STORE OF YOURS... GONNA BE OKAY... WITHOUT YOU? DON'T WANT YOU... RUINING YOUR BUSINESS.
DON'T WORRY, MAMA. I LEFT THINGS IN VERY CAPABLE HANDS.

YOUR POOL GIRL? THAT'S SICK.
YOU DIDN'T SEEM TO THINK SO THE OTHER NIGHT.

OVER AT CLARICE & TONI'S...

MEANWHILE...

suburban subversion

277

THERE'S ONE.
LIT-TLE BOXES ON THE HILLSIDE...
WIDDOW BOXES...

CLARICE, YOU PROMISED TO BE OPEN-MINDED. IT'S NOT **THAT** FAR AWAY, AND THE SCHOOL IS EXCELLENT.
PWAY-GWOUND!

I WANNA PWAY.
LOOK, NO BROKEN GLASS OR GRAFFITI. IS THAT SO BAD?
OKAY. WHY DON'T WE HAVE A PICNIC? WE'LL GO PLAY AND YOU CAN GET SOME SANDWICHES OVER AT THAT DELI.

Salon
Folk Art Gallery
Deli

HI! NICE DAY!
MMM. YEAH.
WHAT'S THIS CHICK SELLING?

WHAT A CUTE LITTLE BOY! YOU MUST WORK FOR SOMEONE NEW. I HAVEN'T SEEN YOU HERE BEFORE.
EXCUSE ME?

I'LL GET YOU ONE TOMORROW. JENNIFER ALREADY THINKS I SPEND TOO MUCH MONEY. A LITTLE MORE WON'T HURT.

HEY, ONE OF MY CREDIT CARDS RAISED MY LIMIT ANOTHER THOU! LET'S GO CHECK OUT THE NEW SKI EQUIPMENT, TOO.

AND LET'S GO BY GIZMO WORLD. I NEED A NEW PERSONAL DIGITAL ASSISTANT.

GREAT!

YOU SHOULD BE GLAD YOU TWO CAN'T GET MARRIED. WHEN SHE CRASHES AND BURNS, YOU WON'T BE LIABLE FOR HER DEBT.

Meanwhile, Ginger is off jobhunting at the Modern Language Association convention.

the long goodbye
©1997 BY ALISON BECHDEL

279
ALBERTA! BRING ME SOME OF THAT PORK GOULASH YOU ALL HAD FOR DINNER.
UH...OKAY, MAMA!
HOME SWEET HOME
XENA

YOU KNOW, ALBERTA... I MEAN JEZANNA. THAT'S WHAT YOU LIKE TO BE CALLED, ISN'T IT? I DON'T THINK I'VE EVER TOLD YOU HOW PROUD I AM OF YOU.
WHOA, MAMA! I THINK YOU'RE HAVING A WEIRD REACTION TO THE MORPHINE.

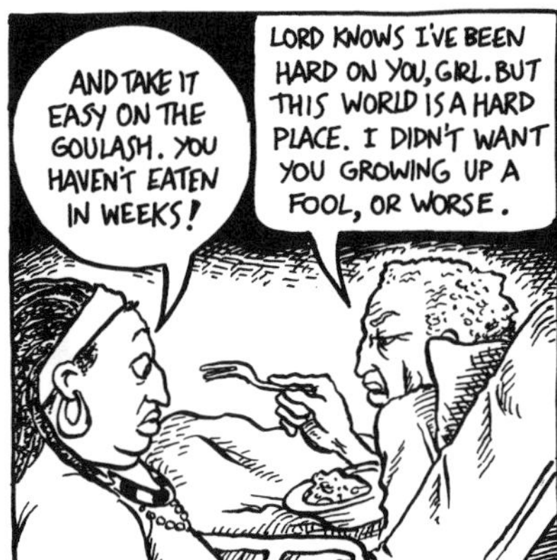
AND TAKE IT EASY ON THE GOULASH. YOU HAVEN'T EATEN IN WEEKS!
LORD KNOWS I'VE BEEN HARD ON YOU, GIRL. BUT THIS WORLD IS A HARD PLACE. I DIDN'T WANT YOU GROWING UP A FOOL, OR WORSE.

AND I DID RIGHT. LOOK AT YOU. YOU'RE A DAMN FINE DAUGHTER, EVEN IF YOU ARE A BULL-DAGGER.
MAMA!

NOW GET ME SOME TABASCO SAUCE.
YES, MA'M!

POOF!

MAMA?

MAMA.

MEANWHILE...
MOMMEEE!
SWEETIE, MOMMY HAS TO GO TO HER NEW JOB NOW. I EXPLAINED THAT TO YOU YESTER-DAY WHEN WE VISITED THIS NICE PLACE.
RAINBOW PRESCHOOL

YOU'RE A BIG BOY, RAFFI! BIG BOYS GO TO SCHOOL. CARLOS WILL PICK YOU UP AT LUNCHTIME.
RAFFI! WOULD YOU LIKE TO PLAY WITH THE BEETLEBORGS?
DON'T GOOOO!
TOVAH
ETHAN
SAM
WILLOW

NOOOO!
DON'T WORRY. HE'LL BE FINE IN FIVE MINUTES.
IT'S NOT HIM I'M WORRIED ABOUT.

TIP O'TH NIB TO AMEY "FÜKENGRÜVEN" RADCLIFFE

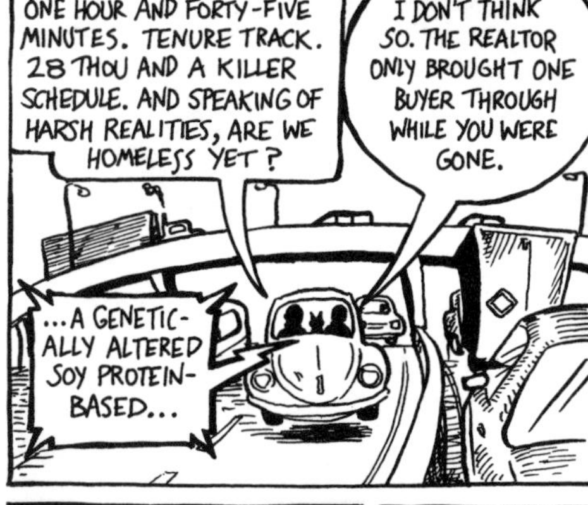

life with father
281
©1997 BY ALISON BECHDEL

TURNIP GREENS! TROTTERS! WHAT A HEARTSTOPPING SPREAD. WISH I STILL ATE MEAT. THE ONLY THING HERE I CAN HAVE ARE THE ROLLS.
DID I EVER TELL YOU ABOUT WANDA BARNES' GIRL THAT WENT VEGETARIAN? IN TWO WEEKS SHE WAS BALD AS A BILLIARD BALL.
A BIG TIP O' THE NIB TO BARBARA SMITH

SHE SHAVED HER HEAD, AUNT YO-LANDA.
THAT'S WHAT SHE TOLD PEOPLE.

HI, BABY. HAS ETTA SETTLED DOWN?
I THINK SO. I NEVER SAW ANYONE GET THE SPIRIT QUITE AS POWERFULLY AS SHE DID TODAY.

TRUST ME. IT WOULDN'T'VE BEEN A CHURCH SER-VICE IF ETTA HADN'T FALLEN OUT.
DON'T BE RUDE. SHE'S GOING TO BE LOOKING AFTER YOUR FATHER NOW.

LISTEN, I LOVE MY FAMILY, BUT I CAN'T WAIT TO GET BACK HOME. TO OUR HOME. ARE YOU REALLY COM-ING WITH ME? FOR GOOD?
I'D BETTER BE. I QUIT MY DAMN JOB.
ALBERTA! GO SAY GOOD-BYE TO THE PREACHER.

REVEREND, THANK YOU FOR THAT MOVING EULOGY. I HAD NO IDEA MY MOTHER GAVE SO MUCH TIME TO THE CHURCH BUILDING FUND.
SHE WAS A GENEROUS LADY. AND IT SOUNDS LIKE YOU TAKE RIGHT AFTER HER. YOUR FATHER JUST TOLD ME HE'S MOVING UP NORTH WITH YOU AND YOUR, UH...FRIEND AUDREY.

HE WHAT? KA-HACK!
THOSE ROLLS ARE AWFUL DRY. GO TRY SOME OF THAT CORNBREAD WITH THE HAM CHUNKS AND BACON DRIPPINGS.
SLAP!

MEANWHILE...
OKAY, DAD, OKAY! NOW WILL YOU GET OFF MY ASS? GOODBYE!

NOW WHAT?
OH, HE WANTS ME TO SEND A CHAPTER OF MY BOOK TO SOME INFLUEN-TIAL OLD FART HE KNOWS.

YOU TWO HAVE TERRIBLE BOUNDARIES, SYDNEY. WHY DO YOU LET HIM GET INTO YOUR BUSINESS LIKE THAT?
I DUNNO. IT'S NOT THAT BIG A DEAL TO KEEP HIM HAPPY.

HE SENT YOU ANOTHER CHECK, DIDN'T HE?
HOW WOULD YOU LIKE A NEW SWEATER? THEY JUST GOT SOME NICE STRIPED ONES IN DOWN AT PAPAYA REPUBLIC.

divert & conquer
282
©1998 BY ALISON BECHDEL

THE MAN'S CLEARLY A SEX ADDICT. HE'S OUT OF CONTROL. LYING, SUBORNING PERJURY...
IT'S THIS PURITANICAL CULTURE THAT'S THE PROBLEM. DO PEOPLE REALLY EXPECT SOMEONE WITH THE RUTHLESS LUST FOR POWER IT TAKES TO BECOME PRESIDENT TO SPEND EVENINGS AT HOME WITH HIS STAMP COLLECTION?
PEEPEE-GATE
SEMEN STAINS
BEVERLY HILLS
NORDIC TRICK
ABDOMINATOR

OH, PLEASE! YOU WOULDN'T BE QUITE SO INDULGENT IF IT WAS NEWT GINGRICH GETTING BLOWJOBS IN THE OVAL OFFICE.
THANK YOU FOR THAT IMAGE.
NY LITERARY AGENT
RITZ-CARLTON

HA! THEY GOT US, SYDNEY! THE WORLD IS TEETERING ON THE BRINK OF GLOBAL DEFLATION, AND HERE WE SIT PRATTLING ABOUT THE PRESIDENT'S PENIS!
CAN I HAVE A SCREW?
CNN RATINGS UP 40%
PARTS LIST

IS THIS GANNETT RAG SHOWING US HOW THE ASIAN BAILOUT BENEFITS BANKS AND CORPORATIONS, BUT DESTROYS LOCAL ECONOMIES? IS DAN RATHER EXPLAINING HOW THE I.M.F.'S STRATEGY ESCALATES THE PROBLEM OF CHEAP FOREIGN LABOR AND THREATENS U.S. WORKERS' JOBS? NO!
WHERE ARE THE PHILLIPS HEADS?
A TIP O' THE NIB TO CHRIS MOES

THE CORPORATE BEHEMOTHS WHO OWN THE NEWS DISTRACT US WITH PRESIDENTIAL PECCADILLOES WHILE THEY PROCEED TO PILLAGE THE PLANET WITH IMPUNITY!

GOOD POINT. WHILE YOU'RE UP, COULD YOU SEE IF I LEFT THOSE SCREWS BY THE PHONE?

YEAH, HERE THEY... UH... ARE.

PLATINUM
MartinaCard
MISTRESS CARD
PREVIOUS BALANCE $11,462
PURCHASES 387.
FINANCE CHARGE 203.9
LATE FEE 12
BALANCE $12,06

SYDNEY! THERE WAS THIS STACK OF CREDIT CARD BILLS LYING ON YOUR DESK! I... I'M SHOCKED! D'YOU REALLY OWE THIS MUCH MONEY?
UHH...

MO... I'M HAVING AN AFFAIR WITH ONE OF MY STUDENTS.
WHAT?!

IT JUST SORT OF HAPPENED. ONE MINUTE WE WERE DISCUSSING GENDER SLIPPAGE, AND THE NEXT, SHE'D SLIPPED RIGHT OUT OF HER AQUA PLAID STRETCH PANTS!
ARE YOU SERIOUS?

UNFORTUNATELY NOT. BUT FOR THE RECORD, YOUR DISTRACTION THEORY IS SOUND.

the iceman cometh
283
©1998 BY ALISON BECHDEL
GINGER! THANK GOD YOU'RE HOME! I WAS SO WORRIED WHEN I HEARD THE WEATHER REPORT. HOW WERE THE ROADS?
FOUR HOURS TO DRIVE A HUNDRED MILES. I CAN'T UNCLENCH MY HANDS.
HOW'D IT GO AT BUFFALO LAKE STATE? ARE THEY GONNA HIRE YOU?
I HAVE A SINKING FEELING THEY MIGHT. SPARROW, YOU'RE NOT GOING OUT ARE YOU?
SHE PROBABLY HAS A DATE WITH HER GENTLEMAN CALLER.
WHAT'S IT FEEL LIKE TO BE STRAIGHT?
LOIS! I... I'M NOT STRAIGHT!
SO WHAT'RE YOU DOING WITH THIS GUY? TALK TO US! YOU'VE BEEN SNEAKING AROUND LIKE A GUILTY TEENAGER!
I DON'T KNOW WHAT I'M DOING! THIS IS VERY CONFUSING, AND YOU'RE NOT MAKING IT ANY EASIER.
ARE YOU SCHTUPPING HIM?
NO.
DO YOU WANT TO?
YES... I THINK. I DON'T KNOW! I REALLY LIKE HIM, BUT... HE'S A MAN!
WELL, THAT'S NOT NECESSARILY A PERMANENT CONDITION.
SHUT UP, LOIS. HOW DOES HE FEEL? WHAT DOES HE WANT?
HE'S A LITTLE WARY, TOO. HE SEEMS TO HAVE A PATTERN OF GETTING INVOLVED WITH WOMEN WHO TURN OUT TO BE LESBIANS.
WHAT IS IT WITH THOSE GUYS?
STOMP STAMP
WUF!
HERE HE IS. SEE YOU LATER.
CLIK!
SPARROW, INVITE HIM IN FOR A SECOND! WHAT'RE YOU AFRAID OF?
AR AR KACK! ARF
YEAH. I PROMISE I WON'T CARVE UP A CUCUMBER WITH A CLEAVER WHILE SHOUTING "DEATH TO THE PATRIARCHY."
LOOK, I'M JUST NOT READY TO HANG OUT PLAYING PARCHEESI WITH ALL OF YOU YET.
HI, STUART! STUART?
WHAT HAPPENED?
M-MY CAR... PHONE POLE... T-TEN BLOCKS AWAY...
THE WHITE COROLLA? I SAW THAT! ARE YOU OKAY?
COME ON IN, LADDY BUCK. I'LL SET UP THE PARCHEESI BOARD.

SPARROW'S SWAIN APPEARS TO BE IN A MILD STATE OF SHOCK.

SHORTLY, IN THE KITCHEN...

Buying the Farm
286
© 1998 BY ALISON BECHDEL
I'M ALL PACKED. I LEFT STUART'S NUMBER BY THE PHONE IN CASE ANYONE NEEDS ME.
SPARROW, PLEASE DON'T DO THIS!
YOU CAN'T BREAK UP THE HOUSEHOLD. WE'RE... WE'RE FAMILY.
MILK BONES
JOY
CARIBOU WOOD
SORROW OF COOKING
CHI
THAT'S THE PROBLEM. LOOK, IT'S ONLY FOR A LITTLE WHILE. I NEED SOME SPACE.
I WAS JUST VENTING WHEN I SAID ALL THAT STUFF ABOUT YOU AND STUART. I'M **OVER** IT!

SHE'S REALLY COME AROUND, SPARROW. I'VE TALKED TO HER.
SHUT UP, LOIS. I WAS **FINE** ABOUT IT TILL YOU STARTED WITH THE HETEROSEXUAL PANIC.
YOU TWO ARE GONNA HAVE TO SORT IT OUT ON YOUR OWN. I NEED TO BE IN A MORE SUPPORTIVE ENVIRONMENT.
SPARROW, WE'RE YOUR FRIENDS! I DON'T THINK IT'S SUCH A GOOD IDEA THAT YOU GO TO STUART'S PLACE. YOU HARDLY KNOW HIM. AND I'D SAY THE SAME THING IF HE WERE A WOMAN!
EXCEPT SHE'D SAY "YOU HARDLY KNOW **HER**."
DING DONG
THAT'S HER. I MEAN **HIM**.
Wurf!

DIGGER, CHILL! YOU'RE GETTING TOO OLD FOR THIS!
LORNA! WHAT DO YOU WANT?
I DIDN'T THINK YOU LADIES WOULD BE HERE. DIDN'T MY OFFICE CALL YOU?
WOOF
Yipe!
ARF

NO, THEY DIDN'T.
WELL, YOU WON'T MIND IF I BRING A CLIENT THROUGH. HE'S LOOKING FOR A RENTAL PROPERTY. IF IT WORKS OUT, YOU COULD GET TO STAY HERE.
GRRR!
COME ON IN, MR. WIENER!

I COULDA TOLD YOU A DOG LIVED HERE. THE YARD'S A MESS. PEOPLE WHO RENT TO DOG OWNERS ARE NUTS.
LISTEN, YOU CAN'T JUST COME IN HERE WITHOUT ANY WARNING!
ARF ARF
ARF

I KNOW, HON. I'LL SPEAK TO MY SECRETARY ABOUT IT. LET'S START WITH THE BASEMENT, MR W.
SEE THERE? LOOKIT WHAT THAT MUTT'S DONE TO THE WOODWORK.
URF!

OKAY, **OUT! I MEAN IT, OR I SET THE HOUND LOOSE!**
WELL! YOUR LANDLORD'LL HEAR ABOUT THIS!
JEEZIZ! BUNCHA **NUT** JOBS.
ARP?
SLAM!

WOW! WAY TA GO, GINGER!
YEAH. THIS'LL BE EXCITING. I'VE NEVER BEEN EVICTED BEFORE.
NO ONE'S EVICTING ANYONE, LADIES. I'M GONNA **BUY** THIS DAMN HOUSE!
POSSESSED GLEAM
WUF!

WHERE IS THE SLUSH of YESTERYEAR?

288

THE MORE OPEN DISCUSSION THERE IS ABOUT SEX, THE MORE WE MOVE BEYOND THE FALSE POLARITY OF WOMEN AS EITHER SEXUAL PREY, OR FRAIL VIRGINS IN NEED OF PROTECTION.

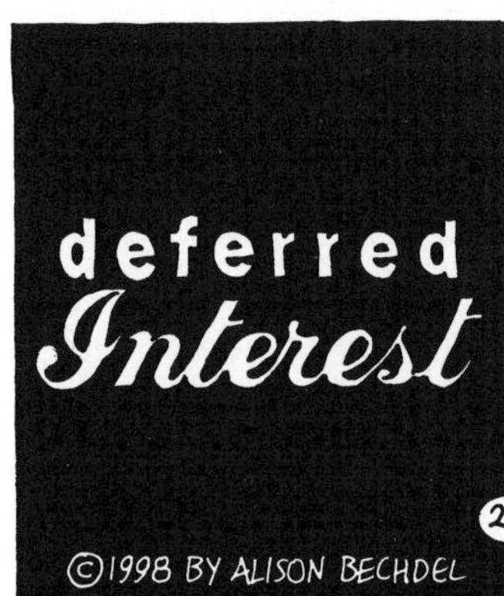
deferred Interest
289
©1998 BY ALISON BECHDEL

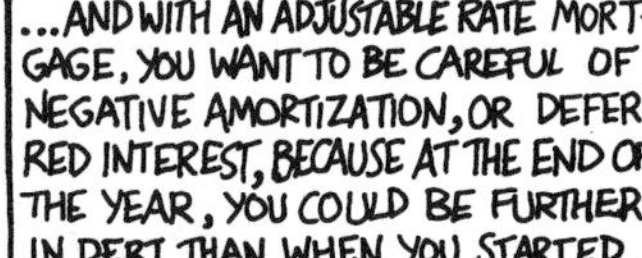
...AND WITH AN ADJUSTABLE RATE MORTGAGE, YOU WANT TO BE CAREFUL OF NEGATIVE AMORTIZATION, OR DEFERRED INTEREST, BECAUSE AT THE END OF THE YEAR, YOU COULD BE FURTHER IN DEBT THAN WHEN YOU STARTED.

GOD, MY HEAD'S SWIMMING. I'M SO GLAD WE'RE BUYING HOUSES AT THE SAME TIME. I DON'T KNOW IF I COULD FIGURE ALL THIS OUT ON MY OWN.

YOU'LL GET THE HANG OF IT. IT'S ACTUALLY REALLY INTERESTING. SO FOR A 30-YEAR FIXED-RATE LOAN, YOU NEED TO PAY 20 PERCENT DOWN, OR YOU HAVE TO BUY MORTGAGE INSURANCE, WHICH...

I THINK IT'S GREAT YOU'RE COMMITTED TO STAYING IN THE NEIGHBORHOOD, GINGER. I DON'T WANT TO LEAVE, BUT...
BUT WE DON'T WANT RAFFI GROWING UP NEXT DOOR TO A CRACK HOUSE.

OKAY. THE BEST DEAL IS A 15-YEAR LOAN. YOU END UP PAYING WAY LESS INTEREST, BUT OF COURSE THE MONTHLY PAYMENTS ARE HIGHER.
I DON'T THINK I COULD AFFORD THAT. BUFFALO LAKE IS ONLY GIVING ME A PITTANCE.
HOW'D YOU DECIDE TO TAKE THE JOB? DIDN'T YOU SAY TEACHING AT A MOSTLY WHITE, SMALL-TOWN STATE COLLEGE SOUNDED LIKE THE NINTH CIRCLE OF HELL?

WELL, HELL STARTED LOOKING PRETTY GOOD. IT'S NOT EXACTLY A BUYER'S MARKET OUT THERE. 463 PEOPLE APPLIED FOR THIS JOB!
LOOK WHAT I GOT, GINGER!
WHOA, RAFFI. THAT'S VERY UH... LETHAL LOOKING.
SO MUCH FOR 'NO MORE WAR TOYS.' SYDNEY GOT HIM THAT. SHE AND MO TOOK HIM TO TOYS R US LAST NIGHT WHILE I WAS AT A FREEDOM TO MARRY MEETING.

HEY, DO YOU HAVE ANY INTEREST IN VOLUNTEERING? IT'S SUCH IMPORTANT WORK!
UM... ACTUALLY, MARRIAGE ISN'T REAL HIGH ON MY AGENDA RIGHT NOW.
TONI, NOT EVERYONE WANTS TO FIGHT FOR THE DUBIOUS RIGHT OF HAVING THEIR DOMESTIC AFFAIRS LEGITIMIZED BY THE PATRIARCHY.

LISTEN, CLARICE, IT'S A MUCH MORE RADICAL ACT FOR TWO WOMEN TO CHALLENGE THE STATE BY GETTING MARRIED THAN TO SIT AROUND MUTTERING ABOUT THE PATRIARCHY.
UM... COULD YOU EXPLAIN THAT STUFF ABOUT "POINTS" AGAIN, AND HOW THEY AFFECT THE INTEREST RATE?
THWACK!
RAFFI!

LATER THAT EVENING...
I LOVE THAT WE'RE FRIENDS WITH GINGER. IT MAKES ME FEEL SO SOPHISTICATED, LIKE WE'RE IN A NOEL COWARD PLAY. WHEN WAS IT YOU TWO HAD THAT AFFAIR? TEN YEARS AGO?

CLARICE?
Real Estate Guide
Century 21

LOVE and WORK part 1

290

BUTCH IN THE STREETS, FEMME IN THE SHEETS? HOW **TOO** TRITE.

SIT BACK & HANG ON AS OUR SPECIAL 2-PART SERIES EXPLORES SOME **MORE PIQUANT** DISPARITIES BETWEEN WORK-PLACE AND BED-ROOM DEMEANOR.

AT WORK, CLARICE HAS LASERLIKE FOCUS,

...AND TONI EXUDES MATURITY.

BUT IN THE BOUDOIR...

AT THE BOOKSTORE, JEZANNA IS A WOMAN OF FEW WORDS,

...BUT IN AN INTIMATE SETTING, SHE'S A BIT MORE VOLUBLE.

OH, **WHERE'D** YOU LEARN TO **DO** THAT? **YES!** DON'T **STOP! @*#!** ME, YOU ***$⊙¢!**

BABE, BEFORE YOUR FATHER MOVES IN, WE NEED TO TALK SOUNDPROOFING.

GINGER HAS AN EYE TO THE FUTURE AT WORK,

...BUT IN BED, SHE'S LIVING IN THE PAST.

ON THE JOB, MO STANDS BY HER PRINCIPLES...

...AND SYDNEY'S OUT OF CONTROL.

BUT IN THE HEAT OF PASSION, MATTERS ARE DIFFERENT.

TO BE CONTINUED...

TO LOVE AND TO WORK. THE TWIN CONDITIONS OF A MEANINGFUL LIFE. BUT IS OUR PERFORMANCE IN ONE ARENA AN INDEX OF OUR PERFORMANCE IN THE OTHER?

JOIN US AS WE SEEK THE ANSWER IN THIS FINAL INSTALLMENT OF OUR PENETRATING INVESTIGATIVE SERIES.

291

SPARROW'S A MODEL OF DECISIVENESS DOWN AT THE SHELTER...

TIPS O' THE NIB TO PATTI McMANAMY & NAT GRANT

AND STUART'S FUNDRAISING ZEAL IS UNFLAGGING.

BUT IN THE RACK, SHE CAN'T DECIDE,

... AND HE FINALLY FLAGS.

THEA'S EASYGOING ON THE JOB...

BUT A BIT MORE PARTICULAR IN BED...

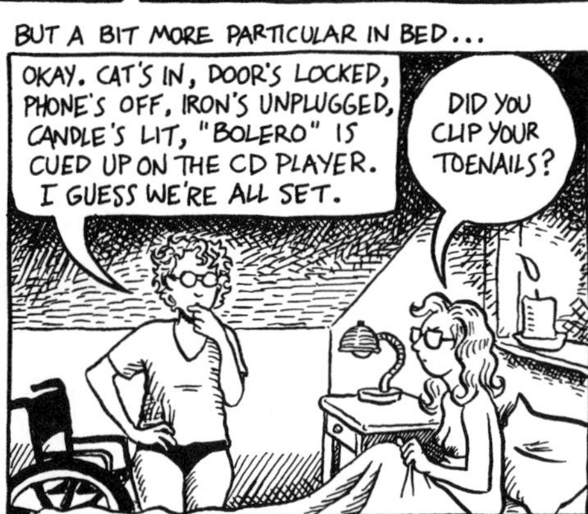

DISORIENTED BY HIS PROLONGED UNEMPLOYMENT, CARLOS IS HAVING SEX WHEN HE SHOULD BE WORKING...

... AND VICE VERSA.

AND LOIS BRINGS TO BOTH WORK AND PLAY...

THIS MODEL REALLY ROCKS IF IT FITS BOTH PEOPLE RIGHT.

THE ULTIMATE ANAL GUIDE TO SEX FOR WOMEN

DIESEL GRUEL POIMS

A CONSISTENT, SERVICE-ORIENTED APPROACH.

an embarassment of condiments
©1998 BY ALISON BECHDEL
292
I HOPE YOU'RE NOT STARVING. TONI ISN'T BACK FROM HER FTM MEETING YET.
OH, TONI'S TRANSITIONING? HERE'S MORE RELISH. I DIDN'T KNOW YOU ALREADY HAD SOME.
NOT FEMALE-TO-MALE! FREEDOM TO MARRY. HERE'S SOME FRUIT-SWEETENED CATSUP.
PICNIC
RELISH
PISS -N- VINEGAR CHIPS

SYDNEE!
COMMANDER SKYWALKER! QUICK! SAND PEOPLE ON THE NORTH RIDGE!

UH... HI, RAFFI.
SHOULD HE BE PLAYING WITH THAT LIGHT SABER? I MEAN, AREN'T YOU CONCERNED ABOUT ALL THESE BOYS MOWING DOWN THEIR CLASSMATES WITH ASSAULT RIFLES?
SQUEAL!

THANKS FOR YOUR CONCERN, MO. I'M NOT THE ONE WHO **BOUGHT** HIM THE DAMN THING.
HEY, I DID EVERYTHING I COULD TO TALK SYDNEY OUT OF IT. BUT SHE'S A **JUGGERNAUT** WHEN SHE'S GOT A VISA CARD IN HER HAND.
CHARCOAL

SHE STILL RACKING UP DEBT?
YEAH. IT'S LIKE SHE **HAS** TO HAVE NEW STUFF ALL THE TIME. HER CLOSET IS LIKE A J. SCREW WAREHOUSE!

REALLY. UM, LISTEN, MO. I NEED TO TALK TO YOU BEFORE TONI GETS HERE...
WHAT'S GOING ON?! IS SOMETHING WRONG? YOU GUYS AREN'T BREAKING **UP**, ARE YOU?

GOD! NO! WILL YOU JUST LISTEN? REMEMBER HOW YEARS AGO I HAD THAT THING WITH GINGER? WELL, I'VE BEEN THINKING ABOUT HER A LOT LATELY...
THINKING AS IN MUSING, OR THINKING AS IN ENTERTAINING FEVERISH SEXUAL FANTASIES?

UM... THE LATTER.
GOD, CLARICE! YOU HAVEN'T SAID ANYTHING TO HER, HAVE YOU?
SKRITCH

OF **COURSE** NOT! WHAT'S COME OVER ME?! IT MUST BE SOME KIND OF **BACKLASH**. WE'RE BUYING A HOUSE, LEAVING THE NEIGHBORHOOD, TONI'S ON THIS "RIGHT TO MARRY" KICK! WE USED TO JOKE ABOUT BEING WARD AND JUNE CLEAVER, BUT IT'S NOT FUNNY ANYMORE. I'M SO **CLAUSTROPHOBIC**, I'M **CHOKING!**

HI! SORRY I'M LATE! I STOPPED BY THE CO-OP FOR BUNS, AND LOOK WHO I FOUND!

UM... HEY.
HEY,..UH.. I BROUGHT SOME RELISH.
I THINK ONE CAN SAFELY SAY THERE'S ENTIRELY TOO MUCH RELISH AT THIS BARBECUE.

home economics

293

BALM BLAST

294

THIS IS NICE. WE DON'T SPEND ENOUGH TIME TOGETHER. UM... SO, ARE YOU GONNA DRAW UP THAT SPENDING PLAN TODAY? YOU KNOW, TO GET YOUR DEBT UNDER CONTROL?

I CAN'T THINK ABOUT IT RIGHT NOW. THE ANTIHISTAMINES ARE STARTING TO KICK IN.

OUT

GCN

HEY! I JUST HEARD A NEW CAT ALLERGY SOLUTION! APPLY **TIGER BALM** AROUND YOUR EYES! I HAVE AN OLD TIN SOMEWHERE IF YOU...

I DON'T THINK SO. I RATHER LIKE BEING ABLE TO SEE.

OUT

HEIL STYLE!

GCN

GOD! HAVE YOU READ ABOUT THIS **"MILLENIUM MARCH"** BROUHAHA? THE HUMAN RIGHTS CAMPAIGN AND THE METROPOLITAN COMMUNITY CHURCH GOT TOGETHER AND UNILATERALLY DECIDED TO THROW A NATIONAL MARCH ON WASHINGTON IN 2000.

A TIDY, CLOSED-PROCESS, TOP-DOWN EXECUTIVE DECISION. NO PUBLIC MEETING, NO DISCUSSION WITH OTHER GAY AND LESBIAN ORGANIZATIONS, NO COORDINATION WITH OTHER PROGRESSIVE GROUPS.

ABSOLUT

OUT

POST-GAY! THE NEW IDEOLOGY FOR FALL!

TWADDLE

THE THEME IS **"FAITH AND FAMILY."** GAG ME WITH A RAINBOW FLAG! OR A **CRUCIFIX!** THAT'S PROBABLY THE LOGO, A RAINBOW CRUCIFIX! I BET THEY'RE PRINTING IT ON SOUVENIR DIAPER BAGS AS WE SPEAK!

WELL, IF THE MESSAGE THAT WE'RE ALL CHURCHGOING MALL PATRONS WINS US MORE SUPPORT, MAYBE IT'S A GOOD STRATEGY FOR THE MOVEMENT.

SEND MONEY PLEASE!

IN

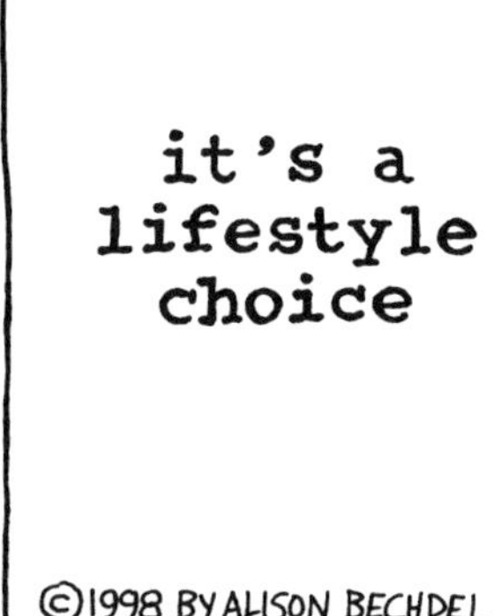
it's a lifestyle choice
©1998 BY ALISON BECHDEL

SPARROW IS STILL SOJOURNING AT STUART'S...
GOD! THAT NEW NEIGHBOR'S DRIVING ME INSANE! HE'S PLAYED THIS MÖTLEY CRÜE ALBUM SIX TIMES SINCE I GOT HOME! AND IS THAT CIGAR SMOKE?!
POOR BABY. SEE YOU LATER. I'M HAVING DINNER WITH LOIS AND GINGER.
Girls, Girls, Girls!
295

SHORTLY...
THANKS FOR COMING, SPARROW. I'VE MISSED YOU SO MUCH.

HOW'S IT GOING, BABE?
GOOD! I MISS YOU GUYS TOO. I'M FEELING MUCH CLEARER ABOUT THINGS WITH STUART, AND I'M READY TO COME BACK.

EXCELLENT! ACTUALLY, THAT'S WHAT WE WANTED TO TALK TO YOU ABOUT.
NOW WHAT? HAVE YOU INSTITUTED VISITING HOURS FOR MALE GUESTS?

HEY, STU CAN MOVE IN AS FAR AS WE'RE CONCERNED. WE JUST WANT YOU TO CO-SIGN THE MORTGAGE AND SHELL OUT FIVE THOU TO HELP BUY THIS PLACE.
WHAT?
TURNS OUT GINGER CAN'T AFFORD THE HOUSE ON HER OWN.

AND MY CREDIT ISN'T SO GOOD SINCE I DEFAULTED ON MY STUDENT LOAN.
COME ON! IT'S A GOOD INVESTMENT! AND NOT JUST FINANCIALLY!

IT'S AN INVESTMENT IN FRIENDSHIP! A COMMITMENT TO SHARING RESOURCES! A TRIUMPHANT BLOW TO THE ALIENATING CORPORATE FORCES THAT ARE STEADILY ERODING HUMAN BONDS!
OKAY. WHAT THE HELL. I'VE GOT SOME MONEY SAVED UP.

!
REALLY?
REALLY. I'VE BEEN GIVING A LOT OF THOUGHT LATELY TO HOW I WANT TO LIVE. IT'S BEEN NICE STAYING AT STUART'S AND HAVING SOME PRIVACY. BUT THAT'S NOT WHAT I WANT PERMANENTLY, THAT KIND OF ISOLATED, COUPLE-FOCUSED EXISTENCE, ALL CUT OFF FROM THE WORLD.

MEANWHILE, IN A DIFFERENT ZIP CODE...
...AND WITH THE ELECTRIC GARAGE DOOR OPENER, YOU DON'T HAVE TO GET OUT OF YOUR CAR TO GO INSIDE!
UH... I THINK WE'RE LOOKING FOR SOMETHING A LITTLE LESS... UH...
HERMETICALLY SEALED.
CENTURY 21
FOR SALE

LATER THAT EVENING...
HI. LISTEN, I'M GONNA STAY HERE TONIGHT.... I KNOW. ME TOO... WHAT?... WELL, I GUESS SO. BUT I DON'T THINK IT'S VERY HEALTHY IF YOU CAN'T BE AWAY FROM ME FOR EVEN ONE NIGHT.

UH... I DO MISS YOU, BUT THAT'S NOT WHY I WANT TO COME OVER.
Girls, Girls, Girls!
MACANUDO EXHAUST
I DON'T CARE IF HE'S DEAD. I STILL WANT TO IMPEACH NIXON

THAT WAS STUART ON THE PHONE. YOU DON'T MIND IF HE STAYS OVER AGAIN, DO YOU? HIS NEIGHBOR SEEMS TO BE HAVING ANOTHER KEG PARTY.

WHATEVER. HE PRACTICALLY LIVES HERE ANYWAY.

STRAY VOLTAGE
©1998 BY ALISON BECHDEL
297
WOW. YOU'RE ONLY WIRED FOR SIXTY AMPS. LOTTA RODENT DAMAGE TOO, I'M SURPRISED THIS PLACE HASN'T BURNED TO THE GROUND.
UH... REALLY?
FUSES

SO, CAN YOU GIVE US AN ESTIMATE?
LEMME GO OUT TO THE TRUCK AND WORK IT UP.

IN A MOMENT...
LOOK, I'M NOT ASKING STUART TO MOVE IN. I'M NOT READY FOR THAT KIND OF COMMITMENT. I DON'T CARE HOW BADLY WE NEED THE MONEY.

SPARROW, THIS IS NO TIME FOR INTIMACY ISSUES. JUST THINK OF IT AS HAVING A TEMPORARY ROOMMATE TILL WE PAY OFF THE REPAIRS.
DON'T LECTURE **ME** ABOUT INTIMACY ISSUES. YOU'RE THE ONE OBSESSED WITH A MARRIED WOMAN. AT LEAST STUART IS **AVAILABLE!**
WHY DON'T YOU ASK **CLARICE** TO MOVE IN, GINGER. YOU'RE GENERATING ENOUGH ELECTRICITY WITH YOUR CRUSH, WE WON'T **NEED** TO REWIRE.

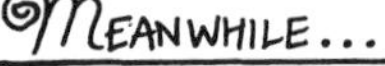

MEANWHILE...

THANKS FOR THE BOXES, MO. TONI'LL CREAM. SHE'S SO EXCITED ABOUT THE MOVE, SHE'S DEVELOPING A CARDBOARD FETISH.
MADWIMMIN BOOKS
NAIAD

YOU DON'T LOOK SO THRILLED.
I'M A WRECK. I'M THINKING ABOUT **GINGER** ALL THE TIME. IT'S CRAZY. I'M AFRAID TONI KNOWS SOMETHING'S WRONG.
THUNK!

CLARICE, YOU'VE GOTTA RECONCILE YOUR FEELINGS ABOUT LEAVING THE NEIGHBORHOOD. IT'S NOT **GINGER** YOU'RE ATTRACTED TO, IT'S WHAT SHE REPRESENTS. THE CO-OP, THE PARK, THE BLOCK FESTIVAL, THE **COMMUNITY!**

OH. SO IT'S REALLY THE **COMMUNITY'S** INNER THIGHS I WANT TO DRIZZLE WITH MAPLE CRÈME ANGLAISE, WHICH I THEN SLOWLY LAP UP WHILE STRADDLING THE TANTALIZING TONGUE OF THE **CO-OP.**
UH... WELL, SORT OF...

MEANWHILE, IN ST. LOUIS, JEZANNA AND AUDREY ARE PACKING UP JEZ'S FATHER TO COME BACK AND LIVE WITH THEM.
IT'S BEEN LONELY WITHOUT YOUR MAMA. BUT I'M GONNA MISS THIS HOUSE.
YOU CAN STILL CHANGE YOUR MIND. WE HAVEN'T SOLD IT YET, AND I CAN ALWAYS RETURN THE U-HAUL.
NUDGE
UH... LOTTA MEMORIES HERE, HUH, DAD?
REMEMBER THIS BURN MARK ON THE BASEBOARD, FROM THE TIME YOU STUCK THAT PIECE OF ERECTOR SET IN THE OUTLET? YOU WERE ALWAYS POKING INTO SOMETHING.
MMM, GIRL!

BACK AT THE RANCH...
OF COURSE, THAT DOESN'T INCLUDE REPAIRING THE WALLS AFTER I'M DONE.
Y'KNOW, MAYBE MY RELUCTANCE TO COMMIT **IS** A TAD UNHEALTHY.
$525 INCLUDING UTILITIES.

Enough Already

©1998 BY ALISON BECHDEL (298)

GET OUT YOUR ROLODEX. AS WE REJOIN OUR WANDERING NARRATIVE, THERE SEEM TO BE A FEW CHANGES OF ADDRESS.

CLARICE AND TONI HAVE EMIGRATED TO THE RIGHT SIDE OF THE TRACKS.

SYDNEY HAS BECOME MO'S NOT-SO-DOMESTIC PARTNER.

JEZANNA, IN A GRUDGING ACT OF FILIAL DUTY, HAS OPENED UP HER HOME TO HER BEREAVED FATHER.

AND IN A QUASI-MARRIAGE OF CONVENIENCE, STUART HAS TAKEN LODGINGS WITH SPARROW AND THE GIRLS.

buyer's remorse
©1998 BY ALISON BECHDEL
301
ONE AUTUMNAL TUESDAY EVE...
WELL, THAT WAS UNPLEASANT. BUT IT HAD TO BE DONE.
OH, THANKS, LOIS! SINCE GINGER STARTED HER NEW JOB, THE DOG SHIT'S REALLY BEEN PILING UP OUT THERE.
UH... I WASN'T CLEANING UP THE YARD. I JUST CAME FROM THE POLLS.
MMM. THAT WAS A NASTY BUSINESS.
CHEESE
MILK
MAY THE LORD HAVE MERCY ON MY SOUL. I VOTED FOR EVERY MARGINALLY LESSER EVIL ON THE TICKET.
YEAH, ME TOO. AND I'M GETTING PRETTY SICK OF THIS ROTTEN TWO-PARTY DEAL. IT'S GOT TO GO.
10% TRIB
MAYBE IT'LL FINALLY HAPPEN, NOW THAT CLINTON'S TOTALLED THE DEMOCRATS, AND THE REPUBLICANS ARE LOST SOMEWHERE BETWEEN LEVITICUS AND THE 19TH CENTURY.
ARF?
I DON'T KNOW. I'M LOSING FAITH IN PEOPLE'S COMMON SENSE. LIKE, WILL YOU EXPLAIN TO ME WHAT THESE LESBIAN AND GAY GROUPS ARE DOING IN BED WITH CONSERVATIVE REPUBLICANS?
ORGANIC COW
QUICHE
HRC ENDORSES ANTI-CHOICE D'AMATO
"WE'D RATHER HAVE GAYS IN THE MILITARY THAN GUN CONTROL"
EGGS
GETTING REAMED. BUT THEY SEEM TO LIKE IT.
HELLO!
LOG CABIN CLUB VOWS TO DEFEAT TWO LESBIAN CONGRESSIONAL CANDIDATES
HEY, SPARROW. HOW'D THE CLOSING GO THIS MORNING?
WE GOT IT! GINGER AND I OFFICIALLY OWN THE HOUSE!
WELL, I JUST HOPE YOU WON'T TAKE ADVANTAGE OF A SIMPLE PEASANT LAD WITH YOUR DEBAUCHED, LANDED GENTRY WAYS.
LATER, AFTER GINGER RETURNS...
TO OUR NEW HOME. CHEERS.
PROSIT.
SKOAL.
FEH!
UH... GREAT NON-ALCOHOLIC WINE, SPARROW. AUSTERE, YET MEAGER, WITH A HINT OF WELCH'S AND A SOBER FINISH.
HEY, WHAT'S THAT PILE OF SAWDUST UNDER THE WINDOW? I THOUGHT WE CLEANED UP AFTER THE ELECTRICIAN.
WE DID.
WEIRD. MAYBE THE FAMILY RESEARCH COUNCIL CAME BY AND PLANTED A LISTENING DEVICE.
WELL, IT'S DEFINITELY SOME KIND OF BUG. I CAN HEAR IT CHEWING.

Mo and Sydney decide to spend the first half of their Christmas vacation with Sydney's father and step-mother.

And the second half with Mo's family.

The drive home is a bit tense...

Meanwhile, their cat-sitters are making an interesting discovery.

...like it's 1999

303

IT'S NEW YEAR'S EVE. MO AND SYDNEY HAVE JUST RETURNED FROM VISITING THEIR FAMILIES, AND IN CONSEQUENCE ARE FEELING A BIT FRACTIOUS.

JEEZ, SPARROW AND STU DIDN'T CLEAN OUT THE CAT BOX **ONCE** WHILE THEY WERE HERE.
GOD, MY KEYBOARD'S ALL STICKY. LOOKS LIKE THEY WERE MESSING AROUND ON MY COMPUTER, TOO.

THEY LEFT THIS INVITATION TO THEIR NEW YEAR'S EVE PARTY. WANNA GO?
UH... SURE. I HOPE THEY DIDN'T GO SNOOPING IN MY FILES.
DEC.

MEANWHILE, PARTY PREPARATIONS ARE AFOOT...

SYDNEY'S HAVING A VIRTUAL AFFAIR? WHO CARES? AND WHAT WERE YOU DOING ON HER COMPUTER?
IT'S MY FAULT. I WAS LOOKING FOR GAMES. YOU KNOW, NASCAR RACING! SOLITAIRE! BUT IN THE FOLDER LABELED 'GAMES...'
...THERE WERE ALL THESE LOGS OF WILD ONLINE SEX WITH ANOTHER WOMAN. SOMEONE NAMED 'GOOD THING.'
PRETZELS

HOW DO YOU KNOW IT'S A WOMAN? FOR ALL YOU KNOW, IT COULD BE CHRISTINE TODD WHITMAN. BESIDES WHICH, IT'S NONE OF OUR BUSINESS.
OH. SO IF STUART HAD SOME BIMBO OVER WHILE I WAS AWAY, YOU WOULDN'T BOTHER MENTIONING IT TO ME?

OH, COME ON! YOU'RE NOT GONNA TELL MO! MAYBE SHE ALREADY KNOWS. MAYBE THEY HAVE AN ARRANGEMENT.
AND IT'S NOT LIKE IT'S A **REAL** AFFAIR.
WHAT'S NOT LIKE IT'S A REAL AFFAIR?

OH, LOIS... WE WERE JUST DISCUSSING, UH... IN A PURELY THEORETICAL WAY... WHETHER AN ONLINE AFFAIR COUNTS.
'COUNTS'? SPARROW, YOU'RE SO 20TH CENTURY.

SOON...

HI, KIDS! WELCOME BACK! HOW'RE THE FOLKS?
UNH.
MPH.

OKAY! TONIGHT'S TOPIC: EXTRA-CURRICULAR SEX— IS IT CHEATING IF IT'S ONLY VIRTUAL?
LOIS! WHY DON'T YOU SEE IF ANYONE WANTS MORE HORSERADISH REMOULADE!
OF COURSE IT'S CHEATING! IT WOULD BE A DIVERSION OF EMOTIONAL ENERGY.

I WOULDN'T CALL IT CHEATING. IT'S MORE LIKE REMOTE, INTERACTIVE MASTURBATION.
HMM... HAS SHE BEEN DOING A LOT OF "ON-LINE RESEARCH" LATELY, MO?

OW! JESUS, SPARROW!
WHOOPS.
DARN. THAT WAS SOME TASTY REMOULADE.

leadership vacuum

 304

the baby question
WHAT'S SYDNEY DOING ON HER COMPUTER SO LATE AT NIGHT?
©1999 BY ALISON BECHDEL 305

SPANKY*? STOP FOOLING AROUND WITH YOUR EMAIL AND COME TO BED!
AAAH!
*SECRET PET NAME

GOD, I THOUGHT YOU WERE ASLEEP! YOU ALMOST GAVE ME A HEART ATTACK!
SORRY. GOT ANYTHING INTERESTING?
CLIK! CLIK!

OH... NOT REALLY. I WAS JUST, UH... RESPONDING TO YET ANOTHER DYKE BABY ANNOUNCEMENT.
SHEESH. I GOT TWO THIS WEEK.
SNIK

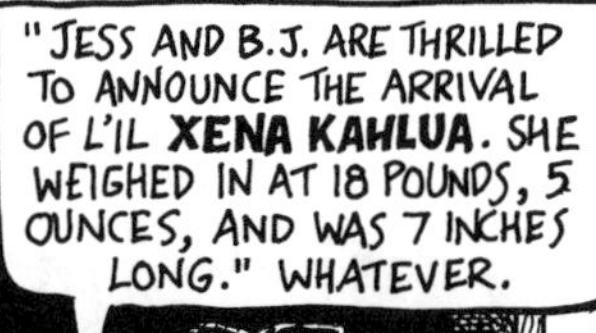
"JESS AND B.J. ARE THRILLED TO ANNOUNCE THE ARRIVAL OF L'IL XENA KAHLUA. SHE WEIGHED IN AT 18 POUNDS, 5 OUNCES, AND WAS 7 INCHES LONG." WHATEVER.

WHY DO THEY ALWAYS TELL YOU HOW BIG IT WAS? SO YOU CAN IMAGINE EXACTLY HOW PAINFUL IT MUSTA BEEN TO SQUEEZE OUT?
FLIK

WHAT IS WITH THIS BREEDING FRENZY?

I MISS THE GOOD OLD DAYS. SMASH THE FAMILY! SMASH THE STATE!

WHAT ABOUT CLARICE AND TONI AND RAFFI? D'YOU WANT TO SMASH THEIR FAMILY?
PLEASE, SYDNEY. I'M EXPRESSING AN IDEOLOGICAL CONVICTION, I'M NOT TALKING ABOUT REAL PEOPLE.
TOM'S of FINLAND

MEANWHILE, GINGER'S PREPARING FOR TRASH DAY.
SPARROW, COULDN'T YOU GUYS DISPOSE OF THIS CONTRACEPTIVE DEBRIS MORE DISCREETLY? IT'S REALLY GROSS.
OH, AND YOUR BLOODY TAMPONS AREN'T?
SPERMEX

I DON'T HAVE MY PERIOD. THOSE MUST BE LOIS'S. OR YOURS.

!
FLIP!

Z
?
APPOINTMENTS

drugstore cowpokes
©1999 BY ALISON BECHDEL
306
ONE SNOWY SATURDAY MORN...
SHE MIGHT BE WHAT?
SHH! SHE DOESN'T WANT STUART TO KNOW TILL SHE'S SURE.
IBU-PRO-FEN
I CAN'T BELIEVE SHE TOLD YOU AND NOT HIM! YOU DIDN'T GET HER PREGNANT!
LOIS, KEEP IT DOWN!
TRO PIC ANA
P-NUT BURR
IBU-PRO-FEN
OH, RELAX. HE WENT OUT WHILE YOU WERE WALKING DIGGER. SO WHAT'S SPARROW GONNA DO?
P.B.
I DON'T KNOW. SHE WAS PRETTY WIGGED OUT. I KNEW ALL THIS HETEROSEXUALITY WOULD COME TO NO GOOD.
ALL I HAVE TO SAY IS, IF THEY BRING A BABY INTO THIS HOUSE, THEY'RE DAMN WELL GONNA PAY MORE OF THE EXPENSES.
OJ
PB
IP
MEANWHILE, DOWN AT THE LOCAL PHARMACY...
I'M SICK OF MESSING AROUND WITH YOGURT. I WONDER IF THIS STUFF THEY'RE ALWAYS ADVERTISING ON "MARTHA STEWART LIVING" WILL KILL ME?
...F...G... AH, THERE WE GO. PREPARATION H!
ROMANCE NOVELS
AUTOMOTIVE
FEMININE HYGIENE
PRESCRIP
FEB. 14
FEB. 14
PROPHYLACTIC SHOPPE
LAXATIVES
ANTACIDS
SNACKS
KOFF KOFF
DIE HARD
HUNG LIKE A TROJAN HORSE SIZE
COMFY TIP
ECONO PAK 1 GROSS
MAGNUM X-LARGE
SUB-ATOMIC SIZE
BUMPS
PETITE
LILLIPUTIAN
RIDGES
BANANA
OH. UH... HI, STUART.
UM... HI THERE.
CHECK OUT
VALENTINE CANDY
VAGICORP YEAST-B-GONE
PREP H RHOID OINTMENT
ER... I'M JUST RUNNING AN ERRAND FOR A... A FRIEND. YEAH.
I HEARD THIS STUFF MAKES A GREAT, UH... WINTER WEIGHT CHAIN LUBE, IF YOU BIKE IN THE SNOW.
INSTRUCTIONS
METAMUCIL
GOD. COULD WE POSSIBLY BE BUYING ANYTHING MORE EMBARRASSING?
LICE EGG REMOVER? AN ENEMA, MAYBE?
HEY, PHUONG! GET ME A PRICE ON THE "MAYBE BABY" PREGNANCY TEST!
JEEZ, THEY SHOULD HAVE PRIVATE CHECK-OUT BOOTHS IN THESE PLACES. LOOK AT THAT POOR LADY!
V.D.
NICOTINE
SUCROSE
THAT'S NO LADY! THAT'S...
SPARROW?
COSMO
TV GUIDE
PREP
AND WE COULD CONVERT THE UPSTAIRS PORCH INTO AN EXTRA ROOM...
I'LL GLUE GLOW-IN-THE-DARK STARS ON THE CEILING. KIDS LOVE THAT. AND WE'LL HAVE TO GET A GATE FOR THE STAIRS, AND PUT THOSE LITTLE COVERS OVER ALL THE ELECTRICAL OUTLETS...

Gossip Failure
©1999 BY ALISON BECHDEL

307
HEY! GUESS WHO'S PICKING UP A FEW PREGNANCY TESTS!
Pillzapoppin' Rx
1156
ANNUAL Truss SALE! % OFF
DON'T FORGET VALENTINE'S DAY
...THIS IS JERRI GROSZ WITH FRESH HAIR.

SPARROW.
TODAY I'LL BE TALKING WITH A GAY MAN IN THE ENTERTAINMENT INDUSTRY...

HOW DID YOU KNOW?
GINGER JUST TOLD ME.
... TO WHOSE EVERY THROAT-CLEARING I WILL RESPOND WITH A COQUETTISH TITTER.

OKAY, BABE. LATER.
GOD, I HATE THAT PHONE.
... AND LATER IN THE HOUR, DAVID BEYONDCOOLGUY WILL EXPLORE THE DANTESQUE IMAGERY OF "TOUCHED BY AN ANGEL."

SHORTLY...
MORNING, JEZ! HEY, GUESS WHO I JUST SAW AT THE DRUGSTORE SHOPPING FOR PREGNANCY TESTS!
MADWIMMIN BOOKS
OPEN

MO, I DON'T HAVE TIME FOR YOUR FOOLISHNESS. THE BOOK BUSINESS IS CONSOLIDATING FASTER THAN THERMONUCLEAR FUSION, AND I'VE GOT A STORE TO KEEP SOLVENT.
GOD! TAKE A BREAK ONCE IN A WHILE! YOU ACT LIKE THE FUTURE OF DEMOCRACY RESTS ON YOUR SHOULDERS.
BUNNS & NOODLE BUYS LEADING WHOLESALE SUPPLIER TO INDEPENDENT BOOKSTORES

YOU THINK IT DOESN'T? JUST WAIT TILL THOUSANDS OF DIVERSE, LOVINGLY TENDED INDEPENDENT BOOKSTORES GET REPLACED BY GENERIC CHAINS, WITH ONE SUBLITERATE BEAN COUNTER DOWN AT CORPORATE HQ SELECTING ALL THE TITLES!
OFFICE
INDEPENDENTS PROTEST TO JUSTICE DEPT.

YOU CAN SAY GOODBYE TO BOOKS BY RISKY OR UNPROVEN AUTHORS, LIKE THE ONES I'VE BEEN HAND-SELLING OUR CUSTOMERS FOR YEARS. WE'LL ALL BE UP TO OUR CEREBRAL CORTEXES IN "CELINE DION'S TITANIC CHEESECAKE RECIPES"!
OFFICE

"IT'S LIKE WENDY'S HAVING TO RELY ON McDONALD'S TO SELL THEM FRENCH FRIES."

AND DON'T COME WHINING TO ME ABOUT THE FUTURE OF DEMOCRACY WHEN NO ONE WILL PUBLISH YOUR SCATHING INDICTMENT OF THE BOOK INDUSTRY!
OKAY, OKAY! I'M ON YOUR SIDE! DON'T GET YOUR JOCKEYS IN A KNOT.
OFFICE
"EAT OUR DUST JACKETS," CHORTLES BUNNS & NOODLE

A BIT LATER...

WELL, LOOK WHO'S SLUMMING! WHAT BRINGS YOU THREE IN FROM THE LAND OF CHEMLAWN?
NICE TO SEE THE INCREASED COMPETITION HASN'T AFFECTED YOUR CUSTOMER RELATIONS SKILLS.
WE JUST STOPPED IN TO HEAR THE LATEST DISH... ER, I MEAN, TO SUPPORT OUR LOCAL INDEPENDENT BOOKSELLER.

WELL, HAVE I GOT SOME NEWS FOR YOU. GUESS WHO WAS RECENTLY SPOTTED PURCHASING A HOME PREGNANCY TEST!
HARRIET! I KNOW! ISN'T IT WONDERFUL?!

HARRIET? MY HARRIET?
UH... IT'S BEEN 7 YEARS, BABE. I THINK THE STATUTE OF LIMITATIONS HAS RUN OUT ON USE OF THE POSSESSIVE.

Sparrow and Stuart return home together after a chance encounter at the drugstore.

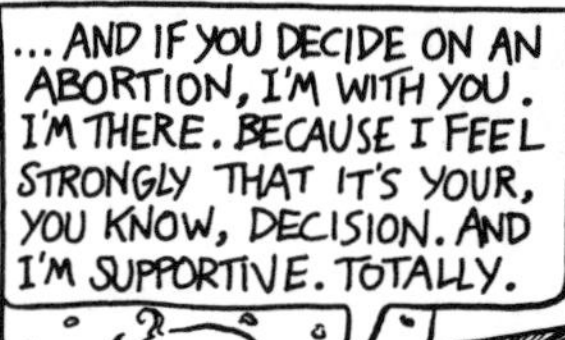

in the family way
309
©1999 BY ALISON BECHDEL

SORRY TO CANCEL OUR DATE, SWEET PEA. BUT I REALLY HAVE TO SEE HARRIET.
TAKE YOUR TIME. I HAVE A LOT OF PLANNING I NEED TO DO, ANYWAY.
ZIP

BYE, THEN.
TA.
File Edit Spin Purée Liquefy Help
ACCT: CraftyGirl@philander.net
To: GoodThing@tryst.com
SUBJ: My office supply fetish
Meet me at the usual time Tuesday for fun with a ream of 24 lb. cream laid paper, half a dozen medium-firm Dixon Ticonderogas, and a few well-placed binder clips.
TIKKITA TIKKA TIKKA TIK

A BIT LATER...
WHEN DID YOU PLAN ON TELLING ME, HARRIET? WHEN THE CONTRACTIONS WERE A MINUTE APART?
LOOK, I KNOW YOU HAVE STRONG FEELINGS ABOUT...WELL, ABOUT EVERYTHING. BUT ESPECIALLY ABOUT THIS. I DIDN'T WANT TO TELL YOU TILL AFTER I WAS PREGNANT.

SAY IT'S NOT TRUE! TELL ME YOU'RE NOT GONNA BECOME ONE OF THOSE "WE'RE JUST LIKE EVERYONE ELSE" CLONES!
LOOK, THIS IS SOMETHING I'VE ALWAYS WANTED. WILL YOU SIT DOWN?

IF THE CHRISTIAN RIGHT WERE SMART, THEY'D CONVERT ALL THOSE EX-GAY OPERATIONS TO LESBIAN-FRIENDLY SPERM BANKS. THEY'D HAVE US ALL SO BUSY ECSTATICALLY PUMPING BREAST MILK, WE'D NEVER NOTICE THEM TAKING OVER THE WHOLE FREAKING WORLD.

OH, PLEASE. IF I WAS AFTER THE MISS MIDDLE AMERICA TITLE, BECOMING A SINGLE LESBIAN MOTHER IS NOT THE WAY I'D GO ABOUT IT.
AND THAT'S ANOTHER THING! HOW ARE YOU GONNA DO THIS ALL BY YOURSELF?
JAVA JONES

WELL, I WOULDN'T MIND HAVING A PARTNER, BUT IT JUST HASN'T HAPPENED. AND I'M NOT GETTING ANY YOUNGER. BESIDES, MILLIONS OF WOMEN DO IT EVERY DAY. HOW DIFFICULT CAN IT BE?

THUMPITTA THUMPITTA CRASH!
RAFFI! WHAT DID I TELL YOU ABOUT ROLLERBLADING ON THE STAIRS?!
RING!

NOT WITHOUT YOUR HELMET!
CLARICE! I GOT YOUR PAGE! WHAT'S WRONG?
YOUR GROWLING CHILD
HERMIONE LEECH

TONI! THANKS FOR CALLING! QUICK QUESTION. RAFFI AND BILLY WERE JUST USING THE BATHROOM TOGETHER, AND, UH...IN SHORT, I FORGET HOW WE DECIDED TO EXPLAIN THE WHOLE UNCIRCUMCISED DEAL. Y'KNOW, SO HE DOESN'T FEEL BAD ABOUT BEING DIFFERENT.

EQUALITY BEGINS AT HOME LOBBY DAY
FREEDOM TO MARRY
VISITORS TO STATEHOUSE SIGN IN →

YOU CALLED ME OUT OF A MEETING WITH THE GOVERNOR FOR THIS? JESUS, CLARICE!
BILLY'S GOT A FUNNY PE-NIS!
I DO NOT!
KLUNKA!
ACTUALLY, BABE, NEVER MIND. I'VE GOT IT UNDER CONTROL.

the Sensuous Bookshop
311
©1999 BY ALISON BECHDEL

ONE AFTERNOON AT MADWIMMIN BOOKS...
DID YOU FIND ABSOLUTELY EVERYTHING YOU'RE LOOKING FOR?
UH... YES. THANKS. I'M ALL SET.
SO DIANE, I'VE NEVER BEEN TO A VEGAN SEDER BEFORE. WHAT DO WE DO ABOUT THE SHANK BONE?
OPEN ME CAREFULLY

OH, WE JUST USE PART OF AN OLD TOY DINOSAUR SKELETON. BUT THE EGG-LESS MATZO BALLS ARE LIKE EATING LEAD SHOT.
Y'KNOW, IF YOU LIKE THIS BOOK, YOU'LL LOVE THE NEW EROTICA ANTHOLOGY, "HOT AND BUTTERED."
LOIS.
NCR
EMILY DICKINSON'S INTIMATE LETTERS

THEA, I'M JUST TRYING TO PROVIDE A SERVICE.
I LIVE TO SERVICE. I MEAN, TO SERVE.
I'LL FINISH THIS. WHY DON'T YOU GO TIDY UP THE BUMPER-STICKER DISPLAY.

IN THE BACK...
AFTER I WATER THE PLANTS, SHOULD I FILL THE WEB ORDERS?
DON'T BOTHER. THERE AREN'T ANY. AND DO YOU KNOW WHY? BECAUSE IF YOU DO A SEARCH FOR OUR WEB SITE, AN AD FOR THE ONLINE BOOKSELLING BEHEMOTH medusa.com SHOWS UP ON THE PAGE.

IT MAGICALLY SAYS "BUY BOOKS ON MADWIMMIN BOOKS." CLICK THE LINK, AND YOU'RE IN THEIR CLUTCHES.

WILL THEY STICK AT NOTHING?!
THOSE ADS ARE PROGRAMMED TO SAY "BUY BOOKS ON" WHATEVER IT IS YOU'RE SEARCHING FOR. IT'S NOT, LIKE, INTENTIONAL.
YEAH, RIGHT. MY ONLY CONSOLATION IS, THEY'RE TROUNCING THE ONLINE SALES OF BUNNS&NOODLE AND BOUNDERS, BOOKS & MUZAK, TOO.
LATEST CASUALTIES: FULL CIRCLE BOOKS, ALBUQUERQUE; RED & BLACK BOOKS, SEATTLE

...AND THEY'RE STILL NOT TURNING A PROFIT.
CUTTHROATS! THEY EVEN HAVE TO WIN AT LOSING.
DESPITE LOSSES, medusa.com STOCK UP 1000%

BYE, BABY. CALL ME WHEN YOU'RE DONE.
'KAY, LATER.
BUMPERSTICKERS
MEAT PEOPLE SUC
got bovine grow hormone?

WHOA! SOPHIE AND MRS. ROBINSON? THE KID'S GOOD!
LOIS, THAT'S HER MOTHER.

OH. WELL THEN, IS SHE AVAILABLE?
DEAR GOD, I HOPE NOT.

DON'T WORRY, JEZANNA. THIS ONLINE SHOPPING FAD WON'T LAST. HOW CAN BUYING A BOOK ON YOUR COMPUTER COMPARE WITH BROWSING THROUGH REAL BOOKS, THE HEFT OF AN ELEGANT VOLUME IN YOUR HAND...
...THE SATISFACTION OF KNOWING YOUR MONEY IS SUSTAINING COMMUNITY, NOT LAYING WASTE TO IT.
...AND LET'S NOT FORGET THE WARMTH OF HUMAN INTERACTION WITH SOMEONE WHO KNOWS EXACTLY WHAT YOU LIKE.

MILLIONS FOR MUMIA
APRIL 24
LESBIAN RIGHTS SUMMIT D.C.

a just war?
or
just a war?

312

MEANWHILE, IN ANOTHER TAX BRACKET...

boy trouble
314
©1999 BY ALISON BECHDEL

MEEMA, LOOK!
OH MY GOD! CALL THE AMBULANCE! THAT'S THE WORST CASE OF FINGER-NAIL FUNGUS I'VE EVER SEEN!

IT'S NOT FUNGUS! IT'S POLISH, SEE? IT'S ALL SPARKLY!
OH, PHEW! WE WON'T HAVE TO AMPU-TATE! THAT'S REALLY COOL, RAF.

EMILY BROUGHT IT TO SCHOOL. I HAVE IT ON MY TOES TOO.
HI, BABE. DID YOU SEE OUR LITTLE FASHION PLATE?

YES, I DID. RAFFI, DID YOU TELL MEEMA WHAT HAPPENED?
NO.
OH. JOY.

WELL, UM, TAYLOR SAID ONLY GIRLS WEAR NAIL POLISH AND SO I, SO I SAID BUT I'M A BOY AND **I'M** WEARING NAIL POLISH, AND SO YOU'RE **WRONG**!
RAFFI, I'M PROUD OF YOU! THAT WAS A VERY SMART THING TO SAY!

AND THEN I KICKED HIM.

MEANWHILE...
AMAZING. YOU'D THINK THAT IN THE STAGGERING AMOUNT OF NEWS ANALYSIS THIS ISSUE HAS GENERATED, SOMEONE WOULD HAVE AT LEAST **MENTIONED** THE INTER-ESTING LITTLE COINCIDENCE THAT ALL THESE PISTOL-PACKIN' PUBESCENTS ARE **MALE**.
USA DISMAY
ALIENATED STUDENTS
LITTLETON MASSACRE
TEEN SHOOTERS
EPIDEMIC OF YOUTH VIOLENC

WHITE BOYS. CAN YOU IMAGINE IF IT WAS GIRLS, OR AFRICAN-AMERICAN KIDS WIPING OUT THEIR HOMEROOMS WITH TEC-9s? ALL THESE LAMENTS ABOUT OUR GENERIC "CHILDREN" WOULD GET AWFUL SPECIFIC AWFUL QUICK.
USA PATÉ
PREZ: "WE MUST TEACH OUR CHILDREN TO RESOLVE CONFLICTS WITH WORDS, NOT WEAPONS. ONCE THEY'RE ADULTS, THEY CAN USE CRUISE MISSILES."
Sale

WELL, MAYBE IT'S JUST THAT EVERYONE TAKES FOR GRANTED THAT BOYS ARE MORE PRONE TO VIOLENCE.
DUH! MALE VIOLENCE IS INVISIBLE. NO ONE WANTS TO LOOK AT IT AS A PROBLEM. THEY'D RATHER BLAME ANYTHING ELSE.
USA MELÉE
IT'S THE SUBURBAN ANOMIE
IT'S THE VIDEO GAMES
IT'S THE MUSIC
IT'S THE INTER-NET
BRING BACK SCHOOL PRAYER

I MEAN, I'M SURE ALL THAT AG-GRESSION CAME IN HANDY BACK IN THE PLEISTOCENE, BUT COME ON! LET'S EVOLVE A LITTLE, BOYS!
UH... RIGHT.
USA HURRAY
MADELINE ALBRIGHT TO MILOSEVIC: NEGOTIATE **THIS**, SLOBO.
MILANOS WITH ECHIN-ACEA

MS. KISSLER THINKS PERHAPS HE'S NOT GET-TING ENOUGH ROUGH-HOUSING AT HOME. YOU KNOW, WHAT WITH HAVING TWO MOTHERS AND ALL.
OH **REALLY?** PERHAPS MS. KISSLER COULD USE A LITTLE ROUGHHOUSING **HERSELF**.

AH, SUMMER VACATION! HAGGARD AND SPENT FROM THEIR STRESSFUL JOBS, SPARROW AND GINGER FINALLY GET SOME TIME OFF TO RECUPERATE.

THEIR HOUSE, THAT IS.
GOD, I HOPE THIS ISN'T LEAD PAINT. I DON'T HAVE ANY BRAIN CELLS TO SPARE.
SPEAKING OF ENVIRONMENTAL HAZARDS...
WAL-MART, AFTER BECOMING THE NATION'S SECOND LARGEST DRUG RETAILER...

HOW'S OUR FRIEND SYDNEY? HAS SHE DUMPED MO FOR THE CYBERSLUT YET?
OH, COME ON! YOU STILL THINK SYDNEY'S HAVING AN AFFAIR JUST BECAUSE...
MAGIC HAT
...BY PUTTING SCORES OF SMALLER STORES OUT OF BUSINESS...

JUST BECAUSE OF THOSE ONLINE CAPERS WITH LITTLE MISS "GOODTHING" I FOUND ON HER COMPUTER? WAKE UP, GINGER!
YEAH, WELL, YOU MAY BE RIGHT AFTER ALL. MO SAYS SYDNEY'S BEEN ACTING WEIRD LATELY, SECRETIVE.
...HAS ANNOUNCED IT WILL NOT BE CARRYING THE 'MORNING AFTER' EMERGENCY CONTRACEPTION PILL.

NOW DO YOU AGREE WE SHOULD WARN HER?
OH, SPARROW! WHAT WOULD WE SAY? "WE THINK YOUR GIRLFRIEND'S SCREWING AROUND ON YOU, BUT WE'RE NOT SURE, AND ANYWAY IT MIGHT ONLY BE VIRTUAL"?
WHEN ASKED IF THEY HAD ANY CONCERN ABOUT USING SHEER CORPORATE FORCE TO IMPOSE THEIR MORALITY ON WOMEN...

VIRTUAL SCHMIRTUAL. HOW LONG WILL THAT LAST? YOU KNOW WHAT LESBIANS ARE LIKE. THEY'LL CHAT ONLINE, THEY'LL PHONE, THEY'LL MEET, THEN SYDNEY'S OUTTA HERE.
WELL, MAYBE.
...BY LIMITING AVAILABLE HEALTH CARE OPTIONS, A WAL-MART SPOKESMAN HAD THIS TO SAY:

I SAY THE SOONER MO FINDS OUT, THE MORE LIKELY IT GETS NIPPED IN THE MODEM. ARE YOU BUSY TOMORROW AFTERNOON?
SPARROW! WE'RE WORKING ON THE HOUSE!
BWAHAHAHA!

WE HAVE TO EAT, DON'T WE?
DIT DIT DIT

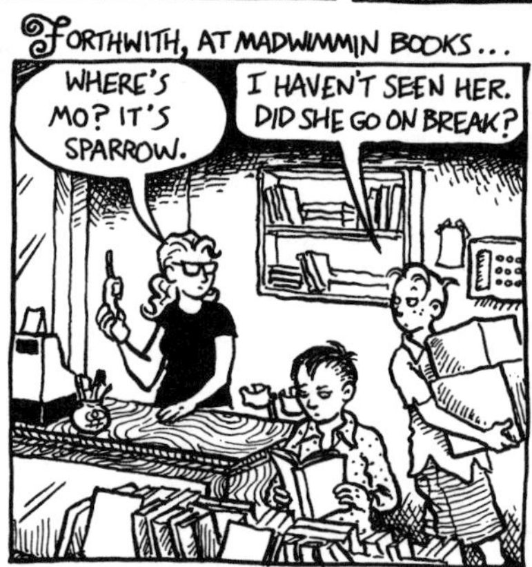

FORTHWITH, AT MADWIMMIN BOOKS...
WHERE'S MO? IT'S SPARROW.
I HAVEN'T SEEN HER. DID SHE GO ON BREAK?

MO? ARE YOU HERE? PHONE!
3MHz

UH...I'M ON THE OLD COMPUTER! I'LL TAKE IT UP HERE!

SHORTLY...
SO SHE'LL HAVE LUNCH WITH US TOMORROW?
YEP. I REALLY THINK WE'RE DOING THE RIGHT THING. SHE DIDN'T SOUND LIKE HER USUAL SELF AT ALL.
BIP

THAT EVENING, MO CONTINUES TO WONDER IF PERHAPS SYDNEY'S ATTENTION IS NOT UNDIVIDED.

ARE YOU GONNA WRITE ALL NIGHT AGAIN?
I'M ON A ROLL WITH THIS PIECE FOR JLQT.* GO TO BED. I'LL BE IN LATER.
* JOURNAL OF LUDICROUS QUEER THEORY

bewitched, bothered, & betrayed

 317

Mo's having trouble falling asleep while Sydney's still up doing God knows what on her computer.

GREAT. WORKING FOR A MULTI-NATIONAL BIOCHEMICAL CORPORATION THAT'S FORCING THE WORLD TO SWALLOW ITS **TRANSGENIC CROPS** IS A VALID CAREER OPTION AS LONG AS YOU'RE **OUT 'N PROUD!**

busted

 318

MO HAS JUST DISCOVERED SYDNEY ENGAGED IN A DISCUSSION OF INTIMATE UNDERGARMENTS WITH AN AS-YET-UNIDENTIFIED THIRD PARTY IN THE HALL CLOSET AT 3 AM.

HMM? DON'T YOU THINK? LIKE SOMETHING MARTHA STEWART MIGHT WEAR UNDER ONE OF THOSE SHAPELESS SWEATERS?

A CATALOG! IT'S... IT'S STUNNING.

NEXT DAY AT MADWIMMIN BOOKS, GINGER & SPARROW ARRIVE A BIT EARLY FOR THEIR LUNCHEON ENGAGEMENT WITH MO.

MEANWHILE, UPSTAIRS...

GoodThing: I love how you've decoupaged my thighs, Ms. Stewart. Now let me help you take off that handsome yet bulky cable-knit turtleneck.

CraftyGirl: Don't be so eager, my little scullion. Do I have to get out the macramé wrist restraints?

GoodThing: Yes, please! Tie me down on your 310 thread count sheets!

ZZZIP!

Mo has been caught in a rather compromising position with the old computer.

LATEST EXPLOITS

320

MO HAS JUST LEARNED THAT SYDNEY PUBLISHED A PARTICULARLY PRURIENT PORTION OF THEIR ONLINE INTERCOURSE IN "PANTHOUSE" MAGAZINE.

MEANWHILE, MO, STILL BRUISED FROM SYDNEY'S "PANTHOUSE" PERFIDY, TURNS FOR SUCCOR TO HER TRUSTY EX, HARRIET.

I GUESS MY TAWDRY DOMESTIC AFFAIRS LOOM PRETTY SMALL NEXT TO THE GREAT MYSTERY OF LIFE.

YEAH, IT'S AMAZING HOW PREGNANCY PUTS ALL THOSE PATHETIC LITTLE DRAMAS INTO PERSPECTIVE.

I.D. fixe?
323
©1999 BY ALISON BECHDEL

YOUR MAIL.
BRIDE'S MAGAZINE?
SPLAP!

IS THERE SOMETHING YOU'D LIKE TO TELL ME, SPARROW? ASIDE FROM THE FACT THAT ORGANZA IS BACK?
OH MY GOD! I BET MY MOM DID THIS! EVER SINCE I CAME OUT TO HER ABOUT STUART, SHE THINKS IT MEANS I'M STRAIGHT. SHE CAN'T UNDERSTAND THAT I'M A BISEXUAL LESBIAN!
BRIDE'S
ORGANZA! IT'S BACK!

WELL, IT'S A NUANCE THAT CAN ELUDE THE BEST OF US.
LOOK, IN A PERFECT WORLD, I WOULDN'T HAVE TO CALL MYSELF ANYTHING. BUT FOR NOW, BI-DYKE WORKS FOR ME, OKAY?
HMO PHOBIC
NGUYEN'S BAGELS

I THINK I'M A BUTCH LESBIAN IN A STRAIGHT MAN'S BODY.
SOFT BUTCH. MAY-BE.
IT'S NOT AS SIMPLE FOR EVERYONE AS IT IS FOR YOU, GINGER! SOMETIMES PEOPLE CHANGE. IDENTITY IS SO MUCH MORE COMPLEX AND FLUID THAN THESE RIGID LITTLE CATEGORIES OF STRAIGHT, GAY, AND BI CAN POSSIBLY REFLECT.

YOU'RE A SWEETHEART, LOIS. SEE YA LATER.
'KAY, JERRY. HAVE FUN.

WHO WAS THAT? DON'T TELL ME YOU'RE SEEING A MAN TOO.
NO, JUST LENDING HIM A TIE. THOUGH HE IS KIND OF HOT.

HE REMINDS ME OF SOMEONE... WHATSERNAME... YOU KNOW, THAT BUFF BABE, YOUR MECHANIC?
GERALDINE, EXACTLY. ONLY NOW HE'S A BUFF TRANS GUY, AND HIS NAME'S JERRY.

ARE YOU SERIOUS? LIKE, WITH SURGERY? AND TESTOSTERONE? GOD, I JUST CAN'T UNDERSTAND THAT!
UH..."SOMETIMES PEOPLE CHANGE"? "IDENTITY IS COMPLEX AND FLUID"? ANY OF THAT RING A BELL?

CHANGING YOUR BODY TO CONFORM TO A RIGID, CONVENTIONAL GENDER IDENTITY IS JUST MORE BINARY THINKING! WHAT WAS WRONG WITH BEING A BUTCH DYKE?
HE DOESN'T FEEL LIKE A BUTCH DYKE. HE FEELS LIKE A GAY MAN.
SKIP FLUID. PRESS "LIQUEFY."
HM

OH MY GOD! GERALDINE FROM RAINBOW AUTOMOTIVE?! I USED TO HAVE SUCH A THING FOR HER! I MEAN HIM... I MEAN.. WOW!
DON'T GET TOO EXCITED, STU. HE GOES MORE FOR THE STUDHORSE TYPE.
HMO PHOBIC

trite and true
324

OKAY, I CAN GET OUT OF DEBT, SPEND A YEAR DOING RESEARCH, ANOTHER YEAR IN BARCELONA OR PARIS WRITING MY BOOK, THE YEAR AFTER THAT TREKKING IN NEPAL, AND STILL HAVE CHANGE LEFT OVER TO BUY A DECENT COUCH.
TIKKA TIKKA TIK
...THE INDONESIAN ARMY HAS RECEIVED OVER A BILLION DOLLARS OF MILITARY AID FROM THE US...

SYDNEY, GIVE IT UP. YOU'RE NOT GONNA WIN A MACARTHUR GENIUS GRANT.
...INCLUDING SECRET TRAININGS FOR THE SPECIAL FORCES WHO DIRECTED ANTI-INDEPENDENCE MILITIAS IN THEIR SLAUGHTER OF TIMORESE CIVILIANS...

I KNOW YOU'RE THREATENED BY MY HIGH LEVEL OF ACHIEVEMENT, MO, BUT THAT'S NO REASON TO BE PISSY.
RIGHT. WELL, YOU SET THE WORLD ON FIRE. I'M GOING OVER TO HARRIET'S.
...AFTER ADMITTING THAT HE'D LOST CONTROL OF HIS TROOPS, INDONESIA'S GENERAL WIRANTO DEMONSTRATED HIS EMOTION ABOUT LEAVING EAST TIMOR BY PUBLICLY CROONING "FEELINGS."
NOT MADE UP!

FOR A SCINTILLATING DISCUSSION OF HER LATEST ULTRASOUND? I THOUGHT SHE WAS BORING YOU SILLY WITH ALL THAT BABY TALK.
HEY, HARRIET'S TRITE OBSERVATIONS ABOUT THE MIRACLE OF A NEW LIFE BEAT LISTENING TO YOU ANY DAY OF THE WEEK.
...THE US COMMANDER-IN-CHIEF OF THE PACIFIC RESPONDED WITH A MOVING RENDITION OF "WIND BENEATH MY WINGS."
MADE UP.

OKAY! YOU'VE MILKED THIS SYDNEY-IN-THE-DOGHOUSE THING JUST ABOUT LONG ENOUGH. WHEN ARE YOU GOING TO STOP BEING MAD?
RING
...SO I WAS THE ONE WITH ALL THE GLORY...

HELLO?
HUH-WO, AUNTIE! DERE'S A WIDDLE BITTY BABY HERE TO TALK TO YOU.
AND YOU WERE THE ONE WITH ALL THE STRAIN...

I'M SORRY. YOU HAVE THE WRONG NUMBER.
CLIK!
MONICA?!
VIRGINIA? NO, IT'S SYDNEY. HANG ON.

I THINK YOUR MOTHER HAS OFFICIALLY LOST IT.
MOM? WHAT'S WRONG?

ROSE HAD THE BABY! A PERFECT LITTLE GIRL! OH, MONICA! SHE LOOKS JUST LIKE YOU DID, ONLY MUCH PRETTIER!
OH MY GOD! REALLY?!
WHAT? WHAT HAPPENED?!

MY SISTER-IN-LAW HAD HER BABY! I'M AN AUNT! MY BROTHER'S A FATHER! MY MOTHER'S A GRANDMA! MY DAD'S A...
I THINK I CAN GENERALIZE FROM THERE.

OH MY GOD! SHE LOOKS LIKE ME! A NEW LIFE! TINY FINGERS AND TOES! IT'S A MIRACLE!
SHE LOOKS LIKE YOU? SNRK!
lunge
SIS? IT'S SCOTT. CAN YOU BELIEVE IT? LPGA, HERE WE COME! MAYBE SHE'LL EVEN BE A LESBIAN! THE BEST GOLFERS ALWAYS ARE, YOU KNOW.

sixty minute man
©1999 BY ALISON BECHDEL

325
YOU WENT TO THE PARK ALREADY? THAT WAS QUICK.
WE ONLY MADE IT TO THE END OF THE BLOCK. SHE'S HAVING A BAD DAY.
OOF! C'MON, PUP. YOU CAN DO IT.

POOR, SWEET DIGGER! ARE YOU STIFF, GIRL?
PANT
PANT
WHITE GUY GOES ON A SHOOTING SPREE

NOT TOO STIFF TO LICK UP SOME CHUNKS FROM A PILE OF BARF BEFORE I COULD STOP HER.
SO LONG, BUCKOS. I'M OFF TO THE FIRST INTERNATIONAL DRAG KING EXTRAVAGANZA IN COLUMBUS.
ANOTHER WHITE GUY GOES ON ANOTHER SHOOTING SPREE

LOIS! YOU'RE NOT GOING ON THE PLANE LIKE THAT!
I WANT TO FULLY IMMERSE MYSELF IN THE TRANSGRESSIVE EXPERIENCE.
YOU SMELL LIKE YOU FULLY IMMERSED YOURSELF IN TRANSMISSION FLUID.
NASCAR
'NOTHER WHITE GUY, 'NOTHER SHOOTING SPREE

JERRY LENT ME ONE OF HIS DIRTY UNIFORMS. WHAT DO YOU THINK? MAX AXLE, FRONT END EXPERT. I'M GONNA LIP-SYNCH TO "I'M YOUR VEHICLE, BABY."
GOD, THIS DRAG KING CRAZE IS SO RETROGRADE! MEN ARE DESTROYING THE PLANET! WHY COMPETE TO SEE WHO CAN MIMIC THEM MOST CONVINCINGLY?!
SEE OUR NEW SHOOTING SPREE SECTION FOR MORE NEWS

UH... BECAUSE I'M GOOD AT IT?
I DUNNO, LOIS. IT JUST SEEMS SO... SO MISOGYNIST. I COULD UNDERSTAND IF YOU WERE CRITIQUING MASCULINE STEREOTYPES INSTEAD OF GLORIFYING THEM, BUT...
NASCAR

ONE COULD ARGUE THAT DRAG IS THE ULTIMATE CRITIQUE OF GENDER STEREOTYPES, AND THUS INHERENTLY FEMINIST...
OH, PUT IT IN A TERM PAPER! LOOK, IT'S JUST A WAY OF EXPRESSING MY MASCULINE SIDE. MAYBE I AM GLORIFYING MASCULINITY. IS THAT SO TERRIBLE?
WOOOOOOO

HEY, WHO USED UP ALL MY ROSEMARY-CUCUMBER CONDITIONER? I NEED IT TO KEEP MY BEARD SILKY!

A REAL MACK-DADDY IS A GLORIOUS THING.
DUDE, JUST RUB A LITTLE CASTROL 30 WEIGHT INTO IT. WORKS FOR ME.

LABOR of LOVE
326
©1999 BY ALISON BECHDEL

REMEMBER, RAF. NO KICKING!
NOT EVEN THE BALL?
ZIP!
CARLOS, MAKE SURE HE USES HIS INHALER IF HE STARTS WHEEZING.

BYE, SWEETIE!
HAVE FUN DOING WHATEVER IT IS YOU GIRLS DO TOGETHER.

I WISH YOU WOULDN'T DISCUSS OUR SEX LIFE WITH HIM.
WHAT SEX LIFE?

OKAY, OKAY. LET'S NOT GET INTO A BIG DISCUSSION. THAT ALWAYS RUINS IT.
NO TALK. SUITS ME FINE.

SHORTLY...
The Distress

OH! IT'S GONNA SNOW TONIGHT! WE HAVE TO BRING IN THE GRILL AND LAWN CHAIRS!
SHHH... NO TALK.
AT HISTORIC DINNER, JERRY FALWELL'S SUPPORTERS AND GAY & LESBIAN CHRISTIANS AGREE TO DISAGREE

TONI, LOOK. IT'S JUST NOT WORKING FOR ME. I HAVE TO BE IN THE MOOD.
IF WE WAITED UNTIL WE WERE BOTH IN THE MOOD AND BOTH HAD TIME, WE'D BE DEAD. THAT'S WHY WE AGREED TO SCHEDULE IT!
EVANGELICALS SAY IT WAS DELICIOUS. GAYS CALL TURKEY TETRAZZINI "AN ABOMINATION."

ALL I CAN THINK ABOUT IS THOSE REPUBLICANS VOTING DOWN THE COMPREHENSIVE TEST BAN TREATY! IT'S LIKE THEY WANT US TO BURN UP IN A NUCLEAR ARMAGEDDON!

AND HOW 'BOUT THE POSSIBILITY THAT OUR NEXT PRESIDENT COULD BE A MAN WITH THE CULTURAL LITERACY OF A HEAD OF ICEBERG LETTUCE? DOESN'T THAT COOL YOUR ARDOR?

GET YOUR STORY STRAIGHT, CLARICE. IS IT THE ELECTION, NUCLEAR HOLOCAUST, OR THE LAWN FURNITURE?
GEORGE W: "ONCE I READ A BOOK BY JOHN LA CARE, ER... CARRIER? WHATEVER. MY CAMPAIGN BUDGET EXCEEDS THE G.N.P."

I BET YOU'D FOCUS PRETTY DAMN QUICK IF IT WAS GINGER LYING HERE INSTEAD OF ME.

UH... THAT'S COMPLETELY UNTRUE! COME BACK, I'M INTO IT NOW!
I'M SURE YOU'LL DO JUST FINE ON YOUR OWN. WHEN YOU'RE DONE, COME HELP ME MOVE THE GRILL.

On a visit to her brother, sister-in-law, and **new niece**, Mo appears to be completely be-sotted.

Holiday on ICE
328
©1999 BY ALISON BECHDEL

'TIS THE SEASON! AT MO & SYDNEY'S...
MO, I DON'T HAVE TIME FOR THIS. I HAVE A HUNDRED PAPERS TO GRADE. I'M JUST GONNA BUY PRESENTS LIKE A NORMAL PERSON.
FINE. FEED THE CONSUMER CAPITALIST MACHINE. ANNIHILATE YOURSELF WITH DEBT.
Buy.com
MOTHRA STEWART LIVING
DO IT YOURSELF GIFTS
PIPE KLEENRS
ELMY'S

IF YOU REALLY CARED ABOUT FIGHTING CAPITALISM, YOU'D TRY POLYAMORY. MONOGAMY IS JUST A DEVICE TO CONSOLIDATE WEALTH BY CREATING LEGAL HEIRS.
MAKE YOUR OWN I.P.O.
QUICK 'N E-Z

DO WE HAVE AN ACETYLENE TORCH?
Things.com
MARTHA STEWART Livi

AT MADWIMMIN BOOKS...
AND THE LAST BOOK ON MY LIST IS "LOVE MAKES A FAMILY," IN HARDCOVER.
YEP, RIGHT HERE. LET ME KNOW WHEN YOU'RE READY TO CHECK OUT. I'LL BE WORKING ON THE WINDOW DISPLAY.
HARRY POTTER & THE GARGANTUAN ROYALTY CHECK
HARRY POTTER

OH, I WON'T BE BUYING ANYTHING. I JUST WANTED TO SEE THE ACTUAL BOOKS BEFORE I ORDERED THEM FROM MEDUSA.COM. THANKS FOR YOUR HELP.
THUMB THUMB
LUV MAKES A MILY

AT SPARROW, STU, LOIS AND GINGER'S DIGS...
BLACK COHOSH TINCTURE.
CHECK.
CANDLES.
FLAX OIL.
CHECK.
CHECK.
KAVA KAVA ROOT.
CHECK.
SUMMONING THE DARK LORD?

JUST MAKING SURE WE'VE GOT THE NECESSITIES ON HAND IN CASE OF A Y2K MELTDOWN.

OH, GINGER! DON'T FORGET TO STOCK UP ON DOG FOOD!
UM... RIGHT.

AND AT MIDTOWN MIDWIFERY SERVICES...
OH, JUST A SLIGHT SNOWBOARDING MISHAP. IT'S NOTHING. HOW ARE YOU FEELING?
NOT SO GREAT, ACTUALLY. I'VE HAD A SPLITTING HEADACHE ALL DAY.
IDITAROD
THE PREGNANT GUIDE TO ULTIMATE LESBIANISM

HMM. REALLY.
MIRIAM? IS EVERYTHING OKAY?

HARRIET, YOUR BLOOD PRESSURE IS AWFULLY HIGH. TO BE ON THE SAFE SIDE, I'M GOING TO SUGGEST THAT TONI TAKE YOU TO THE HOSPITAL IMMEDIATELY.
THE HOSPITAL? BUT... BUT SHE'S NOT DUE FOR ANOTHER WEEK!
I CAN'T GO TO THE HOSPITAL! I HAVE MY LAMAZE CLASS TONIGHT!
RAID GAULOISES

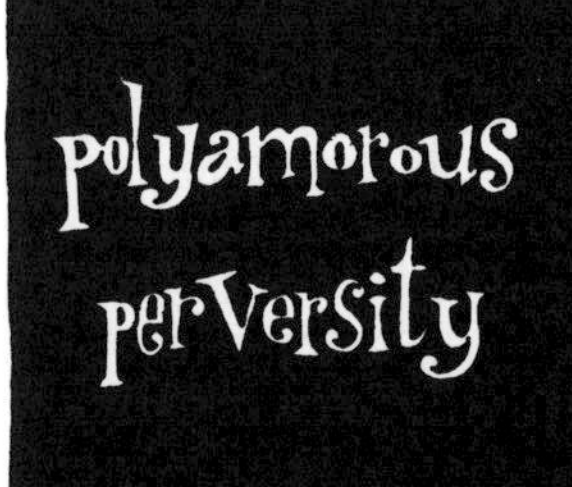
polyamorous perversity

330

MO'S HOLIDAY CRAFTS PROJECT APPEARS TO HAVE BEEN DERAILED.
IF WE WERE POLYAMOROUS, WE COULD EACH DO THIS WITH OTHER PEOPLE, THEN COMPARE NOTES. WOULDN'T THAT BE HOT?
CRAFTSMAN
POLYURETHANE

YOU DRIVE ME CRAZY.
I KNOW.

SOMEWHAT LATER...

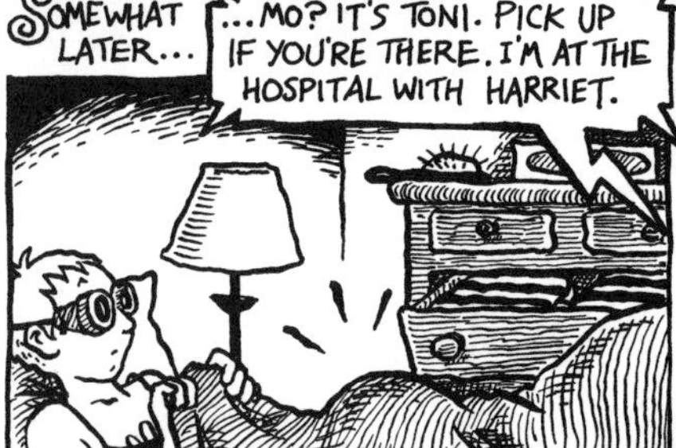
...MO? IT'S TONI. PICK UP IF YOU'RE THERE. I'M AT THE HOSPITAL WITH HARRIET.

A C-SECTION? IS SHE OKAY?
I DUNNO. SHE'S STILL IN THE O.R. THEY SAID THE BABY WAS IN TROUBLE.

SHORTLY...
THANKS FOR COMING ALONG.
...IF YOU ASK ME, THE WORLD TRADE ORGANIZATION DEMONSTRATORS IN SEATTLE WERE A BUNCH OF...

ACTUALLY, MO, I'VE BEEN MEANING TO TALK TO YOU ABOUT HOW INVOLVED YOU'VE GOTTEN WITH HARRIET'S PREGNANCY.
...MISGUIDED 'SIXTIES LEFTOVERS WHO WOULDN'T KNOW A TARIFF FROM A STICK OF DEODORANT...

INVOLVED? SHE'S MY BEST FRIEND!
SHE'S ALSO YOUR EX.
HOSPITAL PARKING
IF YOU WANT TO IMPROVE LABOR AND ENVIRONMENTAL STANDARDS IN DEVELOPING COUNTRIES, THE ANSWER IS FEWER RESTRICTIONS ON TRADE, NOT MORE.

YOU'RE JEALOUS OF HARRIET? GOD! Y'KNOW, YOU COULDN'T HANDLE POLYAMORY!
PARKING $3 IN ADVANCE
CHOMSKY NEOLIBERALISM & GLOBAL ORDER
NO WTO
WHY? BECAUSE I GET PAID A LARGE SALARY BY THE GLOBAL MEDIA CONGLOMERATE THAT OWNS THIS STATION TO TELL YOU SO, THAT'S WHY.

SOON...
MO! LOOK! INSTANT HARRIET JUNIOR!
OH MY GOD! IS HARRIET OKAY?
SHE'S FINE. STILL DRIFTING IN AND OUT FROM THE ANESTHESIA. EVERY ONCE IN A WHILE SHE WAKES UP AND ASKS IF THE BABY'S ALL RIGHT. SHE ASKED FOR YOU TOO, MO.
MOAB

WOW, REALLY? SHE'S BEEN ASKING FOR ME?
HOW VERY TOUCHING.
WELL, TO PUT IT IN PERSPECTIVE, SHE'S ALSO BEEN ASKING FOR OPRAH.
I DO NOT LIKE GREEN EGGS AND HAM.

LUNCH MAKES A FAMILY
©1999 BY ALISON BECHDEL

331
GIVE HER TO ME, MO.
EHHH!
TONI, CAN YOU PUT THIS HERBAL WRAP BACK IN THE MICROWAVE A MINUTE?
RINGG!
CARLOS, WHERE'S MY FRIED EGG SANDWICH?
KEEP YOUR SHIRT ON.
VERMONT SUPREME COURT MAKES LANDMARK DECISION

PESKY SINGLE MOTHERS. YOU'RE RUNNING THIS GREAT NATION INTO THE GROUND.
NOW FEED IT TO ME.

HARRIET, LET'S MOVE TO VERMONT. I COULD MAKE A QUASI-HONEST WOMAN OF YOU.
COVER ME AND ISABEL WITH YOUR HEALTH PLAN, AND WE'LL FOLLOW YOU ANYWHERE.
LESBIAN AND GAY COUPLES DESERVE SAME BENEFITS AS NORMAL MARRIED PEOPLE

MO, IT'S YOUR GIRLFRIEND.
THERE GOES THE HONEYMOON IN STOWE.

I SAID NO MAYO.
NO, I'M GONNA EAT HERE.... SYDNEY, YOU'LL BE FINE! BOIL SOME RAMEN OR SOMETHING!

MEANWHILE...
HELLO, BABY. SORRY I WAS AT WORK SO LONG. HOW'S MY SWEET GIRL?

SHE HARDLY GOT OFF HER BED ALL DAY.
GOD, SPARROW. I DON'T KNOW HOW TO MAKE THIS DECISION. SHE'S SO HAPPY TO SEE ME, BUT SHE CAN BARELY MOVE, AND SHE'S NOT EATING.

ACTUALLY, SHE HAD A FEW BITES OF STEAK EARLIER. I BOUGHT ONE AND COOKED IT FOR HER. THE REST IS ON THE TOP SHELF OF THE FRIDGE IF YOU WANT TO GIVE HER MORE.

YOU COOKED A STEAK? IS THIS THE SAME WOMAN WHO ONCE TRIED TO CONVINCE ME DOGS COULD LIVE ON RICE AND BREWER'S YEAST BECAUSE SHE DIDN'T WANT MEAT IN THE HOUSE?

THAT'S DEVOTION, DIGGER.
LOOK, JUST DON'T TELL STUART I WAS SEARING FLESH IN HIS CALPHALON SAUTÉ PAN. HE'S EVEN MORE OF A PURIST THAN I AM.

HEY, I FINISHED OFF THAT SEITAN ON THE TOP SHELF OF THE FRIDGE. DELICIOUS! WHAT WAS IT MARINATED IN?

CLARICE HAS RUN INTO HER ~~NEMESIS~~ NEIGHBOR BILL AT THE LOCAL PARK WHERE THEIR RESPECTIVE CHILDREN ARE DISPORTING THEMSELVES.

Village IDIOT
333
© 2000 BY ALISON BECHDEL

MO, WHAT ARE YOU **DOING**?! THE DEAN'S RECEPTION IS AT EIGHT! I'M JUST GONNA CHANGE MY CLOTHES, THEN WE HAVE TO LEAVE!
I DON'T FEEL SO GOOD, SYDNEY.
A TIP O' THE NIB TO WILL MARQUESS!

LOOK, I KNOW YOU HATE THESE THINGS, BUT I HARDLY EVER ASK YOU TO COME, AND THIS ONE'S IMPORTANT!
I THINK IT'S THE FLU. GO WITHOUT ME. YOU'LL BE FINE.

GOD, THIS FOURTH YEAR SCRUTINY IS KILLING ME. I WAS HOPING YOU COULD HELP ME SCORE SOME POINTS WITH THE DEAN TONIGHT.
HOW WOULD YOUR LESBO GIRLFRIEND POSSIBLY SCORE YOU POINTS?
ECO-BLOW
POLY-AMORY & YOU

BECAUSE MY PRESSED, STARCHED, LATIN PUN-SPEWING ARCHRIVAL **BETSY GILHOOLY** WILL BE THERE WITH **HER** GIRLFRIEND.
OH, RIGHT. THE ONE YOU'RE COMPETING WITH FOR TENURE.

AND TO TOP IT OFF, NOW THE GIRLFRIEND'S **PREGNANT**. THE DEAN'S VERY BIG ON CHILDREN. EVEN BIOENGINEERED ONES.
RING
HELLO?
MO, I THINK I HAVE THE FLU OR SOMETHING. I CAN'T GET OFF THE COUCH. CAN YOU COME OVER AND HELP WITH ISABEL?
SWINGATRONIC

OKAY, HARRIET. I'LL BE RIGHT THERE.
IF YOU'RE TOO SICK TO COME TO THE RECEPTION, YOU'RE TOO SICK TO GO PLAY HOUSE!
POINK!

HARRIET, MO'S A MESS. YOU'LL HAVE TO FIND ANOTHER NANNY. ... OH, REALLY?... EVERYONE? YOU DON'T SAY...
PC COMPACT FLUORESCENT BULB.

LATER THAT EVENING...
WHAT A NICE WAY TO END THE WORKDAY THESE COLLEGIAL GATHERINGS ARE, DEAN. OR AS I ALWAYS SAY, SIC TRANSIT GLORIA **TUESDAY**! AH HA HA HA HA!
QUITE.

MS. KRUKOWSKI! WHO'S THIS LITTLE CHERUB! I DIDN'T KNOW YOU WERE A PARENT!
WELL, DEAN, TECHNICALLY I'M JUST HELPING OUT A SICK FRIEND, BUT YOU KNOW WHAT THEY SAY— IT TAKES A VILLAGE TO RAISE A CHILD.

OLD DOG NEW TRICKS
334
©2000 BY ALISON BECHDEL

AAAH!

GOD, LOIS! I WISH YOU'D STICK TO ONE DRAG PERSONA.
COOL. YOU REALLY THOUGHT I WAS SOME SKEEVY GUY!
BIRCH BARK
TAMPONS WITH DIOXIN

I KNEW IT WAS YOU, BUT THAT SHIRT TRIGGERED A FLASH-BACK TO MY JUN-IOR PROM.
DAMN. MAYBE BIGGER SIDEBURNS?
DING DONG
1000 SHEETS
HEMPONS

WHAT'S HAPPENIN', PRETTY LADY?

HI, LOIS. CUTE SHIRT. I'M HERE TO SEE DIGGER.
SNICK

GINGER! THE VET'S HERE!
TIME FOR YOUR CHECKUP, BUMBLEPUPPY.
A TIP O' THE NIB TO LASKY, KIRA & WALTER!

MEANWHILE, IN SUBURBIA...
...OH, AND THIS AFTERNOON I FINALLY CONVINCED ANN NEXT DOOR TO HAVE SOME OF US FROM FREEDOM TO MARRY COME SPEAK TO HER ROTARY CLUB CHAPTER.
UH HUH.
FANNING THE ASHES

CLARICE, IF YOU WON'T STOP READING THAT BOOK LONG ENOUGH TO LISTEN TO ME, HOW'S IT SUPPOSED TO HELP OUR RELATIONSHIP?
HAULING THE ASHES

WAIT, I'M JUST CHECKING TO SEE IF THE WORDS "ROTARY CLUB" ARE LISTED IN THE SECTION ON "EXPANDING YOUR EROTIC VOCABULARY."
HOW TO AVOID SEXUAL BOREDOM IN YOUR LONG-TERM RELATIONSHIP

BACK AT GINGER'S HOUSE...
SHE'S WEAK, BUT CLEARLY SHE'S STILL TAKING COMFORT IN EATING AND GET-TING PETTED. YOU'LL HAVE TO DETER-MINE WHEN THE DISCOMFORT STARTS TO OUTWEIGH THE PLEASURE. WHEN IT'S TIME, WE CAN DO IT RIGHT HERE.
HOW IS SHE?

BARAR-ARAR!!
BETTER THAN I THOUGHT.
THANKS, DIGGER. I'LL DEFINITELY KEEP THE MUTTON-CHOPS.

A FINE MESS
335
©2000 BY ALISON BECHDEL

THUD!
CRASH!
MADWIMMIN BOOKS
WE'RE EXPANDING
CAFE OPENING SOON!
café
Open

...AND I WORKED OUT A DEAL WITH THE WOMEN WHO RUN THE CAFÉ NEXT DOOR, AND WE'RE CONNECTING OUR SPACES.
HUH. SO NOW PEOPLE CAN GET COFFEE STAINS AND CRUMBS ALL OVER YOUR BOOKS INSTEAD OF THE ONES AT BUNNS & NOODLE.
STRANGE SISTERS

CHUNK!
EXACTLY. AND IN A COZIER ATMOSPHERE.

HEY, SOPH. HOW WAS SCHOOL?
THE USUAL CZARIST REGIME. OUR GAY/STRAIGHT ALLIANCE IS TRYING TO GET A BUS TO GO TO THE MARCH, AND IT'S LIKE WE SUGGESTED NEUTERING THE FOOTBALL TEAM.

WHAT MARCH?
THE MILLENNIUM MARCH? THE LESBIAN/GAY/BI/TRANS MARCH ON WASHINGTON? AREN'T YOU GOING?

OH, ABSOLUTELY! I'VE ALREADY GOT MY OFFICIAL DISCOUNT CARD, AND MY TICKET TO THE GARTH BROOKS CONCERT! AND I CAN'T WAIT TO SHOP AT THE GAY-FRIENDLY VENDOR BOOTHS! I'M FEELING SO EMPOWERED!
Y'KNOW, YOU THINK YOU'RE SUCH A BIG RADICAL, BUT YOU'RE REALLY JUST A WHINY ELITIST.
THUD!

HEY, THE BIGWIG MARCH ORGANIZERS ARE THE ELITISTS! THEY'RE THE ONES WHO DECIDED TO STAGE THIS DAMN THING WITHOUT CONSULTING THE REST OF THE COMMUNITY.
MO, I'M SORRY THE GOOD OLD DAYS ARE GONE, WHEN EVERYONE SAT AROUND PROCESSING FOR YEARS BEFORE PUTTING UP A FLIER. BUT DON'T TRY AND RUIN THIS FOR ME!

I'M EXCITED ABOUT THIS MARCH AND I'M GOING!
WHAT MARCH?
CRASH
OFFICE

THAT EVENING...
SYDNEY! I THOUGHT YOU WERE GONNA CLEAN THE KITCHEN!
SORRY, BABE. I'VE BEEN WORKING ON THIS LECTURE.
PRETZO RODS
Rice Milk

WELL HOW AM I SUPPOSED TO COOK?!
OH, DON'T BOTHER. I'M NOT HUNGRY.
NUT TER
RICE MILK

WHEW! THE LADY PORCUPINES ARE UP BY ONE AT THE HALFTIME BUZZER! TUNE IN NEXT TIME AS THE TECHNICAL FOULS CONTINUE!

WE LAST LEFT OUR SPORADIC SPORTSFANS AT HALF-TIME.

PLAY APPEARS TO HAVE RESUMED.

GINGER AND CLARICE FLIRT WITH A POSSIBILITY...

Y'KNOW, THERE'S A PICKUP GAME AT THE 'Y' WEDNESDAY NIGHTS. WE SHOULD GO SOMETIME.

THAT SOUNDS REALLY FUN. I HAVEN'T TOUCHED A BALL IN YEARS.

intervention
©2000 BY ALISON BECHDEL
339
6.7
OW!
LOIS! CAN YOU HELP DIGGER? I JUST DID SOMETHING TO MY BACK!
BEING and NOTHINGNESS
C'MON, SWEET GIRL.
CAN YOU HOLD HER UP WHILE SHE POOPS?
OLD FANNY PACK
UH...
WAIT'LL SHE'S READY AND FINDS A SPOT.
LATER...
MONSANTO
GINGER?
UM...WE NEED TO TALK.
I'M SORRY ABOUT THE NEWSPAPERS ON THE KITCHEN FLOOR. I'LL PUT DOWN FRESH ONES AFTER I ICE MY BACK.
IT'S NOT NICE TO GENETICALLY ALTER MOTHER NATURE
IT'S NOT THE PAPERS. LOOK, YOU KNOW HOW MUCH WE LOVE DIGGER, BUT... BUT...
BUT...
BUT WHAT?
WE THINK IT'S TIME.
WH-WHAT?
SHE'S NOT HAVING FUN ANYMORE.
YOU DON'T KNOW THAT! JESUS! GOD FORBID ANYONE SHOULD NEED A LITTLE EXTRA HELP AROUND HERE! WHY DON'T YOU PUT ME DOWN WHILE YOU'RE AT IT?
OW!
GINGER, LOOK AT HER.
JUST GET OUT OF HERE. LEAVE US ALONE.
YOU'RE OKAY, AREN'T YOU, MY LI'L WILDEBEEST?
AREN'T YOU?

the sweet bye-and-bye

6·21

340

THE VET IS COMING AT TWO.

DIGGER'S DEVOTEES HAVE BEEN STOPPING BY ALL MORNING TO PAY THEIR FINAL RESPECTS.

WHO ARE ALL THESE WOMEN PETTING DIGGER?

THAT'S LOIS'S OLD AFFINITY GROUP. WHAT ACTION ARE YOU PLANNING HERE? THE ONE WHERE YOU BLOCKADED THE BANK, OR THE ONE WHERE YOU CHAINED YOURSELVES TO THE FEDERAL BUILDING?

that obscure object of desire
342
© 2000 BY ALISON BECHDEL

AHH... A PERFECT SATURDAY SUMMER'S MORN. HOW BEST TO PARTAKE OF ITS AMBROSIAL PROMISE?
Phoe-be

WHEEEE SKRRRR! DOINK DOINK SCHSCHXXXX! WEL-COME!
WHO'S THAT POKÉMON?!
A.O. HELL
SCIENTISTS CRACK GENETIC CODE... BOOK OF LIFE... GOD ...PINNACLE ...HISTORY OF MANKIND ETC. ETC.

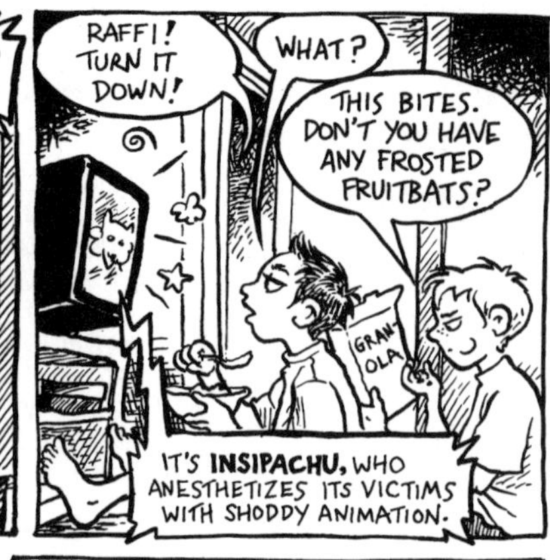

RAFFI! TURN IT DOWN!
WHAT?
THIS BITES. DON'T YOU HAVE ANY FROSTED FRUITBATS?
GRAN-OLA
IT'S INSIPACHU, WHO ANESTHETIZES ITS VICTIMS WITH SHODDY ANIMATION.

WHAT A BEAUTIFUL DAY!
FARE FINDER
DISEASE WILL BE ERADICATED! AGING PROCESS REVERSED! STATIC CLING BANISHED!

WHERE'VE YOU BEEN? I WOKE UP AND YOU WERE GONE.
I WAS FAST WALKING WITH GLORIA. DIDN'T YOU HEAR HER CALL EARLIER?
FOR SALE: CLEAN, CHEAP, SAFE NUCLEAR POWER PLANT
SHIK

GREAT. I'M RESEARCHING PLANE FARES TO VERMONT SO WE CAN GET MARRIED AND YOU'RE OFF CAVORTING WITH ANOTHER WOMAN.
I THOUGHT YOU DIDN'T WANT TO GO TO VERMONT!
TORONTO WOMEN'S BOOK STORE

AND I WASN'T CAVORTING. BUT SO WHAT IF I HAD BEEN? WE DECIDED TO TRY IT, REMEMBER?
WE DECIDED TO TALK ABOUT IT AND MAYBE TRY IT. "FAST WALKING!" SHEESH! WHERE'D YOU GET THAT? "SELF" MAGAZINE?
RAP RAP
UM... HELLO?

ANN! HI!
SORRY TO BARGE IN. I CAME TO GET BILLY.
FedEx

BILLY! IT'S HERE! THE NEW HARRY POTTER BOOK!
GRANOLA

MEDUSA.COM SHIPPED IT OVERNIGHT FOR FREE BECAUSE WE WERE ONE OF THE FIRST 250 BILLION CUSTOMERS TO PLACE AN ORDER.
TORONTO WOMEN'S BOOK STORE
SHRED

WE'RE GETTING YOUR COPY THIS AFTERNOON, RAFFI. REMEMBER?
AT OUR LOCAL INDEPENDENT BOOKSTORE!
BUT I WANT IT NOW.

FIVE MINUTES LATER...
WAY TO SET LIMITS.
IT'S A SPECIAL EVENT, CLARICE. ONE BOOK WON'T SPOIL HIM.
CAN WE GET SOME FROSTED FRUITBATS TOO?

BOOKED
343
©2000 BY ALISON BECHDEL

HI, LOIS.
HI! HEY, RAFFI! HURRY BACK TO THE KIDS' AREA! MO'S JUST ABOUT TO START READING ALOUD!
MADWIMMIN BOOKS & CAFÉ
HARRY PALOOZA! GET THE GOBLET OF FIRE TODAY! FUN, GAMES, SNACKS
DONUTS
JUICE

THAT'S HARRY POTTER.
Kids
CHAPTER ONE.
I KNOW.
HARRY POTTER

GOD, WHAT IS IT WITH THIS BOOK?
BEATS THE HELL OUT OF ME. FOR REALIZED CHARACTERIZATION AND A LUMINOUS YET TRENCHANT LYRICISM, I'LL TAKE THE CAPTAIN UNDERPANTS SERIES ANY DAY OF THE WEEK.
DO NUTS

WELL, I'M HAPPY FOR THE BUSINESS. BUT ALL THIS BESTSELLER HYPE IS SCARY. DID YOU KNOW OVERALL BOOK SALES ARE FLAT, BUT BESTSELLER SALES ARE GROWING EXPONENTIALLY? THAT MEANS PEOPLE ARE BUYING MORE AND MORE COPIES OF FEWER AND FEWER TITLES! BIG SURPRISE, WITH THE SUPERSTORES AND MEDUSA.COM TREATING BOOKS LIKE PORK BELLY FUTURES!
ARE YOU ALL SET?
UM...

MEANWHILE...
WHERE'S YOUR SCAR IF YOU'RE HARRY POTTER?
LOOK, I'M NOT HARRY POTTER, OKAY? NOW SIT DOWN AND LISTEN!
Harry Potty

JEEZ, WE SHOULD BUY SOME NON-BLOCKBUSTERS WHILE WE STILL CAN!
LIKE THIS ONE?
The ETHICAL SLUT
INFINITE SEXUAL POSSIBILITIES

WELL, IF WE'RE SERIOUS ABOUT TRYING TO OPEN UP OUR RELATIONSHIP, A BOOK MIGHT HELP.
RELATIONSHIPS
EBB & FLOW
YAK
BILL & HILL
BLAH
POLYAMORY
THE NEW LOVE WITHOUT LIMITS

HI, GIRLS! TONI, I THOUGHT YOU WEREN'T COMING TILL THIS AFTERNOON!
GLORIA! I...UH, WE...
JANE AUSTEN'S INVESTMENT GUIDE
WOMAN: AN INTIMATE TRIPTIK
TIPPING THE VELVEETA
SOME MYSTERY

WE HAD A LITTLE POWER STRUGGLE AND LOST.
TELL ME ABOUT IT. GOD, I'VE BEEN READING HARRY POTTER TO STELLA FOR MONTHS ON END. I'M DYING FOR A GROWN-UP BOOK. GOT ANY RECOMMENDATIONS?
ONSHIPS
THE RELATIONSHIP WORK BOOK

THIS IS AN ABSOLUTELY TERRIFIC READ. CHANGED MY LIFE.
HUH.
WHAT A LAME-O HARRY POTTER COSTUME.
PATHETIC MUGGLE.
RELA
SHIPS
STRIFE
MONOGAMY A PRECIOUS FLOWER

cognitive dissonance

346

9/13

TONI'S THROWING A LITTLE FÊTE TO OBSERVE THAT MOST HEAVILY FREIGHTED OF BIRTHDAYS.

...BUT A ...WAIT, I HAD IT A MINUTE AGO... OH, YEAH. A GENDERQUEER BOYDYKE GEEK WITH AN OXFORD CLOTH FETISH. HE FOLLOWED LOIS HOME FROM THE DEMOCRATIC CONVENTION PROTESTS.

I'M SO CONFUSED, CARLOS. ONE MINUTE TONI AND I ARE TALKING ABOUT HAVING A CIVIL UNION, AND THE NEXT WE'RE QUESTIONING THE WHOLE CONCEPT OF MONOGAMY.

YEAH, UH HUH... SO WHERE'S THE CONFUSION?

weather
©2000 BY ALISON BECHDEL
9/27
347

ANOTHER SCHOOL YEAR HAS BEGUN.
IT'S ONE OF THOSE DARK, RAINY MORNINGS WHEN THINGS SEEM, AT LEAST FOR THE MOMENT, UTTERLY AND IRREDEEMABLY HOPELESS.
EN ROUTE TO BUFFALO LAKE STATE COLLEGE...
"...HERE! CREEP, / WRETCH, UNDER A COMFORT SERVES IN A WHIRLWIND, ALL / LIFE DEATH DOES END, AND EACH DAY DIES WITH SLEEP."

THAT WAS A POEM ENTITLED "NO WORST, THERE IS NONE. PITCHED PAST PITCH OF GRIEF," BY GERARD MANLEY HOPKINS. AND THAT'S THE WRITER'S ALMANAC FOR MONDAY, OCTOBER SECOND.

MEANWHILE, AT THE CLIFFORD-ORTIZES'...
RAFFI, MOVE IT! WE'RE LATE!
I DID SET IT FOR 6:30. THE ELECTRICITY MUST HAVE GONE OFF.
POKÉMO

AND ON UNIVERSITY HILL...
WHOEVER SCHEDULED GENDER, RACE, AND MINIATURE GOLF: THE SOCIAL CONSTRUCTION OF LEISURE FOR EIGHT O'CLOCK IN THE MORNING SHOULD BE STRAPPED TO A ROTATING WINDMILL FOR ETERNITY.

GREAT. THERE GOES THE BUS.
CAN YOU TAKE HIM? I HAVE TO FINISH A REPORT BEFORE JOAN GETS IN.

UH-UH. CAN'T DO IT. I'VE GOT AN 8:30 TELECONFERENCE WITH THE NRDC AND I CAN'T BE LATE.
SILLY ME, I FORGOT! YOUR COMMITMENTS AUTOMATICALLY OUTRANK MINE.

Y'KNOW, YOU JUST CAN'T ASSUME I'M GOING TO BE THE ONE TO TAKE UP THE SLACK AROUND HERE. MY WORK IS IMPORTANT TOO! MY SCHEDULE IS PACKED!

SHORTLY...
BYE, PORKCHOP. TE QUIERO MUCHO.
¡PERO YO TE QUIERO MÁS!
ELEMENTARY
A TIP O' THE NIB TO CATI MARSH!

HEY, THERE'S STELLA AND HER MOM!
TONI!
HI, STELOCIRAPTOR.
HI, RAFOSAURUS REX.

D'YOU HAVE TIME FOR COFFEE?
ABSOLUTELY, GLORIA!

rules of engagement
348
©2000 BY ALISON BECHDEL

I JUST DON'T GET IT, CLARICE. YOU'VE ALREADY HAD A COMMITMENT CEREMONY. YOU'RE BOTH LEGALLY RAFFI'S PARENTS. YOU'VE BEEN TOGETHER LONGER THAN MELISSA AND JULIE AND ELLEN AND ANNE ALL PUT TOGETHER, TIMES, LIKE, A HUNDRED.

KICK IT, RAFFI!
THE OTHER WAY, SWEETIE!

WHY DO YOU NEED SOME STATE-APPROVED PIECE OF PAPER? I MEAN, A VERMONT CIVIL UNION WON'T EVEN BE VALID HERE.
IT'S NOT ABOUT THE PIECE OF PAPER. IT'S ABOUT CIVIL RIGHTS.

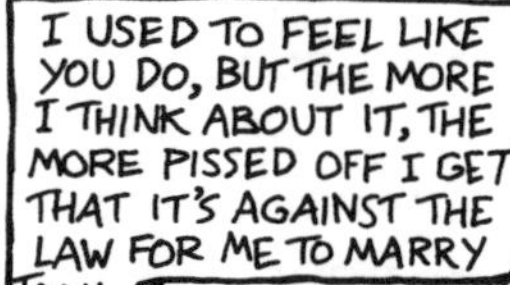
I USED TO FEEL LIKE YOU DO, BUT THE MORE I THINK ABOUT IT, THE MORE PISSED OFF I GET THAT IT'S AGAINST THE LAW FOR ME TO MARRY TONI.

BUT... BUT IT'S AGAINST THE LAW TO PERPE-TRATE FRAUD TOO. YOU'RE NOT PLANNING TO FLY OFF TO VERMONT AND PASS BAD CHECKS!
♪!

WHAT THE HELL KIND OF LOGIC IS THAT?
OH, I DON'T KNOW. DESPERATE.

CLARICE! HEY, I'VE GOT THE LAWN SIGNS.
GREAT, ANN. I'LL COME OVER AFTER THE GAME.
IS THAT YOUR NEIGHBOR? I THOUGHT YOU DIDN'T GET ALONG.

OH, ANN'S NOT SO BAD. HEY, CAN I GIVE YOU A GORE/LIEBERMAN LAWN SIGN?
CLARICE, I FEEL LIKE I DON'T EVEN KNOW YOU ANYMORE! FIRST, AS YOU MIGHT RECALL, I DON'T HAVE A LAWN. AND SECOND, I'M VOTING FOR NADER.

NADER, GREAT. WHY DON'T YOU JUST WRITE IN MUMIA ABU-JAMAL? IT'D BE JUST AS EFFECTIVE AND YOU COULD FEEL EVEN MORE PURE.
OH, REALLY? WELL AT LEAST I'M NOT A S—

A WHAT? GO AHEAD, SAY IT! A SELL-OUT?

A SOCCER MOM.

OH MY GOD! HE'S GOT THE BALL! THEY'RE WIDE OPEN! KICK IT IN, RAFFI! KICK IT IN!

HE HAS GOOD TECHNIQUE, CLARICE, BUT MAYBE YOU COULD WORK WITH HIM A BIT ON STRATEGY, LIKE WHICH END OF THE FIELD TO AIM FOR.
YES!

CRY
CRY
CRY
349
10-25
©2000 BY ALISON BECHDEL

MO AND SYDNEY ARE BABYSITTING...
THANK YOU, SYDNEEE!
RAFFI, NOT IN THE PARKING LOT! WE'LL GO HOME AND PRACTICE IN THE DRIVEWAY!
TOYS 'R' US
SUV 24

WHILE CLARICE AND TONI ARRIVE IN VERMONT.
HUH. IT'S NOT QUITE AS PICTURESQUE AS I WAS LED TO BELIEVE.
DON'T WORRY. OUR B&B IS WAY OUT IN THE COUNTRY.
THE HOME DEPOT
WAL*MART
OLD NAVY
STAPLES
BUNNS & NOODLE
Thrifty CAR RENTAL
MAP O' VERMONT

TWENTY MILES LATER...
SEE? IT IS PRETTY.
PRETTY WHITE.

WELL, IT'S NO SAMBA FEST. BUT THAT'S NOT WHY WE'RE HERE, IS IT?
LOOK. MORE OF THOSE ANTI-CIVIL UNION SIGNS. GOD, THEY'RE ALL OVER THE PLACE.
TAKE BACK VERMONT

DAMN IT, CLARICE! THIS IS SUPPOSED TO BE A FUN, ROMANTIC ADVENTURE! WILL YOU STOP FOCUSING ON EVERY POSSIBLE NEGATIVE?
I CAN'T HELP IT, TONI. I'M A REALIST, NOT A ROMANTIC.

I THOUGHT YOU WANTED TO DO THIS!
I DO! I WANT US TO BE PART OF AN IMPORTANT LEGAL BREAKTHROUGH. BUT I'M SORRY, IT'S JUST NOT A GOOEY HALLMARK MOMENT FOR ME.

FINE. WE'LL PICK UP THE LICENSE, GO TO THE JUSTICE OF THE PEACE, AND GET IT OVER WITH.
MACK
SNURF.

SHORTLY, AFTER A BIT OF PAPERWORK AND THE EXCHANGE OF TWENTY DOLLARS..
...BY THE POWER VESTED IN ME BY THE STATE OF VERMONT, I NOW DECLARE YOU JOINED IN CIVIL UNION.
SUGARBUSH EMU RANCH
MAPLE SYRUP
JUSTICE of the PEACE
Thrifty

WOW.
REALLY?

BWAAAH!
PHOOT
RING!

HELLO?!

TONI? SORRY TO BOTHER YOU, BUT WHICH HOSPITAL WOULD YOU SAY IS THE CLOSEST TO YOUR HOUSE?
WAANH HAAA!
ICE PAK

SPUN
©2000 BY ALISON BECHDEL
352
12-6
CLARICE, ONCE A HARMLESS NEWS JUNKIE, HAS BEEN MAINLINING A DEADLY CONCOCTION OF CNN, MSNBC, AND NPR FOR TWO WEEKS STRAIGHT NOW.

...MEANWHILE, A FLORIDA STATE APPELLATE COURT REJECTED THE GORE CAMPAIGN'S MOTION...

...TO OVERTURN A RULING BY THE LOWER FEDERAL COURT IN MIAMI, WHICH UPHELD A DECISION BY THE 11TH CIRCUIT...
HI! YOU HAD A LONG DAY!
KING ARTHUR

GIMME THE CLICKER.
I'M WATCHING IT!

YOU CAN WATCH UPSTAIRS.
I'M AFRAID TO GO UPSTAIRS AT NIGHT!
...WHICH REVERSED THE STATE SUPREME COURT RULING THAT FEDERAL COURTS DO NOT HAVE JURISDICTION OVER THE CASE.

CLICK! AS BUSH RELAXES ON HIS RANCH NEAR CRAWFORD...
UH OH. THE MEDIA'S LOSING SYMPATHY FOR GORE. THEY'VE STOPPED SAYING BUSH'S RANCH IS NEAR WACO.

MOMMY!
CLARICE! YOU'VE GOT TO STOP! LOOK WHAT YOU'RE DOING TO US!
CLICK! AFTER REPORTS OF DANGLING CHADS BEING EATEN DURING THE MANUAL RECOUNT...

AND WHERE'S THE TURKEY?
WHAT TURKEY?
...REPUBLICANS ARE DEMANDING STOOL SAMPLES FROM ALL BALLOT COUNTERS...

THE FREE-RANGE ORGANIC TURKEY I HAD RESERVED AT THE CO-OP, WHICH CLOSED TEN MINUTES AGO.
OH, #@☆⊘!
YOU SAID #@☆⊘!
CLICK! THE NASDAQ PLUNGED TODAY ON NEWS OF THE REPUBLICAN VICE-PRESIDENTIAL NOMINEE'S HEART ATTACK...

WE'RE HAVING THANKSGIVING HERE TOMORROW! WHAT AM I GOING TO FEED PEOPLE?
...BUT RALLIED BRIEFLY UPON REPORTS THAT GOVERNOR BUSH'S BOIL WOULD NOT LEAVE A SCAR.

GIVE ME THAT!
GO TO THE SUPERMARKET. TAKE RAFFI. LEAVE THE WALKMAN.

LIZ, THEY DON'T HAVE ANY FRESH ONES LEFT, ONLY FROZEN. WHAT SHOULD I DO?
DOES THAT THING HAVE INTERNET ACCESS?
THESE ARE VERY COLD TURKEYS, MEEMA.
.58/LB
LI'L TOM

DEARTH IN THE BALANCE

353

12-20

As the basketball of the presidency rolls precariously around the rim of the electoral college, our longtime friends gather for Thanksgiving dinner.

NEW YEAR'S EVE IS A RATHER DISPIRITED AFFAIR IN THE LOOMING SHADOW OF A BUSH REGIME, BUT OUR PLUCKY FRIENDS MAKE A VALIANT EFFORT.

THE CABINET OF DR. CALIGARI
356
1/31
©2001 by Alison Bechdel

PERHAPS HER ADRENAL GLANDS ARE SPENT FROM THE PROLONGED POST-ELECTION PANDEMONIUM.
PERHAPS IT'S PERIMENOPAUSE.
WHATEVER, CLARICE IS HAVING A HARD TIME HEALING AND MOVING ON.
ENVIRON-MENTAL JUSTICE FUND
BUSH APPOINTEES MORE CONSERVATIVE THAN EXPECTED
A TIP O' THE NIB TO RICK HECHT!

HEY, CONGRATS ON GETTING CERTIORARI IN THAT CANCER CLUSTER CASE, CLARICE. NOW YOU'RE REALLY GONNA KICK THEIR ASS.
SURE.
ASHCROFT FOR ATT'Y GENERAL, NORTON FOR INTERIOR

MEANWHILE, ON THE HOME FRONT...
WHERE'S MY SILLY PUTTY?
YOU CAN PLAY WITH THE SILLY PUTTY WHEN WE'RE DONE WITH YOUR SPELLING HOMEWORK. COME ON, FOCUS. "DISENFRANCHISE."
Spelling Words
·compassionate
·conservative
·coup
·disenfranchise
·filibuster

DON'T STAY TOO LATE. YOU BEEN LOOKING A LITTLE PEAKED.
UNH.
AND FOR LABOR, DEFENSE, TREASURY, AND H.H.S...

RING!
HELLO?
...THE FOUR HORSEMEN OF THE APOCALYPSE

CLARICE? GOOD, YOU'RE STILL THERE. LISTEN, WE'VE HAD A SLIGHT MISHAP HERE, AND I HAVE TO COME DOWNTOWN FOR AN EMERGENCY HAIRCUT. WHY DON'T WE MEET YOU FOR DINNER?

A BIT LATER...
I WISH I'D THOUGHT OF SILLY PUTTY. YOU WOULD'VE LOST THIS MULLET A DECADE AGO.
allure
A TIP O' THE NIB TO TANIA KUPCZAK!

SO HOW'S TRICKS?
OH, OKAY. I'M A LITTLE WORRIED ABOUT CLARICE, THOUGH. SHE'S BEEN IN SUCH A FUNK SINCE THE SUPREME COURT VOTED BUSH INTO OFFICE.

ISN'T THAT THE APPROPRIATE RESPONSE TO BEING FUNKED OVER?
YEAH. BUT LAW IS SOMETHING SHE'S DEVOTED HER LIFE TO. I MEAN, SHE NEVER HAD ANY IDEALISTIC ILLUSIONS ABOUT THE JUSTICE SYSTEM, BUT SHE'D WAKE UP EVERY DAY EAGER TO GO TO WORK. NOW IT'S LIKE, WHY BOTHER?
SAILOR MOON

SOUNDS LIKE DEPRESSION. I BETTER GIVE YOU MY SPECIAL SELECTIVE SEROTONIN REUPTAKE INHIBITOR SALON CUT.
YOU'LL BE SO GORGEOUS, SHE'LL FEEL LIKE SHE'S BEEN ON PAXIL FOR THE PAST TWO MONTHS.

WHAT DO YOU THINK?
I THINK I HAVEN'T SEEN A SCARIER CABINET SINCE WE FOUND THAT EGG SALAD SANDWICH RAFFI HID UNDER THE SINK.
ASHCROFT INSISTS, "I'M NOT A RACIST. I JUST ACT LIKE ONE."

OUT TO EAT. I JUST GOT HOME, BUT SPARROW'S AT YOGA, STUART'S SPINNING, THE HOUSE IS COLD, AND THE LARDER IS BARE.

PERFECT. I SHOULDA BEEN A PAIR OF RAGGED CLAWS SCUTTLING ACROSS THE FLOORS OF SILENT SEAS.

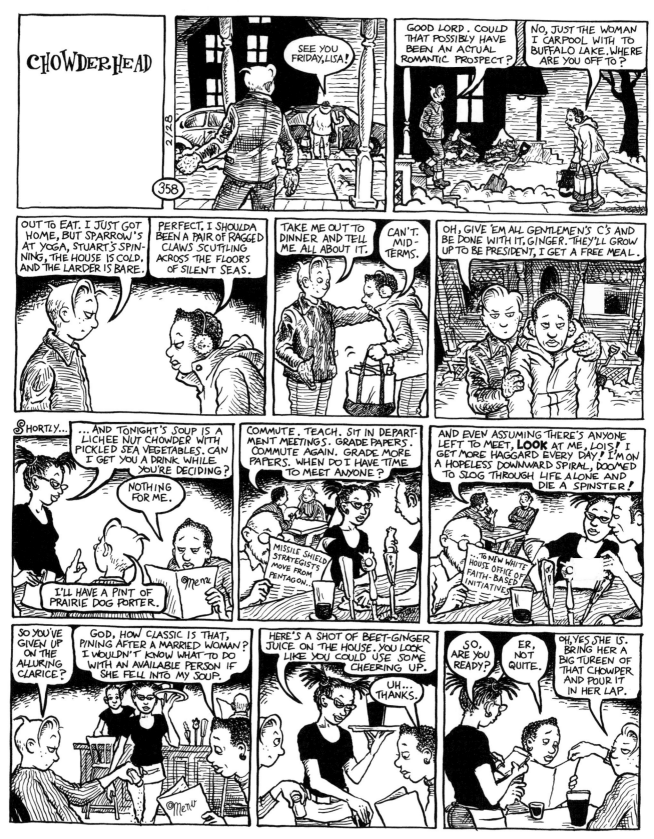

LADiES' MAN
3/14
359
©2001 by Alison Bechdel

WHERE'S JEZANNA? I'M TRYING TO ORDER MORE COPIES OF THE NEW OPRAH PICK, AND THE PUBLISHER SAYS WE HAVE TO PAY OFF OUR BALANCE FIRST.
SHE TOOK - HARUMPH! - SHE TOOK HER DAD TO A DOCTOR'S APPOINTMENT.
MADWIMMIN BOOKS & CAFE

WHAT'S WRONG WITH YOUR VOICE?
I'M GETTING A SORE THR...
VISA

I MEAN, IT MUST BE THE TESTOSTERONE KICKING IN.
YOU STARTED ALREADY? WHY DIDN'T YOU TELL ME?

YOU'D'VE BEEN SO SUPPORTIVE, I'M SURE.
LOOK, THIS ISN'T EASY FOR ME, EITHER. I DON'T WANT YOU TO CHANGE! I LIKE YOU THE WAY YOU ARE!

THAT'S THE WHOLE POINT! THIS IS THE WAY I AM!
THEN WHY ARE YOU WORKING IN A WOMEN'S BOOKSTORE? HAVE YOU TOLD JEZANNA YET? OR ARE YOU GOING TO WAIT UNTIL THE HAIR STARTS SPROUTING FROM YOUR EARS?

LOIS, THIS IS SO STUPID. HOW LONG ARE YOU GOING TO LET HER GO ON THINKING YOU'RE TRANSITIONING?
TILL SHE STOPS BEING SUCH A DICK.

SHORTLY...
YES YOU ARE GONNA DO IT! IF I HAVE TO HOLD YOU DOWN FOR THE DOCTOR, I WILL.
MADWIMMIN BOOKS & CAFÉ
WATCH YOUR MOUTH, GIRL.

SIT IN THE CAFÉ. I'LL GET YOU SOME BOOKS TO READ TILL I'M READY TO GO HOME.

OLD FOOL WATCHES HIS WIFE DIE OF CANCER, THEN REFUSES TO GET A PROSTATE EXAM.
EAT TO BEAT CANC
THE PROSTATE: A FAMILY GUIDE
STOPPING CANCER BEFORE IT STARTS

JEZANNA? IT'S THE BANK RETURNING YOUR CALL ABOUT EXTENDING OUR LINE OF CREDIT.
HUNH. TAKE THESE TO MY DAD, WILL YOU?

UH... MR. RAMSEY? JEZANNA ASKED ME TO GIVE THESE TO YOU.
TELL ME SOMETHING. WHY'S A YOUNG FELLA LIKE YOU WANT TO WORK IN A LADIES' BOOKSTORE?
ANNIE LIEBOVITZ WOMEN SUSAN SONTAG

juiced
3/28
360
©2000 BY ALISON BECHDEL
CLARICE IS STILL NOT QUITE HERSELF...
I'M SO GLAD YOU COULD SEE US, PATRICIA. I DON'T KNOW WHAT TO DO. IT'S LIKE ALL THE JUICE HAS BEEN SQUEEZED OUT OF HER.
HOW LONG HAS THIS BEEN GOING ON?

SINCE THE INAUGURATION.
COULD YOU PLEASE NOT USE THAT WORD?

INAUGURATION?
OR "PRESIDENT," "WHITE HOUSE," "WASHINGTON," "ADMINISTRATION." I CAN'T EVEN TALK ABOUT THE BU– THE SHRUBBERY IN THE YARD WITHOUT SETTING HER OFF.

INTERESTING. WHAT SEEMS TO BE THE PROBLEM, CLARICE?
THAT #*☆@@ BUTTERFLY BALLOT COST GORE 6,607 VOTES! THAT'S TEN TIMES THE NUMBER HE NEEDED TO WIN!
SHE'S DEPRESSED.

LOOK, THIS IS HER IDEA. AS FAR AS I'M CONCERNED, IT'S THE HAPPY PEOPLE WHO NEED THERAPY.
HMM... THE LAST TIME WE MET, YOU TWO TALKED ABOUT FEELING A CERTAIN STAGNATION IN YOUR RELATIONSHIP.

OUR RELATIONSHIP? WHAT'S THAT HAVE TO DO WITH IT? WE'RE LIVING UNDER CONSERVATIVE OCCUPATION! ISN'T THAT ENOUGH TO BE DEPRESSED ABOUT?

I HEAR YOU, CLARICE. I JUST WANT TO MAKE SURE THERE'S NOT SOMETHING ELSE GOING ON, SOME DEEPER ISSUE THAT COULD BE A PRECEDENT.
AAUGH!

PRECEDENT, WITH A "C-E."
FOR EXAMPLE, I KNOW THE TWO OF YOU WERE THINKING OF EXPLORING SOME SORT OF NONMONOGAMY. HAS ANYTHING COME OF THAT?

NO. WE GOT TEMPORARILY SIDETRACKED BY GETTING MARRIED. ANYHOW, SHE'S LOST INTEREST IN EVERYTHING, EVEN THAT PERENNIAL OBJECT OF HER AFFECTION, THE ENCHANTING GINGER.
WHO?

MEANWHILE...
ONE APPLE-ALFALFA TONIC. YOU WANT A SHOT OF GINGER IN THAT, GINGER? IT'S VERY STIMULATING.
UM... SURE, JASMINE. THAT SOUNDS NICE.
THE JUICE BAR & BREWERY

CUP OF CHEER
©2001 BY ALISON BECHDEL
361
4/11

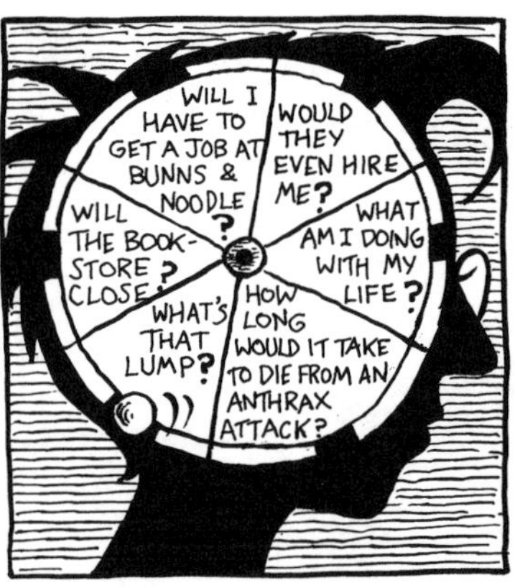
LET'S SEE WHAT MO'S ROULETTE WHEEL OF WORRY HAS LANDED ON TODAY.
WILL I HAVE TO GET A JOB AT BUNNS & NOODLE?
WOULD THEY EVEN HIRE ME?
WHAT AM I DOING WITH MY LIFE?
HOW LONG WOULD IT TAKE TO DIE FROM AN ANTHRAX ATTACK?
WHAT'S THAT LUMP?
WILL THE BOOK-STORE CLOSE?

I CAN'T FEEL ANYTHING. BESIDES, THAT'S YOUR ARMPIT, NOT YOUR BREAST!
YOU'RE SUPPOSED TO CHECK YOUR ARMPITS TOO! DON'T YOU READ THE SHOWER CARD?
DR. LOVE'S BIG BOOK OF BREASTS

I TRY NOT TO. MUST WE KEEP THAT THING HANGING IN THERE ALL THE TIME? IT'S MORBID.
NOT AS MORBID AS CANCER. YOU DO THE EXAM EVERY MONTH, RIGHT?

MORE OR LESS. I'VE GOTTA GO. I HAVE MY SEMINAR TONIGHT, REMEMBER?
I'LL CALL YOU AFTER MY APPOINTMENT.
A TIP O' THE NIB TO PAT FONTAINE!

THAT AFTERNOON...
HMM...
WHAT KIND OF A "HMM" IS THAT? A BIOPSY "HMM"?

NO, NO... YOU'VE GOT A SWOLLEN LYMPH NODE. HAVE YOU BEEN SICK LATELY?
UM... I'VE BEEN A LITTLE CONSTIPATED.

I JUST ASK BECAUSE THE LYMPH NODES CAN SWELL IF YOU'VE HAD A COLD OR AN INFECTION.
BIOHAZARD
JEEZ, I GOT A FLU SHOT LAST WEEK. COULD THAT DO IT?

I'LL BET THAT'S IT, JUST YOUR IMMUNE SYSTEM REACTING TO THE VACCINE. YOUR BREASTS FEEL FINE TO ME, MO. IF IT'S STILL THERE IN THIRTY DAYS, CALL ME, BUT I WOULDN'T WORRY.
REALLY? YOU DON'T EVEN WANT TO DO A NEEDLE ASPIRATION?

SHORTLY...
BOOBS! BELLIES! BUTTS! WE LOVE OUR BOOBS! BELLIES! BUTTS!

SYDNEY? IT'S PROBABLY NOTHING!
BSE
BREAST CANCER NETWORK
WHO NEEDS A MAMMOGRAM?
TIP O' THE NIB TO GEOCITIES.COM/RADICALCHEERLEADERS!

WHAT IS? ACTUALLY, BABE, CAN I CALL YOU BACK? I'M BUSY WITH SOME OF MY STUDENTS.
ATTACK! FIGHT BACK! THIS BOGUS SYSTEM IS WACK!
RADICAL CHEER LEADER
RADICAL CHEER-LEADER

Not-So Quiet Desperation
©2001 BY ALISON BECHDEL
362
4/25

COME ON. YOU CAN'T STAY IN BED ALL WEEKEND AGAIN. I TOLD RAFFI YOU'D TAKE HIM TO GET NEW SNEAKERS.
OH, GOD. TO THE MALL?

CLARICE, I CAN'T TAKE MUCH MORE OF THIS. I AGREE, IT'S HORRIFYING THAT BUSH GOT APPOINTED PRESIDENT. BUT YOU KNOW WHAT? LIFE GOES ON!

AFTER A FASHION. WITH A LITTLE MORE GLOBAL WARMING, CARBON DIOXIDE, AND ARSENIC.

THAT'S WHAT I'M TALKING ABOUT! LOOK AT YOU! YOU'RE AN ENVIRONMENTAL LAWYER AND YOU'RE JUST ROLLING OVER AND TAKING IT!

THEY'RE DISMANTLING ABORTION RIGHTS, SLASHING ENERGY EFFICIENCY, REHEATING THE COLD WAR! AND YOU CAN'T ROUSE YOURSELF TO GO TO THE MALL.
I JUST WANT TO LIE HERE A LITTLE LONGER.

FINE. YOU'RE EXACTLY WHERE THEY WANT YOU.

MEEMA, I DON'T FEEL SO GOOD.
WHAT'S WRONG?

HCHXXCK!
ARE YOU CHOKING?

RAFFI, TALK TO ME!
WHO TURNED OUT THE LIGHTS?

UNHH! MY GUT! I'M DYING!

IT MUSTA BEEN BECAUSE THE PRESIDENT IRRADIATED THE LUNCH MEAT AT SCHOOL.

I'M UP. ARE YOU HAPPY?
I'M GETTING ICE BLUE ADIDAS KOBE'S, OKAY?

365

OUR HAPLESS HOYDENS HAVE DUTIFULLY MUSTERED FOR THE ANNUAL PRIDE WINGDING.

LOIS'S DRAG KING REVUE IS WAITING TO TAKE THE STAGE.

6/7

A TIP O' THE NIB TO YOLANDA!

HEY, GINGER, LOOK! THERE'S JASMINE! GO ASK HER WHAT SHE'S DOING LATER.

AW, LOIS, SHE'S PROBABLY COMING OVER HERE TO SEE YOU.

HAPPY LGBTQWXYZ PRIDE

DUDE, DO YOU HAVE A TAMPON?

GIRLS! GIRLS! GIRLS!
©2001 BY ALISON BECHDEL
367
7/4
WHY DIDN'T YOU TELL ME SHE HAD A KID?!
HOW WAS I SUPPOSED TO KNOW? WHAT AM I, YENTA THE MATCHMAKER? YOU'RE PAYING ME FOR MY SERVICES?
HEY, JONAS, CATCH!
TONK!
OW!
HEY, BIG GUY! YOU'RE OKAY. IT JUST NICKED YOU.
PUT ME DOWN, PLEASE.
SO DIDJA HEAR HOW THIS LESBIAN CLUB, GIRL BAR, APPROACHED THE WNBA TEAM IN LOS ANGELES ABOUT SELLING TICKET PACKAGES, AND THE TEAM SAID "LESBIANS? EW, NO WAY!" NOW THIS SEASON THEY'RE HAVING TROUBLE FILLING SEATS, SO THEY CALL GIRL BAR BACK AND SAY THEY'VE RECONSIDERED.
WHAT AN INSULT. WHERE WOULD WOMEN'S BASKETBALL BE WITHOUT THE WHOLESOME, VIGOROUS, ALL-AMERICAN LESBIAN?
BUD LITE
10% TRIB
PRIDE ISSUE
ABOUT THE SAME PLACE AS THE GIRL SCOUTS.
AMERICAN FAMILY ASSOCIATION ATTACKS GIRL SCOUTS FOR NOT EXCLUDING LESBIANS
HEY, UH... LOUIS. YOU WERE GREAT AT THE RALLY TODAY. UM, ARE THOSE YOUR OWN SIDEBURNS COMING IN? THEY LOOK GOOD.
HUH? OH, JEEZ. I FORGOT TO TAKE THEM OFF. LISTEN, MO. I'M NOT TAKING TESTOSTERONE.
REALLY? SO IF YOU'RE NOT DOING HORMONES, THAT MAKES YOU, LIKE, A NO-HO TRANNY, RIGHT?
JEEZ, SOMEONE'S BEEN DOING HER HOMEWORK, BUT ACTUALLY, I'M NOT TRANSITIONING AT ALL.
WHAT DO YOU MEAN? WHY NOT?
OH, NOW YOU'RE DISAPPOINTED?
MAYBE YOU'RE IN DENIAL. MAYBE IT'S YOUR INTERNALIZED TRANSPHOBIA.
I DON'T THINK SO, DOCTOR. I ENJOY BEING A GIRL. IN A PERVERSE KIND OF WAY.
CAN I PLAY? WHAT ARE YOU GUYS DOING?
WE'RE NOT GUYS, WE'RE POWERPUFFS. YOU CAN BE BUTTERCUP. I'M BLOSSOM. AND HE'S BUBBLES.

notes on
camp
7/18
368

AS HE PICKS RAFFI UP FROM DAY CAMP, CARLOS APPEARS TO HAVE WALKED INTO A LINGUISTIC DEBATE.
¡HOLA, RAFAEL! ARE YOU READY TO GO?
ASK MY UNCLE CARLOS. HE'S GAY, SO HE KNOWS.

BILLY SAID MY BOAT WAS GAY, AND I SAID BOATS CAN'T BE GAY. RIGHT?
UH...

WELL, THAT DEPENDS. DID YOU MEAN HIS BOAT WAS SLEEK AND BEAUTIFUL, BILLY?
HAH! NO! IT'S LAME AND STUPID!

OKAY, THERE'S YOUR PROBLEM. LAME, STUPID THINGS AREN'T GAY. ONLY COOL, EXCELLENT THINGS ARE GAY.

I THOUGHT JUST PEOPLE COULD BE GAY, NOT THINGS.
WORK WITH ME, RAF.
IS HIS SHIRT GAY?

HMM. NO, I'M SORRY TO SAY, RAFFI'S SHIRT IS EXTREMELY UN-GAY.
IS YOURS?

THAT'S AN EXCELLENT QUESTION, BILLY. BECAUSE IT IS GAY ON ME. BUT ON YOUR COUNSELOR OVER THERE, IT'S NOT. CAN YOU TELL ME WHY?
BECAUSE HE'S LAME AND STUPID?

WELL, PERHAPS. BUT I WAS THINKING, NOT ONLY DO I FILL MINE OUT IN A MORE AESTHETICALLY PLEASING WAY, I ALSO WEAR IT WITH AN IRONIC AND TRANSFORMATIVE NOD TO ITS HISTORY AS A SYMBOL OF MALE HETEROSEXUAL LOUTISHNESS. WHEREAS FOR YOUR COUNSELOR, IT WAS PROBABLY THE ONLY CLEAN THING LEFT IN HIS DRAWER.

MY BOAT'S STILL GONNA WIN TOMORROW, BUTTFACE.
WITH THAT HETEROSEXUAL HUNK OF JUNK? I DON'T THINK SO, STINKBUTT!

LATER...
YOU WANT WHAT KIND OF A SHIRT?
A WIFEBEATER. LIKE CARLOS HAS.

UM, TONI? I THINK WE NEED TO HAVE A LITTLE TALK WITH...
I'M ALL OVER IT.
IT'S REALLY GAY.

Not-For-Profit Motive
370
8/15
WHAT ARE YOU THINKING?! SHE HAS A KID!
...AND THAT SLIGHT, CAPTIVATING GAP BETWEEN HER FRONT TEETH.
MEANWHILE, DOWNSTAIRS...
I FEEL DIRTY! IS IT A BRIBE? HUSH MONEY? BLOOD MONEY?
FROM G.W. BUSH YOU'RE A WINNER, LOIS McGIVER!
SIGN IT RIGHT OVER TO THE SHELTER AND YOU WON'T HAVE TO TROUBLE YOUR PRETTY LITTLE HEAD ABOUT IT.
GIVE IT TO THE HOMELESS ALLIANCE AND YOU CAN DOUBLE YOUR IMPACT, THANKS TO THE MATCHING GRANT PROGRAM I SET UP.
HOUSE VOTES: THERAPEUTIC CLONING, NO. DRILLING IN ANWR, YES.
OR YOU COULD SPLIT IT BETWEEN US.
OR I COULD BLOW IT ALL ON... ON... THE MIND REELS. GROCERIES? A MAMMOGRAM?
DING DONG
FUEL EFFICIENCY IN S.U.V.S, NO. EARTH IS FLAT, YES.
HI, LOIS. IS GINGER READY?
LEMME GO SEE.
YOUR DATE WANTS TO KNOW IF YOU'RE READY. I REFRAINED FROM TELLING HER YOU PASSED "READY" SEVERAL YEARS AGO AND WERE NOW WELL INTO THE DESPERATE ZONE.
I CAN'T DO THIS, LOIS! I CAN'T GO OUT WITH A WOMAN WHO HAS A CHILD! I'M TOO YOUNG, I TELL YOU! I HAVEN'T SOWN MY OATS YET!
I THINK YOUR OATS ARE IMPACTED. MAYBE SHE'S NOT LOOKING FOR A SECOND PARENT. MAYBE SHE JUST WANTS TO NAIL YOU.
SHE'S A SINGLE MOTHER! SHE CAN'T GO AROUND NAIL-- HAVING CASUAL SEX WITH PEOPLE.
HOW D'YOU KNOW? AT LEAST FIND OUT WHAT HER INTENTIONS ARE.
GIVE IT AWAY? I DON'T THINK SO. I HAVE A KID TO RAISE.
SEE? I WAS RIGHT! AND THAT'S WHY I CAN'T GO OUT WITH HER!
YOU CAN'T GO OUT WITH ME BECAUSE I SPENT MY TAX REBATE ON A USED COMPUTER FOR JONAS?
IGNORE HER. IT'S THE HEAT.

the Bibliophile

8/29

371

IT'S A LOVELY SUMMER EVENING, AND MO'S NEW BOOK GROUP HAS FAILED TO MATERIALIZE.

Modern Maturity
9/26
373

WHY'S THIS PURCHASE ORDER SITTING IN THE FAX MACHINE?
GOD, I MEANT TO SEND THAT AN HOUR AGO. I JUST GOT MY PERIOD AND I'M REALLY SPACED OUT.

I NEVER USED TO GET LIKE THIS. SPACEY, CRABBY, CAN'T SLEEP. I THOUGHT ALL THAT STUFF ABOUT WOMEN BEING AT THE MERCY OF THEIR HORMONES WAS JUST PATRIARCHAL LIES.
AH HA HA HA HA!

WELCOME TO PERIMENOPAUSE!
MENOPAUSE?! CRIPES, I'M NOT EVEN FORTY YET.
I SAID "PERI." AROUND, ABOUT, NEAR. IT CAN LAST TEN YEARS. THEN THE REAL FUN BEGINS.
MADWIMMIN BOOKS
CIRCUIT CITY

AH HA HA HA HA!
Canon

WHAT'S THIS? YOU'RE APPLYING TO LIBRARY SCHOOL?
SHH! JEEZ! THANK GOD JEZANNA DIDN'T PICK THAT UP.

WHAT, YOU HAVEN'T TOLD HER? YOU'RE JUST BAILING?

I DUNNO. I HAVEN'T FIGURED IT OUT YET.
POTENTIAL
ARIEL SCHRAG

HUH. YOU OF ALL PEOPLE, WORKING INSIDE THE SYSTEM.
WHAT'S MY CHOICE? THERE'S NO OUTSIDE LEFT! YOU CAN BUY "BEST LESBIAN EROTICA" AT THE 7-11.

THE BOOKSTORE'S STRUGGLING. WHY SHOULDN'T I TAKE A CHANCE TO MAKE A DECENT LIVING? I'M NOT GETTING ANY YOUNGER.

TELL ME ABOUT IT.
WHAT HAPPENED, LOIS? LIFE WAS JUST GETTING STARTED.

HI, DAD. HOW'D IT GO?
HIS PSA COUNT'S HIGH. WE'RE PRETTY SURE IT'S ENLARGED, BUT HE STILL WON'T LET THE DOCTOR DO A DIGITAL EXAM.

THEY FIND SOMETHING, THEY'LL WANT TO GO IN AND CUT ME. I'LL END UP LIKE CHARLIE RASKIN, LIMP AS AN EGG NOODLE.
DAD!
THEN AGAIN, MAYBE WE STILL HAVE A FEW GOOD YEARS LEFT.

REAL WORLD
10/3
374
STUDENT CENTER
Café
HOURS 7
ΦKΨ
BUFFALO
LAKE
STATE
POLI

idealpolitik
©2001 by Alison Bechdel
10/24
375

DON'T KNOW MUCH ABOUT HISTORY...
DON'T GIVE ME THAT SELF-FLAGELLATING CRAP, MO. WHAT ARE YOU SAYING, WE BROUGHT THIS ON OURSELVES?!

THAT'S... THAT'S LIKE JERRY FALWELL BLAMING IT ON THE "ABORTIONISTS AND THE FEMINISTS AND THE GAYS AND THE ACLU"!
IT'S NOTHING LIKE THAT! I'M SAYING THAT GIVEN THE VIOLENCE OUR OWN COUNTRY PERPETRATES, WE SHOULDN'T BE SO SURPRISED WHEN SOME OF IT COMES BACK AT US.
CHIPS

BY PLACING THE BLAME ON U.S. FOREIGN POLICY, YOU'RE EXCUSING THESE VICIOUS, FUNDAMENTALIST WACKOS!
NO, I'M NOT. YOU'RE USING THE EXCUSE THAT SINCE THEY'RE RELIGIOUS FANATICS, OUR FOREIGN POLICY HAS NOTHING TO DO WITH IT!

IT'S EGOCENTRIC, REALLY. YOU THINK EVERY TIME SOMETHING BAD HAPPENS IN THE WORLD, YOU'RE SOMEHOW RESPONSIBLE.
NO, YOU ARE.
PISS 'N' VINEGAR

DON'T KNOW MUCH ABOUT GEOGRAPHY...
RAF, WHERE'S YOUR BEACH BALL GLOBE?
WHAT FOR?

BECAUSE I'M FORTY YEARS OLD AND I DON'T KNOW WHERE AFGHANISTAN IS.

IT HAS A LEAK. YOU HAVE TO BLOW IT UP.
UH... UNDER THE CIRCUMSTANCES, I THINK I'D RATHER INFLATE IT.
NUCLEAR OR BIOLOGICAL ATTACK?

THE WHOLE WORLD SHOULD BE JUST ONE COUNTRY, THEN YOU WOULDN'T HAVE TO LEARN ALL THE NAMES AND FLAGS AND STUFF.

BUT I DO KNOW THAT I LOVE YOU.
YOU'RE FASTING? WHAT'S THAT SUPPOSED TO ACCOMPLISH?
IT'S A WAY OF EXTENDING OUR ENERGY TO HEAL AND TRANSFORM THE TRAGEDY.
Café KABUL

AND I KNOW THAT IF YOU LOVED ME TOO...
MMM... STEAMED SCALLION DUMPLINGS WITH YOGURT AND MINT.
INSTEAD OF IGNORING THE PAIN AND DYSFUNCTION IN THE WORLD, WE'RE EMBRACING IT TO HELP US UNDERSTAND HOW TO REACT WITH FORGIVENESS AND COMPASSION.
YEAH, WELL, COMPASSION IS A NICE IDEA, BUT IT'S NOT GEOPOLITICAL REALITY.

WHAT A WONDERFUL WORLD THIS WOULD BE.
THAT'S THE WHOLE POINT. YOU MAKE IT REALITY BY DOING IT. WE CAN CHANGE THE WORLD BY LIVING "AS IF."
AS IF!

Of thee I sing

©2001 BY ALISON BECHDEL

376

IF YOU REALLY WANT TO MAKE THEM HAPPY, QUIT YOUR JOB AND START WEARING A BURQA. OH, AND SINCE YOU'RE QUEER, KNOCK A WALL DOWN ON YOURSELF AND HAVE SOMEONE DRIVE A BULLDOZER OVER IT.

SEE? THIS IS EXACTLY WHAT I'M TALKING ABOUT!

IS STRESS BRINGING OUT THE BEST OR THE WORST IN OUR STOUT-HEARTED WOMEN?

CLARICE IS BECOMING MORE LIKE SHE USED TO BE.

I KNOW IT'S A SCARY TIME, BUT IT'S ALSO AN OPPORTUNITY TO RE-EVALUATE OUR PRIORITIES, TO LIVE MORE FULLY! WE CAN LET FEAR AND DESPAIR SHUT US DOWN, OR WE CAN DO WHAT WE CAN TO MAKE THE WORLD BETTER!

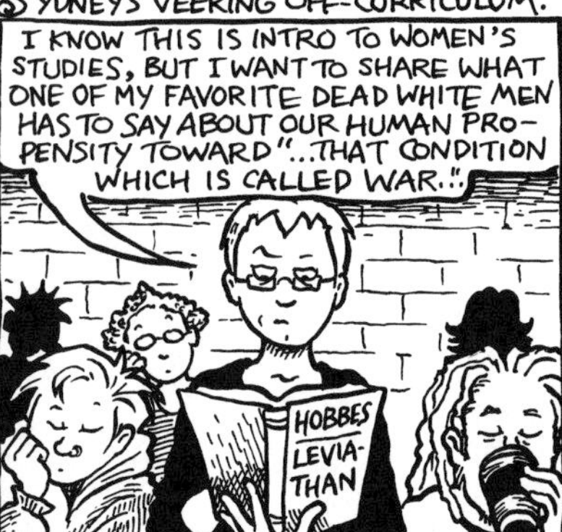

THE ROLE MODEL

12/5

378

HI, EVERY-ONE!

WHO'S THAT?
AN AGGRESSIVE JEHOVAH'S WITNESS?
SHE KINDA REMINDS ME OF SOMEONE...
HI! I'M LAURA BUSH. I'VE BEEN DOING A LITTLE RESEARCH HERE!
OKAY, SO I HAVEN'T BEEN AROUND MUCH.

BUT I WILL BE FROM NOW ON.
OH? WHAT ABOUT YOUR NEW INSTANT FAMILY?
HAVE YOU HEARD OF THE TALIBAN?

GOD, I NEED A TIME-OUT. I RUSHED INTO THINGS WITH JASMINE WAY TOO FAST.
RIGHT. SIX MONTHS BETWEEN MEETING HER AND ASKING HER OUT. I'M SURPRISED THERE WASN'T A SONIC BOOM.
foof

YEAH, BUT THEN JUST AS WE WERE STARTING TO GET INVOLVED, THE ATTACKS HAPPENED. I MEAN, TALK ABOUT EXTENUATING CIRCUMSTANCES!
DID YOU KNOW THEY'VE BEEN BRUTALLY VIOLATING WOMEN'S HUMAN RIGHTS?

DID I HAVE REAL FEELINGS FOR HER OR WAS I JUST CLINGING IN SHEER TERROR TO THE NEAREST PERSON AT HAND?
LET'S PUT A STOP TO IT! AND WHILE WE'RE AT IT, HOW ABOUT THAT SAUDI ARABIA?

SO. YOU ESCAPED YOUR ANXIETY ABOUT THE WORLD BY RUNNING TO JASMINE, AND NOW YOU'RE ESCAPING YOUR FEAR OF INTIMACY BY RUNNING BACK HERE?
YOU CAN'T PLAY AROUND WITH PEOPLE LIKE THAT, GINGER. ESPECIALLY WHEN THERE'S A CHILD INVOLVED!
WOMEN ARE MISERABLY OPPRESSED THERE, TOO! SO WHAT IF WE DEPEND ON SAUDI OIL?

I KNOW THAT! THAT'S WHY I DON'T WANT TO GO ANY FURTHER UNTIL I'M SURE IT'S RIGHT! I DON'T WANT TO SCREW THINGS UP FOR JONAS. GOD KNOWS, HE'S GOT ENOUGH TROUBLES!
DING DONG
I SAY WE GO IN THERE AND- GAK!

HE WANTS TO BE A GIRL, SCHOOL'S TORTURE FOR HIM, HE'S BEEN TO SEE THAT HARRY POTTER MOVIE TEN TIMES ALREADY. THE KID LIVES IN AN ESCAPIST FANTASY.
CLICK

JAS-MINE?!
GINGER, I'M SORRY, BUT LETITIA HAD SOME KIND OF FAMILY EMERGENCY AND JUST DROPPED HIM OFF AT THE RESTAUR-ANT AND I COULDN'T FIND ANYONE ELSE ON SUCH SHORT NOTICE AND I HAVE TO GET BACK TO WORK. I'LL PICK HIM UP AT TEN!

WELL, LOOK! IT'S HARRY POTTER!
I'M HERMIONE. HONESTLY, HAGRID, YOU CAN BE SUCH A DOLT.

Search & Seizure
©2001 by Alison Bechdel
379
12/19
Up on university hill...
SYDNEY, YOU KNOW ALL THAT FLACK THE ADMINISTRATION GAVE ME OVER MY PRESENTATION AT THE ANTIWAR TEACH-IN?
UH.. YEAH.
NOK NOK

WE'RE HAVING A SPEAKOUT FRIDAY ON ACADEMIC FREEDOM AND THE WHOLE CRACKDOWN ON CIVIL LIBERTIES IN GENERAL. CAN I TALK YOU INTO PARTICIPATING?
GEE, GEORGE. I'M CATCHING A FLIGHT IN A COUPLE HOURS. SORRY.

OH, LIKE YOU'D LOVE TO OTHERWISE.
HEY. SEE THIS? THIS IS MY TENURE FILE. SIX YEARS OF PAINSTAKING LABOR. WHY WOULD I COME THIS CLOSE, THEN BLOW IT ALL WITH FIVE MINUTES OF FIST-SHAKING?

LONG LIVE ACADEMIC FREEDOM.
BESIDES, I CAN'T GET TOO EXERCISED ABOUT THIS CIVIL LIBERTIES BUSINESS. IF THE FBI WANTS TO COPY MY HARD DRIVE, THEY'RE WELCOME TO IT. I HAVE NOTHING TO HIDE.
402
SYDN
KRUK

I JUST HAVE TO TURN THIS IN TO THE DEPARTMENT, THEN WE CAN GO.
HELLO, SYDNEY.

HELLO, BETSY.
THANK YOU, DR. KRUKOWSKI, DR. GILHOOLEY. JUST UNDER THE WIRE.
Flump
thunk

Later, at the airport...
DID HERS LOOK BIGGER TO YOU?
WILL YOU DROP IT?

MIND IF I OPEN THIS UP?
NO, GO AHEAD. I DON'T HAVE ANYTHING TO HIDE.
CONCOURSE W →

UM...IT'S NOT LOADED.

Later still, at another airport.
DADDY!
HI, BABY. HAS THAT TWO-BIT AGRICULTURAL SCHOOL GRANTED YOU TENURE YET?

UH.. NOT QUITE.
WE'RE GOING TO HAVE A SPLENDID TIME. I KNOW YOU DON'T SKI, MO. BUT THE CONDO'S GOT A HOT TUB!

SHE DOESN'T GET NAKED EITHER.
OH, PSHAW! WHAT'S SHE HAVE TO HIDE?
WE'RE GOING TO HAVE A SPLENDID TIME.

ARMY OF ONE
©2001 by Alison Bechdel
380
1/2

ON VACATION WITH SYDNEY'S FATHER AND STEP-MOTHER, OUR HEROINE FINDS HERSELF TRAPPED IN A HELLISH VORTEX OF FRIVOLITY AND EXCESS.
HERE'S THE PAPER. SURE YOU DON'T WANT TO COME TO THE SPA, MO?
NO, I'M ALL SET. I JUST HAD MY NOSTRILS WAXED LAST WEEK.
USA HOORAY
THE HUMAN CONDITION

MEANWHILE, ON THE SLOPES...
WHY DON'T YOU SEND SOME OF YOUR ARTICLES TO STANLEY STURGEON, SYD? A LETTER FROM HIM WOULD **CINCH** YOUR TENURE. MENTION MY NAME. WE WERE ON A PANEL TOGETHER ONCE.

RIGHT, DAD. I'M GONNA ASK A WORLD-FAMOUS ACADEMIC WHO MAY OR MAY NOT REMEMBER YOU TO GIVE ME A RECOMMENDATION.
OF COURSE HE'LL REMEMBER ME! HERE, I'VE GOT HIS E-MAIL ADDRESS.
RING!

HANG ON. I HAVE A CALL.
HELLO.
CAN WE GO HOME NOW?

MO, I TOLD YOU YOU'D GO NUTS SITTING AROUND THE CONDO. YOU SHOULD HAVE COME SKIING.
AM I THE ONLY PERSON BOTHERED BY THE CIRCULAR LOGIC OF PUBLIC OPINION POLLS? THE MEDIA'S TOO BUSY KISSING STAR-SPANGLED **BUTT** TO DO ANY CRITICAL OR INVESTIGATIVE REPORTING...
LATEST POLL:
CIVILIAN CASUALTIES? OH, WELL!
INVADE IRAQ? WOO HOO!
MILITARY TRIBUNALS? BRING 'EM ON!
ABM TREATY? NUKE IT!

THEY PRESENT ONE PATRIOTICALLY CORRECT POINT OF VIEW. SO **BIG SURPRISE!** WHEN THEY TAKE A POLL, THAT'S THE ONE PEOPLE SPEW BACK. GARBAGE IN, GARBAGE OUT! WHY DOESN'T ANYONE EVER POLL **ME**?
GOOD
EVIL
DOW ▼47.19
THE RUMSFELD REPORT
CNN
RLD'S LARGEST RUTABAGA
I'M LOSING THE CONNECTION, BABE! SEE YOU LATER! CLICK!

LATER...
WOULDN'T YOU BE MORE COMFORTABLE IN ONE OF THE TERRY-CLOTH ROBES?
SHUT UP.
WINE, MO?

YOU'RE NOT SUPPOSED TO USE THE HOT TUB UNDER THE INFLUENCE OF ALCOHOL.
ISN'T IT NICE, NOW THAT THE TALIBAN HAVE SURRENDERED..

...TO HAVE OUR OWN LITTLE DEPARTMENT FOR THE PROMOTION OF VIRTUE AND THE PREVENTION OF VICE?
HYUK!

SYD, D'YOU HAVE YOUR PALM? LET ME GIVE YOU THAT CONTACT I HAVE AT THE UNIVERSITY OF WICHITA PRESS.

OKAY, OKAY. IF IT'LL GET YOU OFF MY BACK.

MO, A FULL-BODY ALGAE WRAP WOULD DO WONDERS FOR THAT ROUGH SKIN.

just a rhetorical question
385
©2002 BY ALISON BECHDEL
3/13
WHY IS IT THAT SEX WITH A TRUSTED AND FAMILIAR PARTNER,..

EVEN AT ITS MOST ASSIDUOUS...
IT'S NO GOOD. YOU MIGHT AS WELL STOP.
ARE YOU SURE? I DON'T THINK I HAVE A REPETITIVE STRESS INJURY YET...

GOD. MAYBE I SHOULD GO OFF THE DRUG. THIS IS MORE DEPRESSING THAN IT WAS TO BE DEPRESSED.
NOT QUITE. IF YOU WERE DEPRESSED, YOU WOULDN'T BE ABLE TO DO ME. NOW, ENOUGH CHIT CHAT. GET TO WORK.

...ACCESSORIZED,...
MAYBE LOIS HAS ONE?
ARE YOU KIDDING? SHE'D WANT A FULL REPORT OVER BREAKFAST.
MED. TROJ

WELL, JEEZ. WE SHOULD BE OKAY WITH THE CAP AND THE GUNK.
IF YOU'D GET A VASECTOMY, WE WOULDN'T HAVE TO GO THROUGH THIS EVERY TIME.
A TIP O' THE NIB TO LOLA TH' LOVE COUNSELOR

BUT... BUT YOU KNOW I WANT TO HAVE A BABY EVENTUALLY.
SO MAKE SOME DEPOSITS AT A SPERM BANK FIRST. THEN WE CAN INSEMINATE LIKE NORMAL PEOPLE WHEN WE'RE READY.

...OR DEPRAVED,...
NEXT ON MARTHA STEWART LIVING, THREE-WAY SWITCHES AND TIPS ON PACKING.

...CAN'T MATCH THE INTENSITY OF BEING WITH SOMEONE NEW..
JASMINE!
OH. HI.
2 NITE THE VAGINA MONOLOGUES

IT'S NICE TO SEE YOU! YOU LOOK REALLY, UH... NICE!
COME ON, GINGER. DON'T PATRONIZE ME. YOU'VE MADE IT CLEAR HOW YOU FEEL, AND I CAN HANDLE IT.

BUT... BUT I MEANT IT.
FINE. WHATEVER.
'SCUSE ME, DUDES.

NO, REALLY! UM... I MEAN, I THOUGHT MAYBE, UH...
YOU THOUGHT WHAT? THAT YOU'D GIVE MY CHAIN A FEW MORE YANKS?
THIS BATHROOM IS DESIGNATED GENDER-FREE for the evening

...AND HAVING ABSOLUTELY NO SEX AT ALL?
NO! I MEAN, WELL, YES! I MEAN...
YOU ARE TOO *@#ING MUCH!

VAGINA MONOLOGUES
VDAY

deductive reasoning

389

5/8

waterworks
©2002 BY ALISON BECHDEL
390
5/22
TUMS
PENICILLIN SUDZ KILLS GERMS
TOM'S OF FINLAND CURRY FLAVOR
ACME PREGNANCY TEST 2 TESTS
ACME PREGNANCY TEST 2 TESTS
IT COULD BE A FALSE POSITIVE. LEMME DO ANOTHER ONE TO MAKE SURE.
HONEY, YOU DID TWO! THERE AREN'T ANY MORE. BESIDES, CAN'T YOU TELL? I MEAN, DO YOU FEEL DIFFERENT?
DIFFERENT HOW? MYSTERIOUSLY SERENE? ECSTATIC? FILLED WITH @#✱&ING LIGHT?
ACME INSTRUCTIO
UM... OR BLOATED? CONSTIPATED?
STUART, I CAN'T DO THIS! I'M NOT READY! I LIKE MY LIFE THE WAY IT IS! I'M TOO OLD! WHAT ABOUT MY CAREER? WE CAN'T AFFORD IT!
BESIDES! THIS IS WHY HUMANITY'S DOOMED! WHILE GOOD PEOPLE ARE BUSY CLEANING PUKE OFF OF "GOOD-NIGHT MOON," BUSH IS YANKING U.S. SUPPORT FOR THE INTERNATIONAL CRIMINAL COURT! AND JOHN ASHCROFT IS PRAISING THE LORD AND PASSING OUT RIFLES!
I CAN'T BRING A CHILD INTO A WORLD WHERE THE PLAYING FIELD IS TOTALLY TILTED TOWARD TOTALITARIANISM!
HEY, COME ON! WHERE'S THAT UPBEAT IDEALIST I KNOW AND LOVE?
YOU'RE JUST SURPRISED AND CONFUSED. WE NEED TO CALM DOWN AND THINK ABOUT THIS, OKAY?
"WE"? WHO PEED ON THIS STICK, BIG BOY, YOU OR ME?
OOPS! 'SCUSE ME!
LOIS, GET THE @#✱& OUT OF HERE!
CAN YOU TWO GO CHAT SOMEWHERE ELSE? I HAVE TO WHIZ AND THE DOWNSTAIRS TOILET'S STOPPED UP.
OH MY GOD! ARE YOU...
MAYBE BABY 2 tests
YES, OKAY? WE'RE PREGNANT. NOW GET OUT.
I DIDN'T KNOW YOU WERE EVEN TRYING! YOU COULD HAVE AT LEAST MENTIONED IT AT THE LAST HOUSE MEETING. WOW! WE'RE GONNA BE PARENTS!
WHAT IS IT WITH THIS PRONOUN PROBLEM?
I'M THE ONE WHO'S PREGNANT. AND I'M THE ONE WHO'S GOING TO DECIDE WHAT TO DO ABOUT IT.
D-DO ABOUT IT? SNIFF!
UM... IF ANYONE NEEDS ME I'LL BE PEEING IN THE BACK YARD.

MAMMA MIA

391
6/5
HEY, GINGER.
THE SEMESTER'S OVER! PEACE AND QUIET! TIME TO THINK! NO MORE MESSY LITTLE STUDENT DRAMAS, NO MORE CAMPUS POLITICS AND ALL THAT CRAZED JOCKEYING FOR...

...FOR POSITION. JASMINE?
OH, YEAH. RIGHT THERE LOIS. HI, GINGER...
SHE PULLED A MUSCLE IN OUR KICKBOXING CLASS, AND JONAS NEEDED TO GO ONLINE FOR HIS REPORT ON ABBA, SO I SAID HE COULD USE YOUR COMPUTER.

UH...FINE. DON'T LET ME INTERRUPT YOU.
HEY, A LITTLE HEADS UP BEFORE YOU GO IN THE KITCHEN. SPARROW'S PREGNANT, SHE DOESN'T WANT THE BABY, STUART DOES, BUT HE'S TRYING NOT TO COME RIGHT OUT AND SAY SO.
MMM... LOWER.

I HAVE GOT TO GET A CONDO.

I THOUGHT YOU WANTED TO HAVE KIDS!
I THOUGHT I DID, TOO. IT'S A NICE THOUGHT! BUT I DON'T KNOW ABOUT THE REALITY. I MEAN, I'M ALMOST 40! DO YOU KNOW WHAT THE CHANCES OF COMPLICATIONS ARE AT MY AGE?

BUT...DO YOU KNOW WHAT THE CHANCES OF CONCEPTION ARE AT OUR AGE? OUR FERTILITY'S DWINDLING BY THE SECOND! IT'S A MIRACLE THIS HAPPENED AT ALL!
ANNIE LIEBOVITZ JUST HAD A BABY. SHE'S 52!

WELL, I'M NOT ANNIE LIEBOVITZ! AND HE'S NO SUSAN SONTAG!
GASP!

SPARROW, YOU KNEW YOU MIGHT GET KNOCKED UP WHEN YOU STARTED BOUNCING MR. SENSITIVE HERE. TIME TO PAY THE PIPER, BABE.
HEY, IT'S MY BODY! AND WHO THE HELL ARE YOU? THE PRO-LIFE WING OF "POLYAMOROUS PERVERTS OF AMERICA"?

GOD! WHAT ARE YOU PEOPLE GONNA DO NEXT, GO DOWN AND BLOCKADE PLANNED PARENTHOOD?!
SPARROW, I...I WANT TO HAVE THIS BABY! I MEAN, I WANT YOU TO HAVE IT. I MEAN, I WANT US TO HAVE IT.

YOU KNOW, EVERYONE'S AFRAID KIDS ARE GONNA BE ALL THIS WORK, BUT THEY'RE SO GREAT!
YEAH! LOOK AT JONAS!
MOM?

UM, SOMETHING HAPPENED WHILE I WAS DOWNLOADING "DANCIN' QUEEN," AND NOW THERE'S JUST A BLINKING QUESTION MARK ON THE SCREEN.

pro-
lifer-
ation
©2002 BY ALISON BECHDEL

WHILE BROWSING AT THE BOOKSTORE, OUR HEROINE HAS SUFFERED A BRIEF BOUT OF NAUSEA.

6/19
392

OH NO! I FORGOT TO HAVE CHILDREN!
PSORIASIS 10K
APOCA-LYPTICS ANONY-MOUS TUESDAYS 7 PM

HEY, SPARROW. I DIDN'T SEE YOU COME IN. HOW'S IT GOING?
UH...HI, MO. I'M FINE. YOU?
RESTROOM
U.S. AND RUSSIA SIGN "HISTORIC" ARMS CONTROL AGREEMENT

OH, UP AND DOWN. I GOT INTO LIBRARY SCHOOL.
YOU DID? THAT'S GREAT!
RESTROOM
FIRST NUCLEAR TREATY IN HISTORY TO INCREASE RISK OF PROLIFERA-TION

YEAH, AND NOW INDIA AND PAKISTAN ARE POISED TO NUKE US ALL TO KINGDOM COME. BUT I TRY TO LOOK ON THE BRIGHT SIDE. YOU KNOW ME, THE GLASS IS HALF FULL. HALF-FULL OF STRONTIUM-90!
JAPAN: PACIFISM BLOWS. LET'S GO NUCLEAR!

YEAH, WELL, LISTEN. I'M LOOKING FOR BOOKS ON ABORTION. UM, FOR THE LIBRARY AT THE SHELTER. YOU KNOW, RESOURCE GUIDES, WOMEN'S STORIES ABOUT THEIR EXPERIENCES...
SURE, RIGHT OVER HERE.

OH MY GOD! I DIDN'T EVEN CON-GRATULATE YOU! LOIS TOLD ME YOU'RE PREGNANT!
GREAT. WHAT MADE ME THINK I COULD EVER HAVE ANY PRIVACY IN THIS TOWN?
AMERICA A PATRIOTIC YAMMER LYNNE CHENEY
THE NINNY DIARIES

WHAT ELSE DID SHE TELL YOU? THAT I DON'T KNOW IF I WANT TO HAVE THE BABY, AND THAT MY ENTIRE HOUSEHOLD HAS BEEN SUBJECTING ME TO ANTICHOICE HARASSMENT?
WOW, REALLY? SO UM... THESE BOOKS ARE FOR YOU!
BIRTH OR ABORTION ?
ABORTION A WOMAN'S GUIDE

GO AHEAD. CHIME IN WITH YOUR MORAL JUDGMENT.
I'D NEVER JUDGE YOU, SPARROW! I DIDN'T WANT TO SAY ANYTHING, BUT IF YOU ASK ME, IT'S BRINGING A KID INTO THIS WORLD THAT'S IMMORAL.
THE ABORTION RESOURCE HAND-BOOK
LOSS AND RENEWAL

I GUESS I COULD SEE GIVING BIRTH IF ALL WE HAD TO WORRY ABOUT WAS POLLUTION, GLOBAL WARMING, AND RAMPANT MICROBES. BUT THROW WEAPONS OF MASS DESTRUCTION INTO THE MIX, AND WHAT'S THE POINT?
HEALTH
THE CHOICES WE MAKE
U.S. RESUMES PRODUCTION OF NUCLEAR WARHEAD TRIGGERS

THINK ABOUT IT. A LUCKY FEW VAPOR-IZED ON THE SPOT, THE REST OF US DYING IN PROTRACTED AGONY FROM RADIATION SICKNESS IN THE SPECTRAL LANDSCAPE OF NUCLEAR WINTER. WHO IN THEIR RIGHT MIND WOULD EMBRACE LIFE AT A TIME LIKE THIS?
HEALTH
WHAT TO EXPECT WHEN YOU'RE EXPECTING
"HEY, THE MARKET IS HOT," SAYS ENERGY DEPT.
BABY AND

OKAY, THANKS, MO. I THINK I'M ALL SET HERE.
PREGNANCY AFTER 35

cyborg nation
As Sparrow considers her options... ...her housemates are getting edgy.
MADWIMMIN BOOKS & CAFE
7/3
393
PRENATAL PARENTHOOD
ABORTION: A WOMAN'S GUIDE
EMPOWERED PREGNANCY
EXPERIENCING ABORTION
GINGER, CAN I BORROW YOUR CAR? I'M TAKING JONAS AND JASMINE TO A DRIVE-IN MOVIE, AND MINE HAS THAT MOLD PROBLEM.
WHY EVEN ASK? WHY NOT JUST TAKE IT? WHAT THE HELL, LET JONAS DRIVE! LET THE KID CRASH IT, JUST LIKE YOU LET HIM DO TO MY HARD DRIVE.
GOD, MY ENTIRE LIFE HAS COME TO A STANDSTILL. IT'LL TAKE WEEKS OF MY PRECIOUS VACATION TO SHOP FOR A NEW COMPUTER AND GET EVERYTHING SET UP AGAIN.
I MIGHT SPEND THE NIGHT OVER THERE, BUT I'LL HAVE IT BACK BY MORNING.
A TIP O' THE NIB TO TAYLOR ROTHBELL
WAIT, YOU CAN'T TAKE HER CAR! I NEED IT TO GO TEST DRIVE A SUBARU ACROSS TOWN AT 8.
TAKE MINE. SO YOU'RE NOT GONNA HAVE JERRY FIX YOUR COROLLA?
CLASSIFIE
NO, I NEED SOMETHING NEWER IN CASE SPARROW DECIDES TO HAVE THE BABY. I'M ACTUALLY LOOKING AT STATION WAGONS. I ALWAYS SORT OF EQUATED MY DAD WITH OUR STATION WAGON. THEY HAD, LIKE, THE SAME EXPRESSION.
Y'KNOW, STUART, YOU'D MAKE A GREAT FATHER.
OH, GIVE ME A BREAK! PEOPLE SAY THAT ABOUT ANY HALF-SENTIENT MALE AS LONG AS HE'S NOT ACTUALLY A CONVICTED PEDOPHILE.
UM... ACTUALLY, I THINK THEY SAY IT EVEN IF HE IS. BUT I WOULD BE A GOOD FATHER!
WHY BUY SOME BIG HONKING CAR BEFORE YOU KNOW WHAT SPARROW'S GONNA DO? IF SHE DOESN'T HAVE THE BABY, IT'LL BE A CONSTANT REMINDER.
I KNOW, BUT I NEED A CAR NOW!
RIGHT. GOD FORBID ANY AMERICAN GO WITHOUT A VEHICLE FOR MORE THAN A DAY. WOULDN'T WANT TO SLOW THE PACE OF GLOBAL WARMING, OR EASE THE VIOLENCE IN THE MIDDLE EAST. FILL 'ER UP!
UH, I GOTTA GO. I WANT TO GET A GOOD SPOT AT THE DRIVE-IN.
HEY, I DON'T LIKE BEING DEPENDENT ON A CAR. AND WHAT ABOUT THE MILLIONS OF OBSOLETE COMPUTERS THAT GET SENT TO POOR COUNTRIES WHERE THEY LEACH HEAVY METALS INTO THE GROUND WATER JUST SO YOU CAN PLAY SIMS HOUSE PARTY?!
THAT'S NOT ALL I USE IT FOR! MY WHOLE LIFE IS ON THIS THING!
WELL, THAT'S MY POINT! GOD, IS THERE ANY HUMAN ACTIVITY LEFT THAT DOESN'T REQUIRE TECHNOLOGY?
DOOT!
BREAST-FEEDING for FUN & PROFIT
PILATES for PREGNANCY
PRENATA

ARE YOU FINDING THE ACTION-PACKED SUSPENSE OF THIS COMIC STRIP SIMPLY **UNBEARABLE?**

TODAY WE'LL RESOLVE A FEW SUBPLOTS THAT HAVE NO DOUBT KEPT YOU ON TENTERHOOKS FOR WEEKS.

DID STUART GET THAT **STATION WAGON?**

WHAT'S GINGER'S **COMPUTER** SITUATION?

ARE YOU PURSUING JASMINE JUST TO TORTURE ME? LAST I HEARD, YOU WERE INTO **BUTCH DADDIES** AND **TRANS MEN**. SHE'S NOT YOUR TYPE AT ALL!

I HAVE VERY CATHOLIC TASTES. AND BESIDES, JONAS NEEDS A GENDERQUEER ROLE MODEL.

LOIS, LOOK! MOM LET ME WEAR THE TUBE TOP YOU GOT ME!

SWEET.

HAS SYDNEY HEARD FROM THE **PROVOST?**

AND WHAT EXACTLY GOES ON AT **LIBRARY SCHOOL** ANYWAY?

EXCUSE ME. I, UH... JUST HAVE TO TELL YOU, I FOUND YOUR POWERPOINT PRESENTATION ON PRESERVING PATRON PRIVACY UNDER THE **PATRIOT ACT** PROVOCATIVE AND PENETRATING.

GOD, GINGER! HE'S SO COMPLETELY INTO THIS BABY, THERE'S NO ROOM FOR **ME!** WHAT IF I DON'T **LIKE** MILK? WHAT IF THE WAY MY BODY'S CHANGING IS **FREAKING** ME **OUT?**

A TIP O' THE NIB TO MARGIT BERMAN!

I HAVEN'T FELT THIS LONELY AND CONFUSED SINCE I **CAME OUT.**

WELL... DO WHAT YOU DID THEN.

MEANWHILE, JUST DOWN THE STREET FROM BOUNDERS BOOKS AND MUZAK, THE LAST INDEPENDENT BOOKSTORE IN TOWN BITES THE DUST-JACKET.

Intro to Queer Theory
9/25
399
©2002 BY ALISON BECHDEL
THE ARC OF HISTORY IS LONG...

THANKS, ANNE! SORRY I WAS A LITTLE LATE. I HOPE HE WASN'T ANY TROUBLE.
I **WISH** THE TWO OF THEM WOULD GIVE ME SOME TROUBLE. THEY JUST SIT IN FRONT OF THE COMPUTER LIKE... LIKE **LARVAE.**

SO HOW WAS YOUR FIRST DAY OF FOURTH GRADE?

WE'RE GOING TO KEEP JOURNALS AND WE HAVE TO WRITE CURSIVE IN THEM AND WE HAVE COMPUTER LAB EVERY DAY AND AT RECESS A NEW KID TAUGHT US THIS REALLY EXCELLENT GAME.
YEAH?

IT'S CALLED "SMEAR THE QUEER."
WHAT?

YOU THROW THE BALL IN THE AIR AND WHOEVER CATCHES IT RUNS AROUND AND WE ALL TRY TO KNOCK HIM DOWN AND PILE ONTO HIM. SEE MY SCRAPE?
RAFFI! DID YOUR TEACHER KNOW THIS WAS GOING ON? DID SHE SEE THE OTHER KIDS KNOCKING YOU DOWN?!

I DON'T KNOW. BUT I WAS KNOCKING THEM DOWN TOO!
I DON'T EVEN KNOW WHERE TO START! YOU KNOW IT'S WRONG TO GANG UP ON PEOPLE. YOU KNOW "QUEER" IS A VERY MEAN WORD!

THEN HOW COME YOU GUYS ARE ALWAYS SAYING IT?

...BUT IT BENDS TOWARD JUSTICE.

LATER THAT EVENING...
WELL, I'D APPRECIATE THAT. THANK YOU. ... NOT AT ALL. BYE.
WELL?

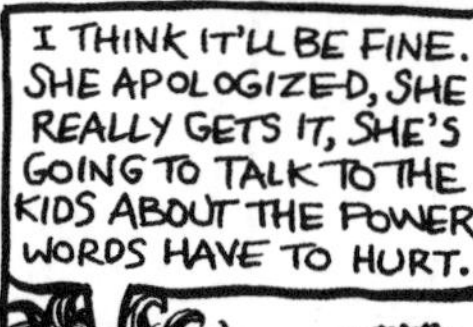

I THINK IT'LL BE FINE. SHE APOLOGIZED, SHE REALLY GETS IT, SHE'S GOING TO TALK TO THE KIDS ABOUT THE POWER WORDS HAVE TO HURT.

BIP

HOW ABOUT THE POWER OF **GANG-TACKLING** TO HURT? #%*@ING RITALIN-RADDLED RIFFRAFF!
CLARICE, CAN WE PLEASE TRY AND WIND DOWN? IT'S BEEN A LONG DAY.

HERE, WE CAN READ THE SAME-SEX COMMITMENT CEREMONY ANNOUNCEMENTS IN THE **TIMES.** GOD, REMEMBER WHEN THEY WOULDN'T EVEN PRINT THE WORD "GAY"?
Sunday Styles

SORT OF.
(APOLOGIES TO DR. KING)

HILARY AND SCHUYLER... CHAPEL AT HOTCHKISS... STANFORD... MBA FROM U. PENN... HOW SWEET! THEY WORK AT THE SAME INVESTMENT BANK IN THE **GLOBAL RAPINE** & **PILLAGE** DIVISION.
OKAY, OKAY. WE CAN READ THE ARTS & LEISURE SECTION.
Sunday Styles
ALL THE NEWS THAT'S SOCIALLY CONNECTED

dis information
10/9
400
©2002 BY ALISON BECHDEL
TONIGHT ON THE LATE SHOW, BRUCE WILLIS AND DONALD RUMSFELD TALK WITH DAVE ABOUT THEIR LATEST PROJECTS.
GOD! GOEBBELS HIMSELF COULDN'T OUT-MARKET THESE GUYS.
just bomb it.
NEWSTIME
BUSH: IF SADDAM WON'T LET WEAPONS INSPECTORS IN, WE'LL HAVE TO INVADE
ARE PEOPLE REALLY FALLING FOR THIS P.R. BLITZ? CAN'T EVERYONE SEE THAT INVADING IRAQ IS JUST A BIG DIVERSION?
IS YOUR HOME SAFE? PROTECT IT FROM DIRT, ANTHRAX, AND NUKULAR WEAPONS WITH OUR NEW, IMPROVED **PRE-EMPTIVE WIPE!**
got regime change?
NEWSTIME
IRAQ: OKAY, OKAY. INSPECTORS CAN COME IN.
DOESN'T IT STICK IN ANYONE'S CRAW THAT THE BUSHITES ARE EXPLOITING THE REAL HORROR OF 9/11, AND THREATENING TO PLUNGE THE ENTIRE GLOBE INTO **ANARCHY**...
NEXT TIME YOU CALL COLLECT, DIAL 1-800-**DIE-IRAQ!**
BUSH: IF SADDAM WON'T SUBMIT TO A COLONOSCOPY BY WEAPONS INSPECTORS WE'LL HAVE TO INVADE.
...JUST TO DISTRACT US FROM THEIR OILY SHENANIGANS AT ENRON AND HARKIN AND HALLIBURTON...
IRAQ: FORGET IT THEN
GLOBAL Wireless WAR
•LONG DISTANCE ROAMING
•UNLIMITED ANYTIME MINUTES
...AND IN THE BARGAIN, MAYBE GET THEIR HANDS ON **MORE** OIL WITH IRAQ'S PETROLEUM RESERVES?!
MOM, BE QUIET. THIS IS A GOOD ONE.
DUDE, YOU'RE GETTIN' A WAR!
BUSH: PHEW! THAT WAS CLOSE.
MEANWHILE, GINGER GRAPPLES WITH THE SEPARATION OF CHURCH AND BUFFALO LAKE STATE.
MS. JORDAN, I JUST WANT TO OBJECT TO OUR ASSIGNMENT FOR THURSDAY. IT'S LIKE, AGAINST THE CONSTITUTION FOR YOU TO MAKE US READ THE KORAN.
IT IS?
WORLD LIT SURVEY syllabus
YEAH. CAUSE YOU'RE LIKE, FORCING RELIGION ON US. SO I REFUSE TO READ IT. NO WAY.
PARTY ON, BRO. ME TOO.
ME TOO.
FINE. YOU CAN EITHER TAKE A QUIZ ON THE READING, OR GIVE ME A THREE PAGE ESSAY EXPLAINING WHY YOU DIDN'T WANT TO DO IT.
THAT IS SO VIOLATING OUR FIRST AMENDMENT RIGHTS.
YEAH.
YEAH.
THIS JOB IS SO VIOLATING MY LIFE, LIBERTY, AND PURSUIT OF HAPPINESS.
BRAND IT AND THEY WILL COME! WHAT EVER HAPPENED TO RATIONALITY? TO COMMON SENSE? TO HUMAN **DECENCY?**
SWEETIE, KEEP YOUR VOICE DOWN. WE DON'T WANT THE NEIGHBORS REPORTING US AS A TERROR CELL.
...SIDE EFFECTS ARE MILD AND INCLUDE INSOMNIA, LOW OIL PRESSURE, AND INCREASED RISK OF TERRORIST ATTACKS...

decline & fall
10/23
401
©2002 BY ALISON BECHDEL

AH, AUTUMN... DEGENERATION, DECAY, NATURE'S EBB, WHEN THE FOLIAGE, LIKE THE HOMELAND SECURITY THREAT LEVEL, RIPENS FROM YELLOW TO ORANGE.

NO, WE DON'T HAVE ANN COULTER'S "SLANDER: LIBERAL LIES ABOUT THE AMERICAN RIGHT."
MADWIMMIN BOOKS
NO WAR IN IRAQ
END OF AN ERA SALE
EVERYTHING MUST GO!

I THOUGHT YOU SOLD BOOKS BY WOMEN.

THAT'S RIGHT. NOT BOOKS BY FRICKIN' FRUIT-CAKES.
I'M **SO** SORRY. WE DON'T HAVE "SLANDER," BUT YOU'LL FIND A COPY OF PEGGY NOONAN'S TRIBUTE TO RONALD REAGAN IN THE "WHO ORDERED THIS?" BIN.

MO, CAN YOU PLEASE NOT PUT US OUT OF BUSINESS ANY FASTER THAN WE'RE ALREADY GOING?
VULTURES! WHERE WERE THEY 6 MONTHS AGO?

GOD, I FEEL SO GUILTY BUYING STUFF FOR 80% OFF.
EXTENDED MASSIVE ORGASM
PLAY YOUR CARDS RIGHT AND I WON'T TELL MO ABOUT THOSE BOOK-BUYING BINGES ON MEDUSA.COM.

I CAN'T BELIEVE THIS PLACE ISN'T GONNA BE HERE ANYMORE. IT SHOULD BE A CULTURAL LANDMARK.
I KNOW. GOD, REMEMBER THAT ADRIENNE RICH READING BACK IN '86, WHEN THE PLACE WAS SO PACKED AND THE ATMOSPHERE WAS SO CHARGED, I **FAINTED?**
IMAGINE ANYONE FAINTING AT BUNNS AND NOODLE. UNLESS MAYBE THEY WERE CHOKING ON A SCONE.
JUST WATCH. NOW THAT THE CHAINS HAVE NO MORE LOCAL COMPETITION, THEY'LL CUT BACK ON THEIR STOCK.
SPARE ME THE DEATH OF LITERATURE SPEECH. IF THERE'S A MARKET FOR A BOOK, WHY WOULDN'T THE CHAINS SELL IT? THIS IS A CAPITALIST COUNTRY, AFTER ALL.
THE EXPECTANT FATHER
THE LESBIAN HOLE SEX BOOK
gender BLUR

EXACTLY. THAT'S WHY BOOKS BY UNKNOWN WRITERS WON'T HAVE THE CHANCE TO **DEVELOP** A MARKET--THEY CAN'T GUARANTEE HUGE SALES.
RIGHT. ALL THE CHAINS CARE ABOUT IS THE BOTTOM LINE, NOT THE HALLOWED WRITTEN WORD, LIKE THIS PLACE. DO YOU HAVE THIS IN PARTY SIZE?
LIBRARY O' LUBRICANTS
MARTHA STEWART'S CRAFT & STOCK TIPS

THANKS FOR BEING HERE ALL THESE YEARS. YOU'VE BEEN SO MUCH MORE THAN JUST A STORE.
YEAH. IF ONLY WE'D CHARGED FOR ALL THAT EXTRA SERVICE, MAYBE A **VELMA'S SECRET** WOULDN'T BE TAKING OVER OUR SPACE.
DOOT

THANKS FOR SHOPPING HERE ALL THESE YEARS.

The Ambassadors
11/6
402
©2002 BY ALISON BECHDEL

...MY MIDDLE NAME? UM, CONSTANCE. AFTER MY AUNT. HANG ON, SOME-ONE'S BEEPING IN.
HELLO?

HI, IT'S ME.
UH... SWEETIE, I CAN'T TALK RIGHT NOW, I'M WORKING ON A PROJECT WITH ONE OF MY CLASSMATES.
I JUST WANTED TO TELL YOU I'LL BE HOME LATE. I HAVE THAT THING AT 6.

OH, RIGHT! YOUR FIRST MAMMO! DON'T WORRY, IT'S NO BIG DEAL. THEY JUST CLAMP YOUR TITS IN A VISE FOR A COUPLE SECONDS.
THANKS. SAY HI TO YOUR LITTLE LIBRARIAN CHUM.
STUDENTS for JUSTICE in PALESTINE
UNIVERSITY HILLEL
INVEST IN ISRAEL

DR. KRUKOWSKI? HAVE YOU SIGNED THE PETITION CALLING FOR THE UNIVERSITY TO DIVEST FROM ISRAEL?
UH... NO.

DR. K! HERE! SIGN OUR PETITION **NOT** TO DIVEST.
SORRY. I FIND PETITIONS TRITE.
RALLY

WHAT AN ASSHOLE.
I COULDN'T AGREE MORE.

LATER THAT SAME DAY, DOWNTOWN...
WHAT'D I MISS?
THIS GUY'S JUST SAYING BUSH'S UNILATERAL FOREIGN POLICY MAKES US LESS SECURE, NOT MORE.
EARTH TO BUSH: DON'T ATTACK IRAQ
USE YOUR WORDS

Y'KNOW, YOU MIGHT WANT TO THINK ABOUT THAT IN TERMS OF YOUR PERSONAL LIFE, GINGER. MAYBE THAT'S WHY YOU DON'T HAVE A GIRLFRIEND.
WHAT?!
NOT IN OUR NAME
U.S. AGAINST THE WORLD? NO THANKS

IT'S LIKE, YOU HAVE TO BE THE ONE IN CONTROL, BUT YOU **CAN'T** BE IN CONTROL IN A COOPERATIVE RELATIONSHIP. SO YOU CUT YOURSELF **OFF**. AND YOU THINK THAT KEEPS YOU FROM GETTING HURT. BUT IN FACT, THE BEST SECURITY STRATEGY IS **DIPLOMATIC ENGAGEMENT** WITH OTHERS.

PERHAPS THIS ALSO EXPLAINS WHY YOU PREFER DOGS TO PEOPLE.
HELLO, BEAUTIFUL!
ANUBIS! HEEL!

HE'S NOT EXACTLY AN ALPHA.
THAT'S OKAY. SHE IS.
WHO'S A PUPPY? WHO'S A GREAT BIG PUPPY?

Swept Away

Conviviality reigns as our eupeptic friends digest the Thanksgiving tofurkey.

11/20

403

A TIP O' THE NIB TO JUDITH LEVINE

female trouble
12/18
405
©2002 BY ALISON BECHDEL

HUH. HAVE YOU TOLD SYDNEY ABOUT HER?
File
me.jpg

YEAH, BUT SHE UNDERSTANDS IT'S ONLY A CRUSH. I THINK FIONA IS JUST THE EMBODIMENT OF MY EXCITEMENT ABOUT THE THINGS I'M LEARNING IN THE PROGRAM.
IF I'D KNOWN THE DEWEY DECIMAL SYSTEM WAS EMBODIED LIKE THAT, I'D'VE GONE TO LIBRARY SCHOOL TOO.
2002-2003

BUT SADLY, WHILE YOU AND YOUR CHIPPY ARE PANTING OVER "CLASSIFICATION SYSTEMS FOR THE ORGANIZATION OF KNOWLEDGE," IT LOOKS LIKE I'LL BE SHOVELING DANIELLE STEELE OVER AT BOUNDERS.
BOUNDERS?! YOU GOT A JOB AT BOUNDERS BOOKS-N-MUZAK?!!
2002-03 COURSE CATALOG

WELL, I APPLIED FOR ONE. LET'S FACE IT. WHAT ELSE AM I FIT FOR?
BUT LOIS...
RRING!
HEY, MAYBE THAT'S THE PUBLIC LIBRARY. I SENT THEM MY RESUMÉ.

HELLO?
SYDNEY KU... KUR... KROTCH-OFFSKI?
NO, SHE'S NOT HERE. CAN I TAKE A MESSAGE?

THIS IS MARCIA AT THE BREAST CENTER. COULD YOU PLEASE ASK HER TO GIVE US A CALL? THANKS! HAVE A NICE DAY! CLIK!

I'M HOPING FOR AN EVENING SHIFT, JUST TO GET OUT OF THE HOUSE. SPARROW AND STUART ARE DRIVING ME NUTS. SHE'S CONVINCED SOMETHING'S GONNA GO WRONG. HE'S MANIACALLY UPBEAT. IT'S LIKE LIVING WITH THOMAS HOBBES AND GIDGET!

MEANWHILE...
I TOLD YOU.
SO IT'S... IT'S NOT JUST BRAXTON-HICKS?
NOPE. IT'S PRETERM LABOR, ALL RIGHT. BUT YOUR CERVIX HASN'T DILATED AT ALL. SO THAT'S GOOD.
SEATTLE MIDWIFERY SCHOOL

GOOD. GOOD IS GOOD.
BUT I HAVE 6 WEEKS TO GO. WHAT DO I DO?
YOU'RE GOING TO NEED COMPLETE BEDREST. THE CONTRACTIONS SEEM TO HAVE SLOWED DOWN. BUT IF THEY START COMING CLOSE TOGETHER AGAIN, I WANT YOU TO CALL DR. HU.
SOUTHERN TRAVERSE
THANKS TO NAN REID, MIDWIFE TO THE COMIX.

THEN WHAT? WHAT'S THE WORST CASE SCENARIO?
WELL, A PREMATURE DELIVERY. BUT LET'S NOT GET AHEAD OF OURSELVES. BEDREST OFTEN DOES THE TRICK.
ECO CHALLENGE

COMPLETE BEDREST! DOESN'T THAT SOUND LIKE FUN?!

THE AWFUL TRUTH

406

1/1

LET'S SEE HOW SPARROW'S BEDREST IS PROGRESSING.

foreign policy

(don't try this at home)

1/29

408

IS YOUR SUPREME AUTHORITY BEING FLAGRANTLY FLOUTED?

ARE YOU TIRED OF TEDIOUS NEGOTIATIONS AND MESSY COMPROMISES?

WHY NOT TAKE A **HARD LINE** FOR A CHANGE? IMAGINE HOW SIMPLE LIFE COULD BE!

START BY USING YOUR WORDS...

... AND SOME SANCTIONS, ...

... BUT THEN, HAUL OUT YOUR **BIG STICK!**

DON'T TRUST ANYONE FURTHER THAN YOU CAN LAUNCH A BALLISTIC MISSILE.

DON'T PANDER TO MALEFACTORS BY PROVIDING ANY INCENTIVE FOR THEM TO CHANGE THEIR BEHAVIOR.

IGNORE BLEEDING-HEART TERRORIST SYMPATHIZERS.

... I HATE YOU, I **HATE** YOU!

POOF!

THEN AGAIN, PERHAPS THERE'S SOMETHING TO BE SAID FOR TEDIOUS NEGOTIATIONS.

LATER...

HEY! HOW COME **YOU** GET TO PLAY?

alienated labor

2/26

410

©2003 BY ALISON BECHDEL

ISN'T THERE **ENOUGH** TO WORRY ABOUT IN LIFE WITHOUT IMPENDING WORLD WAR AND THE FLAGRANT FEAR-MONGERING OF FRAUDULENTLY ELECTED FIGUREHEADS?

this
brief
transit
411
3/12
©2003 BY ALISON BECHDEL

IT'S A DARK AND STORMY NIGHT.

GINGER? ARE YOU JUST GETTING HOME?
IT TOOK ME THREE HOURS! I SHOULD'VE STAYED AT SCHOOL BUT I WAS AFRAID I MIGHT MISS SOMETHING.

WHAT'RE YOU GUYS DOING OUTSIDE?
AND IF WE'RE ALL OUT HERE, WHO'S WITH SPARROW?

SKIS?
HUH. EITHER SHE FOUND SOMEONE TO COME OVER, OR WE'RE BEING BURGLED BY A BIATHLETE.

SPARROW?
UUNNH!

STUART? OH, GOOD. WASH YOUR HANDS AND GET IN HERE! NOW!
NOWWW!

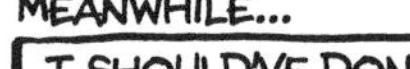
MEANWHILE...

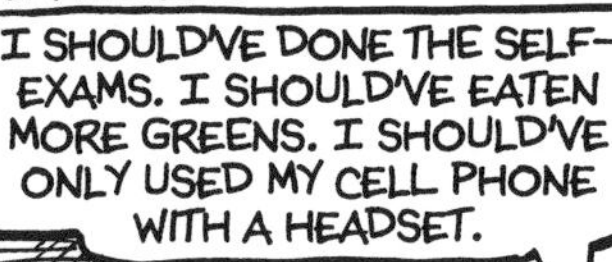
I SHOULD'VE DONE THE SELF-EXAMS. I SHOULD'VE EATEN MORE GREENS. I SHOULD'VE ONLY USED MY CELL PHONE WITH A HEADSET.

HONEY, DON'T BE RIDICULOUS. CELL PHONES GIVE YOU **BRAIN** CANCER, NOT BREAST CANCER.
HOW CAN THIS HAPPEN? WHAT IF I DIE BEFORE MY BOOK COMES OUT?

SHHH.

YEEOW!
I'VE GOT A HEAD...AND A LEG...

OH, SHE'S MAGNIFICENT!

WELCOME, BABY! DO YOU HAVE A NAME?
I'VE BEEN LOBBYING FOR HANS BLIX, BUT NO ONE ELSE SEEMS TOO KEEN ON IT.
EHH!

METAPHOR AS ILLNESS
3/26
412
©2003 BY ALISON BECHDEL
SOME OF OUR FRIENDS ARE IN SHOCK...
THINK OVER THE OPTIONS WE DISCUSSED. BUT YOU NEED TO MAKE A DECISION SOON. WE DON'T WANT THOSE LITTLE TERRORISTS AMASSING ANY MORE RECRUITS BEFORE WE GO IN THERE TO WIPE THEM OUT.
A TIP O' THE NIB TO PAT FONTAINE
GOD, I'M GLAD YOU WERE TAKING NOTES. I COULDN'T FOCUS AT ALL.
CRIPES! WHERE'D SHE STUDY MEDICINE? THE NATIONAL WAR COLLEGE?
EXIT
YOU DIDN'T LIKE HER?
SYDNEY, SHE HAS THE BEDSIDE MANNER OF GEORGE PATTON. I MEAN, GIVEN THAT THE GOAL HERE IS HEALING, I THINK A MORE NON-VIOLENT APPROACH MIGHT BE ADVISABLE.
I DON'T THINK U.N. RESOLUTIONS WORK ON CANCER.
I'M JUST SAYING, THAT IMAGE OF GOING TO BATTLE AGAINST YOUR OWN BODY IS REALLY NEGATIVE. THERE'S SOMETHING SO CUT-OFF ABOUT IT.
YEAH, WELL, I THINK THAT'S THE GENERAL IDEA OF A LUMPECTOMY.
..WHILE OTHERS ARE IN AWE.
I CAN NEVER GO BACK TO WORK.
I HAVE MIDTERMS TO GRADE BUT I CAN'T MOVE.
WELL, SOMEONE HAS TO FACE REALITY. I'M OFF TO THE BOOK MINES. HAVE YOU HEARD THE WEATHER?
...THERE'S NO SUCH THING AS A "SURGICAL" INVASION. SOME PEOPLE SAY SADDAM IS A CANCER THE WORLD NEEDS TO BE RID OF. BUT SOMETIMES THE TREATMENT CAN BE WORSE THAN THE DISEASE.
AND DON'T FORGET THE ACTUAL CANCER OF WAR, THE THOUSANDS OF IRAQI CHILDREN WITH LEUKEMIA FROM EXPOSURE TO DEPLETED URANIUM SHELLS USED BY THE U.S. IN THE 1991--
TURN IT OFF!
OKAY, OKAY. FAR BE IT FROM ME TO BURST THE BLISS BUBBLE.

media-
tion
©2003 By Alison Bechdel
4/14

COMING UP NEXT, COALITION FORCES SHELL A HARDENED PLATOON OF NON-COALITION JOURNALISTS.
KNOCK! KNOCK!
FIX
DOW
PESTILENCE ... CHAOS
VICTORY IS OURS!
ONE COUNTRY DOWN. 236 TO GO
4/23

HI, HARRIET.
HI. I JUST THOUGHT I'D STOP IN AND SEE HOW YOU'RE DOING.

MAN. THANK GOD I'M UNEMPLOYED, OR I DON'T KNOW HOW I'D STAY ON TOP OF THINGS. I SPENT THE WHOLE MORNING E-MAILING CONGRESS AND FORWARDING PETITIONS. THERE'S ALL THIS CORPORATE MEDIA COVERAGE TO MONITOR. I'VE GOT A DIE-IN AT FIVE...

UH...I MEANT, HOW ARE YOU DOING ABOUT SYDNEY.
HANG ON. IT SOUNDS LIKE ONE OF THESE BOOT-LICKING EMBEDS IS ACTUALLY GONNA TALK ABOUT THE CIVILIAN CARNAGE...
LIVE
THE SITUATION IS TERRIBLE HERE. AS AN AMERICAN, I'M EXTREMELY UNCOMFORTABLE. IT'S... WELL, IT'S SICKENING...

...I'M TELLING YOU, I HAVEN'T BATHED IN THREE WEEKS.
NEVER MIND.

LOOK AT THIS. BUSH HAS CREATED SUCH A DIVERSION IN IRAQ, NOBODY NOTICES THE DOMESTIC SITUATION. HE'S USING HIS TAX CUTS AND HIS WAR TAB TO STARVE THE GOVERNMENT. HE'S RE-INSTITUTING FEUDALISM!
...TODAY THE PRESIDENT SUGGESTED THAT THE PESTICIDE METHYL BROMIDE COULD BE A VEGETABLE IN SCHOOL LUNCHES...

HELLO? WHAT ABOUT **YOUR** DOMESTIC SITUATION? YOUR LOVER'S HAVING SURGERY NEXT WEEK!
OH. RIGHT.
CLICK

HI, SYDNEY.
GREAT. WHAT HAVE YOU BOUGHT NOW?
A DVD PLAYER. IF I'M GONNA BE LYING AROUND HERE IN A CHEMOTHERAPY HAZE, AT LEAST I CAN WATCH THE DIRECTOR'S CUT OF "UNCLE BUCK."

Y'KNOW, SHE BROKE UP WITH ME FOR BRINGING HOME A VCR.
SHE WON'T BREAK UP WITH ME! I HAVE CANCER! I CAN DO WHATEVER I WANT.
DVD
WELL...DVD PLAYERS REALLY DON'T COST VERY MUCH.

WHERE SHOULD WE PUT IT, DR. K?
PLASMATRON
32" FLAT SCREEN TV
RXJ128
SCOOTER, ALEX! THANKS. SET IT DOWN ANYWHERE.

HDTV, BABY!
I DON'T EVEN KNOW WHAT THAT **MEANS.**
ANOTHER TRANNY BUTCH ANARCHIST
HEAVY DENIAL TELEVISION.

reflux redux

415

5/7

©2003 By Alison Bechdel

SPARROW'S PARENTS HAVE INVADED-- NOT TO CONQUER, BUT TO LIBERATE.

MOM, WHAT ARE YOU **DOING?**

A TIP O' THE UMBILICUS TO VESA LEHTINEN

JUST TIDYING UP. YOUR FREEZER'S A MESS. I THOUGHT WE COULD HAVE THIS NICE ROAST FOR DINNER.

ROAST?

THAT'S MY PLACENTA! I'M SAVING IT TO BURY IN THE GARDEN WHEN THE GROUND THAWS!

SWEETHEART, I'M GONNA RAKE THE YARD, SO I TOOK THIS RIDICULOUS SIGN DOWN.

NO WAR ON IRAQ

WILL YOU TWO PLEASE STOP TRYING TO HELP?!

MAYBE YOU MISSED THE NEWS--THE WAR'S OVER AND WE WON. C'MERE TO GRANDPA, BABY.

DADDY, NOBODY WON ANYTHING. A LOT OF INNOCENT IRAQIS WERE MAIMED AND SLAUGHTERED, ALONG WITH SOME AMERICAN KIDS WHO JOINED THE MILITARY BECAUSE THEY DIDN'T HAVE A BETTER OPTION.

the basic anxiety
©2003 BY ALISON BECHDEL
5/21
416
I KINDA WISH THEY WERE LOPPING THE WHOLE THING OFF. JUST TO BE SURE.
GIRLS, CAN I GET IN THERE?
NOK! NOK!
MOM, GO BACK TO SLEEP. YOU DON'T HAVE TO GO WITH US. YOU CAN DRIVE OVER WHEN I COME OUT OF SURGERY.
CAN'T WE LOP YOUR MOTHER OFF INSTEAD?
IF YOUR FATHER'S GOING TO BE THERE, SO AM I. I DIDN'T COME ALL THIS WAY AND MISS MY CONFERENCE JUST TO SLEEP IN.
WHAT WAS THAT CONFERENCE AGAIN? REFRESH MY MEMORY.
"BUDDHISM, PSYCHOTHERAPY, AND COMPASSION." I DON'T KNOW WHY YOU FIND THAT SO AMUSING.
SHE'S LIKE A MOTHER TO ME. SORT OF.
WHAT IF SOMETHING GOES WRONG WITH THE ANESTHESIA AND I GET BRAIN DAMAGE? WHAT IF THE SURGEON LEAVES HER ROLEX INSIDE ME?
EMERGENCY
PARKING
I WOULDN'T COUNT ON IT. KNOWING DR. ROMMEL, SHE HAS A SWISS ARMY WATCH. SET TO MILITARY TIME.
MAYBE IT'LL HAVE A LUMINOUS DIAL. AT LEAST THEN I WON'T NEED RADIATION.
JOKING IS AN AVOIDANCE STRATEGY, SYDNEY. TRY TO FACE YOUR FEARS DIRECTLY.
LOOK, THERE'S DADDY!
I'M GOING TO STAY OUT HERE AND HAVE A CIGARETTE. I'LL BE IN IN A MINUTE.
SOME TIME LATER...
... THERE'LL BE A DRAIN IN THE INCISION WHEN YOU WAKE UP. AND DON'T WORRY IF YOU PEE BLUE FOR A WHILE. IT'S JUST THE DYE WE USED TO STAIN THE TUMOR.
KER...KRU... CRUTCHOFFSKI, BREAST CONSERVATION?
HOW ARE WE FEELING?
A BIT LIKE AN ENDANGERED WETLAND.
I WISH IT WERE ME INSTEAD OF YOU.
YEAH. I'M GETTING THE SODIUM PENTOTHAL. YOU HAVE TO GO SIT WITH MY PARENTS.

pump it up
6/4
417
©2003 By Alison Bechdel
SYDNEY MADE IT THROUGH SURGERY. BUT WILL SHE SURVIVE HER MALIGNANT PARENTS AND THE MIASMAL FOG OF CABLE NEWS?

"...AND I PROMISE YOU, WE **WILL** FIND WEAPONS OF MASS DESTRUCTION." THIS HAS BEEN A FOX NEWS ALERT. WE'LL KEEP YOU POSTED ON THIS BREAKING STORY. NEXT...
SO PAUL, HOW'S LOLITA? DID SHE EVER FINISH HER DISSERTATION?

JENNIFER IS FINE. SHE, AH...SHE JUST RECEIVED HER PILATES CERTIFICATION.
SNORT.
"THE VITALITY OF AMERICA'S DEMOCRACY DEPENDS ON THE FAIRNESS AND ACCURACY OF AMERICA'S ELECTIONS."

UH...DOING A LITTLE LIGHT READING, MO?
THE ORIGINS OF TOTALITARIANISM
SO SAID PRESIDENT GEORGE W. BUSH AS HE SIGNED THE **HELP AMERICA VOTE REPUBLICAN ACT** INTO LAW LAST OCTOBER.

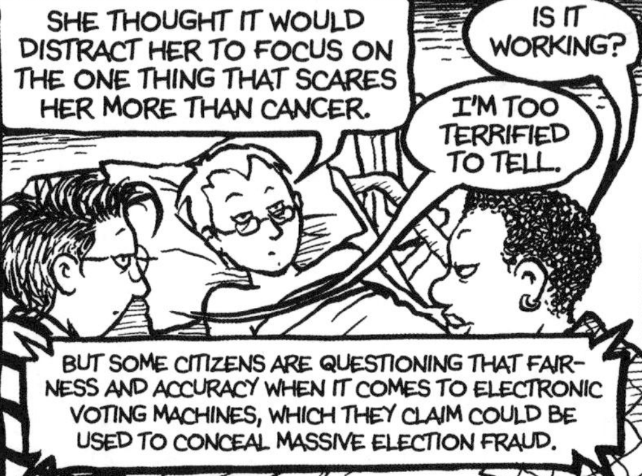
SHE THOUGHT IT WOULD DISTRACT HER TO FOCUS ON THE ONE THING THAT SCARES HER MORE THAN CANCER.
IS IT WORKING?
I'M TOO TERRIFIED TO TELL.
BUT SOME CITIZENS ARE QUESTIONING THAT FAIRNESS AND ACCURACY WHEN IT COMES TO ELECTRONIC VOTING MACHINES, WHICH THEY CLAIM COULD BE USED TO CONCEAL MASSIVE ELECTION FRAUD.

AH! NICE TO SEE YOU AWAKE.
HEY, DR. ROMMEL.
HERE WITH US TO DISPEL THIS HENNY PENNY CONSPIRACY THEORY IS THE CONSERVATIVE REPUBLICAN OWNER OF ONE OF THE LARGEST VOTING MACHINE MANUFACTURERS.

WELL, I GOT GOOD, CLEAR MARGINS. BUT WE WON'T KNOW HOW MEAN THE CELLS ARE UNTIL WE SEE THE PATHOLOGY. I WANT YOU TO REST UP FOR THE FIGHT.

GOD FOR HARRY, ENGLAND AND SAINT GEORGE! TO THE BREACH! TO THE **BREACH!**
UM...CHECK HER MORPHINE PUMP, NURSE.
SHE'S AS LUCID AS I AM. THAT'S "HENRY THE FIFTH."

THE PUMP'S FINE. GO AHEAD AND HIT IT AS SOON AS YOU FEEL ANY PAIN.
SO GINGER, YOU USED TO TEACH WITH SYDNEY AT THE UNIVERSITY?

YEAH. ENGLISH LIT. NOW I'M AT BUFFALO LAKE STATE.
THE STATE COLLEGES PRODUCE A FINE SCHOLAR NOW AND THEN. I DON'T KNOW IF SYD MENTIONED, I'M CHAIR OF THE ENGLISH DEPARTMENT AT CHICAGO UNIVERSITY.

SHE TOLD ME YOU JUST RETIRED.
AND SHE TOLD ME YOU'VE GOT YOUR SHOPLIFTING UNDER CONTROL. I'M GLAD TO HEAR IT.
THIS THING IS GREAT. TOO BAD I DIDN'T HAVE ONE WHEN I WAS GROWING UP.
BEEP

the candidate
2003 BY ALISON BECHDEL

ARE YOU KIDDING ME? HOW COULD THE PROSECUTOR NOT KNOW THE GUY HAS THREE PRIORS?!... NO, NO. I'LL CALL HER TOMORROW... OKAY. BYE.
WAAAAANH
7/2
419

HONEY? DO YOU REALLY THINK YOU SHOULD BE TAKING CALLS FROM WORK? I'M WORRIED THE STRESS IS DECREASING YOUR MILK PRODUCTION.
WAAAH AANH!
BIP

SHE'S SO FUSSY, AND I DON'T THINK SHE'S GAINING ENOUGH WEIGHT.
STUART, SHE WAS FINE AT HER LAST CHECK-UP. AND YOU CAN'T WEIGH HER LIKE THAT!
AANH!

YOU GUYS, WHAT DO YOU THINK? ANOTHER SOCK?
THAT DEPENDS. ARE YOU RUNNING FOR OFFICE?
HIC!

YEAH, TONIGHT'S THE "DEMOCRATS ARE A DRAG" REVUE AT CLUB L. I'M GONNA FLY ONSTAGE WITH A CABLE ATTACHED TO MY, UH... HARNESS.

THEN THE AUDIENCE VOTES AS I SQUARE OFF AGAINST THE DEMOCRATIC CANDIDATES IN AN "ARE YOU HOT" STYLE STRUT-FEST.
IF ONLY ALL CITIZENS WERE AS ENGAGED IN THE POLITICAL PROCESS.

HIGHWAY TO THE DANGER ZONE... DUH DUH DUH...
WAAH!

GINGER, ARE YOU SURE YOU DON'T WANT TO COME? WE STILL NEED A DENNIS KUCINICH. PRO-CHOICE T-SHIRT, A PAIR OF FLIP-FLOPS, YOU'D BE ALL SET.
NAH.

COME ON. I'M WORRIED ABOUT YOU. YOU'RE NEVER GONNA MEET ANYONE HANGING AROUND HERE WITH THE TACTICAL NUCLEAR FAMILY.
ANUBIS!

ANUBIS! **HEEL!**

OFF, ANUBIS! GOD, I'M SO SORRY.
BUT WHAT THE HELL DO I KNOW?

MO'S OFF, WITH SOME RELUCTANCE, FOR A TEN-DAY SESSION AT HER LOW-RESIDENCY LIBRARY SCHOOL PROGRAM.

job lot
8/27
423
©2003 BY ALISON BECHDEL

HOW'S THE STAFF OF THE LATE, LAMENTED MADWIMMIN BOOKS MANAGING TO BRING HOME THE BACON SUB-STITUTE?

THAT'S GREAT, THEA. I KNOW YOU ALWAYS WANTED TO TEACH ART.
YEAH. A LOAD OF CLAY, A JUG OF ELMER'S GLUE, AND A ROOM FULL OF FIVE-YEAR-OLDS. WHAT COULD BE BETTER?
SALE
FAKIN' BACON
PHONY BALONEY
NOT YOUR MOMMY'S PASTRAMI
SHAM CHOPS
I'M NOT TALKIN' TURKEY
WHAT INDEED.

HOW'S THE ESL TEACHING COMING?

GREAT. I HAVE TO TAKE MORE CLASSES BEFORE I'M CERTI-FIED, BUT I'VE GOT A COUPLE GIGS WITH NEIGHBORHOOD PROGRAMS ALREADY.

AND I'M HELPING SOME OF THE SOMALI REFUGEES TO GET SETTLED. THAT'S MADINA, WITH THE BABY. I'M SHOWING HER AROUND THE CO-OP, TRYING TO TRANSLATE A BIT.

?
ALTHOUGH SOME THINGS TAKE MORE TRANSLATION THAN OTHERS.
Organic FILET MIGNON CAT TREATS

MEANWHILE...
HELLO, MO! WHAT BRINGS YOU TO THE TEMPLE OF MAMMON?
I NEED THE LATEST EDITION OF "LIBRARY JOURNAL." I TRIED GOING TO THE LIBRARY--NOVEL THOUGHT!--BUT THEY'VE CUT BACK THEIR HOURS.
PERIODICALS
FOREIGN AFFAIRS
SELF
BOUNDERS BOOKS N' MUZAK

IRONIC, ISN'T IT?
AND I WAS COUNTING ON GETTING A LIBRARY JOB WHILE I FINISH SCHOOL. GOD, WHEN BUSH IS DONE WITH THE ECONOMY, THERE WON'T BE ANY LIBRARIES LEFT. I SHOULD BE GETTING A DEGREE IN DEFENSE CONTRACTING, OR AUTOMOBILE REPOSSESSION.
ANN COULTER
LIBRARY JOURNAL

NOW MY UNEM-PLOYMENT'S ABOUT TO RUN OUT. WHAT'M I GONNA DO?
GET A MAKEOVER AND WRITE A BOOK ON HOW GENOCIDE OR SLAVERY HAS GOTTEN A BAD RAP FROM LIBERALS?
TREASON THE LIBERAL MYTH OF McCARTHYISM
TREASON
LIBRARY JOURNAL

DUDE, IT'S BEEN REAL. I COULDN'T GET TIME OFF FOR THE PHISH CONCERT, SO I QUIT.
plasma

OR THERE MIGHT BE AN OPENING HERE.

AUTUMN: INEXORABLE DECLINE INTO HARD, COLD WINTER,...

OR QUIESCENT SEASON OF SPIRITUAL RENEWAL?

SO FAR, IT'S LOOKING LIKE THE FORMER.

IN THE HALLOWED HALLS OF BUFFALO LAKE STATE...

ZACHARY, THE CLASS SIZE HAS ALREADY BEEN DOUBLED. I JUST CAN'T DO IT.

IN THE BUSTLING WORLD OF COMMERCE...

THE SELF-SERVICE KIOSKS HAVE ENABLED US TO CUT DOWN ON STAFF, BUT SOME CUSTOMERS STILL FEEL THE NEED TO SPEAK TO AN ACTUAL HUMAN. THAT'S WHERE YOU COME IN.

FIND IT YERSELF!

BOUNDERS CUSTOMER SERVICE

AND IN AN OVER-PRICED, UNDER-RENO-VATED APART-MENT ON THE FRINGES OF CAMPUS...

breastiality
10/8
426
©2003 BY ALISON BECHDEL
GINGER, YOU LOOK LIKE SUSAN B. ANTHONY. PUT THIS ON.
WHAT ARE YOU DOING WITH A PUSH-UP BRA?
IT WAS IN MY LOST AND FOUND DRAWER.
LOOK, IT'S NOT A DATE. WE'RE JUST GOING TO THE DOG SHOW. I DON'T EVEN KNOW IF SHE LIKES GIRLS.
WE BOTH HAVE THIS DOG THING, THAT'S ALL.
I GUESS IT'S TRUE. MAKE SODOMY LEGAL AND YOU OPEN THE DOOR TO ALL KINDS OF PERVERSIONS.
SO TELL ME. IF IT'S NOT A DATE, WHY ARE YOU WEARING PROVOCATIVE LINGERIE?
I'M NOT. IT'S TOO SMALL. THIS IS RIDICULOUS.
IT'S SUPPOSED TO DO THAT! LEMME GET YOU A BETTER SHIRT. WE'LL FIND OUT IF SHE LIKES GIRLS OR NOT.
MOMENTARILY, DOWNSTAIRS...
WON'T YOU MISS IT?
I'LL STILL BE NURSING, JUST NOT WHILE I'M AT WORK.
THE ATTACHMENT PARENTING BOOK
I CAN'T STAND THE THOUGHT OF HER IN DAYCARE.
STUART, SHE'LL BE FINE. WILL YOU STOP? WE CAN'T AFFORD FOR YOU TO QUIT YOUR JOB.
HOW COME? IT'S NOT LIKE WE HAVE A LOT OF OVERHEAD HERE. AND I'VE ALWAYS WANTED A HOUSEBOY.
DING DONG!
GOD, GINGER! YOU LOOK HOT!
GINGER! HI!
HI, SAMIA.
SO. YOU TWO KIDS ARE GONNA GO WATCH PEOPLE FEELING UP DOGS?
OH, THIS IS A SERIOUS SPORT. THE BREAST... I MEAN, BEST IN SHOW EVENT IS INCREDIBLY EXCITING.
I HAVE NO DOUBT OF IT.

how quickly they grow
10/22
427
©2003 BY ALISON BECHDEL
I'M SO RELIEVED HIS POLL NUMBERS ARE DOWN, I COULD WEEP.
I JUST WONDER WHAT FRESH HELL THEY'RE PLOTTING TO GET THEM BACK UP AGAIN.
I'M WITH YOU. BUT SYDNEY THINKS WE'RE CYNICAL CASSANDRAS.
YES, I DO. BUT I'M GRIMACING BECAUSE EVERYTHING TASTES SO WEIRD AFTER A TREATMENT. THIS IS LIKE MOLYBDENUM VINAIGRETTE.
SYDNEY, LET ME SEE YOUR HEAD AGAIN.
COOL.
RAFFI, WHY DON'T YOU GO DOWNLOAD SOME BEYONCÉ OR SOMETHING?
NO, STAY, RAF. TELL ME HOW FIFTH GRADE'S GOING.
IT'S OKAY. EXCEPT FOR TAYLOR MAKING FUN OF ME FOR HAVING TWO MOTHERS. I'M GONNA KICK HIS @$$.
RAFFI, LANGUAGE. I KNOW TAYLOR'S A PROBLEM, BUT VIOLENCE ISN'T THE SOLUTION.
YOU'RE GONNA TALK TO HIM LIKE WE DISCUSSED, RIGHT? DO YOU WANT TO PRACTICE WHAT TO SAY?
HOW 'BOUT, "I'M GONNA KICK YOUR @$$, YOU #*&ING @$$HOLE."
MEANWHILE, AT SPARROW & STU'S...
NO, WHEN I WENT BACK TO WORK, ISABEL ADJUSTED FINE TO DAYCARE. I HATED TO LEAVE HER, THOUGH.
I KNOW! I MEAN, WHAT'S THE POINT OF EVEN HAVING A BABY IF YOU'RE JUST GONNA FARM HER OUT TO STRANGERS EVERY DAY?
DON'T LOOK AT ME. IF YOU WANT US TO LIVE ON MY MEASLY SALARY, GO FOR IT.
UH... SWEETIE, DON'T LIFT THE BABY, SHE'S TOO LITTLE.
YOU #*&ING BITCH!
ISABEL!
UH... SHE PICKED THAT UP AT DAYCARE LAST WEEK.
EXCUSE ME. I HAVE A LETTER OF RESIGNATION TO WRITE.

A TIP O' THE NIB TO MICHAEL CRAMER

Enter-tain-ing a Fan-tasy
©2004 BY ALISON BECHDEL
432
1/28
HI.
HI, FUZZY NUT.
--ONE OF THE WIN-NINGEST COACHES-- -CLIK!- DURANGO'S NEW 5.7-LITER HEMI MAGNUM V8 IS A--
WHAT'S THE MATTER, YOU DIDN'T GET ENOUGH RADIATION AT THE HOSPITAL TODAY?
-CLIK!- THE PRESIDENT'S VISIONARY PLAN CALLS FOR A MASSIVE, THROB-BING EXPANSION OF THE U.S. SPACE PRO-CLIK!-
WHOA, STOP A SECOND.
ON MONDAY THE SUPREME COURT UPHELD THE BUSH ADMINISTRATION'S POST 9/11 POLICY OF SECRET ARRESTS AND DETENTION.
ARE WE RECEIVING TRANS-MISSION FROM A PARALLEL UNIVERSE WHERE THE NEWS ACTUALLY TELLS YOU WHAT'S GOING ON?
IT'S "FREE SPEECH TV." THE SATELLITE COM-PANY HAS TO GIVE SOME CHANNELS TO PUBLIC INTEREST PROGRAMMING.
THESE DETAINEES ARE PEOPLE WHO WERE SEIZED OFF THE STREET, THROWN IN JAIL WITHOUT ANY LAWYERS, WITHOUT ANY COURT HEARING...
WOW! IF I KNEW WE COULD WATCH "DEMOCRACY NOW," I WOULDN'T HAVE COMPLAINED ABOUT ALL THE MONEY YOU SUNK INTO THIS HOME ENTERTAINMENT SYSTEM.
LOOK! NEXT, THERE'S A SHOW ABOUT MILITARISM AND GLOBAL-IZATION! THEN THEY'RE COVERING A MEDIA REFORM CONFERENCE!
...AND THEN DEPORTED BECAUSE THEY WERE ARABS OR MUSLIMS.
WHAT PART OF "ENTERTAINMENT" DON'T YOU UNDERSTAND?
-CLIK!- CHARGES AGAINST JACKSON INCLUDE SEVEN COUNTS OF LEWD--
MEANWHILE, AT LA LENTILLE D'OR,... COULD IT BE? GINGER ON AN ACTUAL DATE WITH THE DOG WOMAN?
I'VE BEEN SINGLE FOR A VERY LONG TIME. I'VE GOT A BAD RELATIONSHIP HISTORY. I'M... I'M INTIMACY IMPAIRED.
YOU AMERICAN GIRLS, YOU LOVE TO THINK YOU'RE SUCH BIG TROUBLE.
AND YOU SYRIAN GIRLS?
I'M ALL THE TROUBLE YOU NEED. DO YOU KNOW WHY I INVITED YOU HERE?
FOR THE BRUSSELS SPROUTS TARTARE?
FOR THE LONG, DISCREET TABLE-CLOTHS.
SHORTLY...
DESSERT, LADIES?
UHHHH...
I THINK WE'LL SHARE THE GINGER POT DE CRÈME.

only disconnect
©2004 BY ALISON BECHDEL
434
2/25
HELLO, SHABOOK-ADOOK!
UH... HI! WHAT PUT YOU IN SUCH A GOOD MOOD?
CHECK IT OUT! I GOT THIS FANCY CD PLAYER AND HOOKED THE TV UP TO IT.
OH.
HOSE
I CAN CONNECT IT TO MY LAPTOP TOO. AND MY iPOD, BUT I NEED TO GET A SPECIAL CABLE. GREAT SOUND, HUH?
OKAY! THAT'S IT! I'VE KEPT MY MOUTH SHUT ABOUT ALL THE CRAP YOU'VE BOUGHT SINCE YOU GOT SICK, BECAUSE IT SEEMED TO MAKE YOU FEEL BETTER, IF ONLY FOR A NANOSECOND.
IT IS ESSENTIAL THAT WHEN WE SEE A THREAT, WE DEAL WITH THOSE THREATS BEFORE THEY BECOME IMMINENT. IT'S TOO LATE IF THEY BECOME IMMINENT.
BUT YOU HAVE TO STOP! I DON'T EVEN WANT TO THINK ABOUT HOW MUCH DEBT YOU'RE IN!
Kerry '04
MASS. COURT RULES GAYS CAN MARRY
THAT'S WHY I'M LAUNCHING A GROUND OFFENSIVE ON MASSACHUSETTS.
I KNOW YOU'RE SCARED. BUT ALL THIS STUFF ISN'T GONNA KEEP YOU SAFE. NEITHER IS GOING BANKRUPT!
MR. PRESIDENT, WE'VE GONE FROM A $281 BILLION SURPLUS TO A $521 BILLION DEFICIT. WHY SHOULD THE AMERICAN PEOPLE REHIRE YOU AS CEO?
THE ONLY THING THAT'LL GIVE YOU ANY REAL SECURITY IS REACHING OUT TO PEOPLE. I WISH YOU'D GO TO THAT LESBIAN CANCER SUPPORT GROUP.
PUH-LEASE.
UH...DID I MENTION THIS WAS A DANGEROUS WORLD? AND THAT THERE'S SHADOWY NETWORKS AND ROGUE NATIONS AND DANGEROUS MADMEN AND, UH, LOTSA DANGER?
THEN TALK TO ME! Y'KNOW, YOU SURROUND YOURSELF WITH ALL THESE COMMUNICATION DEVICES, YOU'RE OBSESSED WITH "CONNECTIVITY." BUT YOU WON'T CONNECT WITH ME!
YES, ACTUALLY, ABOUT 521 BILLION TIMES.
LET'S GET MARRIED.
WHAT?
WE'LL GO TO BOSTON OR FRISCO OR TORONTO OR... OR BELGIUM, AND GET MARRIED.
IS THIS A PROPOSAL, OR SOME KIND OF POST-MODERN INTIMACY AVOIDANCE STRATEGY?
BOTH. RATHER CLEVER OF ME, YOU HAVE TO ADMIT.

milk man
©2004 BY ALISON BECHDEL
435
3/10
I DON'T THINK I CAN LEAVE FOR AT LEAST ANOTHER HOUR.
WELL, SHE POLISHED OFF THE LAST BOTTLE. AND YOU KNOW SHE WANTS YOU AT BEDTIME.
WHOOSH! SLURP!
ACME PUMP CO.
A TIP O' THE NIP TO KIRSTEN BERGGREN
GIVE HER SOME RICE MILK.
SHE'S NOT GONNA FALL FOR MILK-RELATED PROGRAM ACTIVITIES.
IS SHE HUNGRY NOW? WHY'S SHE CRYING?
NO, IT'S LOIS. SHE'S DOING RUMSFELD AT THE CLUB TONIGHT. I BETTER GO.
HAA-ANH...
LOIS!
GEE GOSH-DARN WILLIKERS, LITTLE LADY! YOU'D THINK YOU'D NEVER SEEN A RUTHLESS NEOCON PSYCHOPATH HELL-BENT ON CONVULSING THE FRAGILE WORLD IN A FRENZY OF LAWLESS AGGRESSION BEFORE!
WAAAH!
STUART, THANKS SO MUCH FOR KEEPING JONAS. HE'LL PROBABLY JUST READ TILL BEDTIME.
SHE'LL PROBABLY JUST READ UNTIL BEDTIME, AND MY NAME'S BRITNEY.
I'M SORRY, SWEETIE. I'LL TRY TO REMEMBER TO CALL YOU "SHE," BUT NO WAY WILL I CALL YOU BRITNEY. WE NEED TO DISCUSS THE NAME CHANGE FURTHER.
WHY IS SHE NEGOTIATING WITH HIM?! HE NEEDS TO LEARN TO ADJUST.
RIGHT. I'LL SEND HIM TO GITMO IN THE MORNING.
AND YOU'RE NOT HELPING MATTERS WITH THIS DRAG KING BUSINESS.
IF YOU WEREN'T WEARING A SKIRT, SIR, I'D TAKE EXCEPTION TO THAT REMARK.
SO, UH... TIGER, WHAT'RE YOU READING? ANOTHER HARRY POTTER?
"TRANSGENDERISM AND INTERSEXUALITY IN CHILDHOOD AND ADOLESCENCE." IT'S VERY FASCINATING.

get me to the clerk on time

©2004 BY ALISON BECHDEL

436

3/24

IN THE FIRST BLUSH OF HER ROMANCE WITH SAMIA, GINGER HAS BECOME A BIT LAX IN THE CLASSROOM DISCIPLINE DEPARTMENT.

betrothal or betrayal?
©2004 BY ALISON BECHDEL
437
CLARICE AND TONI ARE GETTING MARRIED, BUT THEIR WITNESSES ARE DIVIDED.
CITY HALL
SYDNEY, I'M NOT GONNA MARRY YOU! I DON'T BELIEVE IN IT!
I DON'T BELIEVE IN GAY MARRIAGE.
EVE NOT STEVE
GOD HATES YOU
EYEWITNESS NEWS
MO, THIS IS ABOUT EQUAL PROTECTION, PURE AND SIMPLE. D'YOU BELIEVE IN **THAT**?
WHAT'S THE BIG DEAL? MARRY YOUR GIRLFRIEND.
MARRIAGE LICENSES
YEAH.
I WON'T BE COMPLICIT WITH THE ENSHRINEMENT OF **COUPLEDOM** AS A PRIVILEGED CIVIC STATUS.
RIGHT. YOU'VE SO ENSHRINED YOUR OWN **OPPRESSION** AS A PRIVILEGED CIVIC STATUS, EQUALITY WOULD BE A **DOWNGRADE**.
LOOK, I JUST DON'T WANT THE NATIONAL **SECURITY STATE** IN **BED** WITH ME! AND BESIDES, WHILE WE STAND HERE FRETTING ABOUT OUR TROUSSEAUS, THE BUSHITES ARE **LIQUIDATING** THE **REPUBLIC**!
I'M **BORED**.
MARCH FOR WOMEN'S LIVES APR. 25 D.C.
RAF, LOOK AT ALL THESE PEOPLE. WOULDN'T IT BE A GREAT OPPORTUNITY TO SIGN FOLKS UP FOR THE KERRY CAMPAIGN?
KERRY'S **BORING**.
AND IF YOU'RE SO GUNG-HO TO GET MARRIED, WHY AREN'T YOU BACKING KUCINICH OR SHARPTON, WHO ACTUALLY SUPPORT YOUR **RIGHT** TO?
BECAUSE I LIVE IN THE REAL WORLD, NOT IN MY **NAVEL**. ADULTS MAKE COMPROMISES. THAT'S HOW PROGRESS HAPPENS. THAT'S WHY SUPPORT FOR CIVIL UNIONS HAS BECOME THE CONSERVATIVE FALLBACK!
C'MON. LET'S DO IT BEFORE SOMEONE SAYS WE CAN'T.
SYDNEY, YOU JUST WANNA REGISTER AT POTTERY BARN.
Y'KNOW, THIS IS AN IMPORTANT EVENT FOR ME. COULD YOU GO SQUABBLE ELSEWHERE?
WHAT DO YOU WANT? A **PRE-NUP** SAYING YOU'RE NOT RESPONSIBLE FOR ANY FUTURE **CHEMO** BILLS I MAY INCUR?
!

SNUG AS A BUG
a cautionary parable for do-it-yourselfers
©2004 BY ALISON BECHDEL

4/21
438
D'YOU SMELL THAT? I THINK THE CARPET'S MILDEWED.
SOMETHING'S DEFINITELY FUNKY. BUT IT SEEMS TO BE COMING MORE FROM BEHIND THE WALL.
IRAQ

SOME NEW CARPET WOULD MAKE THE PLACE REALLY SNUG. PLUS I'VE ALWAYS HATED THIS COLOR.
I THINK WE SHOULD HAVE SOMEONE LOOK AT THE WALL FIRST.
COMMON SENSE
NEOCON-SERVATIVE AGENDA

YEAH. WE SHOULD LIKE, CALL THREE CONTRACTORS AND COMPARE BIDS.
MY DAD CARPETED OUR WHOLE HOUSE BY HIMSELF. I CAN DO THIS!
U.N.
STUART! WHAT ARE YOU DOING?
U KNOW WHO
RRIP!

OKAY, OKAY. I VOTE FOR NEW CARPET.
WHATEVER.
CONGRESS
TONY BLAIR
TOXIC MOLD .COM
OLD EUROPE
DON'T COME CRYING TO ME WHEN THE ROOF CAVES IN.

WHOA, THERE! ISN'T THAT A BIT HIGH? IT'S ONLY $6.99 A SQUARE YARD.
IT'S PRICED PER SQUARE FOOT, BRO. TRY MULTI-PLYING BY 9.
"$87 BILLION"
$727.54
HOME DESPOT

CHAOS
SWEETIE, STAY AWAY FROM THE...
GAH.

...SHARP TACKS.
CASUALTIES
AAAH!

NICE JOB.
GOD, THE FUMES ARE MAKING ME WOOZY.
IT JUST HAS TO OFFGAS FOR A FEW DAYS. WE'LL LEAVE THE WINDOWS OPEN.
DEPLETED URANIUM
KOFF

SURE, GET ANOTHER QUOTE. BUT DON'T WASTE ANY TIME. THE WORSE THE LEAK GETS, THE MORE TOXIC MOLD YOU'RE GONNA HAVE BEHIND THIS WALL. AND WHO KNOWS WHEN THE ROOF MIGHT CAVE IN.

HOW MUCH?
YOU GUYS? I THINK THE NEW CARPET'S MILDEWED FROM THE RAIN COMING IN.
UNINTENDED CONSEQUENCES

LICENTIOUS BEHAVIOR

5/15

439

FOR THE NONCE, NO NUPTIAL NOOSE FOR OUR NATTERING NABOBS OF NETTLE-SOMENESS.

YET PART OF YOU IS RELIEVED WE CAN'T, BECAUSE IF MY CANCER COMES BACK, YOU CAN JUST LEAVE.

WHY WOULD I LEAVE? DID I LEAVE THIS TIME? **GOD**, SYDNEY. YOU HAVE **ME**, WHY DO YOU NEED A PIECE OF PAPER? MARRIAGE IS NOT SOME KIND OF **INSURANCE** POLICY.

Shameless

6/16

442

SAMIA HAS UNWITTINGLY AGREED TO TEACH ARABIC TO ONE OF GINGER'S MORE RIGHTWARD-LEANING STUDENTS.

SO I SHOULDN'T MENTION YOUR PREDILECTION FOR CROOKNECK SQUASH?

IT'S AT THE OTHER END OF THE PARK, TO PROTEST HOW PRIDE HAS GOTTEN SO CORPORATE. I THINK WE SHOULD MAKE IT MORE INCLUSIVE, THOUGH. **AMERICAN** SHAME!

EXCELLENT.

I'LL BE PROUD WHEN BUSH IS GONE

HONK!

evildoer

siren thong

446

8/11

There've been a few changes at the home of Jasmine and her son Jonas.

JANIS! Will you shut that off and get up here? You need to finish packing.

He wants to grow breasts like Mommy

Ladies' Home Journal
John & Teresa Kerry

And this is Sparrow's rain jacket. And some fleece stuff of mine.

You're really doing great with all this, you know.

I dunno. I miss my angelic little boy who played with dolls. Now I'm living with this... this **VALLEY GIRL** who steals my clothes and ignores me.

Britney

But on the upside, all my anxiety about being a single mother raising a young black man in this culture has completely disappeared.

power to the people
448
9/8
©2004 BY ALISON BECHDEL

SOMEWHERE IN THE BLOGOSPHERE...
subversive parenting
notes from a stay-at-home dad

About Me
Name: Stuart Goodman
8.29.04
virtually active
Jiao Raizel and I are canning tomato sauce and watching the RNC protest on C-SPAN, listening to the rally on streaming radio, and monitoring the indymedia site for breaking news. Wish I was there with my housemate Lois, but this is almost better because I'm getting my canning done at the same time.

SEE DADDY'S LATEST POST? ARE WE WIRED, OR WHAT?
PWEE.
MILK

LET'S CALL LOIS FOR A MARCH UPDATE!
NYC

HELLO?
LOIS! ME AGAIN. HOW'S IT GOING?
THANKS NEW YORK
BUSH
POVERTY IS A WEAPON OF MASS DESTRUCTION
NO WAR

GOD, IT'S *#@ING INCREDIBLE!
FUSH
GOOD BUSH

I KNOW! HEY, BE CAREFUL. THERE ARE RIOT COPS ADVANCING ON THE MOUSE BLOC ACTION IN TIMES SQUARE.
THIS IS WHAT DEMOCRACY LOOKS LIKE!
WHAT?
NYC

I SAID... HEY, HOLD UP YOUR PHONE SO I CAN CHANT ALONG WITH THE CROWD FOR A SECOND.
STU, I CAN'T HEAR YOU AT ALL.
TELL ME WHAT DEMOCRACY LOOKS LIKE!
nu'clē-ar
SUV=WAR
STOP TORTURING PEOPLE YOU FREAKS
SUPPORT THE TROOPS VOTE BUSH OUT!
GOP GO HOME
DARN GOOD LIAR
TAKE BACK THE FUTURE
BUSH IS A TUSH
PINK BLOQUE

THIS IS WHAT DEMOCRACY LOOKS LIKE!
4 MORE MONTHS
BAD BUSH

RUMBBLE!
NEW YORK
WOW. I CAN SENSE THE ELECTRICITY IN THE ATMOSPHERE! I FEEL SO...

KRAK!

...CONNECTED.

impolitic

9/22

449

©2004 BY ALISON BECHDEL

AS GOVERNMENT OF THE PEOPLE, BY THE PEOPLE, FOR THE PEOPLE APPEARS TO BE IN DANGER OF PERISHING FROM THE EARTH, OUR PLUCKY PATRIOTS ATTEMPT CPR.

...SO THANKS FOR COMING TO MY PARTY AND FOR MAKING A DONATION TO MoveOn PAC INSTEAD OF PRESENTS.
HAPPY ELEVENTH, RAF. I'M PROUD OF YOU FOR GETTING SO INVOLVED IN THE POLITICAL PROCESS.
Barbecue BUSH
OH, PUH-LEEZE! CUE THE VIOLINS.

CLARICE HAS SOME NERVE TURNING HER KID'S BIRTHDAY INTO A FUNDRAISER!
IT WAS RAFFI'S IDEA. I THINK IT'S GREAT.
JEEZ, MO! I'M DELIGHTED TO GIVE MONEY. DEMOCRACY ITSELF IS AT STAKE.
HAMM 9

BUT THAT'S JUST IT! IT'S NOT DEMOCRACY IF YOU HAVE TO **BUY** IT! I RESENT BEING MADE COMPLICIT IN THE...THE CORRUPT **PUTRESCENCE** THAT IS OUR ELECTORAL SYSTEM.
HAVE YOU SEEN TONI?
HUH. NOT IN A WHILE.
RRIP

"*What is the first part of politics?* **education.** *The second?* **education.** *And the third?* **education.**"
~*Michelet*

10/6

450

SCHOOL'S BACK IN SESSION, AND NOT A MOMENT TOO SOON CONSIDERING IT'S THE EVE OF AN ELECTION IN WHICH A MINUTE TIP OF THE IDEOLOGICAL BALANCE COULD USHER IN A RIGHT-WING ICE AGE.

NOTHING RANG A BELL FOR ANY OF YOU? LIKE, SAY, THE DECEPTIVE AND EUPHEMISTIC USE OF LANGUAGE? THE SURVEILLANCE? THE TORTURE? THE ONGOING WAR? THE ERASURE OF HISTORY AND MEMORY?!

MEANWHILE, CLARICE IS SUPPLE-MENTING THE CURRICULUM AT RAFFI'S MIDDLE SCHOOL WITH HER OWN UNIT ON THE FACTS OF LIFE.

WHAT'S A LESBIAN REPUBLICAN TO DO?

HEY, THE **CHENEYS** ARE THE RHETORICAL CONTORTIONISTS! THEY MANAGED TO SIMULTANEOUSLY GAY-BASH THEIR OWN DAUGHTER **AND** BLAME IT ON KERRY! IT MAKES MY BRAIN HURT!

THEY WERE JUST TRYING TO PROTECT HER. **MY** PARENTS ARE THREATENING TO CUT OFF MY TUITION.

MEANWHILE, BACK AT THE COLLECTIVE...

THIS K-8 SCHOOL HAS BEEN OKAY FOR HER. BUT WHAT ABOUT NEXT YEAR?

IF ONLY WE HAD A QUEER HIGH SCHOOL.

Marriage engagé

11/17

453

AS CLARICE, TONI, AND RAFFI ENTERTAIN GUESTS, RIFTS SEEM TO BE EMERGING IN THE MARRIAGE EQUALITY MOVEMENT... NOT TO MENTION IN SOME MARRIAGES.

pilgrim's regress

12/1

454

IN KEEPING WITH OUR NATION'S NEW MORAL MANDATE, THIS COMIC STRIP HAS CHANGED ITS FORMAT TO **RELIGIOUS ALLEGORY**.

CAN OUR HEROINE FIND HER WAY TO SALVATION DESPITE THE MANY ABSTRACT-CONCEPTS-EMBODIED-IN-HUMAN-FORM THAT LITTER HER PATH?

HERE SHE IS, **MS. SECULAR HUMANIST**, FLOUNDERING IN THE SLOUGH OF DESPOND.

SHE SETS OUT ON HER QUEST, STOPPING TO VISIT NEIGHBOR **OBSTINATE**.

WHY'S THE MEDIA IGNORING THIS? WHY ARE WE ALL JUST ROLLING OVER? MY **MOTHER** COULD HACK AN ELECTRONIC VOTING MACHINE. I **REFUSE TO ACCEPT** THE ELECTION RESULTS!

I WISH I COULD REFUSE TO ACCEPT THIS CREDIT CARD BILL. TELL ME YOU DIDN'T GIVE $500 TO THE DNC AT THE LAST MINUTE.

THEN, IT'S ON TO NEIGHBOR **PLIABLE**.

IT'S UP TO US TO BREAK THROUGH THIS CULTURAL POLARIZATION. TO CONNECT WITH RED STATERS, WE NEED TO GET COMFORTABLE TALKING ABOUT OUR FAITH.

MS. LITTLE-FAITH AND **MS. LOVE-LUST** WEIGH IN.

YEAH, I'M SURE TELLING SOME KNUCKLE-DRAGGERS ABOUT YOUR KABBALAH MEDITATION GROUP WOULD HEAL THE RIFT RIGHT UP.

LOOK. PEOPLE VOTED REPUBLICAN BECAUSE OF THE GAY MARRIAGE THING. THEY'RE TERRIFIED OF SEX.

UPON FLEEING, OUR HEROINE RUNS INTO **GIANT DESPAIR**.

...I SWITCH TO MY FEAR OF BEING ROUNDED UP AND SHIPPED TO A GULAG FOR INTELLECTUALS. IN KENTUCKY.

ONWARD SHE TREKS, BUT BEFORE REACHING HER FINAL GOAL, OUR PILGRIM MUST PASS THROUGH THE TEMPTATIONS OF **VANITY FAIR**.

ON SECOND THOUGHT, MAYBE SHE'LL HANG HERE FOR A WHILE.

...CIA AND STATE DEPARTMENT PURGING DISSIDENTS... VOTING IRREGULARITIES... WAR CRIMES... IRAN'S NUCLEAR PROGRAM...

CAN I HAVE A SWIG OF THAT?

CLINK

AMY GOODMAN

VANITY FAIR EMINEM PARIS HILTON LEO

LOCH NESS 90 PROOF

nothin' left to lose
12/29
456
©2004 BY ALISON BECHDEL

AH, THE MALL. AMERICA'S AORTA.
I MADE A HAIKU! "WANDERING, DAMNED SOULS NEED SOMETHING, BUT AREN'T SURE WHAT— NEXT STOP, CINNABON."
OKAY, SETTLE DOWN. I'M ALMOST DONE.
crombie
PA-RUM-PA-PUM-PUM
Victo
ENLIST NOW AND GET A REBATE ON YOUR BODY ARMOR!
YOU CAN!
GO GUARD
CRAP

SYDNEY?
CHERYL! UH... HOW ARE YOU?
TARPIT

I'M DOING OKAY. I REALLY APPRECIATED YOUR CONDOLENCE BASKET.
MO, THIS IS CHERYL, MY RADIATION TECH.
OH. HI. SYDNEY TOLD ME ABOUT YOUR SON. I'M SO SORRY.

WELL, IT HELPS KNOWING HE DIED DOING SOMETHING SO IMPORTANT. WE TEND TO FORGET THAT FREEDOM ISN'T FREE.
UHH...

YOU'RE SO RIGHT.

BUT I'M STAYING BUSY. I'M SENDING CARE PACKAGES TO OTHER SOLDIERS. LOOK AT ALL THIS STUFF THEY NEED! TOYS FOR KIDS, SOCKS, BATTERIES..

SHORTLY...
I GUESS FREEDOM HAS AN A.P.R. OF 18.99%
SHUT UP AND GO FIND THE BEEF JERKY.
MAGLITE
books

MEANWHILE, RAF'S TWO MOMMIES ARE AWOL.
MEEMA, COME ON! YOU SAID YOU'D PLAY CRANIUM WITH US.
HACKEDVOTE.ORG
•MEDIA LOCKDOWN?
•E-VOTE TAMPERING
•VOTING WHILE BLACK
•RAMPANT OHIO "IRREGULARITIES"
MORE

I'LL COME WHEN MOMMY GETS OFF THE PHONE.

HEY, WE CAN'T ROLL OVER NOW. IF WE GIVE AN INCH ON MARRIAGE, NEXT THING YOU KNOW THEY'LL BE SHOVING CREATIONISM AND "ABSTINENCE" DOWN OUR THROATS!

MOM, COME ON!

HANG ON, GLORIA—
SWEETIE, I'LL COME WHEN MEEMA GETS OFF THE COMPUTER.

I'LL BE OVER BEHIND THE QUICKIE MART SCORING SOME CRANK.
HAVE FUN.
WEAR YOUR HAT.

IN THE SEASON OF GREATEST DARKNESS, OUR QUASI-INTENTIONAL FAMILY ADMITS A STRAY EVANGELICAL TO THEIR MULTI-PURPOSE FESTIVAL OF LIGHTS.

below the law
1/26
458
©2005 BY ALISON BECHDEL

WHAT'S CLARICE WATCHING?
THE ELECTIONS IN IRAQ?
AS MILITARY HELICOPTERS HOVER OVERHEAD, CITIZENS PRESENT IDENTIFICATION PAPERS TO HEAVILY-ARMED SECURITY FORCES...

A REPORT ON THE TSUNAMI DAMAGE?
THE SCALE OF DEVASTATION IS INCONCEIVABLE!

OR NEITHER?
GOD HELP US.
I DO SULLENLY SWEAR THAT I, UH... THAT I WILL FATEFULLY EXECUTE THE CONSTITUTION OF THE UNITED STATES...
MEEMA, HE'S GONNA BE AROUND FOR FOUR YEARS. IF YOU DON'T CALM DOWN YOU'LL GIVE YOURSELF A RUPTURE.

I'M SORRY, RAFFI. I DON'T MEAN TO UPSET YOU.
BUT THE MAN'S A FASCIST TORTURE FREAK AND HE'S DESTROYING AMERICA!

YOU'RE OVERREACTING. HE JUST WANTS TO PROTECT US FROM TERRORISTS.

MY SON, LET ME EXPLAIN A LITTLE LEGAL PRINCIPLE WE CALL "HABEAS CORPUS."
DUMP!

GET IN.
WHY?
HUMOR ME.

COMFY?
VERY.
GOOD. YOU'LL BE IN THERE INDEFINITELY.
SNAP
MOMMY WILL LET ME OUT WHEN SHE GETS HOME.

NOT IF I DRAG YOU TO THE GARAGE AND TELL HER YOU'RE SPENDING THE NIGHT AT BILLY'S.
I THINK THAT'S CHILD ABUSE.

TELL IT TO THE JUDGE! OOPS! NO, SORRY. THERE WON'T BE A TRIAL.
WHAT IS YOUR POINT? ANYONE CAN PUT THEIR KID IN A TRUNK. I'M NOT A TERRORIST!

THAT'S WHAT THEY ALL SAY. BUT YOU'LL CHANGE YOUR TUNE AFTER I BLAST YOU WITH LITE ADULT CONTEMPORARY ALL NIGHT LONG.

I JUST CALLED... TO SAAY... I LO-OVE YOU...
OKAY, IT'S TIME TO MAKE ANOTHER DEPOSIT TO MY THERAPY FUND.

2/9

459

Ah, Valentine's Day, when we celebrate the life-affirming bliss of the erotic bond.

At Mo and Sydney's...

O conspiracy!

(Julius Caesar, II, i, 77)

2/23

460

CLARICE IS ON THE PROGRESSIVE™ DIET.

HER APPETITE IS COMPLETELY GONE, AND SHE WORKS HERSELF INTO A LATHER DAILY.

... AND THE BEAUTY OF IT IS, BUSH DOESN'T **NEED** THOUGHT POLICE. WE POLICE OURSELVES! EVERYONE'S SO AFRAID OF BEING LABELED A "CONSPIRACY THEORIST," THEY SHUT THEIR BRAINS DOWN!

UH OH. KEEP TALKING, BUT I HAVE TO LOOK BUSY.

NATIONAL REVIEW

FLEX

GUNS & AMMO

FORBES

THE BUSHITES SEEM TO THINK REALITY IS JUST A BIG **WAD** OF **GUM** THEY CAN CHEW INTO ANY SHAPE THEY LIKE.

WHAT IF WE **ALL** LIED THROUGH OUR TEETH LIKE THAT?

THERE ARE SO MANY DIFFERENT FUN TECHNIQUES: DENIAL.

THE COMMON OR GARDEN-VARIETY WHOPPER.

THE OPPOSITE GAME-- DRIVE THE WHOLE FAMILY MAD!

THE RETRO-FIT

DON'T LET THOSE PESKY, AGREED-UPON CONVENTIONS STAND IN YOUR WAY!

DISMISS!

COME NOW, MO. MONOGAMY'S A QUAINT, OBSOLETE PARADIGM.

EVADE!

SYDNEY, JUST TELL ME! DID YOU HAVE AN AFFAIR?

I DON'T RECALL SPECIFICALLY.

ONCE YOU BELIEVE YOUR LIE, THERE'S NO STOPPING YOU!

AND IF REALITY **STILL** INSISTS ON REARING ITS UGLY HEAD. THERE'S ALWAYS THE DOUBLE-REVERSE BACK FLIP.

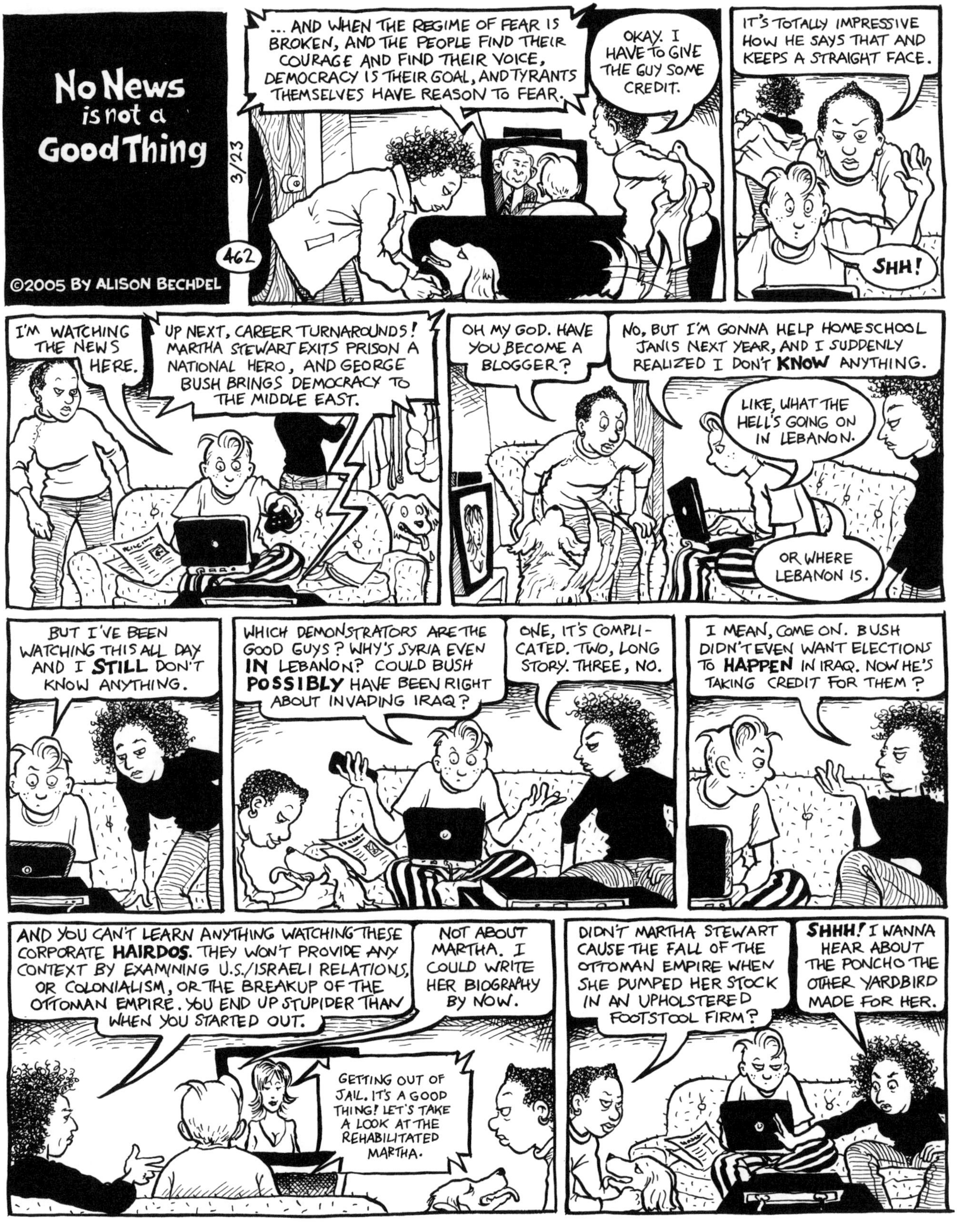

No News is not a Good Thing

3/23

462

... AND WHEN THE REGIME OF FEAR IS BROKEN, AND THE PEOPLE FIND THEIR COURAGE AND FIND THEIR VOICE, DEMOCRACY IS THEIR GOAL, AND TYRANTS THEMSELVES HAVE REASON TO FEAR.

OKAY. I HAVE TO GIVE THE GUY SOME CREDIT.

IT'S TOTALLY IMPRESSIVE HOW HE SAYS THAT AND KEEPS A STRAIGHT FACE.

SHH!

I'M WATCHING THE NEWS HERE.

UP NEXT, CAREER TURNAROUNDS! MARTHA STEWART EXITS PRISON A NATIONAL HERO, AND GEORGE BUSH BRINGS DEMOCRACY TO THE MIDDLE EAST.

OH MY GOD. HAVE YOU BECOME A BLOGGER?

NO, BUT I'M GONNA HELP HOMESCHOOL JANIS NEXT YEAR, AND I SUDDENLY REALIZED I DON'T **KNOW** ANYTHING.

LIKE, WHAT THE HELL'S GOING ON IN LEBANON.

OR WHERE LEBANON IS.

BUT I'VE BEEN WATCHING THIS ALL DAY AND I **STILL** DON'T KNOW ANYTHING.

WHICH DEMONSTRATORS ARE THE GOOD GUYS? WHY'S SYRIA EVEN **IN** LEBANON? COULD BUSH **POSSIBLY** HAVE BEEN RIGHT ABOUT INVADING IRAQ?

ONE, IT'S COMPLICATED. TWO, LONG STORY. THREE, NO.

I MEAN, COME ON. BUSH DIDN'T EVEN WANT ELECTIONS TO **HAPPEN** IN IRAQ. NOW HE'S TAKING CREDIT FOR THEM?

math anxiety
©2005 BY ALISON BECHDEL
4/6
463
IF NOT NOW, WHEN?
CLARICE, WE GO THROUGH THIS EVERY YEAR. WE HAVE A CHILD TO PUT THROUGH COLLEGE. I DON'T WANT TO HAVE TO WORRY ABOUT THE I.R.S. SEIZING OUR HOUSE.
SKECHERS
THEY HARDLY EVER TAKE HOUSES! AND I DON'T THINK ANYONE'S GONE TO JAIL FOR IT SINCE THOREAU.
CAN YOU HELP ME WITH THIS MATH PROBLEM?
NOT RIGHT NOW, SWEETIE. I'M IN THE MIDDLE OF TAX STUFF.
I'LL HELP YOU, RAF.
YOU GET TOO CARRIED AWAY.
READ THE PROBLEM, BUCKO.
I HAVE TO MAKE A PIE CHART, AND I'M NOT SURE OF...
NO KIDDING?! I WAS JUST ABOUT TO SHOW MOMMY A PIE CHART! LOOK! THIS'LL BE VERY EDUCATIONAL!
US MILITARY SPENDING
THIS CIRCLE REPRESENTS THE FEDERAL BUDGET. CAN YOU TELL WHAT PROPORTION GOES TO PAY FOR KILLING PEOPLE IN OTHER COUNTRIES?
UM, ABOUT HALF?
VERY GOOD! BUT DOESN'T THAT SEEM KIND OF PSYCHO? WOULDN'T IT BE A BETTER WORLD IF WE ALL PUT A STOP TO WAR BY REFUSING TO PAY FOR IT?
YOUR TAX DOLLAR!
THEY'D LEVY FINES. THE INTEREST WOULD RACK UP. WE CAN'T TAKE THAT KIND OF FINANCIAL RISK.
AS IT IS, WE'RE ONE MEDICAL EMERGENCY AWAY FROM DEBTOR'S PRISON. THANKS TO THIS CRAZY REPUBLICAN BANKRUPTCY BILL AND BUSH'S PLAN TO PIRATIZE SOCIAL SECURITY.
SPEAKING OF CONSERVATIVE FAMILY VALUES, GLORIA CALLED EARLIER ABOUT SOME FREEDOM TO MARRY THING. YOU SHOULD GET BACK TO HER.
OH. THANKS.
I'M SORRY, RAF. TELL ME ABOUT YOUR PIE CHART.
WELL... MAYBE WE COULD REFUSE TO PAY PART OF OUR TAXES, AS A SYMBOLIC GESTURE.
REALLY?
CAN WE REFUSE TO PAY ENOUGH TO BUY ME AN X BOX?

MEANWHILE, CLARICE EXPLAINS A THING OR TWO.

my sweet impressionable you
5/4
465
©2005 BY ALISON BECHDEL
THE EVIDENCE SPEAKS FOR ITSELF. ON A FACULTY OF 250, THERE ARE ONLY 15 OPENLY REPUBLICAN PROFESSORS.
WHAT ARE YOU PROPOSING? IDEOLOGICAL DIVERSITY THROUGH AFFIRMATIVE ACTION? THAT'S REAL CONSERVATIVE.
STUDENTS FOR ACADEMIC FREEDOM
I'M PROPOSING THAT IMPRESSIONABLE STUDENTS HEAR ALL SIDES OF THE ISSUES. DOES THAT THREATEN YOU?
IF ALL SIDES INCLUDES CREATIONISM AND HOLOCAUST DENIAL AND THE NOVELS OF AYN RAND, THEN YEAH, I GUESS IT DOES.
4:22 PM. PROFESSOR GINGER JORDAN MOCKS ONE OF MY INTELLECTUAL HEROINES.
?!
I'LL JUST POST THIS LITTLE INCIDENT TO THE ACADEMIC FREEDOM COMPLAINT CENTER.
CYNTHIA, IF YOU REALLY WANT MORE REPUBLICANS ON THE FACULTY, TRY GETTING OUR SALARIES QUADRUPLED.
RRIP!
MEANWHILE, IN THE CEREAL AISLE...
FOZZY FOO BAAAAPS!
SWEETIE, YOU DON'T REALLY WANT THOSE. YOU JUST THINK YOU DO BECAUSE A COMMERCIAL TOLD YOU TO.
THAT WAS PERSUASIVE. YOU SHOULD GO INTO MARKETING.
OH, HI, MO. IT'S AMAZING. SHE HAS A VOCABULARY OF 50 WORDS, AND THREE OF THEM ARE "FROSTED FRUIT BATS."
AAAIEEE
J.R.! LOOK! HOW 'BOUT A NICE STRING BEAN?
NO!
HEY, I HEARD YOU'RE GRADUATING FROM LIBRARY SCHOOL NEXT WEEK. CONGRATS!
THANKS. IT'S REALLY EXCITING. BUT I'M BUMMED SYDNEY WON'T BE ABLE TO COME WITH ME. ONE OF OUR CATS IS SICK.
CAN'T LOIS CATSIT?
NO, IT'S KIND OF A DICEY OPERATION. WE HAVE TO GIVE HER INSULIN INJECTIONS TWICE A DAY.
FOO BAAPS.
CALLING DR. SYDNEY...
#@$&! VIRGINIA!

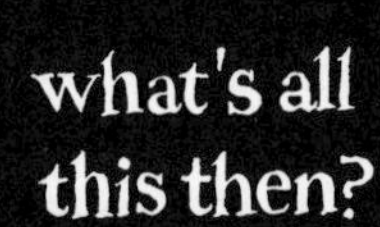

5/18

466

To: madeleine.zeugma@dartridge.edu
Cc:
Subject: Pompous circumstances
Attachments: none

I'm home googling student papers and watching Mo's graduation via webcast. Having fond memories of the day I got my Ph.D. Remember going at it in your office in our academic robes? And how you got that big blue blot on your doctoral hood from lying on that fountain pen?

x
Sydney

MO HAS A MASTER'S DEGREE.

IN LIBRARY AND INFORMATION SCIENCE.

NOW SHE'S SHARING A GRADUATION NIGHT FUTON WITH FIONA, THE DIGITAL SERVICES SPECIALIST.

YOU WOULDN'T BE DOING IT TO SYDNEY, YOU'D BE DOING IT TO ME. THAT'S THE WHOLE POINT!

HMM. I SEE YOUR LOGIC.

MEANWHILE, THE LONELY CYNTHIA HAS PARLAYED A RIDE WITH THE LOCAL LGBT CYCLING GROUP INTO DINNER, THEN COFFEE, WITH ONE CYCLIST IN PARTICULAR.

THESE CONSERVATIVE EVANGELICALS WHO WANT TO MERGE CHURCH AND STATE WILL SCREW THIS COUNTRY **WAY** MORE THAN AL QAEDA COULD EVER DREAM OF. WE'VE GOT TO STOP THE **REPUBLICAN MULLAHS!**

YEAH, RIGHT. GOOD ONE, CYNTHIA.

NO, REALLY. AND IT'S SO HARD TO MEET PEOPLE. I TRIED THE RAINBOW REPUBLICANS, BUT THEY WERE ONLY **FISCAL** CONSERVATIVES.

WILL PASSION PRE-EMPT PRINCIPLE?

PERHAPS.

PERHAPS NOT.

Divorced from Reality
468
©2005 BY ALISON BECHDEL

THE PRESIDENT REPEATEDLY LINKED THE WAR IN IRAQ TO 9/11 AND SAID WE MUST DEFEAT THE TERRORISTS ABROAD BEFORE THEY ATTACK US AT HOME. IN BUSINESS NEWS, OIL PRICES TOPPED $60 A BARREL...
7/13
♪ WEEZ ON BUS GO ♪ WOWND AN' WOWND...
WHAT ARE WE DOING?

...AND A CHINESE COMPANY'S BID FOR U.S. OIL GIANT UNOCAL TRIGGERS CONCERN THAT CHINA MAY GAIN STRATEGIC ENERGY RESERVES.
WE'VE REACHED PEAK OIL! THE BRUTE STRUGGLE FOR THE DREGS HAS BEGUN! YET HERE WE ALL SIT IN OUR AIR-CONDITIONED SARCOPHAGI!

WHAT KIND OF A WORLD AM I LEAVING YOU? LISTEN TO ME, JIAO RAIZEL. WE'RE STOPPING THE MADNESS RIGHT NOW.
WHIMPER...

MEANWHILE, IN AN UNSUSTAINABLY DESIGNED SUBURB...
FINALLY! IT TOOK US LONG ENOUGH TO GET TOGETHER AGAIN.
I KNOW! CAN YOU BELIEVE IT'S BEEN SIX MONTHS SINCE OUR TRIP TO CHICAGO?

GOD, THAT WAS FUN. DIDN'T THE KIDS HAVE A GREAT TIME?
YEAH. YOU TWO SHOULD'VE COME. ALL THAT WORK YOU DID TO STOP THE MARRIAGE AMENDMENT WAS WASTED ANYHOW.
ANA, THAT'S SO NOT TRUE. YES, THE BILL PASSED. BUT WE DID CRUCIAL WORK, AND WE'LL STOP IT IN THE NEXT SESSION.

OH, I MADE YOU GUYS A COPY OF THAT PHOTO OF RAF AND STELLA AT THE AQUARIUM. COULD YOU GET IT, TONI? IT'S ON THE MICROWAVE, WITH GLORIA'S PANTIES.
GLORIA'S WHAT?

I GUESS I LEFT THEM HERE WHEN YOU WERE IN CHICAGO. REMEMBER, I STAYED OVER HERE WHILE TONI AND I WERE PLANNING THE RALLY?

MUSTA BEEN ONE HELL OF A RALLY.
NO KIDDING. IF THESE TWO WEREN'T THE POSTER CHILDREN FOR MARRIAGE EQUALITY, WE MIGHT HAVE REASON TO BE SUSPICIOUS.

AND ON THE SHOULDER OF A MAJOR ARTERY...
WE BUY CARS & TRUCKS
FAST CASH FOR CARS
2.39
2.54
2.79
THERE! NO MORE DENIAL FOR US!
HONNK!

Wonk Wank
©2005 BY ALISON BECHDEL
469
7/27
TO YOUR MASTER'S DEGREE.
ANY JOB LEADS YET?
NOPE. I'M STILL AT BOUNDERS, PEDDLING LESBIAN ROMANTIC FICTION TO THE MASSES.
CAFÉ CROW
WHAT?
WE MUSTA MOVED TWO PALLET LOADS OF "THE TRUTH ABOUT HILLARY" THIS WEEK ALONE.
SYDNEY, WHAT ARE YOU DOING DOWN THERE? ARE YOU TEXTING MADELEINE AGAIN?
I'M JUST SEEING HOW HER MAMMOGRAM WENT. RELAX, I'M NOT THE ONE HAVING THE AFFAIR.
I'M NOT HAVING AN AFFAIR.
SO, I'M WATCHING MO'S GRADUATION ONLINE, RIGHT? AND WHEN SHE AND HER "FRIEND" FIONA WIN THE REFERENCE GEEK AWARD, THEY GO INTO A BIG LIPLOCK ONSTAGE!
MO GETS HOME FROM HER TRIP, AND I START TEASING HER, "YOU KISSED FIONA!"
AND SHE SCREAMS, "I CONFESS! I'M SORRY! IT'LL NEVER HAPPEN AGAIN!" TURNS OUT SHE REALLY DID KISS FIONA! THEY SLEPT TOGETHER!
YOU DID?!
NOTHING HAPPENED. YES, THERE WAS A BRIEF KISS, BUT THEN WE WENT TO SLEEP.
WHAT A WASTE OF OPPORTUNITY.
REMINDS ME OF CYNTHIA AND HER VIRGINITY PLEDGE.
YOU KNOW GINGER'S STUDENT, CYNTHIA, THE NEOCON YOUTH?
SHE SIGNED THIS PLEDGE AT HER CHURCH WHEN SHE WAS 15, AND SHE'S CONTINUING TO HONOR IT NOW THAT SHE'S COME OUT!
WHAT EXACTLY CONSTITUTES VIRGINITY IN A LESBIAN CONTEXT?
I KNOW! I MEAN, DOES THIRD BASE COUNT?
SYDNEY!
UH... I DON'T KNOW ANYTHING ABOUT BASEBALL. UNLESS YOU WANT TO HEAR MY REFUTATION OF GEORGE WILL'S THEORY ABOUT THE JEFFERSONIAN ROOTS OF THE INFIELD FLY RULE.

©2005 BY ALISON BECHDEL

in the GOOD OLD SUMMER-TIME

8/24

471

AH, THE SIMPLE PLEASURES OF THE SEASON!

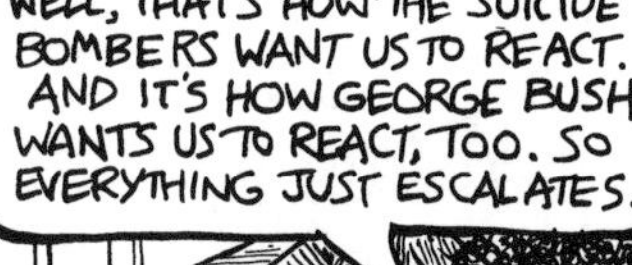

WELCOME! WE'RE FROM CAMP TRANS, AND WE'RE TALKING TO FESTIE-GOERS ABOUT THE...

LOIS! YOU OLD DOG!

INCLUDE ALL SELF-IDENTIFIED WOMEN

A TIP OF THE QALAM TO SOPHIE AND DREW

* WE HELD HANDS AND WATCHED THE ENTIRE FIRST SEASON OF "BUFFY THE VAMPIRE SLAYER" LAST NIGHT.

As the turbid, oil-slicked tide of American public opinion begins to turn against the war, our friends are caught in the undertow of their own personal affairs.

UH... I'LL TAKE A LOOK, BUT I DON'T THINK I HAVE IT. HEY, D'YOU WANT TO ROOM TOGETHER AT THE MLA CONVENTION AGAIN THIS YEAR?

IMPOSSIBLE DESIRES
NO FUTURE
PLEASURE and DANGER

And near a motley clot of big-box shops...

DRIVETIME DRIVE-BY

9/21

473

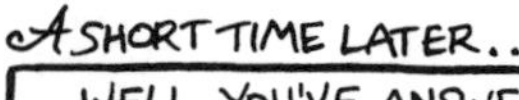

infra-struc-ture

10/5

From gulf to stormy gulf, the American empire is in a shambles.

474

Meanwhile, at Mo and Sydney's...

And at Clarice and Toni's...

Back at Ginger's place...

Schools for Scandal
10/19
475
©2005 BY ALISON BECHDEL
IF YOU WON'T SEE A THERAPIST WITH ME, I'M LEAVING.
MO, I CAN'T HAVE THIS CONVERSATION NOW. I HAVE A MEETING IN TWO MINUTES.
CAT-A-MUCIL
BESIDES! I KEEP TELLING YOU, MADELEINE WAS A... A CANCER THING. I JUST NEEDED TO CONNECT WITH SOMEONE WHO UNDERSTOOD.
YOU HAD CANCER TWO YEARS AGO. IT'S NOT A PERMANENT GET-OUT-OF-JAIL-FREE CARD.
HANG ON. I'M HAVING A HOT FLASH.
SO, WHAT IS IT, SYDNEY? ARE YOU IN OR OUT?
I'M IN! HYPNOTHERAPY, AROMATHERAPY, WHATEVER YOU WANT. I HAVE TO GO. I'M LATE FOR THE PROVOST SEARCH COMMITTEE.
GOOGLE
MEANWHILE, ANOTHER TROUBLED COUPLE IS IN MIDDLE SCHOOL.
DON'T WORRY. GLORIA SAID SHE'D LEAVE BY SIX-THIRTY. WE WON'T RUN INTO HER.
I'M NOT WORRIED ABOUT RUNNING INTO **HER**. SHE SHOULD BE WORRIED ABOUT RUNNING INTO **ME**.
N.H.M.S. OPEN HOUSE WELCOME
A FEW MOMENTS LATER...
DAD! CAN I HAVE FIFTY MORE DOLLARS FOR THE HURRICANE RELIEF FUND? IF WE HIT EIGHT THOUSAND, THE PRINCIPAL HAS TO GET HIS HEAD SHAVED.
TEN. THAT'S IT. I'M TAPPED OUT.
ME TOO.
COME ON, MOM. AFTER THE TSUNAMI, MRS. JANSEN NICKED HIS SCALP AND IT BLED ALL OVER THE PLACE.
RAF, IT'S CHARITY. NOT A BLOOD SPORT.
global warming
SO, SAD NEWS ABOUT ANA AND GLORIA, HUH? I FEEL BAD FOR STELLA. SWEET KID.
ANA AND GLORIA ARE BREAKING UP?
OH. I ASSUMED YOU KNEW.
THE GAY DIVORCE RATE AT THIS SCHOOL IS SKY-ROCKETING. FROM ZERO TO THIRTY-THREE PERCENT, OVERNIGHT.
MEANWHILE...
...THEN AFTER WE AGREE ON A PROCEDURE FOR SOLICITING NOMINATIONS AND APPLICATIONS...
...ER, DR. KRUKOWSKI? I DON'T KNOW HOW YOU DO THINGS IN THE ENGLISH DEPARTMENT, BUT I'D LIKE TO SUGGEST THAT WE REMAIN FULLY CLOTHED WHILE WE'RE SERVING ON THIS COMMITTEE.
!

FIXED
©2005 BY ALISON BECHDEL
476
11/2
MAN. TALK ABOUT CHICKENS COMING HOME TO ROOST. THIS BIRD FLU THING IS PERFECT. OUR MONEY AND SUV'S AND MISSILE DEFENSE FANTASIES CAN'T SAVE US. HOGGING ALL THE ANTIVIRALS CAN'T SAVE US. ONCE A POOR COUNTRY GETS SICK, WE'RE ALL GOING DOWN!
The Daily Distress
ANOTHER, BIGGER HURRICANE
PANDEMIC
CHENEY-RUMSFELD CABAL
NOW THAT'S GLOBALIZATION!
HA! DID YOU SEE "DILBERT"?
BUSH WITHDRAWS MIERS, NOMINATES FETUS TO HIGH COURT
Comics
MINDLESS ENTERTAINMENT IS THE HANDMAIDEN OF FASCISM. HOW CAN YOU READ THE FUNNIES AT A TIME LIKE THIS?
A TIME LIKE WHAT? THE WORLD'S NOT GOING TO HELL ANY FASTER THAN IT EVER WAS.
BUSH DOESN'T RULE OUT ATTACK ON SYRIA
SEE OUR NEW GOP INDICTMENT SECTION
SPEAKING OF HELL, HAVE YOU CALLED ANY OF THOSE COUPLES THERAPISTS YET?
WHY DO I HAVE TO CALL THEM?
TSUNAMI REPORT
BUSH DOESN'T RULE OUT ATTACK ON VENEZUELA
IRAQ DEATHS HIT 2K
YOU'RE THE ONE WHO HAD THE AFFAIR.
I DID CALL ONE GUY. HE WASN'T ON YOUR LIST. I GOT HIS NAME FROM CARLOS.
ETHNIC CLEANSING IN NEW ORLEANS
A MAN?
HE'S GAY. CARLOS SAID HE REALLY HELPED HIM AND DANIEL.
TORTURE
YEAH, RIGHT. HELPED DANIEL ACCEPT THE FACT THAT CARLOS WILL NEVER BE MONOGAMOUS.
WE DIDN'T GET INTO PARTICULARS.
GOD! YOU ARE SO INTELLECTUALLY DISHONEST! YOU'RE LIKE THE BUSH ADMINISTRATION, FIXING THE INTELLIGENCE TO SUPPORT YOUR SELF-SERVING POLICY.
WELL THEN, SINCE YOU LET ME GET AWAY WITH MY OBVIOUS BULLS**T FOR SO LONG, THAT MAKES YOU LIKE THE DEMOCRATS--COMPLICIT.
I DON'T KNOW WHY YOU STAY WITH ME.
FAILURE OF LEADERSHIP, I GUESS.

477

11/16

THERE'VE BEEN SOME COMMUNICATION PROBLEMS LATELY AT CLARICE AND TONI'S HOUSE.

MEANWHILE, IN ANOTHER ADOLESCENCE...

strange bedfellows
11/30
478
©2005 BY ALISON BECHDEL

IN THE HALLS OF BUFFALO LAKE STATE...

BUT THE REASON YOU'RE ABLE TO SIT HERE BEING ALL LIBERAL AND TOLERANT IS BECAUSE OTHER PEOPLE ARE OUT THERE USING FORCE-- AND TORTURE WHEN NECESSARY--TO GET TERRORISTS OFF THE STREETS AND PROTECT YOU FROM FUTURE ATTACKS!
NORTON ANTHOLOGY

THAT'S SO **BOGUS!** TORTURE DOESN'T PRODUCE GOOD INTELLIGENCE! EVEN IF THE PEOPLE YOU'RE TORTURING **ARE** ACTUAL TERRORISTS, AND NOT FARMERS OR JAYWALKERS, LIKE MOST OF THE **83,000** PEOPLE WE'VE DETAINED IN THE PAST FOUR YEARS!
ANARCHO VEGAN

GOD! **ENOUGH!** I CAME HERE TO STUDY FOR THE HARLEM RENAISSANCE FINAL, NOT TO WATCH YOU TWO FLIRT.

THE PASSION OF THE CHRIST

MEANWHILE, AT THEIR PROFESSOR'S DOMICILE...
SAMIA? CAN I COME OVER? I HAVE FORTY HARLEM RENAISSANCE PAPERS TO GRADE AND I CAN'T HEAR MYSELF THINK.
SPARROW! I'M BUSY!
WE'LL BE QUICK! SHE'S GLUED TO THE TV!
PUBLIC BROADCAST CHIEF PROMOTES CONSERVATIVE VIEWS AT PBS
BUT...BUT MR. RUMSFELD, HOW CAN WE ATTACK IRAQIS WITH CHEMICAL WEAPONS WHEN ONE OF THE ARGUMENTS REPEATEDLY GIVEN FOR THE INVASION WAS THE FACT THAT SADDAM USED CHEMICAL WEAPONS AGAINST HIS OWN PEOPLE?

YEAH! COME ON OVER!
Y'KNOW, MAYBE IF YOU HELPED OUT A LITTLE AROUND HERE, I'D FEEL MORE AMOROUS!
ELMO, YOU LITTLE DICKENS, WE DIDN'T ATTACK OUR OWN PEOPLE WITH CHEMICAL WEAPONS! WE ATTACKED **IRAQIS** WITH **WHITE PHOSPHORUS.** THAT'S AN **INCENDIARY** WEAPON! CAN YOU SAY "INCENDIARY"?

A SHORT WHILE LATER...
YOU COULD HAVE THIS KIND OF PEACE AND QUIET ALL THE TIME IF WE MOVED IN TOGETHER.
MAYBE YOU'RE RIGHT. I'M TOO OLD FOR THAT CHAOS.

BZZZZT!
BAM!
BAM!
BAM!
ARAR
ARF!

HEY, BABY! OPEN UP!
AMMAR? I THOUGHT YOU WERE IN TOLEDO!
WHO THE HELL'S THAT?
WOOF

BAM
BAM!
UH...MY HUSBAND.
RROWF!

AND BACK AT THE DORM, CYNTHIA IS DEEP IN STUDY.

abject relations

12/14

479

YOU BETTER WATCH OUT, YOU BETTER NOT CRY, YOU BETTER NOT POUT, I'M TELLING YOU WHY... SYDNEY'S MOM IS COMING TO TOWN!

Silent Night
UPDATE
A BIG TIP O' THE NIB TO SIMON AND GARFUNKEL
480
©2005 BY ALISON BECHDEL

SILENT NIGHT...
12/28
THE "UNITED STATES GOVERNMENT" DOES NOT "AUTHORIZE" OR "CON-DONE" "TORTURE" OF "DETAINEES."

HOLY NIGHT...
SEE? EVERYONE CELEBRATES THE RE-TURN OF THE LIGHT!
THE PRESIDENT SAID BOTH SIDES IN THE DEBATE BETWEEN EVOLUTION AND INTELLIGENT DESIGN SHOULD BE TAUGHT...

ALL IS CALM...
FEDERAL AIR MARSHALS SHOT AND KILLED THE MENTALLY ILL PASSENGER WHEN HE REFUSED TO LIE ON THE GROUND...

ALL IS BRIGHT...
MAUL OF AMERICA
IN NEW ORLEANS, POOR AND AFRI-CAN AMERICAN CITIZENS CONTINUE TO BEAR THE BRUNT OF HURRICANE KATRINA WITH FORCED EVICTIONS AND SKYROCKETING RENT...

ROUND YON VI-IR-GIN...
COME ON! WHY NOT?
I TOOK A PLEDGE.
A SECRET PENTAGON DATABASE LISTS A MEETING OF QUAKER ANTI-WAR ACTIVISTS IN FLORIDA AS A "THREAT."

MOTHER AND CHILD... HOLY INFANT SO TENDER AND MILD
PLEASE LET ME START ON AN ANDROGEN INHIBITOR BEFORE I GROW A MUSTACHE!
LIGHT!
THE GERMAN CITIZEN WAS SEIZED BY THE CIA, BEATEN, DRUGGED, AND HELD IN A SECRET PRISON IN AFGHANISTAN FOR FIVE MONTHS BEFORE THE AGENCY REALIZED THEY HAD THE WRONG PERSON.

SLEEP IN HEA-VEN-LY PEA-
TODAY THE PRESIDENT DEFENDED HIS ILLEGAL DOMESTIC SPYING PROGRAM AS A VITAL TOOL IN THE WAR ON TERROR.

-EACE ...
THE AMERICAN PEOPLE EXPECT ME TO DO EVERY-THING IN MY POWER...

SLEEP IN HEA-VEN-LY PEACE.
...TO PROTECT THEM AND THEIR CIVIL LIBERTIES. AND THAT IS EXACTLY WHAT I WILL CONTINUE TO DO SO LONG AS I'M THE PRESIDENT OF THE UNITED STATES.

PSY-OPS
©2006 BY ALISON BECHDEL
481
1/11
GET THIS. BECAUSE IRAQIS, FOR SOME INEXPLICABLE REASON, DON'T TRUST AMERICAN INFORMATION, THE PENTAGON RUNS PRO-U.S. STORIES IN ARABIC NEWSPAPERS AND HIDES THE FACT THAT THEY'RE WRITTEN BY THE U.S. MILITARY!
CREDIBILITY PROBLEM SOLVED!
SPEAKING OF CREDIBILITY, HOW'S YOUR GIRLFRIEND'S HUSBAND, GINGER?
SAMIA HAS A HUSBAND?! NO ONE TELLS ME ANYTHING!
MARRIED WOMEN ARE HOT.
SHE'S NOT MARRIED MARRIED. IT WAS A LONG TIME AGO. SHE NEEDED TO GET HER FAMILY OFF HER BACK, HE NEEDED A GREEN CARD. OR SO SHE SAYS.
WHAT'S HE DOING HERE NOW?
HE LOST HIS JOB AND HE'S KIND OF AT LOOSE ENDS. SAMIA'S PUTTING HIM UP FOR A WHILE.
WAIT. SHE NEVER TOLD YOU ABOUT HIM?
NO! SO WHO KNOWS WHAT ELSE SHE HAS UP HER SLEEVE? ANOTHER GIRLFRIEND? A BOYFRIEND?
AHH. SO IT BEGINS.
WHAT?
YOUR INEVITABLE INTIMACY FREAKOUT.
OR MAYBE SAMIA USED TO BE SAMIR.
MEANWHILE, SYDNEY'S UNLOADING SOME BAGGAGE.
OKAY! BUH BYE!
ACME AIRLINES
I HOPE YOU'LL REALLY APPLY YOURSELF TO COUPLES COUNSELING. IT'S HARD TO REBUILD TRUST AFTER AN AFFAIR. LOOK WHAT HAPPENED WITH YOUR FATHER AND ME.
WELL, DAD WAS HAVING MORE THAN AN AFFAIR. MORE LIKE FIFTY.
NO, I MEAN MY AFFAIR. I NEVER SHOULD HAVE TOLD HIM ABOUT IT.
SHIK
YOUR AFFAIR?!
AND IF I'D KNOWN WHAT YOU WERE UP TO SOONER, I'D HAVE ADVISED YOU TO TAKE IT TO YOUR GRAVE.
SUPER SHUTTLE
BUH BYE.

FLASH BACK
1/25
482
©2006 BY ALISON BECHDEL
OUR INTREPID HOME-SCHOOLERS VENTURE INTO THE UNIVERSITY OF THE STREETS.

THIS SUCKS! I THOUGHT WE WERE DOING HISTORY THIS AFTERNOON!
THIS IS HISTORY, JANIS! TODAY'S LESSON IS, "THOSE WHO CANNOT REMEMBER THE PAST ARE CONDEMNED TO REPEAT IT."
UNFORTUNATELY, SO ARE THOSE WHO CAN.
in

IF BUSH HAS GOOD CAUSE TO SPY ON PEOPLE, HE CAN GET A WARRANT. THE ONLY REASON TO BREAK THE LAW AND DO IT SECRETLY...
'NOTHER BUNGEE, PLEASE.

A TIP O' THE NIB TO FREEWAYBLOGGER.COM
...IS IF HE'S MONITORING JOURNALISTS OR ACTIVISTS, IN A DESPERATE ATTEMPT TO COVER UP THE FACT THAT HE MISLED THE COUNTRY INTO WAR FOR POLITICAL PURPOSES. WHO'S THAT REMIND YOU OF?
THE WATERGATE GUY, OKAY? I GET IT! NOW CAN WE GO HOME?
impeach
5th Ave
JANIS, STOP WHINING. WHEN I WAS A GIRL, I HAD TO MISS NUMEROUS EPISODES OF THE PARTRIDGE FAMILY THANKS TO THAT GUY'S IMPEACHMENT HEARINGS.

YO, BEYONCÉ! WANNA SMOKE THE BONE?

HEY! HAVE A LITTLE RESPECT!
WASN'T TALKIN' TO YOU, FUGLY.

WHAT'S "SMOKE THE BONE"?
SOMETHING THAT IF SOMEONE WOULD ONLY DO TO GEORGE BUSH MIGHT MAKE IT ACTUALLY POSSIBLE TO IMPEACH HIM.
ach
PUNKS.

HISTORY'S IN RE-RUNS ELSEWHERE, TOO.
ASHLEY! FOR SOMEONE WHO CLAIMS TO BE A FEMINIST, YOU'RE ACTING A LOT LIKE A FRAT BOY!

I GIVE UP. IF YOU DON'T WANNA HAVE SEX, I'M GOING TO MY PETA MEETING.
CAN I... CAN I COME WITH YOU?

OH MY GOD!

THAT EXPLAINS IT! YOU DIDN'T TAKE A VIRGINITY PLEDGE, CYNTHIA. YOU'RE AN AGENT!
Campus Review
FBI COUNTER-TERROR AGENTS SURVEIL P.E.T.A., GREENPEACE

for worse
2/8
483
©2006 BY ALISON BECHDEL

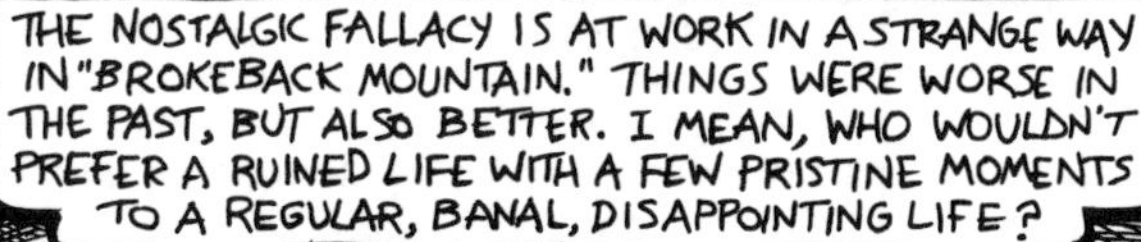
THE NOSTALGIC FALLACY IS AT WORK IN A STRANGE WAY IN "BROKEBACK MOUNTAIN." THINGS WERE WORSE IN THE PAST, BUT ALSO BETTER. I MEAN, WHO WOULDN'T PREFER A RUINED LIFE WITH A FEW PRISTINE MOMENTS TO A REGULAR, BANAL, DISAPPOINTING LIFE?

EVERYONE BUT **YOU?** WILL YOU STOP ANALYZING THE BEJEEZUS OUT OF THAT MOVIE? YOU'RE RUINING IT FOR ME. SPEAKING OF RUIN.

IMAGINE THE CINEMATOGRAPHY IF ENNIS AND JACK **HAD** BEEN ABLE TO LIVE TOGETHER. SWEEPING VISTAS OF THEIR COUPLES THERAPIST'S OFFICE.
127
ACME
PSYCHOTHERAPY
ASSOCIATES

WELL, LOOK WHAT THE CAT DRUG IN!

I DIDN'T KNOW YOU TWO CAME HERE! WHO DO YOU SEE?
NO ONE YET. WE'RE JUST AUDITIONING THIS GUY CARLOS RECOMMENDED.
NEWSTIME
IS PREZ ABOVE THE LAW?

UH...TWO WOMEN SEEING A MAN. ABOUT THEIR **RELATIONSHIP?**
I THOUGHT IT'D BE REFRESHING. A SORT OF TABULA RASA APPROACH.
GOD. WHAT THE HELL ARE WE **DOING** IN HERE? WE COULD BE RUNNING THE COUNTRY! **BUSH** ISN'T IN THERAPY. **SAMUEL ALITO** ISN'T IN THERAPY.
U.S. SNOOZE
CONSTITUTION in CRISIS?

BUT WOULD YOU WANT TO BE IN A RELATIONSHIP WITH ONE OF THEM?
HEY, WE'RE **ALL** IN A RELATIONSHIP WITH THEM. AND IT @@#ING **SUCKS!**
ABSOLUTE POWER
COURT SHIFTING TO RIGHT

ANYHOW, SYDNEY THINKS THIS GUY IS MORE LIKELY THAN A WOMAN TO TELL HER IT'S OKAY TO DO WHATEVER SHE WANTS WHENEVER SHE WANTS.
WHAT'S **WRONG** WITH DOING WHATEVER YOU WANT WHENEVER YOU WANT?

SHE'S A BIG FAN OF THE UNITARY EXECUTIVE THEORY.
AND **YOU'RE** A RELATIONSHIP ORIGINALIST! YOU REFUSE TO ADAPT THE PARADIGM TO CHANGING CIRCUMSTANCES!
LET'S HOPE YOUR THERAPIST IMPEACHES YOU BOTH.

girls gone mild
3/22
484
©2006 BY ALISON BECHDEL
SUSPICIOUS OF CYNTHIA'S VIRGINITY PLEDGE, ASHLEY HAS BROKEN THINGS OFF.
BUT CYNTHIA'S TRYING TO WOO HER BACK.

"PLAN B"! HMPH! IF WOMEN DON'T WANT TO GET PREGNANT, TRY "PLAN A"! ABSTINENCE.
AND IF YOU WANT TO CONVINCE ME YOU'RE NOT A JUNIOR FBI AGENT, YOU'RE GONNA HAVE TO TRY HARDER.
CROCKERY SHED
BOUNDERS
BOOKS-N-MU
HELP PASS THE PLAN B ACT
NARAL Pro-Choice America
TELL THE FDA TO APPROVE OVER-THE-COUNTER CONTRACEPTION

HEY, I'M SPENDING SPRING BREAK DOING PRO-CHOICE OUTREACH! WHY WOULD I DO THAT IF I DIDN'T REALLY CARE ABOUT YOU?
YOU'RE PROBABLY SPYING ON THIS GROUP, TOO.
PETA
HELP PASS THE PLAN B ACT
NARAL Pro-Choice
TELL THE FDA TO APPROVE OVER-THE-

I WAS NOT SPYING ON YOUR PETA ACTIVITIES! LISTEN, I'M EVEN HAVING SECOND THOUGHTS LATELY ABOUT GEORGE BUSH!
REALLY?
PETA

TOTALLY! EXPANDING STATE POWER TO ADVANCE HIS OWN AGENDA? HOW LIBERAL CAN YOU GET?

MEANWHILE...
EXECUTIVE DIRECTOR OF THE STATE NARAL OFFICE? THAT WOULD BE A REALLY DEMANDING JOB.
I'LL TAKE COCKNAZIS FOR $500, ALEX.
A TIP O' THE NIB TO SUSIEBRIGHT.COM

IT WOULD MEAN LONGER HOURS, BUT ALSO MORE MONEY. AND NEW CHALLENGES!
YOU HARDLY SPEND ANY TIME WITH JIAO RAIZEL AS IT IS!
DING DONG
OCTAVIA BUTLER
CHIPS
YOU MAY HAVE BEEN RAPED BY YOUR OWN FATHER, BUT YOU CAN'T GET AN ABORTION IN SOUTH DAKOTA...

GINGER? IT'S YOUR GIRLFRIEND. AND HER HUBBY.

HI, BABY! COME TO THE PARK WITH US! IT'S SPRING!
...UNLESS THE GOVERNOR DEEMS YOUR LIFE TO BE IN THIS.

I'D LIKE TO, BUT I'M TOO BUSY GRADING PAPERS. WAY TOO BUSY.
WHAT IS JEOPARDY?

BACK ON TH' STREET...
WHAT CAN I DO TO CONVINCE YOU?
I THINK YOU KNOW. AND IT DOESN'T INVOLVE "PLAN A."

IF THE ONLY THING WORSE THAN NOT HAVING A JOB IS HAVING A JOB, OUR HEROINE FINDS HERSELF IN AN EXCRUCIATING LIMBO.

A TIP O' THE NIB TO AMY RUBIN

A TIP O' THE NIB TO RUTH HOROWITZ

ultimata

4/19

486

HMM. PEAK OIL, A MILITARY QUAGMIRE, CATASTROPHIC CLIMATE CHANGE, STRATOSPHERIC DEBT, A LOOMING PANDEMIC... WHAT'S A NATION TO DO?

MEANWHILE, IN THE GROVES OF ACADEME...

bully for you
5/3
487
©2006 BY ALISON BECHDEL
I CAN'T KEEP TAKING OFF WORK LIKE THIS. IF WE CAN'T GET AN EVENING SLOT, I'LL HAVE TO QUIT THERAPY.
WE'LL TALK TO PATRICIA ABOUT IT.
...IF THERE'S A LEAK OUT OF MY ADMINISTRATION, I WANT TO KNOW WHO IT IS. AND IF THE PERSON HAS VIOLATED LAW, THE PERSON WILL BE TAKEN CARE OF.
WE'RE LATE. WHERE IS HE?
OVER THERE. WITH YOUR MISTRESS. WHAT'S SHE WANT?
NETHER HTS. M LE SCHOOL
UH...HI, GLORIA.
HI. LISTEN, YOU KNOW THAT ANTI-BULLYING WORKSHOP WITH THE LGBT YOUTH GROUP THAT THE SCHOOL WAS SUPPOSED TO HAVE TODAY?
A COUPLE PARENTS FREAKED OUT, SO THE PRINCIPAL CANCELED IT AT THE LAST MINUTE.
ARE YOU KIDDING?
NO. WE HAD TO GO BACK TO SOCIAL STUDIES.
LEMME GET THIS STRAIGHT... THE PRINCIPAL WAS BULLIED INTO CANCELING AN ANTI-BULLYING WORKSHOP?
BASICALLY. I WAS JUST GONNA GO TALK TO HIM.
JEEZ...WE'RE ON OUR WAY TO THE SHRINK.
FORGET IT. WE'LL COME WITH YOU.
ARE YOU GONNA BULLY THE PRINCIPAL TOO?
MEANWHILE, ON UNIVERSITY HILL...
HURRY UP. WE'RE GONNA BE LATE FOR THE SHRINK-MAN.
OKAY, OKAY. I JUST HAVE TO FINISH THIS EMAIL.
SYDNEY? CAN I GET YOU TO JOIN MY RELAY FOR LIFE TEAM?
RELAY FOR LIFE? WHAT'S THAT, SOME KIND OF ANTI-ABORTION JAMBOREE?
NO, NO, IT'S A CANCER FUNDRAISER. YOU GET TEAMS TOGETHER, AND WALK OR RUN AROUND A TRACK ALL NIGHT. IT'S VERY INSPIRATIONAL.
NO WAY. I'LL GIVE YOU TEN BUCKS, BUT I DON'T DO INSPIRATIONAL.
I THINK WE SHOULD TALK TO RICHARD ABOUT YOUR CANCER ISSUES.
I THINK THAT YOU NEED TO USE "I" STATEMENTS.

your children are not your children
©2006 BY ALISON BECHDEL

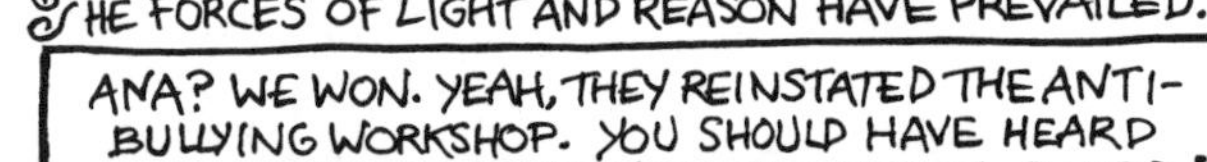
THE FORCES OF LIGHT AND REASON HAVE PREVAILED...

5/11
488
ANA? WE WON. YEAH, THEY REINSTATED THE ANTI-BULLYING WORKSHOP. YOU SHOULD HAVE HEARD YOUR DAUGHTER SPEAKING TO THE SCHOOL BOARD!
DLE SCHOOL

I'M SO PROUD OF BOTH YOU GIRLS FOR TALKING IN FRONT OF THAT CROWD. YOU WERE A BIG REASON THE VOTE WENT THE WAY IT DID.
DAD! OW!

I WAS SURPRISED RAF DIDN'T GET UP THERE TOO. I DIDN'T REALIZE HE WAS SO SHY.

HOW COME YOU DIDN'T GIVE A BIG GAY SPEECH, LESBO-BOY?
#@$ YOU, DILLWEED.
TAYLOR! LET'S GO!

MEANWHILE, SYDNEY'S ALLAYING SOME EXISTENTIAL DREAD BY BROWSING THE LATEST ELECTRONICS...
...OKAY, I'LL BE HOME SOON... OH, MAN! MY OLD RADIATION TECH JUST SPOTTED ME... THE WOMAN WHOSE SON WAS KILLED IN IRAQ. GOTTA GO.
46-64" TV'S
SYDNEY!
MILITARY COUP AT CIA
S&P ▲ 0.50
CNN
IF THE MAINSTREAM MEDIA INSISTS...

CHERYL! NICE TO SEE YOU. HOW'VE YOU BEEN?
I'M GETTING BY. IT'S ALMOST THE SECOND ANNIVERSARY OF BRENT'S DEATH, SO THAT'S KINDA HARD.
The DANGER of GRAPE-FRUIT JUICE
DOW ▼ 3.77
THAT STEPHEN COLBERT'S BUSH ROAST WASN'T FUNNY...

UHH... YEAH, JEEZ, I CAN'T IMAGINE...

BUT IT'S LUCKY I RAN INTO YOU! I'M ORGANIZING A TEAM FOR THE RELAY FOR LIFE, YOU KNOW, THE CANCER FUNDRAISER? I'D LOVE TO HAVE YOU ON IT.
31%
DO THEY MAKE A SOUND?

I THINK YOU'LL FIND IT VERY INSPIRATIONAL!
ARMY NATIONAL GUARD

AND JASMINE SAYS NO TO DRUGS.
LOIS, I DON'T WANT HER DOING ANYTHING IRREVOCABLE. LOTS OF GENDER-VARIANT KIDS GROW UP TO BE NON-TRANSGENDER.

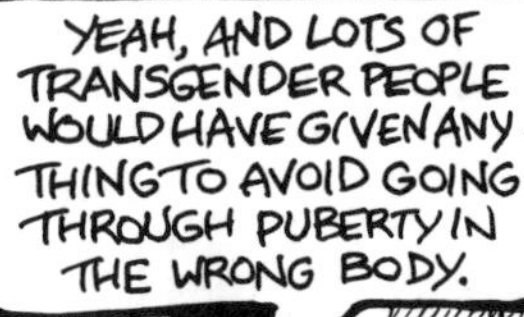
YEAH, AND LOTS OF TRANSGENDER PEOPLE WOULD HAVE GIVEN ANYTHING TO AVOID GOING THROUGH PUBERTY IN THE WRONG BODY.

AND YOU KNOW, THE MORE SHE CONFORMS, THE SAFER SHE'LL BE.
HEY, I DON'T NEED YOU TO TELL ME THAT. BUT I HAVE HIGHER HOPES FOR MY CHILD THAN CONFORMITY, OKAY?

©2006 BY ALISON BECHDEL

489

5/31

IT'S ROUGH SLEDDING FOR THE ASSOCIATES AT ACME PSYCHOTHERAPY.

HE WAS A HAPPY KID UNTIL HE STARTED MIDDLE SCHOOL.

THAT WAS RIGHT ABOUT THE TIME SHE FOUND OUT ABOUT THE THING WITH GLORIA.

OH, SO IT'S **MY** FAULT? FOR FINDING OUT ABOUT THE "THING"?!

AND IN THE NEXT OFFICE...

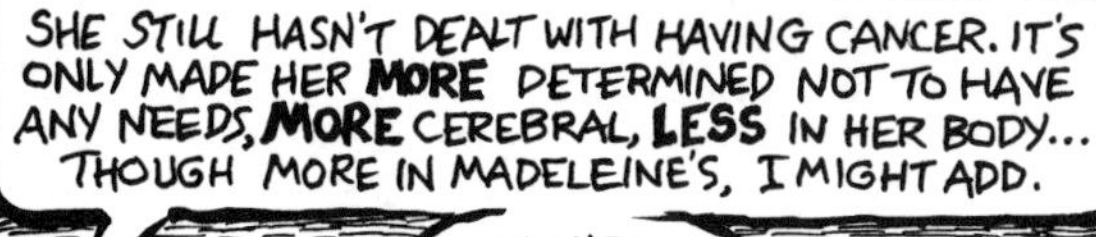

WHY DON'T YOU TELL **US**, SYDNEY? WHAT **ARE** YOU FEELING?

UHH... I FEEL SORT OF DISCURSIVELY DISPERSED, YOU KNOW? DECENTERED, UNTHEORIZED... EVEN A TAD **HYPHENATED**.

MEANWHILE, ANOTHER COUPLE GETS A THERAPEUTIC WORKOUT FROM AN UNEXPECTED SOURCE...

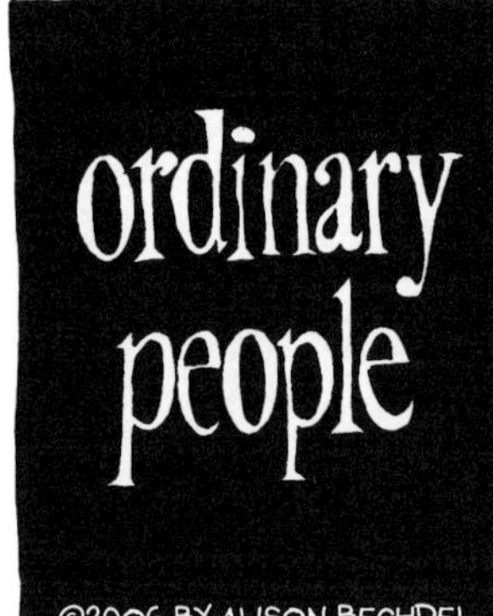
ordinary people
490
©2006 BY ALISON BECHDEL

7/12
@#&*! THIS FISH IS STICKING.
MO, DON'T CHOP THE CARROTS LIKE THAT. CUT THEM IN LITTLE STRIPS.

UH...ARE YOU GUYS OKAY, TONI? YOU SEEM A LITTLE...
RAFFI! FOR THE THIRD TIME, SET THE TABLE!
...TENSE.

IN A MINUTE!
YOU SAID THAT FIFTEEN MINUTES AGO.

DIE, YOU NAZI MOTHER!
RAFFI!
A TIP O' THE GAMEPAD TO SAM HOROWITZ

HE'S PLAYING ONLINE.
OH.

YOU TOO, I SEE. CAN'T STOP RASPBERRYING MADELEINE FOR ONE EVENING?
RAF, YOUR MOMS ARE KINDA STRESSED OUT. MAYBE YOU SHOULD GIVE THEM A HAND.
OKAY.

ABIGAIL, I HAFTA GO. I'LL SEE YOU AT THE MALL LATER.
YOU'RE NOT SEEING ANYBODY AT THE MALL LATER. WE HAVE DINNER GUESTS.

I HAVE TO SEE HER! SHE'S GOING AWAY TO HER DAD'S FOR THE REST OF THE SUMMER!
CLARICE, DON'T BE RIDICULOUS. OF COURSE HE CAN GO.

NO ONE LISTENS TO ME. I DON'T KNOW WHAT I'M EVEN DOING HERE.

I WISH YOU GUYS WOULD GET DIVORCED. THEN I COULD BE NORMAL.

survivor's benefits
7/26
491
©2006 BY ALISON BECHDEL
I DON'T KNOW WHY YOU GUYS WANTED TO COME. IT'S JUST GONNA BE A SENTIMENTAL SPECTACLE OF SYNTHETIC CATHARSIS.
IT WAS THIS, OR WATCH SAMIA AND AMMAR CAULK THE TUB.
ICAN CANCER SOCIE
Relay for Life
WALK / JOG / RUN
ALL-NIGHT FUNDRAI
SWEETIE, I THINK IT'S REALLY GREAT THAT YOU'RE DOING THIS. I WANT TO SUPPORT YOU!
SUPPORT!
JUST GIMME A HALF-HOUR TO DO THIS SURVIVOR'S LAP THING, THEN I'M OUTTA HERE.
A TIP O' THE NIB TO CHRISTINE JENKINS
DISEASE AS COMMODITY. CONSUMPTION AS CHARITY. FIND A CURE, FORGET ABOUT THE CAUSE. WHY'D I LET CHERYL GUILT-TRIP ME INTO THIS OBSCENE CHARADE?
SYDNEY! COME JOIN THE TEAM!
BREAST
PROSTATE
MELANOMA
CERVICAL
LUNG
TESTICULAR
RACE for the CURE
BRENT'S BATTALION
CANCER WRISTBANDS $5
WE'RE STARTING. HERE'S YOUR T-SHIRT AND BALLOON.
MY BALLOON? WHY'S THERE A "THREE" ON IT?
IT'S HOW MANY YEARS YOU'VE SURVIVED!
AT FIRST I THOUGHT IT WAS HOW MANY YEARS OLD I WAS EXPECTED TO FEEL WALKING AROUND WITH A BALLOON ON A STRING. ISN'T THIS **INFANTILIZING**?
BRENT'S BATTALION
DEAN HAVERSTICK!
I DIDN'T KNOW YOU, UH...THAT YOU...
COLORECTAL, STAGE TWO. NOT THE SORT OF THING ONE TRUMPETS ABOUT. I'M FINE NOW.
AS THE EVENING LENGTHENS...
SYDNEY!
A TIP O' THE NIB TO AMY RUBIN!
I FORGOT YOU WERE STILL HERE! HEY, I'M GONNA STAY. I'M REALLY BONDING WITH THE DEAN. SHE'S CONFESSING A BOUT OF LESBIANISM IN HER RADCLIFFE DAYS.
I JUST HOPE THAT BOUT'S IN REMISSION.

PROXY WAR
©2006 BY ALISON BECHDEL
492
8/9
ANOTHER DAY, ANOTHER DEMO.
GOD, IT'S HOT.
SWIMMING, DADDY!
NO, SWEETIE. THE FOUNTAIN'S DIRTY.
STOP THE MASSACRE IN LEBANON
JEWISH VOICE for PEACE
END THE WAR ON GAZA
CEASE FIRE NOW!
SWIMMING!
HERE WE GO.
SWIM-MING!
UH... WE'LL BE BACK IN A FEW. WE'RE GONNA GET SOME WATER.
IS SOME-ONE HAVING A TANTRUM?
OH. SHE'S JUST A LITTLE FRUSTRATED.
WAIL!
JVP
WHEN MY KIDS HAD TANTRUMS, I'D GIVE THEM A FLICK ON THE FACE. NOT HARD, JUST ENOUGH TO SNAP THEM OUT OF IT.
IGNORING HER REALLY WORKS BEST, TRUST ME.
I SUPPOSE YOU THINK THAT'S A GOOD WAY TO HANDLE TERRORISM, TOO.
?!
JEWISH VOICE for PEACE
1559? WHAT ABOUT 242?
I SUPPOSE YOU THINK BRUTALIZING CIVILIANS IS A BETTER PLAN! HEY, IT WORKED IN IRAQ, RIGHT? EVERYTHING'S COPACETIC THERE!
COLLECTIVE PUNISHMENT IS IMMORAL
SWIMMING!
LEMME TELL YOU SOMETHING. A BOOT ON THE NECK ONLY MAKES THINGS WORSE!
TERRORIST LOVER.
FACE FLICKER!
STUART!
GOD, I THOUGHT YOU WERE GONNA HEAD-BUTT THAT LADY. WHO WAS SHE?
THE PRESIDENT OF MOTHERS FOR A NEW AMERICAN CENTURY, BY THE SOUND OF IT.
DAAAH!
DADDY'S HAVING A TIME OUT.

OR, HOW TO GET AWAY WITH DOING WHATEVER YOU WANT WHENEVER YOU LIKE.

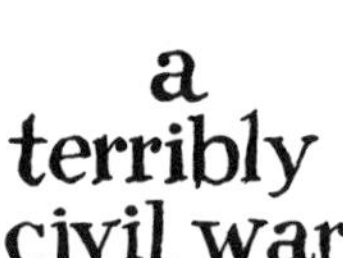

2006 BY ALISON BECHDEL

HARD KNOCKS U
©2006 BY ALISON BECHDEL
495

BACK TO MIDDLE SCHOOL...
9/20
STELOCIRAPTOR! WORD UP?
HEY, RAFOSAURUS REX. SEVENTH GRADE SUCKS.

EIGHTH TOO. MAJOR SUCKAGE.
PLUS MY MOMS HAVE BEEN DRIVING ME CRAZY SINCE THEY BROKE UP.

HUH. I THINK MINE MIGHT BE SPLITTING UP TOO.
GET OUT! YOU ARE SUCH A **BITER**! YOU'RE TOTALLY COPYING ME.

BACK TO LIBERAL ARTS SCHOOL...
LIKE, THE U.N. DEFINES TERRORISM TO INCLUDE WAR CRIMES. THAT MEANS ALMOST EVERY GOVERNMENT IN THE **WORLD** IS A TERRORIST!
What is TERRORISM?

GOOD POINT, ASHLEY. SO IS THAT A USEFUL DEFINITION? CYNTHIA?
MS. JORDAN, WHY ARE WE DISCUSSING TERRORISM?

THIS IS ENGLISH, NOT POLITICAL SCIENCE! YOU'RE ABUSING YOUR POSITION WITH THIS KIND OF INDOCTRINATION.
OH, COME ON! IT'S A TOTALLY APT TOPIC. WE'RE STUDYING THE PERSUASIVE USE OF LANGUAGE!

WELL, GOSH KNOWS YOU'RE THE EXPERT ON **THAT**, MS. PLEASE-PLEASE-WHY-WON'T-YOU-HAVE-SEX-WITH-ME.
What is TERRORISM?

BACK TO HOMESCHOOL.
OKAY. GEOMETRY'S OVER, TIME FOR GENDER AND SOCIETY.

DID YOU FINISH YOUR ESSAY ON THE MICHIGAN WOMYN'S MUSIC FESTIVAL'S ANTI-TRANS POLICY?

LOIS, YOU HAVE TO CONVINCE MOM TO LET ME TAKE HORMONES. I'M ALMOST FIFTEEN!

I KNOW. THANK GOD YOU'RE A LATE BLOOMER. NOTHING SPROUTING YET.
I'M NOT A LATE BLOOMER. I'VE BEEN TAKING ANTI-ANDROGENS FOR THE PAST SIX MONTHS.

A TIP O' THE NIB TO SAMUEL LURIE
WHAT? WHERE'D YOU GET THEM?
PLEASE. THIS **IS** AMERICA! NOW, I CAN TAKE STREET HORMONES, OR WE CAN DO THIS RIGHT. WHAT'S IT GONNA BE?

sleep's sister

10/4

496

life 2.0
10/18
497
©2006 BY ALISON BECHDEL
THANKS FOR COMING OVER, TONI. SEE? I TRY TO OPEN THE FREEDOM TO MARRY DATABASE AND IT SAYS "FILE CORRUPT."
I CAN FIX THIS. I JUST HOPE STELLA DOESN'T MIND HANGING OUT WITH RAFFI FOR A WHILE.
MEANWHILE, UPSTAIRS...
MAYBE YOU'LL BELIEVE ME ONCE YOU SEE THIS.
NO WAY!
Shoont!
I SAW GLORIA THIS AFTERNOON AT THE GROCERY STORE.
THAT'S NICE. DID YOU HAVE SEX WITH HER?
YEAH, IN THE DAIRY CASE.
SHE'S NOT DOING SO GOOD. ANA MOVED OUT LAST WEEK. STELLA'S HAVING A HARD TIME AND DOESN'T WANT TO GO TO SCHOOL. IT SOUNDS AWFUL.
WELL, GLORIA SHOULD HAVE THOUGHT OF THAT BEFORE SHE...
RAFFI! WHAT ARE YOU DOING?!
ARE YOU SPYING ON US?
CLICK
SEE? TOLD YOU.
THEY HAD SEX AT THE GROCERY STORE?!
NO, DIPTARD! THAT PART WAS A JOKE. BUT SOMETHING'S GOING ON.
YOU KNOW WHAT WE SHOULD DO?
WHAT?
THEY'RE AWFULLY QUIET.
PIRATES of the CARIBBEAN
KIDS? ARE YOU HUNGRY?
NO THANK YOU!
UH... NOTHING!
YouTube BROADCAST YOURSELF!
VIDEO UPLOAD SUCCESSFUL

SCANDAL IN THE HOUSE
©2006 BY ALISON BECHDEL

ONCE AGAIN, CLARICE GETS HER HOPES UP...
11/1
498
WELL, THE HOUSE IS IN THE BAG. NOW IF ONLY THIS HAS ENOUGH LEGS TO TAKE THE SENATE.
LA CAGE AU FOLEY
DERANGED PEDOPHILE
SECRET GAY NETWORK
MIDTERMS

THANK GOD FOR CREEPY, INDISCREET, PAGE-HARRASSING, CLOSETED GAY REPUBLICAN CONGRESSMEN.

WHY ARE YOU SO FIXATED ON THIS? WE HAVE REAL PROBLEMS TO DEAL WITH.
TONI, AMERICANS DON'T CARE ABOUT 600,000 DEAD IRAQIS, OR THE INTRICACIES OF THE ABRAMOFF SCANDAL, OR THE FACT THAT CONGRESS JUST OKAYED TORTURE AND DITCHED HABEAS CORPUS!
THEY CARE ABOUT DIRTY IM'S! AND IF THAT SWEEPS THE GOP OUT OF POWER, **THEN** WE CAN TACKLE THOSE REAL PROBLEMS!

I WAS REFERRING TO THE REAL PROBLEMS OF OUR SEPARATION.
RINNG!

HELLO?
OH, HI, STELLA. YEAH, HANG ON.

RAFFI! CAN YOU STOP THE SLAUGHTER FOR A SECOND AND SPEAK TO STELLA?

HEY.
YOU'RE STILL ALIVE. I GUESS YOUR PARENTS DIDN'T NOTICE WE PUT UP THAT VIDEO OF THEM FIGHTING ABOUT MY MOM.
SINCE WHEN DOES HE CONDUCT HIS CONVERSATIONS PRIVATELY?
GLORIA THINKS THEY HAVE SOMETHING GOING ON.

YEAH, **DUH**. THERE'S ONLY A MILLION VIDEOS ON YOUTUBE. WHY SHOULD ANYONE NOTICE **THAT** ONE?
Slip Knot

STELLA, CAN YOU MOVE? I HAVE TO FINISH THE FREEDOM TO MARRY NEWSLETTER AND EMAIL IT OUT TONIGHT.
HMM. **UNLESS**...
EQUALITY newsletter
GREAT. ANOTHER BRIGHT IDEA.

AS CONGRESSMAN FOLEY'S INSTANT MESSAGES SHOW, THERE ARE VERY SERIOUS DANGERS WHEN CHILDREN GO ONLINE...
PUNDIT PANIC

HOIST
11/15
499
©2006 BY ALISON BECHDEL

SO... IF WE'RE REALLY DOING THIS, IT'S WEIRD TO KEEP SLEEPING TOGETHER.
YOU TAKE THE BED. I'LL STAY ON THE COUCH. I CAN'T IMAGINE EVER SLEEPING AGAIN ANYWAY.

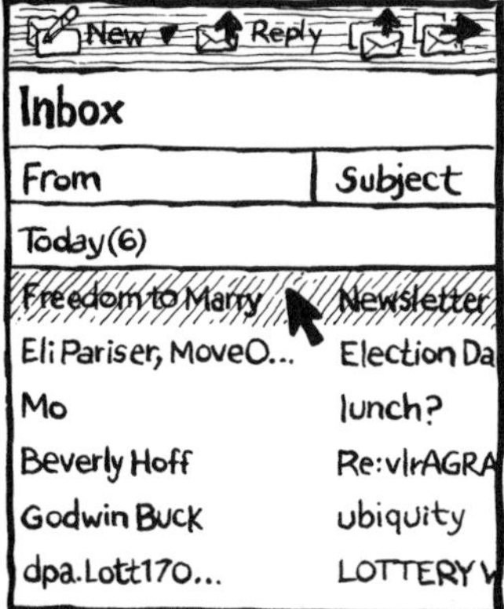
New
Reply
Inbox
From
Subject
Today(6)
Freedom to Marry
Newsletter
Eli Pariser, MoveO...
Election Da
Mo
lunch?
Beverly Hoff
Re: vlrAGRA
Godwin Buck
ubiquity
dpa.Lott170...
LOTTERY

!

I SAW GLORIA THIS AFTERNOON AT THE GROCERY STORE.
YouTube
THAT'S NICE. DID YOU HAVE SEX WITH HER?

CLARICE!
MMM. COME TO BED.
WAKE UP!

YOU HAVE TO SEE THIS.

THIS IS WHAT STELLA AND RAFFI HAVE GOING ON! IT WENT TO EVERYONE ON THE FREEDOM TO MARRY MAILING LIST!
I CAN'T BELIEVE RAFFI WOULD DO SOMETHING SO...
YouTube

...SO BRILLIANT. YOU HAVE TO ADMIT, IT'S RATHER NEAT. HOIST BY YOUR OWN PETARD!

BUT THAT DOESN'T MEAN HE'S NOT CUT OFF FROM EVERY CONCEIVABLE ELECTRONIC DEVICE UNTIL HE LEAVES FOR COLLEGE.
THAT MUST BE GLORIA!
RING

TONI? LIZ FARKAS-McLAUGHLIN. DID YOU SEE THE NEWSLETTER GLORIA JUST SENT OUT? THERE'S A VERY CURIOUS LINK ON IT...

who's your daddy?

CYNTHIA IS SPENDING THANKSGIVING BREAK AT THE HOME FOR WAYWARD EVANGELICALS.

IF IT WAS A CHOICE, WHY ON EARTH WOULD THE PASTOR OF AN EVANGELICAL GIGACHURCH **CHOOSE** TO BE **GAY?**

MEANWHILE, MO AND SYDNEY ARE PAYING A VISIT TO SYD'S DAD AND STEPMOM.

MEANWHILE, FREEDOM TO MARRY IS HOLDING AN EMERGENCY BOARD MEETING.

love & other calamities

1/24

502

WHAT'S THE ANSWER FOR OUR EMBATTLED COUPLE?

FLUX
2/7
503
© 2007 BY ALISON BECHDEL
WHERE ARE THE SNOWS OF YESTER-YEAR?

DANDELION, DADDY!
WOW. FLOWERS IN JANUARY!
WE'RE ALL GONNA DIE.

HEY, DO YOU GUYS WANT TO GO LOOK AT A HOUSE WITH US?

YOU AND SAMIA ARE HOUSEHUNTING? DOES THAT MEAN HUBBY IS OUT OF THE PICTURE?
THE GUIDE TO REFERENCE BOOKS

WELL... NOT EXACTLY. BUT IF THE TWO OF YOU COME ALONG, THERE WON'T BE ROOM IN THE CAR FOR AMMAR.

GINGER, WHAT THE HELL IS GOING ON WITH THAT LITTLE MÉNAGE?

SAMIA AND I ARE PLAYING EMOTIONAL CHICKEN. SHE'LL MAKE AMMAR LEAVE WHEN I LEAVE SPARROW AND STUART AND LOIS, BUT NOT BEFORE.
THAT COULD BE QUITE A PILE-UP IF NOBODY SWERVES.
SNO-TUBE

WHATEVER. SO WILL YOU COME SEE THIS PLACE TODAY?
NO, WE NEED TO SPEND TIME WITH VIRGINIA. WE'VE BOTH BEEN AT WORK ALL WEEK AND SHE'S NOT DOING WELL. SHE MISSES HER SISTER.

OH, RIGHT. I'M SORRY.
CAN'T SPARROW OR STUART OR LOIS GO WITH YOU?

NO! THEN THEY'D KNOW I WAS HOUSEHUNTING!
GINGER, YOU'VE GOTTA FACE THE MUSIC EVENTUALLY.

LET GO, MOVE ON! NOTHING LASTS FOREVER.

THE USES OF INTELLIGENCE
2/21
504
©2007 BY ALISON BECHDEL

HEY! DR. JORDAN! I'M IN! I GOT THE CIA INTERNSHIP!
THAT'S, UH, GREAT, CYNTHIA.
THE Hortense Schmendrick LECTURE SERIES
WAR & LIES: FABRICATED INTELLIGENCE FROM IRAQ TO IRAN

AFTER GRADUATION, I'LL BE SPENDING THE SUMMER AT THE GEORGE BUSH CENTER FOR INTELLIGENCE, DOING THE WORK OF THE NATION!
THE WORK OF THE NATION.

THANKS FOR SETTING ASIDE YOUR KNEEJERK DISAPPROVAL LONG ENOUGH TO WRITE ME A DECENT RECOMMENDATION.

I'M JUST GLAD YOU'VE DECIDED TO GO TO GRAD SCHOOL IN THE FALL, BEFORE SETTLING ON TORTURE AND RENDITION AS A PERMANENT CAREER.

YOU HAVE SO MUCH PROMISE, CYNTHIA. THERE ARE BETTER WAYS TO CONTRIBUTE THAN GATHERING INFORMATION FOR SOME FUTURE PRESIDENT TO MANIPULATE AND MISUSE.

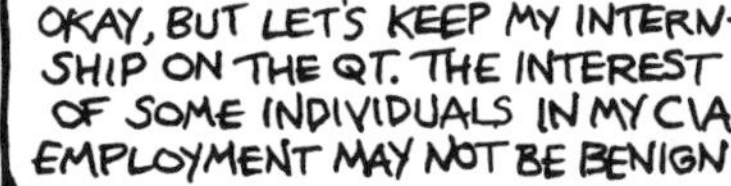
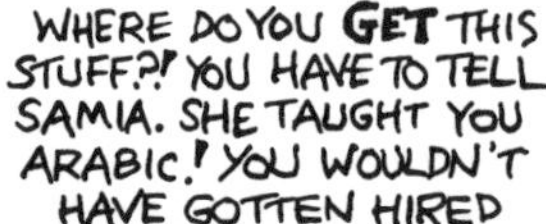

HEY, YOU CAN SIT HERE IN YOUR IVORY TOWER, BUT THE TRUTH IS, THERE ARE BAD PEOPLE OUT THERE.
HERE ARE SOME NOW! SAMIA AND AMMAR ARE MEETING ME FOR THE LECTURE. D'YOU WANT TO SIT WITH US?

OKAY, BUT LET'S KEEP MY INTERNSHIP ON THE QT. THE INTEREST OF SOME INDIVIDUALS IN MY CIA EMPLOYMENT MAY NOT BE BENIGN.
WHERE DO YOU GET THIS STUFF?! YOU HAVE TO TELL SAMIA. SHE TAUGHT YOU ARABIC! YOU WOULDN'T HAVE GOTTEN HIRED WITHOUT HER.

WHY DOES SHE HAVE AMMAR HANGING AROUND ALL THE TIME. DOESN'T HE BUG YOU?
UH... THEY HAVE A COMPLICATED HISTORY.

SAY THE WORD, AND I'LL LOOK INTO HIS GREEN CARD SITUATION WHEN I'M AT HEADQUARTERS.
CYNTHIA!

LEMME GET BACK TO YOU ON THAT.

togetherness
©2007 BY ALISON BECHDEL

SO WE'LL MEET YOU RIGHT HERE AFTER THE MOVIE'S OVER AT 4:35. GOT IT? REPEAT IT BACK TO ME.
OVER THERE, AT 4:53.
IN THE LOBBY, AT 5:34.
MAUL
INFINIPLEX
SMOKIN' ACES
LAST KING OF SCOTLAND
THE QUEEN
JACK FROST
TEN
ROYAL FLUSH
3/7
505

OKAY, FIRST THE OFFICE SUPPLY STORE TO GET TICKETS FOR THE RAFFLE.
THE QUEEN

DOESN'T IT STRIKE YOU AS STRANGE THAT WE'RE BOTH STILL WORKING FOR THIS GAY MARRIAGE ORGANIZATION EVEN THOUGH WE'VE JUST LEFT OUR PARTNERS?
WELCOME TO
STAPLED
NO.

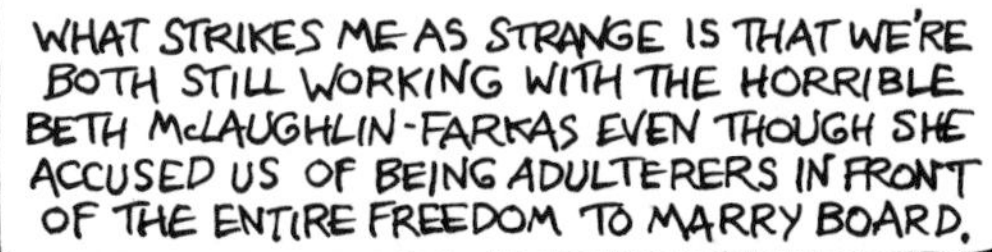
WHAT STRIKES ME AS STRANGE IS THAT WE'RE BOTH STILL WORKING WITH THE HORRIBLE BETH McLAUGHLIN-FARKAS EVEN THOUGH SHE ACCUSED US OF BEING ADULTERERS IN FRONT OF THE ENTIRE FREEDOM TO MARRY BOARD.

MP3·GPS
DVD·CDR
ZIP·PDA
LCD·DLP
WTF
ENVELOPES for LIFE
ENVELOPES
5000

NOW EVERYONE THINKS WE'RE CARRYING ON. AT THIS RATE WE MIGHT AS WELL BE.
ENVELOPES for your NEXT 5 REINCARNATIONS

IT'S SO WEIRD BEING SINGLE AFTER ALL THESE YEARS. SINGLE! WHAT DOES THAT MEAN?
GEL
GRIP

GOD. YOU CAN'T EVEN BUY A SINGLE PEN ANYMORE.
SOB!
G2
ONE GROSS
THEY SKIP! THEY BLOT! BUT YOU HAVE 144!

TONI! I'M SORRY TO GO ON LIKE THIS WHEN IT'S STILL SO RAW FOR YOU!

WHAT HAPPENED, GLORIA? MY LIFE USED TO BE SO TOGETHER.
IT WILL BE AGAIN. DON'T WORRY.
GRIP GEL

OH, PLEASE. CAN'T YOU PEOPLE CONTROL YOURSELVES?

UHHH... HI BETH. LIZ.
ELSPETH.

...but she digresses.
©2007 BY ALISON BECHDEL
506
3/21
SYDNEY'S SPRING BREAK MIGHT BREAK HER.
SYDNEY! COME SEE IF YOU THINK THIS WOULD BE A GOOD COLOR ON ME.
IN A MINUTE, MOM. I'M DOING YOUR RECYCLING.
SHOCKER! FBI ABUSED PATRIOT ACT!
WHO KNEW? WOUNDED VETS GET SUBSTANDARD TREATMENT!
PINOT GRINGO
HI.
HI, SWEETIE. HOW'S IT GOING?
GOD. MOM IS SO NEEDY. I HAVEN'T BEEN ABLE TO GET ANY WORK DONE ON MY DIGRESSION PAPER, AND THE PANEL IS FRIDAY!
MYSTERY! WILL BUSH PARDON LIBBY?
THAT'S TOO BAD. LISTEN, I'M WORRIED ABOUT VIRGINIA. I THINK MAYBE IT'S NOT SO MUCH THAT SHE MISSES VANESSA, BUT THAT SHE'S FEELING SURVIVOR'S GUILT.
MO, SHE PROBABLY HAS A HAIRBALL. I HATE IT WHEN YOU ANTHROPOMORPHIZE.
BEEP!
OH, MAN. MY DAD'S CALLING. I GOTTA GO.
HELLO, PATER.
STRAND
HI, SYD. I JUST WANTED TO SEE WHEN YOU WERE PLANNING ON GETTING HERE.
DAD! I'M SPENDING THE BREAK AT MOM'S, REMEMBER? THE NARRATIVE CONFERENCE IS HERE THIS WEEKEND. I'LL SEE YOU IN JUNE. I TOLD YOU THIS LAST WEEK!
CLINK!
STRAND
MAGNUM
ER... I MUST'VE ENTERED THE DATES WRONG. I HAVEN'T GOTTEN USED TO THIS NEW BLACKBERRY.
SYDNEY! I CAN'T FIGURE OUT THIS WEB BROWSER YOU INSTALLED. I LIKED THE OLD ONE.
I HAVE TO GO. I'LL CALL YOU LATER.
LOOK. ALL YOUR BOOKMARKS ARE RIGHT HERE. SEE?
MADELEINE!
I'M SO EXCITED ABOUT SEEING YOU THIS WEEKEND I CAN'T FOCUS ON THE ETHICS OF NARRATIVE DIGRESSION. SAY SOMETHING TO DAMPEN MY ARDOR SO I CAN FINISH THIS PAPER.
MOTHERR!
OOPS.

Secrets and Spies
507
©2007 BY ALISON BECHDEL

FOUR YEARS INTO THE WAR, ALLIANCES ARE GETTING ODD.
I'M GLAD TO SEE YOU'VE COME TO YOUR SENSES ABOUT THE WAR, ASHLEY.
AS IF! I'M HERE TO SUPPORT QUEER TROOPS, NOT THE WAR, YOU CIA SPOOK.
FIRE PACE HIRE GAYS
GENERAL PACE IS IMMORAL
QUEERS ARE FABULOUS

WHO TOLD YOU ABOUT THAT?! ARE YOU TRYING TO **OUT** ME?!
WHAT'S IMMORAL?

HEY, CYNTHIA! DIDJA HEAR BIBLE STUDY IS CANCELED TONIGHT? WE'RE HOLDING A VIGIL AGAINST THE INHUMANE TREATMENT OF DETAINEES.
SHE CAN'T MAKE IT. SHE'LL BE CRAMMING FOR "ENHANCED INTERROGATION TECHNIQUES."
CAMPUS FELLOWSHIP
VIGIL 2NITE

MEANWHILE...
SAMIA! GINGER!
FOR SALE
RE/MAX

ARE YOU LOOKING AT THIS PLACE? WE'LL BE NEIGHBORS!
FOR SALE
call LIZ
RE/MAX

HI, SYDNEY. I DUNNO. IT NEEDS A LOT OF WORK.
ARE YOU JUST GETTING BACK FROM THE CONFERENCE? HOW WAS IT?
OH, MAN.

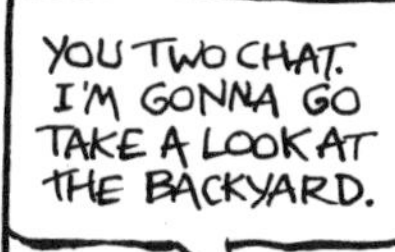
YOU TWO CHAT. I'M GONNA GO TAKE A LOOK AT THE BACKYARD.

THIS THING WITH MADELEINE IS GETTING OUT OF CONTROL.

GOD, SYDNEY. I'M TOO OLD FOR THIS. AND SO ARE YOU! I'M TIRED OF KEEPING YOUR SORDID SECRETS.
SYDNEY! YOU'RE HOME!

UH...HI, SWEETIE! HI, STUART. HOW WAS THE MARCH?
IT WAS **SOMETHING!** J.R. ALMOST GOT ARRESTED. SHE WANDERED OFF AND FELL ASLEEP AT THE DIE-IN.
TROOPS OUT NOW
IMPEA

WAY TO GO, J.R.!
GINGER, I THOUGHT YOU WERE AT BUFFALO LAKE ALL DAY. WHAT'RE YOU DOING HERE?

YOUR LITTLE HOUSE-MATE'S GROWING UP! SHE AND SAMIA ARE THINKING OF BUYING THIS PLACE!
YOU **ARE?!**

GOOD POINT, RAFFI.

YET CURIOUSLY, AGAINST THE SWEEPING BACKDROP OF HISTORY... EVERYDAY LIFE PRETTY MUCH CONTINUES.

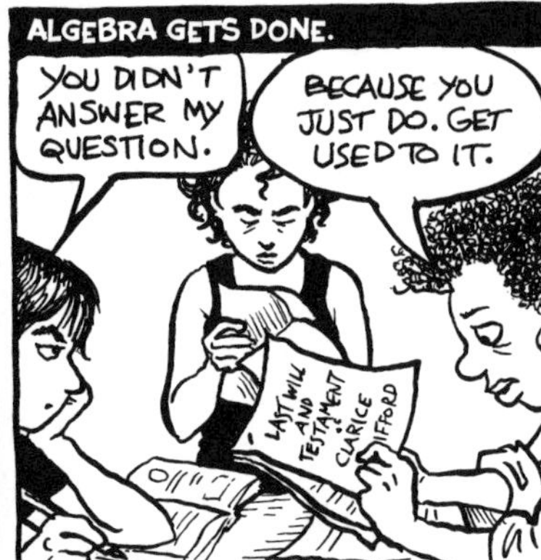

doctor, doctor
©2007 BY ALISON BECHDEL
509
6/13
HI, PAUL! IT'S MO. IS SYDNEY THERE? SHE'S NOT ANSWERING HER CELL.
REFERENCE
AH, THE MELLIFLUOUS TONES OF MY DAUGHTER'S FAIR CONSORT, KEEPER OF THE FLAME OF LITERACY! HOW GOES THE LIBRARY?
NYRB
I THINK YOU'RE OVERREACTING. HE'S SEVENTY! IT'S JUST PART OF GETTING OLDER.
JENNIFER! HE RAN MY CELL PHONE THROUGH THE DISHWASHER! HE NEEDS TO SEE A DOCTOR. IF THEY CATCH IT EARLY, THERE'S STUFF THEY CAN DO.
SYD! TELEPHONE. IT'S MADELEINE.
WE NEED TO TALK ABOUT THIS.
MADDY! GOD, I MISS YOU SO MUCH. I'M SURROUNDED BY CRAZY PEOPLE AND I'VE BEEN HAVING THE MOST OBSCENE FANTASIES ABOUT YOU.
LADY? HEY! I SAID I CAN'T FIND THE SPORTS ILLUSTRATED SWIMSUIT ISSUE.
MADDY? MADELEINE, ARE YOU THERE?
MEANWHILE...
JANIS, COME HELP ME CARRY THE PICNIC TABLE OUT OF THE GARAGE.
I CAN'T. I'LL GET ALL MUSCLEY. PLUS I JUST DID MY NAILS.
ELLE
The End Times
Y'KNOW, THIS IS GETTING OLD.
DR. TAUBMAN SAID IT'S CRUCIAL AT THIS STAGE THAT I NOT BECOME TOO MASCULINE.
BRINGING WORLD TO BRINK OF THERMO-NUCLEAR HOLY WAR...
JANIS, MOVE IT! YOU'RE ON MY LAST NERVE WITH THE BIMBO ROUTINE. WOMEN ARE STRONG AND CAPABLE, NOT JUST OBJECTS OF DESIRE.
OKAY, OKAY! NO NEED TO GO ALL ALICE WALKER ON ME.
...HASN'T MADE US SECURE ENOUGH, SAYS BUSH
SISTERHOOD IS POWERFUL!
I LIKED HER BETTER WHEN SHE WAS TAKING THE BOY HORMONE-INHIBITORS, AND BEFORE SHE STARTED ON THE GIRL HORMONES.
BUT RESTARTING ARMS RACE WITH RUSSIA MIGHT DO TRICK

Are You My Mother?
2007 BY ALISON BECHDEL
510
7/11
SYDNEY'S JIG IS UP.
LOOK, EXCEPT FOR THAT ONE TIME AT THE NARRATIVE CONFERENCE, IT'S BEEN PURELY VIRTUAL.
FIVE SUPREME COURT JUSTICES TODAY WENT ON A WILDING SPREE...
WELL, EXCEPT FOR THAT OTHER TIME AT THE MLA CONVENTION.
I JUST DON'T GET IT! WHAT IS SO EROTICALLY COMPELLING ABOUT THAT GNARLED LITTLE SHREW? YOU NEED TO FIGURE OUT YOUR FIXATION ON UNAVAILABLE OLDER WOMEN IN POSITIONS OF AUTHORITY!
iFone

OH. BY THE WAY, I CAN'T GO TO COUPLES COUNSELING TONIGHT. DEAN HAVERSTICK SIGNED ME UP TO ROW ON HER DRAGON BOAT CREW.
THE LAWLESS GANG OVERTURNED PRECEDENT, TORCHED INDIVIDUAL RIGHTS, EVISCERATED LANGUAGE...
DOOT DOOT
iFone

MEANWHILE... HOW'S THE SEPARATION GOING?
DO YOU HAVE ANY PLANS FOR TOMORROW NIGHT?
NO. D'YOU WANT TO DO SOMETHING?
...AND DEFECATED ON WIDELY VALUED SOCIAL AND ECONOMIC POLICIES OF THE LAST CENTURY.

OH. NO, I MEAN, I WAS GONNA GO SEE THE MICHAEL MOORE MOVIE WITH GLORIA. AND RAFFI HAS THAT ALL-DAY FIELD TRIP SO SOMEONE NEEDS TO PICK HIM UP AT SEVEN.
WHAT'S GOING ON WITH YOU TWO?
RING!
THE DANGEROUS BOOK FOR BOYS

NOTHING! UM, D'YOU WANT TO COME TOO? MAYBE CARLOS COULD GET RAFFI.
RING! RING!
RAF! ANSWER THE PHONE!

BECAUSE I CAN'T KEEP LIVING HERE IF YOU'RE INVOLVED WITH SOMEONE. THAT WAS OUR AGREEMENT!
H'LO?
OH, I'M SORRY. I MUST HAVE THE WRONG NUMBER.

NO, HANG ON. IT'S THE RIGHT NUMBER!
IT'S MO!

MO?
GOD! WHEN DID RAFFI'S VOICE CHANGE?

IT'S BEEN HAPPENING GRADUALLY. KIND OF LIKE THE DISINTEGRATION OF MY ENTIRE LIFE. GOD, I CAN'T TAKE ONE MORE DAY OF THIS. I'M SO GLAD YOU CALLED.

OH, UH. SURE. I JUST WANTED TO CHECK IN AND SEE HOW YOU WERE DOING.

summer of
vice
8/8
511
©2007 BY ALISON BECHDEL

WHAT ARE OUR FRETFUL FRIENDS UP TO THIS LAZY AUGUST SUNDAY?
NO GOOD, APPARENTLY.

EXPLORING S/M
WHAT ARE YOU DOING ON MY COMPUTER?
READING YOUR EMAILS WITH MADELEINE.

HOW VERY DICK CHENEY OF YOU. WILL I BE RENDERED TO A BLACK SITE IN ROMANIA AFTER BRUNCH?

YOU TOLD HER YOU LOVED HER.
MO, THAT'S JUST A FIGURE OF SPEECH! I LOVE YOU.

SABBATH-BREAKING
DO YOU REALLY WANT IT?
YES.
HARRY POTTER AND THE VICIOUS VEEP

ARE YOU SURE YOU'RE READY?
YES! YES! DO IT!

OKAY, BETH. WE ACCEPT THEIR COUNTEROFFER.
BUT THEY'RE STILL GOING TO FIX THE LEAKY DOWNSTAIRS TOILET, RIGHT?

PREACHING AND NOT PRACTICING
MO, WHY DO YOU STAY WITH HER WHEN SHE TREATS YOU LIKE THAT?
PROBABLY FOR THE SAME REASON YOU KEEP LIVING WITH TONI EVEN THOUGH YOU'RE MAKING EACH OTHER MISERABLE.

HELL, PROBABLY FOR THE SAME REASON THE BUSH ADMINISTRATION CLINGS TO THEIR IRAQ POLICY.

I HAVE TO DISAGREE WITH YOU THERE. I'M PRETTY SURE HALLIBURTON'S NOT MAKING A CENT OFF THE IMPLOSION OF MY LIFE.

LIVING IN A DREAM.

SO THIS IS REALLY IT. I KNOW IT'S HARD, BUT TRUST ME, NO ONE'S SADDER THAN I AM. I'LL BE MOVING RIGHT AFTER MY CLOSING ON THE THIRTIETH.
OH. I KINDA THOUGHT YOU'D BE OUT SOONER. I'M EXPANDING OUR OFFICES INTO YOUR ROOM NOW THAT THE MOVEMENT'S FINALLY GAINING SOME TRACTION.
PETITIONS
IMPEACH CHENEY
IMPEACH

GINGER RETURNS HOME FROM BUFFALO LAKE STATE TO FIND A VISITOR.

fortunate
fall
©2007 BY ALISON BECHDEL

THE PLANET'S ON A GREASED POLE TO HELL...
10/3
513
World News
ALL OPTIONS REMAIN ON TABLE, BUSH SAYS
DOLLAR HITS NEW LOW
WAR COSTS $720 KABILLION A DAY
YEAH, IT'S .07 PERCENT OF THE LAND AREA. BUT THEY'VE GOT 90% OF THE CHROMIUM 6 EMISSIONS.

BUT IS PERSONAL PARADISE LOST FOR OUR PLUCKY PALS?
SIGH.
LOOK, I KNOW THIS IS BORING. BUT RICHARD SAID WE NEED TO DO STUFF TOGETHER.
PICK YOUR OWN

I'M SORRY I CAN'T SIT AROUND PROBLEMATIZING POSITIONALITY IN "THE TURN OF THE SCREW," OR WHATEVER THE HELL IT IS YOU DO WITH MADELEINE.
MO, THAT'S NOT WHAT I WANT.

I'M SORRY I CAN'T SIT AT HOME KNITTING ANTIMACASSARS, OR WHATEVER IT IS YOU WANT ME TO DO WITH YOU.
THAT'S NOT WHAT I WANT!

BUT I LOVE THAT YOU KNOW WHAT AN ANTI-MACASSAR IS.
ISN'T THAT THE BEST WORD EVER?

I DUNNO. BETTER THAN UNCTUOUS?
HMM. OR ISTHMUS?
DIRNDL.
SYZYGY!
OH GOD! SYZYGY!

GARY, I GOTTA GO SPEND SOME TIME WITH MY EX AND THE KID... YEAH, WE'RE STILL LIVING TOGETHER.... I KNOW, IT'S NUTS. IT KEEPS US FROM MOVING ON WITH OUR LIVES. BUT WHAT CAN YOU DO IN THIS HOUSING MARKET?
BREAKING NEWS
FAMILY VALUES SENATOR FOUND IN MISSIONARY POSITION WITH OWN WIFE

HEY!

COWABUNGA!

MEANWHILE, IN THE BUSHES...
THEN AGAIN, I'VE ALWAYS BEEN FOND OF PAROXYSM.

SCARY PROSPECTS
©2007 BY ALISON BECHDEL
514
10/31
MO! SYDNEY! HAPPY HALLO-WEEN!
EXCELLENT HILLARY COSTUME, SPARROW! VERY CREEPY.
I JUST GOT HOME FROM WORK. THIS IS WHAT I WEAR NOW THAT I'M LOB-BYING AND FUNDRAISING FOR NARAL ALL DAY.
HEY! HOW COME YOU GUYS DIDN'T DRESS UP?
HEY LOIS.
WE DID. I'M A VICTIM OF THE BREAST CANCER INDUSTRY.
AND I'M A GOOD GERMAN, STANDING IDLY BY AS MY COUNTRY PERPETRATES ATROCITIES IN MY NAME. I LOOK LIKE EVERYONE ELSE.
SHOP for the CURE
I BETTER GO TURN UP THE MUSIC.
NICE PARCEL.
ASTRA ZENECA
LOOK 'OO'S 'ERE, FLEUR! OFFER OUR FRIENDS A COCKROACH CLUSTER! BUTTERBEER?
NICE HARRY POTTER OUTFIT, MO.
SHUT UP, JANIS.
HI! I'M A PRO-GRESSIVE! SIGN MY IMPEACHMENT PETITION?
CAN I INTEREST YOU IN OUR MAGAZINE?
The WATCH-TOWER
JESUS, GINGER! YOU SCARED THE CRAP OUTTA ME.
SAMIA?
WE'RE THE DAUGHTERS OUR PARENTS ALWAYS WANTED. HAVE YOU MET MY HUSBAND?
SO DO YOU MISS HAVING GINGER AROUND NOW THAT SHE AND SAMIA GOT THEIR OWN PLACE?
YEAH, IT SUCKS. THIS USED TO BE A GROUP HOUSE-HOLD. NOW IT'S SPARROW AND STU'S ROLE-REVERSED NUCLEAR FAMILY CIRCUS.
HEY, I HEARD ABOUT YOU AND TONI. YOU DON'T LOOK SO GOOD.
I'M NOT DOING SO GOOD. I GOTTA GET OUT OF THAT HOUSE.
THERE'S A ROOM TO LET AT THE HOME FOR WAYWARD ADULTS. JUST SAY THE WORD.

just
say
yes
11/14
515
©2007 By ALISON BECHDEL

IT'LL BE BETTER THIS WAY, YOU'LL SEE.
AM I GONNA HAVE TO SLEEP THERE?

NO. EVENTUALLY I'LL GET MY OWN PLACE WITH A ROOM FOR YOU. THIS IS JUST TEMPORARY.
GOOD. 'CAUSE THOSE PEOPLE ARE WEIRD.
RAF, YOU LOVE LOIS AND STUART AND SPARROW.

THEY'RE STILL WEIRD.
WELL, YEAH. BUT IN A GOOD WAY.

Nothing. Whatev.
Nov 13 7:20
That wuz sum xtreme weed. RU still high?
Nov 13 6:58 pm
I am the ganja master!!!!!
Nov 13 6:34 pm
sick bro. LMAO.
WHAT TH'... RAFFI!

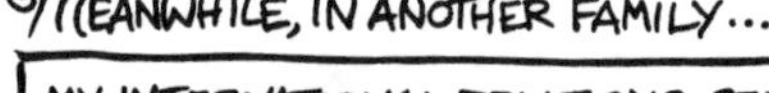
MEANWHILE, IN ANOTHER FAMILY...

MY INTERNATIONAL RELATIONS SEMINAR IS SO FRUSTRATING. YOU'D THINK BY GRAD SCHOOL PEOPLE WOULD HAVE SEEN THE LIGHT OF REALISM.

... BUT NO, THEY'RE ALL LIVING IN A FUZZY DREAM OF PEACE AND INTERNATIONAL LAW.
UH, CYNTHIA, WE'RE GONNA TURN IN EARLY.

OH. OKAY. I'LL BE UP LATE WITH THUCYDIDES.
GOD, WE'RE NEVER ALONE!

SHE NEVER GOES OUT, NEVER GETS DRUNK OR HIGH. NOT TO MENTION LAID.
THIS IS ONE TROUBLED KID.

BUT YOU SPIED ON ME.
YOUR MYSPACE PAGE WAS JUST SITTING THERE. I THINK YOU WANTED TO TELL US, AND I'M GLAD YOU DID.

YOU'RE TOO YOUNG TO SMOKE POT, RAF. END OF STORY.
YOU SMOKED POT.

AND LOOK AT ME NOW. DIVORCED PARENT OF A JUVENILE DELINQUENT.
PLUS YOU SUCK AT HALO 3.

FAILED STATE
11/28
516
©2007 BY ALISON BECHDEL

CLARICE IS FEELING A MITE HOMESICK.
IS YOUR ROOM OKAY? DID YA FIGURE OUT THE WIFI?
YEAH, I'M ALL HOOKED UP. IT'S KINDA COLD IN HERE, THOUGH.

OH, WE KEEP THE THERMOSTAT AT 64. YOU'LL GET USED TO IT. JUST PUT ON A HAT.
IMPEACH

SPARROW'S WORKING LATE AND LOIS IS OVER AT JASMINE'S, SO IT'S JUST GONNA BE US FOR DINNER.
PAKISTAN
...UNDER THE STATE OF EMERGENCY, GENERAL MUSHARRAF HAS DISMISSED THE SUPREME COURT AND DETAINED...

KINDA REFRESHING, ISN'T IT, TO SEE SOMEONE COME STRAIGHT OUT AND TELL PEOPLE HE'S SUSPENDING HIS COUNTRY'S CONSTITUTION?!
CAN YOU GRAB MY KASHA VARNISHKES?
The Distress
WATER-BOARDING
WIRETAPPING
ATTORNEY SCANDAL
HABEAS CORPUS

SHORTLY...
UH... PLEASE PASS THE SALT.

SORRY. NO SALT, SOY SAUCE, OR COFFEE. WE'RE TRYING TO EAT LOCAL ALL WINTER. YOU'LL GET USED TO IT.
LOCALVO

SO. I'M SORRY THINGS DIDN'T WORK OUT BETWEEN YOU AND TONI. Y'KNOW. I'VE NEVER REGRETTED MAKING MY FAMILY MY TOP PRIORITY. HEY, I HAVE AN IDEA!
LOCALVORE

WHY DON'T YOU INVITE TONI AND RAFFI TO OUR SOLSTICE RITUAL!
I WANT FROSTED FRUIT BATS.

SWEETIE, I EXPLAINED TO YOU, THAT CEREAL COMES FROM THOUSANDS OF MILES AWAY.
I WISH I WAS FOUSANDS OF MILES AWAY.
KUCINICH 2008
HOLD THAT THOUGHT. I'LL BE RIGHT BACK.

TONI!
HEY. HOW'S IT GOING OVER THERE?
I'M BEING FROZEN, STARVED, PREACHED AT, AND FORCED TO TAKE PART IN A RITUAL! IT COULDN'T BE GOING WORSE!

CAN WE DO THIS LATER? GLORIA AND STELLA ARE HERE FOR DINNER.

OH. OKAY. BYE.

in the bleak midwinter
12/12
517
©2007 BY ALISON BECHDEL

STUART'S SOLSTICE RITUAL IS UNDER WAY...
WHY DID I LET YOU DRAG ME TO THIS WIT-LESS AFFAIR?
BECAUSE YOU'RE STILL ATONING FOR YOUR WITLESS AFFAIR.
... IT'S THE DARKEST HOUR OF THE YEAR, POSSIBLY THE DARKEST HOUR OF OUR NATION. AND THINGS AREN'T LOOKING ANY TOO BRIGHT FOR THE PLANET, EITHER...
SO CLARICE, HOW D'YOU LIKE LIVING HERE?
I'M ECSTATIC. I CAN'T IMAGINE WHY YOU MOVED OUT.

UH...IT'S NICE RAFFI CAME TONIGHT. IT MUSTA BEEN HARD LEAVING HIM AND TONI.
IT WAS. I'M SORRY, GINGER. DON'T MIND ME. I'VE BEEN IN A CLINICAL DEPRESSION SINCE DECEMBER 12, 2000.

...PEOPLE CREATED SOLSTICE RITUALS BECAUSE THEY WERE AFRAID THE SUN WOULD NEVER COME BACK TO THE SKY. AND LEMME TELL YA, AFTER SEVEN YEARS OF BUSH, I KNOW HOW THEY FELT...
THOSE TWO SEEM BACK ON TRACK. HAS SYDNEY REALLY QUIT THAT FOOLISHNESS WITH MADELEINE?

YEAH. MO FINALLY LAID DOWN THE LAW. I THINK IT KINDA TURNED SYDNEY ON.

...AND AS THE LENGTH-ENING DAYS TRIUMPH OVER THE DARKNESS, MAY PEACE TRIUMPH OVER WAR, MAY...
STUART? D'YOU REALLY WANT TO APPLY THAT SOLAR MODEL TO HUMAN BEHAVIOR? AFTER ALL, DARKNESS TRIUMPHS OVER THE LIGHT IN JUNE.

UNLESS YOU MEAN THAT WAR IS INEVITABLE, A KIND OF CYCLICAL, BATAILLEAN SQUANDERING OF EXCESS ENERGY—A VIEW WITH WHICH I'M INCLINED TO AGREE.

I'M JUST SAYING.

AND NOW I'D LIKE YOU ALL TO JOIN ME IN A SONG I'M SURE YOU KNOW...

♪ HERE COMES THE SUN, DOO DO DO DO...
I'M GOING OVER TO THE DARK SIDE NOW.
WHEN DID YOU EVER LEAVE THE DARK SIDE?

have yourself a high def little christmas
518
©2007 BY ALISON BECHDEL
12/26
BLOW, BLOW, THOU WINTER WIND.
JUST DON'T KNOCK OUT THE CABLE.

YOU'RE GONNA LOVE THIS, DAD! YOU'LL BE ABLE TO COUNT JIM LEHRER'S NOSE HAIRS....WHAT TH'?
YOU DON'T HAVE THE CABLE BOX HOOKED UP RIGHT.
SO JENNIFER... HOW'S PAUL'S MEMORY?
SONY
BLOVIA
40 LCD
Egg Nog
HE'S FINE! I WISH YOU AND SYDNEY WOULD STOP FUSSING.

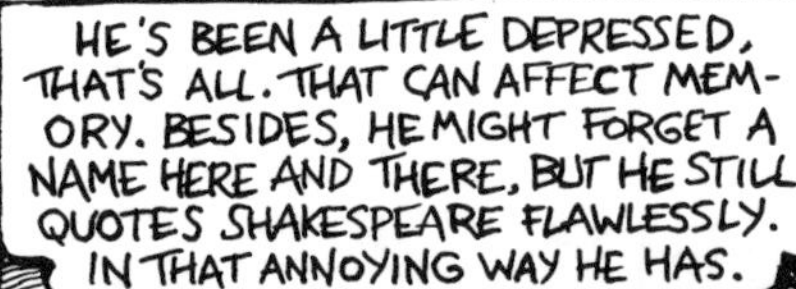
HE'S BEEN A LITTLE DEPRESSED, THAT'S ALL. THAT CAN AFFECT MEMORY. BESIDES, HE MIGHT FORGET A NAME HERE AND THERE, BUT HE STILL QUOTES SHAKESPEARE FLAWLESSLY. IN THAT ANNOYING WAY HE HAS.

VSOP

DAD! QUIT MESSING WITH IT! YOU DON'T UNDERSTAND HOW THIS...
OKAY, SO THEY'RE NOT TRYING TO BUILD NUKULAR WEAPONS.

...WORKS.
BOMB IRAN
BOMB IRAN
BOMB
ALL THE MORE REASON TO BOMB 'EM NOW, BEFORE THEY START.

SO YOUNG, AND SO UNTENDER?
SO YOUNG, MY LORD, AND TRUE.
HEY, MY SURGE IS A SUCCESS! THINGS'RE A TAD BIT BETTER'N THEY WERE AT THEIR WORST!

HOW SHARPER THAN A SERPENT'S TOOTH IT IS TO HAVE A THANKLESS CHILD.
BITE ME.

CLARICE IS HOME FOR THE HOLIDAYS, TOO. SORT OF.
IF THAT'S ALL THE PRESENTS, I'M GOING OVER TO BILLY'S. I WANNA SEE WHAT HALO 3 LOOKS LIKE IN HD.
WELL... GUESS I SHOULD BE GETTING BACK TO THE BOARDING HOUSE.

NOO! I WANT YOU TO BE HERE FOR DINNER!
SURE, WHY DON'T YOU STAY. IT WOULD GIVE ME AN EXCUSE NOT TO GO TO THE McLAUGHLIN-FARKASES' OPEN HOUSE.
GEE, I DUNNO. STUART'S MAKING SOY NOG TONIGHT.

YAY! SEE YA LATER!
WANNA WATCH A MOVIE? I HAVE A NON-HD DVD OF "THE BISHOP'S WIFE."

HD? OR NOT HD?
DAD, SHUT UP. I'M TRYING TO FIGURE OUT HOW TO CALIBRATE THIS THING.
BLOVIA
AND THUS THE NATIVE HUE OF RESOLUTION IS SICKLIED O'ER WITH THE PALE CAST OF THOUGHT.

THE FUNDAMENTAL THINGS
©2008 BY ALISON BECHDEL
519
AT AN LGBTQA GRAD STUDENT MIXER...
HI, CYNTHIA, POLITICAL SCIENCE.
NICE TO MEET YOU, JILL, MASS COMMUNICATION.
AND IN AN ACRONYMLESS LIVING ROOM...
AM I GLAD YOU'RE HOME.
RIF!
SCIENCE NEWS
MORE THAN USUAL, MY SULTRY COSMOGENIC NUCLIDE EXTRACTOR?
YES. I'M FINDING THIS ARTICLE ABOUT THE MECHANICS OF THE VENUS FLYTRAP STRANGELY AROUSING.
INDEED?!
WHERE'S OUR LITTLE BUNDLE OF JOY?
NOT YOU, ANUBIS! YOU REALLY ARE A BUNDLE OF JOY.
SHE WON'T BE HOME TILL 9. SHE'S GOING TO SOME GRAD STUDENT DINNER.
GREAT! MAYBE SHE'LL FINALLY GET A LIFE AND WE CAN STOP SNEAKING AROUND LIKE TEENAGERS.
I DUNNO. IT KINDA PERKS THINGS UP.
AT THE ACRONYMOUS EVENT, THINGS GROW ACRIMONIOUS.
SO I SUPPOSE YOU THINK IT'S A GOOD IDEA TO INVADE IRAN, TOO.
I THINK WE NEED TO TAKE A HARD LINE WITH THEM. I MEAN, THEY'RE EXECUTING GAY PEOPLE!
RUDY 2008
I DON'T UNDERSTAND SO-CALLED PROGRESSIVES WHO DEMONIZE BUSH, AND TIPTOE AROUND ISLAMIC FUNDAMENTALISM.
EXCUSE ME, I HAVE TO GO, UH, RECHARGE MY FERRET.
ELSEWHERE, THINGS GROW ACROBATIC.
GOD... MAYBE WE SHOULD =GASP!= GO UPSTAIRS AND TAKE OFF OUR CLOTHES...
NO! DON'T STOP! I'M...
CLO-OH! OHHHHHSE!
STOMP!
RATTLE
CLICK
ARAR ARF!
CYNTHIA! I THOUGHT YOU WERE EATING OUT!
APPARENTLY NOT. WHAT ARE YOU GUYS UP TO?
WANT TO ORDER A PIZZA?

come-back Kids

1/23

520

DID YOU SEE THE LATEST VIDEO I POSTED? OF J.R. DOING HER CHINESE FLASH CARDS? I THINK SHE HAS A REAL KNACK FOR LANGUAGES.

SNURRP!

THAT'S GREAT, SWEETIE. BUT I DON'T HAVE TIME TO CHECK YOUR BLOG EVERY TWENTY MINUTES. I'M PREPARING MY COMMENTS FOR THIS PANEL TONIGHT ON THE HYDE AMENDMENT.

HYDE: 30 YEARS IS ENOUGH! FUND ABORTION

DAMN, I FORGOT ABOUT THAT! I HAD A SPECIAL DINNER PLANNED!

MEANWHILE...

GOD, I'M AN IDIOT.

GLORIA, THINK OF THE KIDS. THEY'VE HAD SO MUCH UPHEAVAL IN THEIR LIVES. THEY CAN'T HANDLE ANY MORE CHANGE RIGHT NOW.

DUMBASS.

SMEGMAFACE.

MUCUSOID MOUTHBREATHER.

LATER, AT THE BLOGGERY...

WITH TAUTOLOGICAL REASONING...

BY MEANS OF AN ELECTORAL COLLEGE...

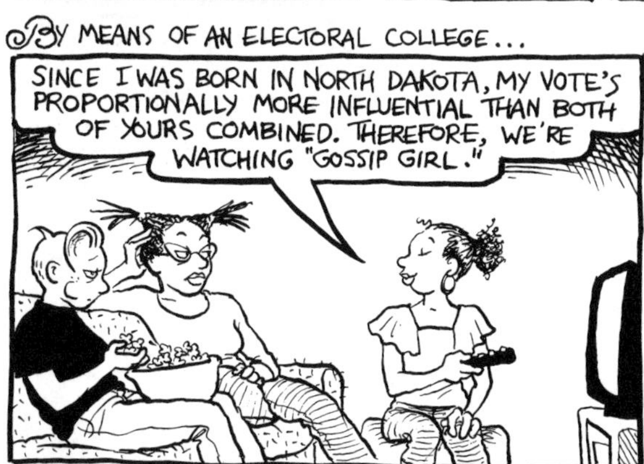

WITH FRONT-LOADED PRIMARIES...

LABORING UNDER THE DELUSION WE HAVE FREE CHOICE.

TIPS O' THE NIB TO VAL ROHY & KATIE SULLIVAN

ENTRUSTING VITAL PROCEDURES TO SHODDY TECHNOLOGY...

OF COURSE THERE'S NO REAL WAY TO BE SURE THE SCAN REFLECTS *YOUR ACTUAL* BRAIN, AND THERE'S A ONE IN TEN CHANCE THE MACHINE WILL FAIL ALTOGETHER. BUT HOP ON UP HERE!

SOUNDS GOOD, HUH DADDY?

iMRItronic By ~~DIEBOLD~~ ACME IMAGING SOLUTIONS RUNS ON WINDOWS!

...AND JUST HOPING THERE ARE NO ALTERCATIONS.

DEMANDING CHANGE!

WORKING FOR CHANGE!

HOPING FOR CHANGE!

AND...

IT LOOKS PRETTY MUCH THE SAME AS BEFORE.

HUH. WE COULD TRY REARRANGING THE DECK CHAIRS.

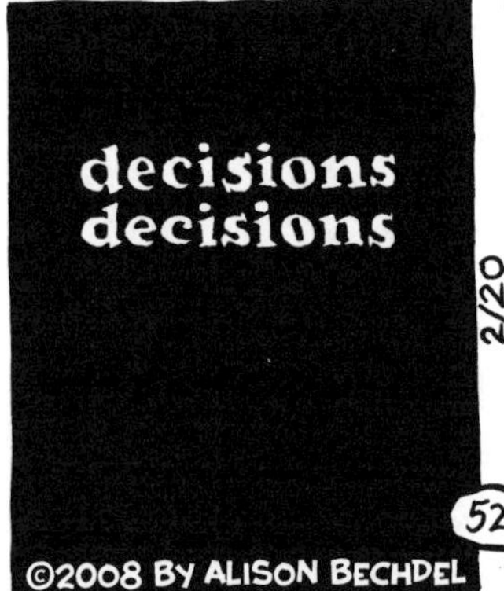
decisions decisions
2/20
522
©2008 BY ALISON BECHDEL

OH, THE RAREFIED CHOICES FACED BY THE MODERN CONSUMER...
EAT PESTI-CIDES?
ORGANIC
Raw Cane Sugar
FAIR TRADE
Raw Cane Sugar
OR EXPLOIT WORKERS?

'SCUSE ME, MA'AM!
DOMINO
DOMINO
THEORY SUGAR
FAIR TRADE
!

LOIS!
HEY, YOU LOOK KIND OF LIKE A VERY GOOD FRIEND OF MINE, ONLY OLDER.
Splenda
Splenda
DOMINO

YOU'RE GETTING A LITTLE LONG IN THE TOOTH YOURSELF. WHERE THE HELL HAVE YOU BEEN?
I BEEN IN THE SALT MINES, BABE.

DID YOU KNOW I GOT PROMOTED TO ASSISTANT STORE MANAGER AT BOUNDERS?
NO!

YEAH. I'M TOO BUSY BEING THE MAN TO DO ANY DRAG KINGING. I'M RAISING A TEENAGER. I'M PRACTICALLY MARRIED TO JASMINE. AM I STILL POLYAMOROUS IF I HAVEN'T BEEN WITH ANYONE BUT HER FOR THREE YEARS?

D'YOU HEAR ME? THIS IS NOT MY BEAUTIFUL HOUSE! THIS IS NOT MY BEAUTIFUL WIFE! HOW DID I GET HERE?
UH...

HEY, MO.
HI JASMINE, HI JANIS!
Lipidos
THEY'RE OUT OF TORPIDOS, SO I GOT THESE.

HUH. CLARICE TOLD ME YOU WERE ONLY EATING LOCAL FOOD.
THAT'S JUST AT MY PLACE. WHEN I WANT TO ESCAPE THE RHUBARB WINE, I GO TO THESE GUYS' HOUSE.

GIRL POWER.
BLACK POWER.
EXPERIENCE.
CHANGE.
TRACK RECORD!
ON THE WAR?
HILLARY
OBAMA

AND WHEN I WANT TO ESCAPE THE POLITICAL RHUBARB, I GO BACK HOME!

It's a great night for sleep-ing. It must be the air...

parental unit
524
©2008 BY ALISON BECHDEL

3/19
OUR CAREER GALS HAVE TAKEN THE SAME BUS AFTER WORK.
YOU NEED TO TALK TO HIM EVERY DAY! I CAN'T DO THIS ON MY OWN.
TONI, I DO TALK TO HIM EVERY DAY! I SAID I'D CALL BACK. HE WAS WITH HIS FRIENDS..
2753

HIS STONER FRIENDS. OH. I GOTTA GO, GLORIA'S CALLING.
7312
WHAT-EVER.

TROUBLE?
SNEP
NOT AS MUCH AS I HAD LIVING THERE. I KINDA LIKE PARENTING VIA REMOTE.

SOUNDS APPEALING.
DON'T GET ME WRONG, I MISS RAFFI. BUT I DON'T MISS THE NUCLEAR FAMILY MADNESS.
OBA
OBAMA '08
VOTE OBAMA
STAND FOR CHANGE
Hillary '08
VOTE
HILLARY
VOTE Hillary

IT'S SO NICE TO KNOW I HAVE THE WHOLE EVENING TO MYSELF. NO RELATION-SHIP DRAMA! NO KID ANGST!

WHY NOT? YOU DID IT!
THAT WAS A TOTALLY DIFFERENT SITUATION. PLUS I WAS IN COL-LEGE! YOU'RE ONLY SIXTEEN!

YOU'RE SUCH A HYPOCRITE! HOW DO YOU EXPECT ANY-THING TO EVER CHANGE?

STOMP
STOMP
SLAM!
UH... DRUGS? OR SEX?
NEITHER.
BOTH.

SHE WANTS TO JOIN THE SPEAKER'S BUREAU OF THE QUEER YOUTH GROUP AND GO INTO SCHOOLS TO TALK ABOUT BEING TRANS.
UHH... SO WHAT'S THE PROBLEM?

WHAT'S THE PROB-LEM?
GOD, A HIGH SCHOOL'S THE LAST PLACE YOU'D WANT TO SEE JANIS.
10% TRIB
CALIFORNIA HATE CRIME: 15-YR. OLD GENDER NON-CONFORMING BOY KILLED BY CLASSMATE

THANK YOU, CLARICE. I'M GLAD SOMEONE GETS IT.
UHH...SURE, JASMINE.
10% TRIB

DON'T INVEST YOUR TAX REBATE CHECK! SPEND IT IMMEDI-ATELY!

rent
©2008 BY ALISON BECHDEL
4/16
526

AS THE CAMPAIGN SEASON DRAGS ON, CIVILITY IS BEING STRETCHED TO A GOSSAMER FILAMENT.

ANTIWAR ACTIVISTS GROW BELLICOSE.
OBAMA DOESN'T HAVE THE EXPERIENCE TO BEAT McCAIN. AND BELIEVE ME, ONCE THE BUSHIES START A WAR IN IRAN, WE'RE GONNA **NEED** TO BEAT McCAIN.
SPARROW, ARE YOU ON OXYCONTIN? RED STATERS HATE HILLARY WITH THE WHITE HOT PASSION OF A BILLION BILIOUS RUSH LIMBAUGHS. THEY'LL MAKE **MINCEMEAT** OF HER.

LOOK. I DON'T EVEN CARE THAT HILLARY'S SUCH A HAWK. WE NEED A WOMAN PRESIDENT BECAUSE IT'LL EMPOWER GIRLS TO BE LEADERS, AND THAT'S OUR ONLY HOPE FOR **EVER** DISMANTLING THE PATRIARCHY.
A TIP O' THE NIB TO HOLLY RAE TAYLOR

EXES ARE GETTING EX-IER.
GOD, MADELEINE. CONDOLEEZZA **RICE** IS A WOMAN. WOULD YOU VOTE FOR **HER?** I CAN'T BELIEVE YOU'VE FALLEN PREY TO THE ESSENTIALIST FALLACY!
BLUE BOOK

AT LEAST I HAVEN'T FALLEN PREY TO THE **SAVIOR** FANTASY. IF I HEAR ONE MORE PERSON WAX RHAPSODIC ABOUT HOW OBAMA INSPIRES THEM, I'LL COUGH UP A GIANT HAIRBALL OF **HOPE**.

CHILDREN ARE DIVIDED AGAINST THEIR PARENTS.
I JUST WANT TO UNDERSTAND. IF THEIR POSITIONS ARE VIRTUALLY IDENTICAL, WHY ARE YOU SO SOLD ON OBAMA?
HE'S A MAC!
SHE'S A PC!
NEED WE SAY MORE?

PROFESSIONALS ARE NOT SO PROFESSIONAL.
I JUST CAN'T SUPPORT HER, NOT AFTER SHE AND BILL SACRIFICED THE WELL-BEING OF MILLIONS OF KIDS AND SINGLE MOMS WITH THEIR "WELFARE REFORM" PLAN.

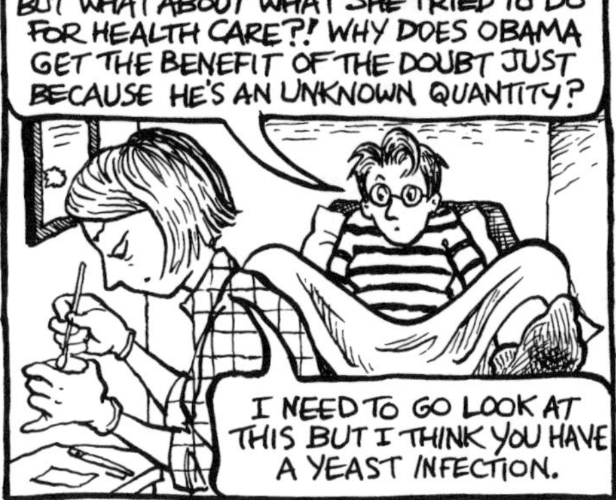
BUT WHAT ABOUT WHAT SHE TRIED TO DO FOR HEALTH CARE?! WHY DOES OBAMA GET THE BENEFIT OF THE DOUBT JUST BECAUSE HE'S AN UNKNOWN QUANTITY?
I NEED TO GO LOOK AT THIS BUT I THINK YOU HAVE A YEAST INFECTION.

HOW WILL IT ALL **END?**
GIRLIE MAN, MANLY GIRL. IT'S ALL THE SAME TO ME.
J.R., SING THE SONG I TAUGHT YOU.
YES WE CAN! **YES WE CA-A-N!**

sing, cuccu

527

5/14

SUMER IS ICUMEN IN. BUT IT DOESN'T LOOK LIKE OUR FRENETIC FRIENDS WILL BE GETTING MUCH OF A FURLOUGH.

SYD'S DONE READING... BUT NOT WRITING.

In conclusion, I think the main factor underlying the spread of the protestant work ethic has been the fact that it's such a widely pervasive concept.

B-

FINITO!

HEY, DR. K. I WAS HOPING TO TAKE *THE SOCIAL CONSTRUCTION OF LEISURE* FROM YOU NEXT FALL, BUT IT'S NOT LISTED.

UKOWSKI

NOK NOK

A SCHOLARLY NIB CITATION TO VAL ROHY!

WHAT A LIFE. NOTHING TO DO BUT RELAX, AND WRITE!

HEY, I SENT IN THE SECURITY DEPOSIT FOR THE CABIN ON LAKE MINNEKOOPA! WE'RE ALL SET FOR JULY.

WAIT! IS THERE INTERNET ACCESS? CAN I AT LEAST USE MY iPHONE? I'VE GOTTA PUMP OUT A **CHAPTER** A **MONTH** TO MAKE THIS DEADLINE!

CAFE CUCKOO

CAN I GET A SABBATICAL FROM MY GIRLFRIEND?

INDEX

***BOLDFACE** INDICATES FIRST APPEARANCE

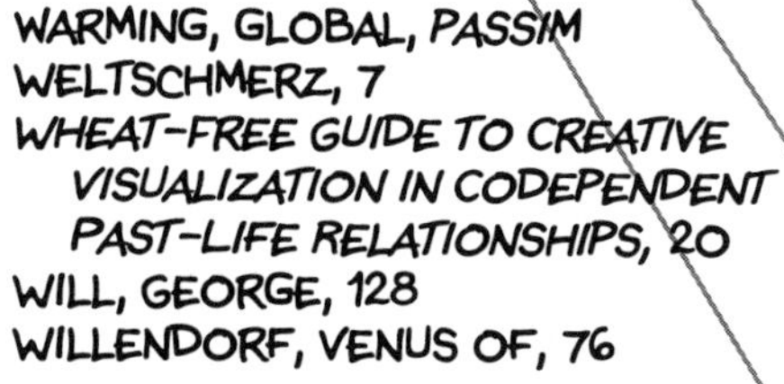

ACKNOWLEDGMENTS

I'M DEEPLY GRATEFUL TO ALL THE PEOPLE WHO HAVE WORKED TO CREATE AND MAINTAIN THE PUBLISHED SPACES WHERE MY WORK HAS APPEARED OVER THE YEARS. IN PARTICULAR, I'D LIKE TO THANK THE 1983 WOMANEWS COLLECTIVE, THE MANY, MANY DEDICATED EDITORS OF LESBIAN AND GAY NEWSPAPERS THROUGHOUT THE EIGHTIES AND NINETIES AND AUGHTS, AND NANCY BEREANO, THE VISIONARY FOUNDER OF FIREBRAND BOOKS. AND I PROSTRATE MYSELF IN GRATITUDE TO MY AGENT SYDELLE KRAMER AND MY EDITOR DEANNE URMY AT HOUGHTON MIFFLIN HARCOURT. WITHOUT THEIR ALARMINGLY SUPERHUMAN EFFORTS, THIS VOLUME OF COLLECTED WORK WOULD NEVER HAVE MATERIALIZED.

ABOUT THE AUTHOR

ALISON BECHDEL, A CAREFUL ARCHIVIST OF HER OWN LIFE, BEGAN KEEPING A JOURNAL WHEN SHE WAS TEN. SINCE 1983, SHE HAS BEEN CHRONICLING THE LIVES OF VARIOUS CHARACTERS IN THE *DYKES TO WATCH OUT FOR* STRIP, "ONE OF THE PREEMINENT OEUVRES IN THE COMICS GENRE, PERIOD" (*MS.*). THE STRIP IS SYNDICATED IN DOZENS OF NEWSPAPERS, TRANSLATED INTO SEVERAL LANGUAGES, AND COLLECTED IN A SERIES OF AWARD-WINNING BOOKS. *UTNE* MAGAZINE HAS LISTED *DTWOF* AS "ONE OF THE GREATEST HITS OF THE TWENTIETH CENTURY." AND *THE COMICS JOURNAL* SAYS, "BECHDEL'S ART DISTILLS THE PLEASURES OF *FRIENDS* AND *THE NATION*; WE RECOGNIZE OUR WORLD IN IT, WITH ITS SORROWS AND IRONIES."

IN ADDITION TO HER COMIC STRIP, BECHDEL HAS ALSO DONE EXCLUSIVE WORK FOR A SLEW OF PUBLICATIONS, INCLUDING *MS.*, *SLATE*, *ENTERTAINMENT WEEKLY*, AND MANY OTHER NEWSPAPERS, WEBSITES, COMIC BOOKS, AND 'ZINES.

SHE IS ALSO THE AUTHOR OF THE BEST-SELLING *FUN HOME: A FAMILY TRAGICOMIC*, A NATIONAL BOOK CRITICS CIRCLE AWARD FINALIST. *TIME* NAMED *FUN HOME* THE NUMBER ONE BEST BOOK OF 2006, CALLING IT "A MASTERPIECE ABOUT TWO PEOPLE WHO LIVE IN THE SAME HOUSE BUT DIFFERENT WORLDS, AND THEIR MYSTERIOUS DEBTS TO EACH OTHER."

BECHDEL MAINTAINS A WEBSITE AT WWW.DYKESTOWATCHOUTFOR.COM.

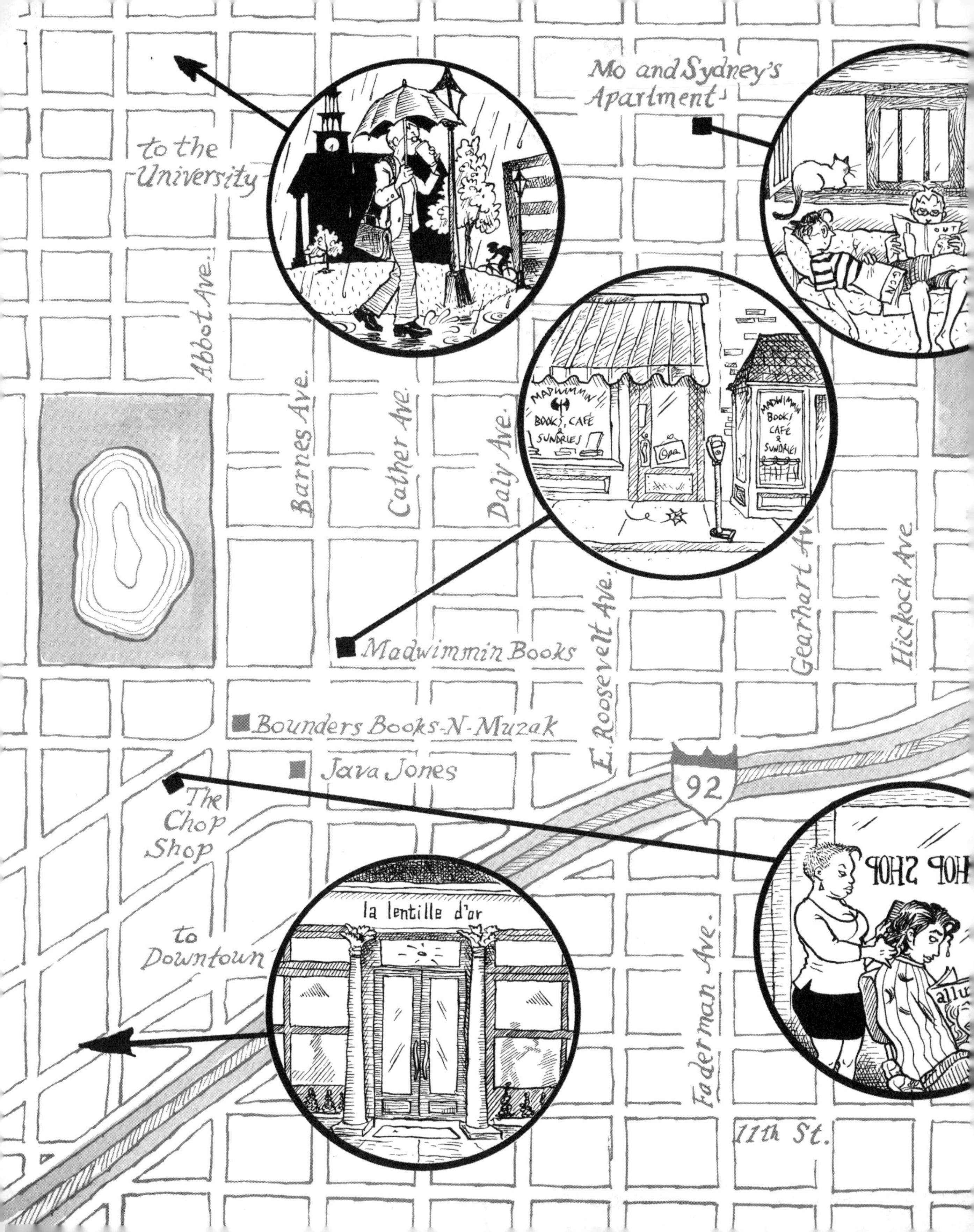

to the University
Mo and Sydney's Apartment
OUT
Abbot Ave.
Barnes Ave.
Cather Ave.
Daly Ave.
MADWIMMIN BOOKS, CAFÉ & SUNDRIES
Open
MADWIMMIN BOOKS CAFÉ & SUNDRIES
E. Roosevelt Ave.
Gearhart Ave.
Hickock Ave.
Madwimmin Books
Bounders Books-N-Muzak
Java Jones
92
The Chop Shop
HOP SHOP
la lentille d'or
to Downtown
Faderman Ave.
11th St.